External Debt and Capital Flight in Sub-Saharan Africa

External Debt and Capital Flight in Sub-Saharan Africa

Editors

S. Ibi Ajayi
Mohsin S. Khan

IMF Institute
International Monetary Fund
Washington, D.C.

Production: IMF Graphics Section
Cover design: In-Ok Yoon
Typesetting: Alicia Etchebarne-Bourdin

Cataloging-in-Publication Data

External debt and capital flight in Sub-Saharan Africa / S. Ibi Ajayi, Mohsin S. Khan, editors. — Washington, D.C. : International Monetary Fund, IMF Institute, 2000.

p. ; cm.

Includes bibliographical references.
ISBN 1-55775-791-7

1. Debts, External — Africa, Sub-Saharan. 2. Capital movements — Africa, Sub-Saharan. I. Ajayi, Simeon Ibidayo. II. Khan, Mohsin S. III. IMF Institute.

HJ8826.E98 2000

Price: $26.00

Address orders to:

International Monetary Fund, Publication Services
700 19th Street, N.W., Washington, D.C., 20431, U.S.A.
Tel.: (202) 623-7430 Telefax: (202) 623-7201
E-mail: publications@imf.org
Internet: http://www.imf.org

Contents

Preface

The economic problems afflicting Africa in general are many and varied. Among these, the twin problems of mounting external debt and large-scale capital flight have been at the forefront since at least the 1980s. The papers in this volume analyze these problems for a selected group of sub-Saharan African countries. All the studies were sponsored by the African Economic Research Consortium (AERC) in the period 1989–97. The various analyses of the different countries are brought together here to highlight common themes, and to compare and contrast the experiences of different countries. The issues raised in these papers still remain relevant to the countries today, and indeed apply to many other African countries as well.

The AERC commissioned us to put the papers together in a book in 1997. It is our hope that the materials in the book will serve not only as good reference points for the generation of scholars working in the areas of external debt and capital flight in sub-Saharan Africa, but also to policy analysts and policymakers as well. Our special thanks go to the former Executive Director of AERC, Professor Benno Ndulu and the former AERC Director of Research, Dr. Ibrahim Elbadawi for initiating the idea of this book and their subsequent support for the project. Special thanks also go to the International Monetary Fund for accepting to publish the book as a service for its member countries.

S. Ibi Ajayi
Mohsin S. Khan

1 Introduction

S. Ibi Ajayi and Mohsin S. Khan

It is generally expected that developing countries, facing a scarcity of capital, will acquire external debt to supplement domestic saving. The rate at which they borrow abroad—the "sustainable" level of foreign borrowing—depends on the links among foreign and domestic saving, investment, and economic growth. The main lesson of the standard "growth with debt" literature is that a country should borrow abroad as long as the capital thus acquired produces a rate of return that is higher than the cost of the foreign borrowing. In that event, the borrowing country is increasing capacity and expanding output with the aid of foreign savings.

In theory, it is possible to calculate the sustainable level of foreign borrowing, based, for example, on the terms, maturity, and availability of foreign capital. In practice, however, the task is nearly impossible, since such information is not readily available. Thus, various ratios, such as that of debt to exports, debt service to exports, and debt to GDP (or GNP), have become standard measures of sustainability. Even though it is difficult to determine the sustainable level of such ratios, their chief practical value is to warn of potentially explosive growth in the stock of foreign debt. If additional foreign borrowing increases the debt-service burden more than it increases the country's capacity to carry that burden, the situation must be reversed by expanding exports. If it is not, and conditions do not change, more borrowing will be needed to make payments, and external debt will grow faster than the country's capacity to service it.

Countries in sub-Saharan Africa have generally adopted a development strategy that relies heavily on foreign financing from both official and private sources. Unfortunately, this has meant that for many countries in the region the stock of external debt has built up over recent decades to a level that is widely viewed as unsustainable. For example, in 1975 the external debt of sub-Saharan Africa amounted to about $18 billion. By 1995, however, the stock of debt had risen to over $220 billion. The standard ratios reflect this huge buildup of debt. The region's aggregate debt-export ratio rose from 51 percent in 1975 to about 270 percent in 1995 (excluding South Africa, the ratio was above 300 percent). For all low- and middle-income developing countries, the average ratio of debt to exports was less than 150 percent. Similarly, the debt-GNP ratio for sub-Saharan Africa was 14 percent in 1975, but by 1995 it had reached more than 74 percent. Although debt-service ratios have remained relatively low because of the highly concessional nature of external financing provided to Africa, many countries in the region have been unable to service their debt without recourse to rescheduling under Paris Club arrangements or by accumulating arrears.

The massive growth in external debt in sub-Saharan Africa over the past two decades has given rise to concerns about the detrimental effects of the debt on investment and growth, principally the well-known "debt overhang" effect. Furthermore, there is now considerable evidence that the buildup in debt was accompanied by increasing capital flight from the region. In other words, sub-Saharan Africa was simultaneously an importer and an exporter of capital.

What is the relationship between foreign borrowing and capital flight? Two hypotheses have gained currency in the literature. First, there is the straightforward view that it is the government that engages in foreign borrowing while the private sector shifts its funds abroad. This theory undoubtedly has some validity, since the bulk of financing to Africa has been contracted by governments and comes from donor countries and multilateral agencies. And of course capital flight is purely a private sector activity. The drain of foreign exchange resources through capital flight creates a greater need for governments to borrow abroad.

A second hypothesis, proposed originally by Khan and Ul Haque (1985), argues that the perceived risk of investment in developing countries is higher than that elsewhere. Residents of developing countries can expect risk-free compensation for the additional risk on their investment at home; Khan and Ul Haque (1985) describe this risk as "expropriation risk." That is, domestic residents face the possibility that their assets may be expropriated by the government, through outright nationalization, taxes, or exchange controls, whereas the risk on similar assets held abroad is negligible. An exogenous or policy-induced shock that raises the perceived level of risk could therefore result in capital flight; at the same time the government would be forced to go abroad to obtain financing to cover not only the original imbalance but also the loss of resources through capital flight.

It is useful to consider what governments can do in a situation of foreign borrowing and capital flight. Obviously, providing a stable financial and macroeconomic environment would reduce domestic uncertainty. Experience has shown that foreign borrowing and capital flight were most pronounced in those countries that had higher and more variable rates of inflation, larger fiscal deficits, and overvalued currencies. These factors produced the incentives for governments to overborrow and for domestic investors to shift their funds abroad. Adopting sound macroeconomic policies would thus seem to be a key element in reducing reliance on foreign savings and in inducing capital flight. This strategy, as pointed out by Fischer, Hernández-Catá, and Khan (1998), is increasingly being followed by a number of African countries.

The international economic community can also play an important role in lowering the debt burden of sub-Saharan African countries. Recognizing this, the IMF and the World Bank in late 1996 implemented the Heavily Indebted Poor Countries (HIPC) Initiative, to help remove the debt overhang and restore the sustainability of the debt of eligible countries within a reasonable time frame. The HIPC Initiative stipulates that, after a three-year track record of effective economic reform under an IMF-supported program, the international financial community, including the IMF, the World Bank, and official creditors, will provide sufficient debt relief to reduce the external debt to sustainable levels, subject to the recipient country completing a further three-year period of strong policy performance. Once the process is under way, it is expected that eligible countries will exit from debt rescheduling and be in a position to tap global capital markets. Steps were taken in 1997 to implement the HIPC Initiative for four countries in sub-Saharan Africa: Burkina Faso, Côte d'Ivoire, Mozambique, and Uganda.

To address the twin issues of external debt and capital flight in sub-Saharan Africa, it is necessary to understand the nature of the problem at the country level. The chapters in this volume represent an attempt to provide such an analysis for a selected group of sub-Saharan African countries at different times in the 1990s. All of these studies were sponsored by the African Economic Research Consortium (AERC) and are brought together here to compare and contrast the experiences of different countries. The chapters are grouped into two parts. The five chapters on external debt cover Nigeria, Ghana, Uganda, Kenya, and the sub-Saharan African countries as a group. The other four chapters, on capital flight, examine the experiences of Nigeria, Uganda, Tanzania, and Kenya.

The chapters on external debt deal with the following common set of questions:

- What is the size of the external debt, and how has it evolved over time?
- What is the composition of the debt, particularly between official and private sources?
- What were the causes of the buildup in the debt?

- What are the effects of the debt on domestic economic performance?

In a similar vein, the chapters on capital flight look at the following questions:

- How is capital flight measured?
- What is the magnitude of capital flight?
- What are the conduits of capital flight?
- What are the causes and consequences of capital flight?
- How can capital flight be stemmed or reversed?

External Debt

Chapter 2, by S. Ibi Ajayi, examines Nigeria's external debt, including its size, structure, source, type, and composition. The chapter analyzes the indexes for measuring the debt burden and examines alternative debt scenarios. It distinguishes between the internal and external factors influencing external debt accumulation, identifies the changes in the international environment necessary to alleviate the debt burden, and examines the relationship between export performance and the debt burden. After reviewing the structure of the Nigerian economy and its political history, the chapter concludes that Nigeria's debt crisis is the result of structural defects inherent in the economy since independence. The chapter finds that the indicators of the debt burden have been relatively high. The behavior of these indicators, under varying assumptions, are explored using a growth-cum-debt model. The external and internal causes of debt accumulation are tested econometrically, and the results show the most important variables to be the real effective exchange rate and the terms of trade. The chapter ends with some policy prescriptions for dealing with the debt crisis.

In Chapter 3, Barfour Osei focuses on the implications of Ghana's external indebtedness for sustained economic growth. The study attempts to provide a better understanding of Ghana's external debt problem in order that adequate and effective debt measures can be sought. The chapter contains a description of the main features of Ghana's external debt, including its size, type, sources, structure, and terms. The chapter also assesses the sustainability of the external debt and evaluates its impact on the country's economic growth. The focus of the analysis is on external debt in the period 1983–90, during which Ghana pursued an economic recovery program and adopted an IMF-approved structural adjustment program. Using various indicators of the debt burden and concentrating on two of these, the debt-service ratio and the debt-GNP ratio, the author finds that the external debt burden has been at critical levels since 1983. This situation can be attributed directly to the country's inability to generate sufficient foreign exchange through export earnings, and to the low rate of return on investments to which borrowed funds are applied. Although it has continued to service its debt, Ghana has maintained an unstable fiscal stance. The chapter concludes that debt is one of the factors constraining the rapid growth of the Ghanaian economy. To continue to service its debt, Ghana needs to pursue programs of export expansion, widen the base of its nontraditional exports, and introduce measures to increase domestic saving.

Chapter 4, by Barbara Mbire Barungi and Michael Atingi, analyzes Uganda's external debt problem and its implications for sustainable growth. The chapter examines the size of Uganda's external debt, empirically assesses the internal and external factors influencing external debt accumulation, and analyzes the country's debt-servicing capacity and the sustainability of its external debt. A special effort is made to link debt to economic growth. Major findings are the acuteness of the debt-servicing obligation of the country and the fact that a large proportion of Uganda's debt is not eligible for rescheduling. Of great concern is whether the economy can sustain a growth rate of 5 percent per year while maintaining adequate domestic investment, given the heavy reliance on foreign capital inflows. Debt payments have been identified as the fundamental cause of slow economic growth. Debt relief is not enough, and continued government commitment to structural reforms and sound debt management is essential. Although the need to continue with the ongoing restructuring of the economy and promote further growth is clear, whether Uganda can keep to this challenging path without accumulating more external debt is not so apparent.

In Chapter 5, N.K. Ng'eno analyzes the case of Kenya, focusing on the extent of the debt problem, including the size, structure, and sources of the stock of debt. The causes of the external debt problem are separated into external and internal factors. Additionally, the available debt management strategies are discussed, and the sustainability of Kenya's debt is highlighted. The chapter notes that the external debt of Kenya and the indicators of the debt burden have been very high since 1980. The external causes of the debt burden are identified as the deterioration in the terms of trade and the worldwide recession, whereas the main internal causes are public sector deficits and exchange rate misalignment. To calculate the sustainability of Kenya's debt, two solvency indexes were calculated using the debt-export and debt-GNP ratios. The chapter claims that the external debt of Kenya is sustainable.

Chapter 6, by Milton A. Iyoha, begins with an analysis of the poor performance of sub-Saharan Africa since the onset of the external debt crisis in 1982. After an analysis of the scope, nature, and severity of sub-Saharan Africa's external debt, the chapter uses a simulation approach to investigate the impact of external debt on economic growth for the region. In particular, it undertakes policy simulations (using alternative debt reduction scenarios) to analyze the effect of the external debt on investment and output in sub-Saharan Africa for the period 1970–97. The chapter concludes that there is a significant debt overhang as well as a crowding-out effect. In other words, the large stock of external debt and heavy debt-service payments have had depressing effects on investment. From the policy simulations under alternative debt stock reduction scenarios, the chapter concludes that debt reduction measures bring about corresponding reductions in the total debt stock, the debt-GNP ratio, and the debt-service ratio and have positive impacts on investment and growth of real GDP.

Capital Flight

In Chapter 7, S. Ibi Ajayi examines the magnitude and conduits of capital flight from Nigeria in the period 1970–88 using alternative measurement methodologies. The chapter identifies the main macroeconomic and other factors responsible for capital flight, considers the major consequences of capital flight on the domestic economy, and examines the linkages between capital flight and external debt. The data indicate that Nigeria's capital flight may be episodic. For example, there is evidence of more capital flight in the oil boom years than in other years. And even though there seems to have been more capital flight during the military era, it is difficult to come to any conclusions as to whether capital flight actually occurred more under the military than under a civilian regime, not only because the military has been at the center stage of governance since independence, but also because the economic fortunes of Nigeria were not the same under the two regimes. The chapter also discusses different causes of capital flight. The mechanisms of capital flight identified include monetary instruments, bank transfers, precious metals and collectibles, misinvoicing of trade transactions (usually involving the local affiliates of multinational companies), and transfers by business owners engaged in international trade through the black market and through commissions and agents' fees. The chapter examines the linkage between capital flight and external debt and examines policies for containing capital flight.

In Chapter 8, Razaq A. Olopoenia estimates capital flight from Uganda for the period 1971–94, during which Uganda experienced both economic and political crises as well as regime changes. Various definitions of capital flight and their implied measures are used in the study. From the estimates, eight variants of capital flight measurement are derived, four of which are based on the concept of normal capital outflows whereas the other four are based on the concept of unrepatriated external earnings. All the estimates indicate fairly significant levels of capital flight during the period covered. The estimates also indicate variations in the degree of capital flight that reflect changes in the economic and political situations in the country. Substantial capital outflows are reported for the periods 1971–74, 1976–79, and 1981–87. These periods were characterized by political and economic instability. Reverse capital flows have been observed during the 1990s (except for 1994), when both political and economic conditions improved. The stock of residents' external assets ranged from 5 percent of the external debt stock in 1971 to 86 percent in 1979. The ratio declined consistently from 1988 to 1993, however, when it fell to 30 percent, less than half its 1987 level. Attempts to identify the factors that influence the flow of capital were not encouraging. The regression model identified the rate of inflation as the only statistically significant variable influencing capital flight. This might be associated with the way the measurements have been derived and the poor quality of the data.

Chapter 9, by Timothy S. Nyoni, focuses on capital flight from Tanzania during the period 1971–93. Given the controversy surrounding the definition of capital flight, the author chooses to define capital flight as all resident capital outflows rather than abnormal outflows only. Resident capital outflows from Tanzania are measured by three approaches: the balance of payments, the residual, and cross-border bank deposits. The chapter argues that the Morgan Guaranty Trust measure is preferred, since it is more comprehensive and dominates the other two. Important mechanisms of capital flight include corruption, trade misinvoicing, and smuggling. From the econometric analysis, the main cause of capital flight in Tanzania is the differential between the growth rates of the United Kingdom and Tanzania. Other influences include domestic inflation, external and political shocks, lagged capital flight, and parallel-market premiums. The chapter concludes that, to control capital flight, it is important in the first instance to get the macroeconomic fundamentals right.

Finally, in Chapter 10, N.K. Ng'eno analyzes the magnitude of capital flight in Kenya using different methods of estimation and empirically determines the causes of capital flight, with an emphasis on the role of macroeconomic variables. The author concludes that the World Bank and Morgan Guaranty Trust methods provide the best estimates for Kenya. By these estimates, capital flight peaked in the years of balance of payments crisis, implying that capital flight was used to hedge against the poor economic conditions. Trade misinvoicing is a problem in Kenya. Evidence from the study shows that underinvoicing of imports is greater than underinvoicing of exports, suggesting that trade policy plays a role in the misinvoicing of trade. Using a simple regression model, the chapter finds that a real appreciation of the currency encourages capital flight. It also suggests that, in the absence of credible reforms, growth of the economy would lead to increased capital flight: the increase in incomes would simply provide the means for increased accumulation of foreign assets. Appropriate macroeconomic policies are the principal way to reduce capital flight.

In summary, the chapters in this volume provide a wealth of data and some useful insights for individual sub-Saharan African countries on external debt and capital flight. What emerges from the studies on external debt is that the authors generally consider the size of the debt, in all the countries considered, to be so high as to be unsustainable. All the authors view policies of debt reduction as unambiguously good, in that reducing the debt burden would yield positive benefits in terms of both investment and growth. In addition, all the countries studied experienced large-scale capital flight, caused mainly by inappropriate domestic macroeconomic policies. Thus, the remedy for capital flight would be the adoption of sound macroeconomic policies, including lower fiscal deficits, reduced monetary expansion, positive real interest rates, and an appropriately valued exchange rate. All in all, the sub-Saharan African countries require international assistance to get control over their external debt burden, and they need to follow sensible domestic policies to limit the loss of critical foreign exchange resources through capital flight. By 1997 it was already evident that this type of strategy was emerging in a few sub-Saharan African countries. This process clearly needs to be strengthened and widened to cover other countries in the region, so that sub-Saharan Africa as a whole can see a sustained higher rate of economic growth and improved living standards for its population.

References

Khan, Mohsin S., and Nadeem Ul Haque, 1985, "Foreign Borrowing and Capital Flight: A Formal Analysis," *Staff Papers*, International Monetary Fund, Vol. 32 (December).

Fischer, Stanley, Ernesto Hernández-Catá, and Mohsin S. Khan, 1998, "Africa: This Is a Turning Point?" paper presented at the American Economic Association meeting, Chicago, January 3–5.

Part I

External Debt

Macroeconomic Approach to External Debt: The Case of Nigeria 2

S. Ibi Ajayi

One of the greatest problems facing many sub-Saharan African countries is the amount of their external indebtedness. This problem is becoming more acute for a number of reasons. First, the debt is enormous relative to the size of the economy and can lead not only to capital flight but also to the discouragement of private investment. Second, debt-servicing payments absorb a major proportion of annual export earnings. Meeting debt-servicing obligations eats significantly into whatever other facilities can be provided to improve the welfare of the country's citizens; it therefore has macroeconomic implications. This raises the question of whether a country can grow fast enough to maintain debt obligations and maintain adequate domestic investment. Third, the burden of debt for a large number of sub-Saharan countries threatens not only the execution but also the prospects of success of adjustment programs. Fourth, the current system of debt management has a dire impact on an economy's overall output. This assumes a significant magnitude when the time expended by chief executives of debtor countries involved in the various phases of rescheduling negotiations is considered.

It has been claimed that debt payments have been neither the fundamental cause of Africa's slow growth nor the cause of its other difficulties. The debt problem is nevertheless becoming more acute as the proportion of debt payments ineligible for rescheduling is rising rapidly. The implication of this is clear, as discussed previously. In addition, the cost of debt transfer from scheduled debt repayments into lower, manageable payments is growing. The external indebtedness of African countries is an obstacle "to the restoration of the conditions needed for growth" (World Bank, 1988, p. xix).

Sub-Saharan African countries fall into different groups when the issue of debt is discussed. The two most significant groups are the debt-distressed countries and the heavily indebted ones. Experiences differ, however, not only between these groups but also among countries in the same group. It is in this light that an explanation of the debt crisis must necessarily be country specific. Two West African countries, Côte d'Ivoire and Nigeria, belong to the group of 17 heavily indebted countries. The focus of this chapter is on Nigeria.

Objectives

The broad objectives of this chapter are to

- analyze trends in and causes of debt accumulation and servicing;
- determine debt-service ratios and debt-servicing capacity;
- calibrate a debt viability model and provide appropriate scenarios; and
- draw policy implications.

Specifically, the chapter will

- examine Nigeria's debt, including its size, structure, source, type, and composition;
- analyze indexes for measuring the debt burden and debt-servicing capacity;
- distinguish between the internal and external factors influencing external debt accumulation;
- identify the changes in the international environment necessary to alleviate the debt burden; and
- examine the relationship between export performance and the debt burden.

General Economic Background

A study on the macroeconomic aspects of debt in Nigeria is not complete without a preliminary discussion of the structure of Nigeria's economy and political history. The present problems of Nigeria, including the accumulation of debt, cannot be divorced from the structural defects inherent in the economy at independence in 1960 and the political economy of development since independence.

At the time of independence, Nigeria was heavily dependent on agriculture as the mainstay of the economy. Shortly after independence, about 64 percent of GDP originated in the agricultural sector. The contribution of this sector systematically declined, however, until it reached an all-time low of about 17 percent in 1982.

Nigerian oil came vigorously on the economic scene in 1970, when Nigeria became a member of the oil-producing nations. From then on, oil became the catalyst in Nigeria's growth. Nigeria benefited immensely from the sharp petroleum price increases in 1973–74 and again in 1979–80. By 1976 oil had become the major source of government revenue and the main foreign exchange earner, accounting for over 80 percent of both. Consequently, the relative importance of oil increased at the expense of other sectors.

These revenues provided the basis for significant increases in government expenditure designed to expand infrastructure and improve non-oil productive capacity. Indeed, the large oil revenues "not only provided government with the financial resources to undertake new programs and projects and to expand oil programs, but they affected the very institutions which were to make policy and the nature of centralization of authority and decision making in Nigeria" (Bienen, 1983, p. 2). Pressures on expenditure were exerted from all sides. The creation of more states meant more expenditure on infrastructure. In spite of spending on some important projects, some projects were undertaken without sufficient attention being paid either to their economic viability or to the executive capacity of government (Tallroth, 1987). Of importance in the success (or failure) story is the increase in government expenditure, especially on construction and urban services, which was accompanied by price and wage increases that drastically reduced producers' incentives in the non-oil tradable sector.

A result of the neglect of agriculture in the first instance, coupled with an appreciation of the currency, the naira, was that agricultural exports fell. Imports became relatively cheaper in the domestic market as a result of the government's attempt to curb inflation. Nigeria became a major food importer, and its dependence on oil gave it the character of a monoproduct economy.

One of the features of the economy during the oil boom of the 1970s was its high degree of openness. The economy depended heavily on the external sector in its manufacturing development strategy. Consequently, capital-intensive technology and assembly-type industries dependent on imported inputs were stimulated, and Nigeria had a high import-GDP ratio. Indeed, the need to protect a given level of availability of consumer goods became so pervasive that it was difficult to cut expenditures in this area. During most of the 1970s, budgetary expenditures were greater than the fast-rising income from oil.

There occurred a slump in the oil market in 1978. This precipitated an economic downturn despite the fact that the danger of maintaining a monoproduct economy based on exports of an exhaustible resource had been evident earlier. The reawakening in the oil market in 1979–80 was a reassurance that all was not lost. However, the breathing space provided was in the end very short-lived (Ajayi, 1986).

After 13 years of military rule, a civilian regime arrived on Nigeria's political scene in 1979. The oil market weakened in the 1980s, bringing about a reduction in export earnings. But with the new constitutional system, and with intensification of inappropriate macroeconomic policy (plus a system of tariff protection and import licensing) resulting in a further appreciation of the naira, large external borrowing became inevitable after the country's foreign exchange reserves had been substantially run down. The large external borrowing of the late 1970s continued, with substantial increases between 1978 and 1983.

The government resorted to austerity measures in 1982 and 1983 but relied heavily on controls and regulations rather than correcting the structural distortions. This worsened the situation. With a new government in power in 1985, policies changed toward a desire to combine austerity with adjustment. Between 1985 and 1986 the external debt increased by about 20 percent. The year 1985 was crucial not only because of the economic malaise afflicting the economy and the urgent need for adjustment, but also because of the national debate surrounding the acceptance of IMF lending. The dramatic fall in oil prices in 1986 increased the urgency of reform, and Nigeria put a structural adjustment program in place in July of that year.

Dimensions of the External Debt Problem

How much does Nigeria owe? There is a general belief among Nigerians that Nigeria does not know how much it owes. In other words, the genuineness of the debts is in dispute. The genuineness is related not only to false claims but also to serious accounting problems with some debt transactions. In its 1986 budget, the federal government made the following statement (Federal Republic of Nigeria, 1986, p. xi):

> In respect of external debt management, Government affirms its readiness to honour its obligations to clearly-established creditors, consistent with available foreign exchange resources accruing to the country and with the dictates of national survival. In this respect, Government has decided that no more than 30% of such resources will be taken up in 1986 for external debt servicing. We believe that this is a realistic estimate considering recent revelations in the JMB affair and the foreign exchange scandals with the implication that not all purported external debts would eventually be certified.

Conceptual and Practical Problems

There are both conceptual and practical problems in estimating foreign debt (Krueger, 1987). First, current account deficits can be financed—if only temporarily—by running down reserves or selling foreign assets. To the extent that large payment imbalances are financed in this way, any estimate of the change in debt understates the true rate of increase in the debt. The most appropriate concept for analyzing the sustainability of debt is therefore a net concept. However, only gross data are available in published form.

Second, currency revaluation can significantly affect the amount of debt outstanding. Therefore the increase in debt in a particular year may not necessarily equal the amount of external funds borrowed.

Third, it is important to realize that different types of debts do exist. Debt at concessional terms is different from debt at commercial terms. The rate at which funds are borrowed is also important.

Another conceptual problem of measurement arises from the inconsistency of the debt figures published by official sources. For data published in Nigeria, consistent time series are often not available. What are often found are data series that cannot be meaningfully analyzed on a consistent basis. Publications of the World Bank and the IMF also often have the same defects; for example, the figures for debt sometimes depend on which World Bank publication is being used. Changes in the figures sometimes reflect improvement of measurement standards.

Most of the statistics used for this chapter are nevertheless drawn from World Bank publications and denominated in U.S. dollars. Even though some justification can be made for using Nigeria's official sources, if only to show the magnitudes of change in naira terms given the variation in the exchange rate, there are advantages in using World Bank publications. The first is that some of the statistics used here are not generally available from domestic official sources. When such data exist, they are often not current or consistent. Inconsistent data series make comparisons difficult. Second, international comparisons are easier to make when a common currency such as the dollar is used.

Finally, it is important to recognize attempts made to reduce debt (Frydl and Sobol, 1988). Debt reduction can be brought about through negotiated changes in the terms and conditions of contracted debt. Steps such as debt rescheduling and retiming of interest payments may reduce the amount of interest to be paid in any given year. Other debt reduction mechanisms include debt conversion, debt-equity swaps, and debt buybacks, which reduce the present value of debt-service obligations.

Since April 1986 Nigeria has taken steps to restructure its debt. For commercial banks (multilateral), a total of $4.7 billion was restructured in April 1986 and November 1987. In March 1989, $6.0 billion was restructured. A total of $13.3 billion in debt to official creditors was restructured between October 1986 and March 1989 (World Bank, 1990b).

The Magnitude of Nigeria's External Debt

Table 1 shows the size of Nigeria's external indebtedness in both current-dollar and constant-dollar values for the period 1970–88. From

Table 1. Nigeria: External Debt, 1970–88

	In Current Dollars		In Constant Dollars	
	In millions of dollars	Change from previous year (In percent)	In millions of dollars[1]	Change from previous year (In percent)
1970	567		1,817	
1971	651	14.8	1,979	8.9
1972	732	12.4	2,062	4.2
1973	1,205	64.6	2,757	33.7
1974	1,274	5.7	2,085	–25.1
1975	1,144	–10.2	1,702	–17.6
1976	906	–20.8	1,332	–21.7
1977	3,146	247.2	4,257	219.5
1978	5,091	61.8	6,270	47.3
1979	6,216	22.1	6,398	2.0
1980	8,855	42.5	7,511	17.4
1981	12,018	35.7	10,405	38.5
1982	12,815	6.6	11,692	12.4
1983	18,422	43.8	17,646	50.9
1984	18,435	0.1	18,109	2.6
1985	19,324	4.8	19,324	6.7
1986	23,164	19.9	22,402	15.9
1987	30,039	29.7	26,373	17.7
1988	30,718	2.3	. . .	. . .

Sources: World Bank (1990a, 1990b); World Bank data; and IMF, *International Financial Statistics Yearbook, 1989*.

[1]Calculated as the nominal value of external debt deflated by the World Unit Import Value Index, 1985=100 (Dornbusch and Helmers, 1988).

1970 to 1973 Nigeria's external debt in current dollars grew at very high rates, particularly in 1972–73. The external debt in current dollars fell between 1975 and 1976 but has risen steadily since then. Whereas nominal debt grew by about 44 percent from 1982 to 1983, growth in constant dollars was more pronounced, at about 51 percent. From 1985 to 1986, the growth rate of nominal debt was about 20 percent, but only about 16 percent in constant dollars.

The growth rate of external debt fell between 1975 and 1976, but the debt rose astronomically between 1976 and 1977 and continued rising from 1978 until 1983. Even though the percentage indebtedness increased between 1983 and 1988, it was of a different magnitude. The growth in external debt in constant dollars shows a fairly similar pattern to that in current-dollar terms. To explain the sharp jumps during 1977, 1978, 1980, 1981, and 1983, one needs to recognize developments within the Nigerian economy. The period of the 1970s can be regarded as one of successful growth, and Nigeria benefited from the oil price shock of 1973–74, when the price of oil quadrupled. In 1972–73 and 1973–74 exports grew by 94 percent and 138 percent, respectively. Over the entire 1970–80 period, exports grew annually at an average rate of 41 percent, while imports grew at an annual rate of 35 percent. In 1978, however, there was a glut in the international oil market. Nigeria's exports fell by about 13 percent, and imports increased by about 64 percent. Given the country's creditworthiness, it was not difficult to obtain external credit, and borrowing seemed sustainable because of the worldwide inflation and the consequent negative real interest rates.

Between 1979 and 1983 a number of developments affected Nigeria's level of indebtedness. The civilian regime that came to power in 1979 did not fail to avail itself of the opportunity and attraction of external borrowing. Developments in the external sector also helped increase the debt. Consequent to the second oil price increase in 1979, the stance of macroeconomic policy in the industrial countries changed. The anti-inflationary macroeconomic policy they adopted caused worldwide recession, the highest real rates of interest in the postwar era, and sharply falling prices of commodities (Krueger, 1987). Between 1980 and 1983 the value of Nigeria's exports fell at an annual average rate of 6.5 percent. In 1981, 1982, and 1983 the value of exports fell by 29, 35, and 16 percent, respectively. In 1980 Nigeria began borrowing from private sources. The share of private borrowing rose to 85 percent in 1980–82, compared with only 31 percent in 1970–72 (Table 2). Debt at floating rates, which was only 0.7 percent of total debt in 1973–75, was 48.6 percent in the 1980–82 period. Simultaneously, the interest rate paid on new commitments rose by 39.5 percent between 1975 and 1978, and by about 11 percent between 1981 and 1983. Between 1975 and 1980, private creditors' average terms for new commitments also rose by about 67 percent.

Structure, Source, Type, and Composition of External Debt

There are various ways of characterizing external debt. First, external debt can be classified on the basis of the status of the donor, generally divided into official and private debts. Official debts are those obtained from national governments or their agencies or from international agencies like the World Bank and the IMF. Private debts consist of those obtained from private creditors and include Eurodollar loans, suppliers' credit for exports, and loans from private commercial banks.

Another useful classification is the maturity structure of external debt. Short-term debts are those with an original maturity of one year or less. Long-term debts are generally subdivided into public or pub-

Table 2. Nigeria: Composition of Long-Term External Debt Outstanding, 1970–87
(In percent of total)

Type of Debt	1970–72	1973–75	1980–82	1987
Debt from official sources	68.8	. . .	14.6	44.6
Debt from private sources	31.2	. . .	85.4	55.4
Debt at floating rates	. . .	0.7	48.6	48.8

Source: World Bank (1989b, p. 154).

licly guaranteed debt and private nonguaranteed debt. Publicly guaranteed external debt is usually defined as the external debt obligation of a private debtor that a public entity guarantees for repayment.

Over the last few years, a number of structural changes have occurred relating to Nigeria's external debt. Two of these are significant: the composition of external debt outstanding and the terms of borrowing at fixed or floating rates. Table 2 showed the composition of debt outstanding between 1970 and 1987 from different sources. External debt from official sources was about 69 percent, while that from private sources was about 31 percent in 1970–72. In 1980–82, debt from official sources declined to about 15 percent while debt from private sources rose to about 85 percent. This represents a structural change in the sources of funding. As official loans were difficult to obtain, Nigeria found private sources attractive and borrowed from them at floating interest rates. In 1987, debt from official sources fell from its 1970–72 level to about 45 percent, while the share from private sources was about 55 percent.

Another important aspect of Nigeria's debt relates to the variation in the share of debt at floating rates between 1973 and 1987. Between 1973 and 1975 less than 1 percent of total long-term debt was at floating rates. This share rose to about 49 percent in 1980–82 and stayed at about that level in 1987.

Thus, two significant characteristics of Nigeria's debt structure are the increase in debt contracted at floating interest rates and the decrease in the share of official loans. One of the macroeconomic implications of floating rates is an ever-rising debt service. This will have great implications for resource use and hence for growth.

External debt can further be broken down into public and publicly guaranteed debt, private nonguaranteed debt, and short-term debt. The significant changes for these groupings occurred in the period 1980–88 (Table 3).

As can be seen from Table 3, public and publicly guaranteed debt increased from 79 percent of total debt in 1980 to about 99 percent in 1988. On the other hand, the share of private, nonguaranteed loans declined from about 21 percent in 1980 to about 1 percent in 1988. Short-term debt steadily declined, from 40 percent of total external debt in 1980 to about 20 percent in 1982 and finally to about 6 percent in 1988.

Table 4 gives information on the average terms of new commitment for the period of interest. In general, the average interest rate rose between 1971 and 1973. It rose again after a drop in 1974 and continued rising for most of the period between 1978 and 1983. The maturity structure of loans also varied between 1970 and 1988. In the early 1970s the average maturity was about 20 years. This dropped thereafter to an average of 9.7 years between 1978 and 1983 but increased again between 1984 and 1988. In the early 1970s the percentage of loans at concessional rates was higher than in the late 1970s and early 1980s. Also, the share of debt at variable interest rates as a proportion of public debt outstanding and disbursed was less than 3 percent between 1970 and 1977. By 1978 it had risen to about 61 percent. In 1988, the ratio stood at 42 percent, a significant increase from the 1970 level.

To consider these changes, we should discuss the changes in composition between official and private creditors in total debt service, interest payments, principal payments, debt outstanding and disbursed, debt outstanding and undisbursed, commitments, disbursements, net flows, and net transfers. According to the *World Debt Tables* (World Bank, 1990a, p. xiii), the terms listed above are defined as follows: "Disbursements are drawings on loan commitment during the year specified. Net flows (or net lending or net disbursements) are disbursements minus principal repayments. Net transfers are net flows minus interest payments of disbursement minus total debt service payments."

In 1974 the share of private creditors in total debt service was 66 percent (Table 5). This rose to 83.5 percent in 1976 but declined thereafter. By 1984, however, it had risen to a peak of 96.2 percent. By 1986 it stood at about 73 percent. Of interest payments due in 1974, about 14.3 percent were paid to private creditors (Table 6). This share declined to about 6 percent in 1978. Between 1974 and 1978 most interest payments were made to official creditors. After 1978 the situation changed. Total interest payments to private creditors and the share paid to them rose substantially, with the latter reaching a peak of about 91 percent in 1982. By 1988 the share stood at about 51 percent.

The share of principal repayments to private creditors was 80 percent in 1974 (Table 7). This rose steadily until 1976, when the share stood at 92 percent. The share fell between 1977 and 1979, after which

Table 3. Nigeria: Public, Private, and Short-Term Debt, 1980–88

	Total External Debt	Long-Term Debt						Short-Term Debt	
		Public and publicly guaranteed		Private nonguaranteed		Total			
	(In millions of U.S. dollars)	In millions of U.S. dollars	Share (In percent)	In millions of U.S. dollars	Share (In percent)	In millions of U.S. dollars	Share (In percent)	In millions of U.S. dollars	Share (In percent)
1980	8,855	4,205	79.3	1,097	20.7	5,302	59.9	3,553	40.1
1981	12,018	6,244	82.3	1,347	17.7	7,591	63.2	4,427	36.8
1982	12,815	8,969	67.2	1,313	12.8	10,282	80.2	2,533	19.9
1983	18,422	12,066	90.3	1,300	9.7	13,306	72.6	5,056	27.4
1984	18,435	11,290	89.0	1,400	11.0	12,690	88.8	5,744	31.2
1985	19,324	12,934	90.1	1,416	9.9	14,350	74.3	4,974	25.7
1986	23,164	19,046	97.9	400	2.1	19,446	83.9	3,718	16.1
1987	30,039	28,026	98.8	352	1.2	28,377	94.5	1,662	5.5
1988	30,718	28,630	98.8	357	1.2	28,967	94.3	1,752	5.7

Source: World Bank (1989b, 1990b).

Table 4. Nigeria: Average Terms of New Debt Commitments, 1970–88

	Interest Rate (In percent)	Grant Element (In percent)	Maturity (In years)	Grace Period (In years)	Concessional Debt as Share of Total Public Debt (In percent)	Variable-Interest-Rate Debt as Share of Total Public Debt (In percent)
1970	6.0	21.5	14.3	3.9	64.6	2.8
1971	4.5	40.3	24.9	6.4	62.9	2.2
1972	6.1	26.1	22.7	5.8	58.7	1.6
1973	6.6	24.0	23.0	7.5	35.9	0.9
1974	4.4	41.7	24.2	7.2	36.9	0.8
1975	7.6	13.3	17.5	4.3	43.6	0.7
1976	8.5	8.2	18.6	4.1	57.5	0.7
1977	8.2	10.7	19.7	5.2	55.9	0.7
1978	10.1	–1.1	8.1	3.1	21.7	60.8
1979	10.7	–1.6	9.6	3.8	15.2	68.8
1980	10.6	–2.5	10.9	3.6	11.7	68.5
1981	9.2	4.4	10.3	4.1	7.1	57.3
1982	10.0	–0.3	9.9	3.7	4.5	50.5
1983	10.2	–1.3	9.2	3.0	3.6	52.0
1984	9.8	–0.2	11.8	2.6	3.5	45.6
1985	9.0	4.3	12.6	3.6	3.3	41.7
1986	9.0	8.0	16.7	4.4	2.8	54.3
1987	7.9	10.8	14.9	4.4	3.2	49.5
1988	7.9	13.6	16.0	4.6	2.1	41.8

Source: Author's calculations from data in World Bank (1989b, 1990b).

Table 5. Nigeria: Total Debt Service, 1970–88

	In Millions of U.S. Dollars			In Percent of Total	
	Total	Official	Private	Official	Private
1970	55.60	31.60	24.00	56.83	43.17
1971	32.80	. . .	0.00	. . .	. . .
1972	64.50	40.80	23.70	63.26	36.74
1973	102.30	. . .	0.00	. . .	. . .
1974	169.20	57.40	111.80	33.92	66.08
1975	246.60	66.70	179.90	27.05	72.95
1976	374.80	62.00	312.80	16.54	83.46
1977	106.20	79.50	26.70	74.86	25.14
1978	105.70	87.50	18.20	82.78	17.22
1979	237.80	103.60	134.20	43.57	56.43
1980	544.40	118.30	426.10	21.73	78.27
1981	934.40	120.10	814.30	12.85	87.15
1982	1,456.50	143.40	1,313.10	9.85	90.15
1983	2,060.00	215.20	1,844.80	10.45	89.55
1984	3,162.80	121.80	3,041.00	3.85	96.15
1985	4,003.40	774.60	3,228.80	19.35	80.65
1986	1,624.40	430.90	1,193.50	26.53	73.47
1987	983.00	480.00	503.00	48.83	51.17
1988	1,984.00	987.00	997.00	49.75	50.25

Source: World Bank, *World Debt Tables*, various issues.

it started to rise, reaching a peak of 96 percent in 1984. A substantial reduction occurred after 1984, and the private creditor share was only about 37 percent in 1988.

Patterns of debt outstanding and disbursed, debt outstanding and undisbursed, commitments, disbursements, net flows, and net transfers (not shown) reveal that in almost all cases the share of private creditors predominated from about the middle or late 1970s.

Nigeria's external debt by source is shown in Table 8. For the period for which statistics are available, Eurodollar loans became important beginning in 1978, rising to a share of 65 percent in 1982. Table 9 shows a simplified accounting of Nigeria's external debt by type for the period covered in this study. Trade arrears started exerting a very strong trend in 1982 and formed the largest type of debt by 1984. Until then debt incurred in the international capital market formed the largest component. The table also illustrates the important relationship between bilateral and multilateral external debt. Until 1982, bilateral debt was more important than multilateral debt. By 1982, however, the value of multilateral debt had shot up significantly, and it rose to about three times the size of bilateral loans in 1988. From

Table 6. Nigeria: Interest Payments, 1970–88

	In Millions of U.S. Dollars			In Percent of Total	
	Total	Official	Private	Official	Private
1970	19.80	16.00	3.80	80.81	19.19
1971	9.20	. . .	0.00	. . .	. . .
1972	26.30	22.50	3.80	85.55	14.45
1973	32.60	. . .	0.00	. . .	. . .
1974	35.70	30.60	5.10	85.71	14.29
1975	41.10	36.80	4.30	89.54	10.46
1976	39.00	35.00	4.00	89.54	10.46
1977	44.20	41.90	2.30	94.80	5.20
1978	50.30	47.20	3.10	93.84	6.16
1979	180.30	59.40	120.90	32.95	67.05
1980	443.70	66.50	377.20	14.99	85.01
1981	564.70	64.80	499.90	11.48	88.52
1982	819.20	75.50	743.70	9.22	90.78
1983	1,042.70	123.00	919.70	11.80	88.20
1984	1,172.00	157.80	1,014.20	13.46	86.54
1985	1,256.00	172.60	1,083.40	13.74	86.26
1986	391.20	163.80	227.40	41.87	58.13
1987	524.00	340.00	184.00	64.89	35.11
1988	1,386.00	682.00	704.00	49.21	50.79

Source: World Bank, *World Debt Tables*, various issues.

about 43 percent in 1984, the federal government share of external loans rose to about 84 percent in 1987 (Table 10). The international capital market share of this debt was about 50 percent in 1984; it steadily declined thereafter until 1987, when it stood at 25 percent, but it remained the predominant source. For state government debt, while the international capital market remained the major source, its share declined from about 12 percent of total external debt in 1982 to 10 percent in 1987.

External Debt Burden, Debt-Service Ratios, and Debt-Servicing Capacity

The debt burden of a country inevitably imposes a number of constraints on its growth prospects. The burden of principal and interest payments, for example, drains the nation's resources and curtails the possible expenditure of resources on other productive ventures. This is even more constraining, considering that the incomes from which debts are to be serviced are very small. This gives rise to three macroeconomic problems: earning foreign exchange, finding extra budget

Table 7. Nigeria: Principal Repayments, 1970–88

	In Millions of U.S. Dollars			In Percent of Total	
	Total	Official	Private	Official	Private
1970	36.00	15.60	20.40	43.33	56.67
1971	...	...	0.00	...	...
1972	38.20	18.30	19.90	47.91	52.09
1973	...	...	...	...	...
1974	133.50	26.80	106.70	20.07	79.93
1975	205.50	29.90	175.60	14.55	85.45
1976	335.90	27.00	308.90	8.04	91.96
1977	61.90	37.60	24.30	60.74	39.26
1978	55.40	40.30	15.10	72.74	27.26
1979	57.50	44.20	13.30	76.87	23.13
1980	100.70	51.80	48.90	51.44	48.56
1981	369.77	55.30	314.47	14.96	85.04
1982	637.30	67.80	569.50	10.64	89.36
1983	1,017.30	92.20	925.10	9.06	90.94
1984	1,990.80	83.70	1,907.10	4.20	95.80
1985	2,747.40	602.00	2,145.40	21.91	78.09
1986	1,233.20	267.10	966.10	21.66	78.34
1987	307.00	140.00	167.00	45.60	54.40
1988	483.00	306.00	177.00	63.35	36.65

Source: World Bank, *World Debt Tables*, various issues.

resources for debt service, and adjusting to a reduction in spendable resources.

To reduce the debt burden and increase debt-servicing capacity, there is a need for an increase in exports and a reduction in world interest rates, among other things. This raises some basic macroeconomic issues relating to international trade and costs. To the extent that the increasing protectionism of the developed countries prevents entry of developing country commodities into world markets, and rising real interest rates are maintained, the debt burden of many developing countries may not abate. Thus, part of getting out of debt is related to events in the international sector (Ajayi, 1989a).

A number of macroeconomic aggregates and debt data are often used to assess the external situation of any given country. These ratios generally offer measures of the cost of, or the capacity for, debt servicing. The following ratios are often used:

- total debt service to exports of goods and services (referred to here as DSR_1);
- interest payments to exports of goods and services (DSR_2);

Table 8. Nigeria: External Debt by Source, 1969–82

(In percent of total external debt)

	1969	1970	1971	1972	1974	1975	1976	1977	1978	1979	1980	1981	1982
Contractor finance	22.98	20.52	17.25	11.57	0.00	0.00	0.00	0.00	0.00	0.00	0.00	0.00	0.00
Austria	0.00	0.00	0.90	0.35	0.00	0.00	0.00	0.00	0.00	0.00	0.00	0.00	0.00
African Development Bank	0.00	0.00	0.00	0.00	0.00	0.00	0.00	0.00	0.00	0.00	0.13	0.10	0.08
Canada	0.00	0.00	0.00	0.00	1.61	2.86	7.69	0.00	2.84	2.02	1.74	1.39	1.21
France	0.00	0.00	0.00	0.00	0.00	0.00	0.00	8.79	0.00	0.00	1.05	1.41	3.10
Germany	0.00	0.00	0.00	0.00	12.41	11.23	10.12	9.36	2.72	14.34	15.06	19.17	13.09
Hungary	0.00	0.00	0.00	0.00	0.00	0.00	0.00	0.00	0.00	0.00	0.56	0.42	0.34
Israel	0.23	0.11	0.00	0.00	0.00	0.00	0.00	40.14	0.00	0.00	0.00	0.00	0.00
Italy	10.35	9.92	9.29	6.12	4.16	3.60	3.20	0.00	0.90	0.65	0.51	0.39	0.34
Japan	0.00	0.00	1.46	2.14	2.45	7.23	7.85	3.29	2.40	1.89	1.32	0.96	1.14
Netherlands	2.16	2.17	2.13	1.48	3.26	2.92	2.72	8.51	0.75	0.56	0.47	0.36	0.31
Soviet Union	0.00	0.00	0.00	0.13	0.37	0.54	0.45	0.47	0.05	0.04	0.00	0.00	0.00
United Kingdom	33.11	33.18	30.46	20.27	16.66	14.55	11.45	2.92	3.48	1.63	2.04	1.57	1.78
United States	10.58	11.74	16.13	18.00	14.61	14.43	13.75	13.81	3.67	3.06	2.63	2.05	1.78
World Bank	22.98	20.52	17.25	39.79	37.84	36.01	34.78	0.00	12.32	10.17	9.60	7.70	6.99
Eurodollar loans	0.00	0.00	0.00	0.00	0.00	0.00	0.00	0.00	50.11	63.78	58.42	56.52	65.08
Others	0.00	0.68	2.02	2.10	6.64	6.63	6.46	1.46	20.75	0.86	5.96	7.54	5.26

Source: Central Bank of Nigeria, *Annual Report and Statement of Accounts*, various issues.

Table 9. Nigeria: External Debt by Type, 1970–88
(In millions of naira)

Debt Type	1970	1971	1972	1973	1974	1975	1976	1977	1978	1979
Bilateral	100.2	106.1	124.0	150.9	182.8	200.7	233.1	350.3	210.6	405.9
Multilateral	37.9	37.9	102.1	107.1	122.0	126.0	119.4	140.2	154.3	163.9
International capital market	. . .	. . .	. . .	. . .	. . .	. . .	. . .	. . .	641.0	1,027.8
Trade arrears	. . .	. . .	. . .	. . .	. . .	. . .	. . .	. . .	. . .	. . .
Refinanced	. . .	. . .	. . .	. . .	. . .	. . .	. . .	. . .	. . .	. . .
Unrefinanced	. . .	. . .	. . .	. . .	. . .	. . .	. . .	. . .	. . .	. . .
Others (unguaranteed state or private loans)	350.7	70.5	37.3	18.9	17.6	23.2	22.1	6.4	259.8	13.9
Total	488.8	214.5	263.4	276.9	322.4	349.9	374.6	496.9	1,265.7	1,611.5

Debt Type	1980	1981	1982	1983	1984	1985	1986	1987	1988
Bilateral	483.8	656.1	163.2	179.3	351.3	365.1	1,159.1	1,986.9	3,308.1
Multilateral	181.6	181.9	503.4	566.4	1,271.2	1,283.5	4,670.2	8,782.3	9,991.8
International capital market	1,090.2	1,317.5	5,474.4	5,026.5	6,003.1	7,726.4	21,725.3	40,546.3	54,563.3
Trade arrears	. . .	. . .	1,891.7	4,283.4	6,598.4	7,438.2	102,597.3	47,593.6	61,194.2
Refinanced	. . .	. . .	. . .	1,524.6	1,155.0	1,273.9	94,152.6	32,869.7	. . .
Unrefinanced	. . .	. . .	1,981.7	2,758.8	5,443.4	6,164.3	8,444.7	14,723.9	. . .
Others (unguaranteed state or private loans)	11.2	175.7	669.7	522.1	312.6	477.4	1,300.0	1,898.0	5,898.3
Total	1,866.8	2,331.2	8,819.4	10,577.7	14,536.6	17,290.6	14,451.9	100,789.1	133,956.3

Source: Central Bank of Nigeria, *First Bank Quarterly Review*, March 1990, pp. 25–26.

Table 10. Nigeria: External Debt Outstanding, 1982–87
(In percent of total)

	1982	1983	1984	1985	1986	1987
Federal	54.64	55.00	42.80	80.75	74.68	84.38
International capital market	50.25	36.94	25.61	31.25	32.98	25.06
World Bank	3.18	25.79	6.993	5.09	9.29	5.92
Bilateral	1.22	0.86	1.39	1.39	2.02	1.46
Capital interest on rescheduled debt	0.00	0.00	0.00	0.00	0.00	2.13
Refinanced debts and promissory notes	0.00	14.41	8.87	7.37	10.02	20.47
Accrued interest on letters of credit	0.00	0.00	0.00	0.00	0.00	2.13
Letters of credit	0.00	0.00	0.00	35.65	20.37	24.61
Guaranteed state enterprise loans	0.00	0.00	0.00	0.00	0.00	2.69
State	22.89	18.92	15.72	19.72	25.32	14.67
International capital market	11.83	10.58	9.79	13.44	19.44	10.44
World Bank	2.87	2.56	2.86	2.34	1.97	2.81
Bilateral	0.63	0.83	0.66	0.72	0.08	0.49
Unguaranteed SGS loans	7.59	4.94	2.41	2.76	3.14	0.93
Unguaranteed private sector loans	0.00	0.00	0.00	0.00	0.00	0.96
Payment arrears	22.47	26.06	41.48	0.00	0.00	0.00

Source: Central Bank of Nigeria, *Annual Report and Statement of Accounts*, various issues.

- debt outstanding and disbursed to exports of goods and services (DSR_3);
- debt outstanding and disbursed to GNP (DSR_4);
- total debt service to GNP (DSR_5);
- interest payments to GNP (DSR_6);
- reserves to debt outstanding and disbursed (DSR_7);
- total external debt to exports of goods and services (DSR_8); and
- total external debt to GNP (DSR_9).

Table 11 shows the trends in these variables for the period 1970–88. The various indexes depict the debt burden and the debt-servicing capacity of Nigeria. The ratio of external debt to income and the ratio of external debt to exports of goods and services are two of the most important indexes. The most convincing evidence of a country's ability to

Table 11. Nigeria: Indicators of Debt Burden and Debt-Servicing Capacity, 1970–88

(In percent)

	DSR_1	DSR_2	DSR_3	DSR_4	DSR_5	DSR_6	DSR_7	DSR_8	DSR_9
1970	7.16	2.09	42.28	4.41	0.73	0.21	30.69	42.28	4.31
1971	4.73	1.49	32.39	4.38	0.64	0.20	55.61	32.39	4.38
1972	4.10	1.38	31.61	4.29	0.56	0.19	39.89	31.61	4.29
1973	6.11	1.04	32.17	6.29	1.19	0.20	38.51	32.17	6.29
1974	1.91	0.42	12.68	3.82	0.58	0.13	431.07	12.68	3.82
1975	2.95	0.50	12.52	2.84	0.67	0.11	461.07	12.53	2.84
1976	3.67	0.40	8.29	1.83	0.81	0.09	521.08	8.29	1.83
1977	1.04	0.39	7.42	1.75	0.25	0.09	379.59	23.70	5.59
1978	1.29	0.57	22.93	4.30	0.24	0.11	50.02	44.14	8.29
1979	2.17	1.43	21.83	5.12	0.51	0.33	126.95	34.34	8.06
1980	4.15	3.28	19.10	5.35	1.16	0.92	180.93	31.91	8.90
1981	9.09	5.87	38.58	8.17	1.92	1.24	40.81	61.08	12.93
1982	16.17	9.70	79.83	11.21	2.27	1.36	15.25	99.50	13.97
1983	23.60	13.04	123.03	15.18	2.91	1.61	7.20	169.57	20.92
1984	33.62	15.71	102.50	13.96	4.58	2.14	11.44	148.72	20.28
1985	38.75	12.76	105.98	16.23	5.93	1.95	11.61	142.72	21.85
1986	29.55	11.80	281.66	42.43	4.45	1.78	5.56	335.52	50.54
1987	13.08	7.58	362.78	118.45	4.27	2.48	4.11	384.03	125.39
1988	29.26	18.76	374.54	100.95	7.89	5.06	2.25	397.18	107.06

Source: Author's calculations using data in World Bank (1989b, 1990a, 1990b).

Note: Variables are defined as follows:

DSR_1 = ratio of total debt service to exports of goods and services (TDS/XGS)
DSR_2 = ratio of interest payment to exports of goods and services (INT/XGS)
DSR_3 = ratio of outstanding and disbursed debt to exports of goods and services (DOD/XGS)
DSR_4 = ratio of debts outstanding and disbursed to GNP (DOD/GNP)
DSR_5 = ratio of total debt service to GNP (TDS/GNP)
DSR_6 = ratio of interest payments to GNP (INT/GNP)
DSR_7 = ratio of reserves to debt outstanding and disbursed (RES/DOD)
DSR_8 = ratio of total external debts to exports of goods and services (EDT/XGS)
DSR_9 = ratio of total external debts to GNP (EDT/GNP).

service foreign debt is the stream of foreign exchange it earns. This is perhaps one of the reasons why "international lenders see the ratio of a nation's debt to exports as an important debt-burden indicator" (Sweet, 1987, p. 9).

One way of looking at the debt problem is in terms of debt service (interest plus amortization) and interest payments in relation to exports and GNP. There can be no doubt that these and some others to be discussed shortly are indicators of the debt burden (Feeder and Just, 1977). Between 1970 and 1980 Nigeria's ratio of debt service to GNP (DSR_5) averaged about 0.7 percent per year. Since 1980 the rate has been on the increase, reaching about 8 percent in 1988.

When the ratio of debt service to exports (DSR_1) is considered, we find two distinct periods: one in which the ratio was less than 8 percent and another in which it was more than 8 percent. The ratio grew to about 39 percent in 1985, representing a very high debt burden. It declined to 13 percent in 1987 but rose again to 29 percent in 1988. In other words, the creditworthiness of Nigeria was in doubt between 1982 and 1986, when this ratio was very high.

Two other significant ratios are the ratios of total external debt to exports (DSR_8) and to GNP (DSR_9). In 1970 and 1972, the first years of the petroleum earnings surge, the debt-export ratio (DSR_8) stood at 42 percent and 32 percent, respectively. It declined thereafter to about 8 percent in 1976 before it started an upward turn, reaching 170 percent in 1983, and 397 percent by 1988. Total external debt as a ratio to GNP (DSR_9) was less than 10 percent between 1970 and 1980. Since the early 1980s, this ratio has been rising, reaching a value of 125 percent in 1987. The ratio declined to 107 percent in 1988.

We can compare the performance of Nigeria's external debt-export ratio and external debt-GNP ratio with that of sub-Saharan Africa as a whole (Table 12). Nigeria's debt-export ratio was better than that of the region up to the late 1980s, when Nigeria's relative situation worsened. Whereas the debt-export ratio for sub-Saharan Africa was 352.4 percent in 1987, it was 384.0 percent for Nigeria. Nigeria also had a better debt-export ratio than the average for the 15 heavily indebted poor countries (a group to which it belongs) until 1987, when conditions deteriorated.

Although Table 12 expresses external debt as a ratio to GDP, and Table 11 expresses it as a ratio to GNP, the two figures are comparable. Nigeria performed better than the sub-Saharan African countries as a group and better than the 15 heavily indebted poor countries for the periods for which comparable data are available. The data also show that Nigeria's debt burden is very high.

In order to assess the impact of the debt problem, ignoring the equity issues, one must ask whether the issue of debt is one of liquidity

Table 12. Debt Burden Indicators for Sub-Saharan Africa and Other Debt-Distressed Countries, 1970–87
(In percent)

	1970[1]	1975[1]	1980	1982	1985	1986	1987
Ratio of external debt to exports of goods and services							
Africa	72.6	71.2	108.7	108.4	230.4	315.0	. . .
Sub-Saharan Africa	65.5	65.2	94.1	190.9	253.6	335.6	352.4
Countries with recent debt-servicing problems[2]	131.7	111.0	155.6	247.0	282.3	322.6	317.0
15 heavily indebted countries[3]	162.5	133.9	169.5	271.9	301.2	361.0	347.6
Ratio of external debt to GDP							
Africa	15.9	19.5	31.9	41.4	50.3	58.1	. . .
Sub-Saharan Africa	14.1	17.1	27.2	38.7	51.2	62.8	81.6
Countries with recent debt-servicing problems[2]	18.7	18.8	34.2	44.6	51.1	51.7	54.2
15 heavily indebted countries[3]	19.6	18.5	33.1	43.0	47.0	49.2	51.3

Sources: Greene and Khan (1989); Greene (1989).

[1]Estimated.

[2]Average for capital-importing countries that experienced external arrears in 1985 or that rescheduled debt during 1984–86.

[3]Average for Argentina, Bolivia, Brazil, Chile, Colombia, Côte d'Ivoire, Ecuador, Mexico, Morocco, Nigeria, Peru, the Philippines, Uruguay, Venezuela, and Yugoslavia.

or solvency problems. The liquidity problem refers to the inability of a country to service debts now, in the amount initially contracted, whereas the solvency issue relates to the "question of whether the value of a country's liabilities exceeds the ability to pay any time" (Dornbusch, 1986a, p. 138). When examined critically, "a solvency problem would mean that the real interest rate on the marginal external loan exceeded the increase in national income made possible by this loan. A liquidity problem would mean that the borrower would be unable to obtain the foreign exchange to make the debt service payments on schedule" (Aliber, 1980, p. 1).

The liquidity and solvency problems raise a number of macroeconomic issues that can be neither ignored nor underrated. The first is whether countries (in both the medium and the long run) can continue to service their debt as contracted and continue to enjoy, at the same time, growth in per capita incomes. The general belief is that this will depend on domestic policies as well as on the scope for effective resource mobilization in terms of both import substitution and export promotion. The extent of a country's success depends on the world economic environment, particularly monetary policy and fiscal policy, as they affect interest rates and the extent of protectionism in world trade. "It is generally believed that if the real interest rates rapidly turn to low levels and the growth of the world trade is strong and sustained, and protectionism is not an issue, then the debt problems can be solved" (Dornbusch and Helmers, 1988, p. 139).

The second macroeconomic issue is related to the intricate balance between pure economics and politics. Given the interwovenness of the two, to what extent are the level of economic activity and living standards depressed in order to generate the needed foreign exchange for servicing debt?

Given the discussion on the liquidity or solvency issue of debt, when did it become apparent that Nigeria had a debt problem? What was the nature of the problem, liquidity or solvency? The first question has been answered from the array of indicators previously discussed. Drawing from the literature, there are many ways of assessing whether a liquidity or a solvency problem exists. One of the ways of determining solvency is to calculate an index of solvency (Cohen, 1985). Given the definition of solvency presented earlier, and following Eaton and Taylor (1986) and Krueger (1987), a country is insolvent when it is incapable of servicing its debt in the long run. By this definition, when debt exceeds the expected discounted present value of the borrower's income stream, the country is insolvent. Most recent authors have focused on export growth as the main variable for measuring the income stream. Thus the simple rule for solvency is that the export growth rate should be greater than the interest rate (Eaton and Taylor, 1986). In other words, if the rate of growth of exports is represented by n, and the interest rate on debt by r, "if $r < n$ then the country's wealth is, in present value terms, infinite and there is no solvency problem: any fraction, however small, of its revenues can repay any level of initial debt in finite time" (Cohen, 1985, p. 143). From Table 13, the average for the period shows that there is no evidence of insolvency in the period 1970–88; the average for the period is about 9 percent.

Lack of liquidity occurs when a country does not have enough cash on hand to pay current obligations, that is, when the maximal income lies below a debt-service obligation in some particular time period (Eaton and Taylor, 1986). There are many indexes that can be used to gauge the liquidity of a nation, such as the relationship between debt and export earnings. One can also look at the difference between net

Table 13. Nigeria: Solvency and Liquidity Calculations, 1970–88

	$n - r$[1] (1)	External Net Debt (In millions of U.S. dollars) (2)	Exports of Goods and Services (In millions of U.S. dollars) (3)	Liquidity Difference (4 = 3 – 2)
1970	–0.06	393	1,341	+
1971	0.45	289	2,041	+
1972	0.09	440	2,316	+
1973	0.55	741	3,746	+
1974	1.64	–4,229	10,048	+
1975	–0.17	–4,126	9,130	+
1976	0.11	–3,815	10,924	+
1977	0.13	–593	13,277	+
1978	–0.23	3,768	11,535	+
1979	0.46	1,199	18,100	+
1980	0.43	–738	27,754	+
1981	–0.38	8,920	19,675	+
1982	–0.45	11,247	12,880	+
1983	–0.26	17,459	10,864	–
1984	0.04	15,983	12,381	–
1985	0.00	17,658	13,540	–
1986	–0.58	22,083	6,904	–
1987	0.05	28,874	7,822	–
1988	–0.09	30,067	7,734	–
Average	0.06			

Source: Author's calculations using data from World Bank (1989b, 1990b).
[1]n is growth of exports and r is the interest rate.

debt (total indebtedness minus foreign reserves) and export earnings and use this to calculate liquidity. If this is done, we find that Nigeria's liquidity problem started in the early 1980s (Table 13).[1] Indeed, the liquidity problem emerged in 1983, when Nigeria began searching for solutions to its economic problems, culminating in rescheduling and the search for loan accommodation and structural adjustment.

Debt Burden and Export Performance

To examine the relationship between the debt burden and export performance, it is important to remember the well-known stability condition: "If the rate of growth of exports exceeds the interest rate, a permanently positive resources gap can be reconciled with a limited

[1]It is assumed that only foreign earnings are used to meet debt obligations.

debt/export ratio" (Simonsen, 1985, p. 103).[2] In other words, we can calculate the rate of unsustainable borrowing as the excess of the percentage rate of growth of debt over the percentage rate of growth of exports of goods and services.

The calculations in Table 14 reveal an interesting story. They show that unsustainable borrowing occurred in 1973, 1977, 1978, and 1981–83, and from 1986 to 1988. The rates of growth of debt in those years were greater than the rate of growth of exports. The story is similar when we use net indebtedness u^*, which is defined as the excess of growth in net external indebtedness over exports. Table 14 shows the relationship between export growth and the interest rate, in an attempt to illustrate that Nigeria's liquidity problem developed in 1983. The parameter reveals that in the years 1978, 1981–83, and 1986, the country was becoming relatively overindebted.

In conclusion, the stability of the debt-export ratio in the long run requires that the rate of growth of exports be higher than the rate of interest on the debt. Thus, of great importance is the "value" of the interest rate at which new loans are contracted when the old ones are being renewed. This parameter is outside the control of borrowers in many cases, because interest rates are determined in the international market, where the debtor country has little say. The other parameter of importance is exports, whose growth can be influenced domestically depending on the macroeconomic policy being pursued, as well as by a favorable international economic environment. An international environment with high growth potential is crucial to promotion of the export sector, as is the absence of protectionism.

Capital Flight and the Real Capacity to Service Debt

Private capital flight in developing countries has received much attention in recent times as a contributor to debt problems. This is particularly true when capital-scarce developing countries borrow heavily in international capital markets. It is generally believed that capital flight is indeed counterproductive.

---

[2]If $Z = D/X$, $x = \dot{X}/X$ and $g = G/X$, where Z is the debt-export ratio, x is the growth of exports, and g stands for the resource gap as a proportion of exports, then

$$\dot{Z} = (i - x)\,Z + g.$$

If Z is kept unchanged over time, this equation implies a sustainable resource gap:

$$g = (x - i)\,Z,$$

which is positive for $x > i$. In this case the resource gap can be sustained indefinitely without the country being pushed into a position of relative overindebtedness.

Table 14. Nigeria: Selected Indicators of Debt and Export Performance, 1970–88

	u	*u**	*CD*	*x*	*tc*	*g*
1970	...	...	...	...	75.7	–2.5
1971	35.0	76.3	14.8	49.9	83.1	14.6
1972	2.7	–37.0	12.4	15.2	87.7	2.6
1973	–2.9	–6.7	64.6	61.7	100.7	17.7
1974	162.5	838.9	5.7	168.2	198.9	20.8
1975	1.1	–6.7	–10.2	–9.1	101.9	–2.1
1976	40.5	27.2	–20.8	19.6	98.2	2.0
1977	–225.7	106.0	247.2	21.5	94.1	3.1
1978	–74.9	722.3	61.8	–31.1	76.8	–10.1
1979	34.8	125.1	22.1	56.9	112.9	15.8
1980	10.9	214.9	42.5	53.3	125.9	13.7
1981	–64.8	1,008.5	35.7	–29.1	77.4	–23.2
1982	–41.2	–97.1	6.6	–34.5	65.3	–44.7
1983	–59.6	–70.9	43.9	–15.7	73.3	–44.7
1984	14.0	16.7	–0.03	14.0	103.6	6.0
1985	4.5	5.4	4.8	9.4	125.8	0
1986	–68.9	–74.1	19.9	–49.0	108.0	–194.6
1987	–16.4	–17.5	29.7	13.3	99.5	19.2
1988	–3.4	–5.3	2.3	–1.1	88.5	–35.7

Source: Author's calculations.
Note: Variables are defined as follows:

u = unsustainable borrowing defined as the excess of the percentage growth rate of debt over that of exports
*u** = unsustainable borrowing defined as the excess of the percentage growth rate of net debt over that of exports
CD = percentage growth of debt
x = rate of growth of exports
tc = transfer coefficient defined as the ratio of exports to imports
g = $(x - i)\,z$—where x is the growth rate of exports, i is the interest rate, and z is the debt-export ratio.

The macroeconomic argument against capital flight is that it is "a perverse exportation of domestic savings and foreign exchange that given the insufficiency of both in low income countries has consequences that may severely hinder their potential for growth" (Lessard and Williamson, 1987, p. 136). Capital flight intensifies the shortage of foreign exchange and of the savings necessary to finance investment projects; capital held abroad could serve a more useful purpose at home.

The existing literature on the causes of capital flight refers to overvaluation of the domestic currency as the most important macroeconomic factor (Dornbusch, 1985). Others include domestic inflation and interest rates (Cuddington, 1986), the domestic economic growth rate

(Conesa, 1987), and external incentives provided by foreign banks and governments (Khan and Ul Haque, 1987). However, for a lot of developing countries capital flight is related more to being in "power" and having access to domestic and foreign money, and it is an issue that goes beyond the straightjacket economics that is often used to explain its magnitude.

The term "capital flight" itself is subject to debate, and there is no precise method of measuring it (Lessard and Williamson, 1987). Three approaches are nevertheless often used: the balance of payments accounts approach, the residual approach, and the increase in the recorded foreign bank deposits owned by the residents of a country (this is usually published by the IMF).

There are no calculated values on the first two approaches for capital flight in Nigeria. Using the IMF statistics, however, the capital flight of the country can be approximated by the cross-border bank deposits of nonbanks by resident depositors.[3] This is used herein as the measure of capital flight. These statistics have inherent limitations that may underestimate capital flight, since substantial funds are held in assets other than bank deposits, and some funds are held in bank deposits outside the major reporting financial centers. The nationality of the depositor is also often not known or not reported correctly. In some cases the national identity and name of some foreign depositors are never made public.

Limited as the statistics may seem, they are nevertheless suggestive and point to the magnitude of the problem. Some useful information derived for the period 1981–88 is shown in Table 15. The first observation is that a substantial amount of money is kept abroad that could assist in the implementation of the nation's macroeconomic policy. Cross-border deposits by Nigerians as a ratio to GNP amounted to 1.3 percent in 1984, and 9.6 percent and 6.8 percent in 1987 and 1988, respectively. If these funds were held at home, they could positively affect the real capacity to service debt.

Some interesting aspects of these figures must be mentioned. Nigerian cross-border deposits of nonbanks by Nigerian residents fell between 1981 and 1982, between 1983 and 1984, and between 1987 and 1988. Between 1986 and 1987 they rose by $620 million, but they fell by $350 million between 1987 and 1988. These fluctuations are very difficult to explain. One explanation is that some of the deposits went into real estate or other investments abroad. Another explanation, however, is that, consequent to the adjustment of the exchange rate in 1986,

[3]I thank Mohsin Khan for directing me to this source of statistics.

Table 15. Nigeria: Cross-Border Deposits of Nonbanks by Domestic Residents, 1981–88

	In Millions of U.S. Dollars	Change from Previous Year (In millions of U.S. dollars)	As Share of External Debt (In percent)	As Share of GNP (In percent)
1981	1,540	. . .	12.8	1.6
1982	1,380	160	10.8	1.5
1983	1,380	0	7.5	1.6
1984	1,170	–210	6.3	1.3
1985	1,500	330	7.8	1.7
1986	1,680	180	7.3	3.7
1987	2,300	620	7.7	9.6
1988	1,950	–350	6.3	6.8

Sources: IMF, *International Financial Statistics Yearbook, 1989*; and World Bank (1990b).

some of the funds that were moved between 1986 and 1987 returned to Nigeria to take advantage of the depreciated naira.

Debt Viability: Growth-cum-Debt Model Scenario

The behavior of the indicators of debt burden under varying assumptions also requires analysis. How do some indicators of debt behave under different assumptions or scenarios? To answer this question we use the growth-cum-debt model developed by Solis and Zedillo (1985), the details of which are in Appendix I. The model uses a simple growth dynamic equation of the type

$$D_t = D_{t-1}\,(1 + \gamma),$$

where D_t = total external debt, and γ is a constant that is varied in each scenario.

The equations solved are Equations (4) and (9) in Appendix I for different possible paths for D_t and r_t. The value of γ is varied in the scenario from –0.05 to 0.07. Three possible values of the interest rate (r = 0.04, 0.08 and 0.10) are used.

Assuming various values for the reciprocal of the incremental capital-output ratio (σ) and for different rates of interest r, simulations were run for the period 1989–95. The indicators used are labeled as DB_1, DB_2, and DB_3, where

DB_1 = the debt-GNP ratio

DB_2 = the interest-export ratio

DB_3 = the resource transfer.

The variables DB_1, DB_2, and DB_3 are further defined as

$$DB_1 = \frac{D}{GNP}$$

$$DB_2 = \frac{r_t D_{t-1}}{XGS}$$

$$DB_3 = \frac{(D_t - D_{t-1}) - (r_t D_{t-1})}{GNP},$$

where D is external debt and r_t is the interest rate. The results are shown in Table 16.

Considering first the high-interest-rate scenario (r = 10 percent), zero growth in the external debt is consistent with an average growth rate of GNP of about 1.9 percent. The debt-GNP ratio (DB_1) would fall to 139.6 percent, which is still very high. The debt-service ratio (DB_2) would be about 32.8 percent, and the resource transfer (DB_3) would be negative at 14.2 percent.

We can also examine the scenarios for the cases where r = 8 percent and r = 4 percent. A zero growth in external indebtedness when r = 4 percent is consistent with a 2.2 percent growth rate of GNP and a reduction of the debt-GNP ratio to 140.6 percent. The resource transfer would continue to be negative, at 5.7 percent of GNP; the debt-service ratio DB_2 would be 13 percent.

When the interest rate is 8 percent, the following picture emerges. Zero growth in the external debt is consistent with an average GNP growth rate of 1.96 percent. The debt-GNP ratio will fall to 139.9 percent. The resource transfer (which is negative) is more than twice the value observed when r = 4 percent.

In terms of this model, a doubling of the interest rate has the same effect on growth of GNP. Only about 0.19 percent is lost when the interest rate is increased to 8 percent from 4 percent, and only about 0.09 percent is lost when the interest rate is increased to 10 percent from 8 percent. This is perhaps not too surprising since the effect of a rise in interest rates is divided between consumption and saving (Solis and Zedillo, 1985). The rise in the interest rate has larger impacts in terms of DB_2 and DB_3, which in all cases are higher. Thus variations in interest rates have effects on debt burdens and debt-service capacity.

Although a zero growth rate for external debt is not only optimistic but somewhat unrealistic, it nevertheless gives a base for the purpose

Table 16. Nigeria: Results of the Growth-cum-Debt Model

γ	g (–)	DB_1	DB_2	DB_3
		$r = 0.04$		
0.07	0.0021	180.075	15.499	5.154
0.06	0.0212	173.862	15.078	3.349
0.05	0.0212	167.850	14.735	1.632
0.04	0.0213	162.032	14.392	0.000
0.03	0.0213	156.405	14.057	–1.551
0.02	0.0214	150.961	13.731	–3.024
0.01	0.0214	145.696	13.413	–4.421
0.00	0.0215	140.605	13.103	–5.747
–0.01	0.0215	135.683	12.801	–7.003
–0.02	0.0216	130.923	12.506	–8.193
–0.03	0.0216	126.323	12.219	–9.318
–0.04	0.0217	121.876	11.940	–10.383
–0.05	0.0217	117.579	11.667	–11.389
		$r = 0.08$		
0.07	0.0189	179.026	30.897	–1.704
0.06	0.0190	172.874	30.175	–3.323
0.05	0.0191	166.981	29.471	–4.859
0.04	0.0192	161.155	28.784	–6.317
0.03	0.0193	155.579	28.114	–7.698
0.02	0.0194	150.183	27.462	–9.007
0.01	0.0195	144.964	26.825	–10.245
0.00	0.0196	139.916	26.205	–11.416
–0.01	0.0197	135.034	25.601	–12.522
–0.02	0.0198	130.313	25.012	–13.566
–0.03	0.0199	125.749	24.438	–14.551
–0.04	0.0200	121.336	23.879	–15.478
–0.05	0.0201	117.071	23.335	–16.352
		$r = 0.10$		
0.05	0.0180	166.458	36.838	–8.068
0.02	0.0184	149.799	34.327	–11.966
0.00	0.0187	139.575	32.757	–14.221
–0.02	0.0189	130.011	31.265	–16.227
–0.05	0.0192	116.819	29.169	–18.811

Source: Author's calculations.
Note: Calculations are based on an incremental capital-output ratio (σ) of 0.40.

of comparison. Similarly, by taking $\sigma = 4$ percent, a very productive economy is assumed. There is perhaps a need to be optimistic in view of various adjustments taking place in the Nigerian economy and the need to put a lid on Nigeria's past extravagance. It is within this context that the model analyzed is meaningful.

Causes of External Debt Accumulation

There is no shortage of literature on the causes of the developing country debt crisis. It is often said that the debt accumulation has been brought about by the overambitious attempts of many governments to speed up growth, prompted by international creditors who were also overly generous. Many creditors overstated the potential capabilities of the debtor countries to meaningfully absorb and pay for debts. Commenting on the origin of the debt crisis in 1982, Dornbusch and Fischer (1985) concluded:

> Imprudent borrowing policies in the debtor countries and imprudent lending by commercial banks had a chance encounter with extraordinarily unfavorable world macroeconomic conditions that exposed the vulnerability of the debtors and the creditors.

In the same vein, Guttentag and Herring (1985) blame the commercial lenders and their regulators. Different authors have emphasized different aspects of the debt crisis. For example, Cline (1985) focuses on the global macroeconomic considerations, and Sachs (1985) stresses not only the importance of the global shocks but also the country-specific factors. Greene (1989) combines both external and internal factors in his description of the causes of sub-Saharan Africa's debt.

One prominent aspect in all these views is that the sources of debt accumulation and the reaction to it differ from one developing country to another. However, there are common themes, such as budget deficits, misaligned exchange rates (generally overvaluation), economic mismanagement, deteriorating terms of trade, and rising real interest rates. Although these are intertwined, the causes of debt accumulation generally fall into two categories: domestic factors (usually merged under the general term of poor performance of macroeconomic policy) and external factors. The division into these two seemingly watertight compartments is not correct, however. Indeed, external factors do impinge crucially on what happens domestically. The same is true of internal (domestic) factors. As Khan and Knight (1983, p. 830) point out, "external factors such as changes in terms of trade may also exert a systematic influence on the real effective exchange rate so that it is not always a reflection of domestic factors alone."

External Factors

A host of external factors, including oil shocks, rising interest rates, and declining terms of trade, are key elements responsible for debt accumulation. When the price of oil increased substantially between 1973 and 1974, Nigeria benefited and public expenditure was expanded sharply. When the price of oil fell, expenditures were not reduced commensurately; the buoyant economy arising from previous periods gave a high credit rating to Nigeria, allowing it to borrow heavily in the period 1978–79. When the second oil shock came in 1979, the industrial countries adopted an anti-inflationary policy stance. The period 1979–82 was one of recession, resulting in a declining value of exports from 1981 to 1983 at a much faster rate than that of imports. Indeed, Nigeria's terms of trade by 1977 and 1988 were, respectively, 46.2 percent and 59.9 percent below their 1980 level. Borrowing was necessitated by declining export earnings and increasing import requirements. Nigeria's import substitution strategy depended on importation of raw materials, equipment, machinery, and food.

Interest rates rose in the 1980s, affecting Nigeria in particular since it made significant use of commercial borrowing. As discussed earlier, the share of private borrowing rose to 85 percent in 1980–82. Similarly, debt at floating rates rose to about 49 percent of total debt in the same period, and interest rates on new commitments also rose, by about 11 percent between 1981 and 1983.

Growth in industrial countries has both direct and indirect effects on developing economies. It has a direct impact by increasing demand for exports from developing countries. Thus, rapid growth in the industrial world pulls up the growth of these economies. A healthy international environment is a sine qua non for strong economic growth, particularly in the developing world (Ajayi, 1989a). The indirect effect is on the terms of trade of developing countries (Khan and Knight, 1983).

In summary, the external factors contributing to Nigeria's debt crisis were

- the cumulative impact of world price shocks—the first resulting in an expansionary policy necessitating heavy borrowing, and the second in restrictive fiscal and monetary policies and thus in rising real interest rates;
- a decline in the terms of trade; and
- liberal lending policies of the international commercial banks.

Domestic Factors

The problems posed by the external factors were exacerbated in most cases by the adoption of wrong macroeconomic policies. Two such domestic errors were those attributed to fiscal irresponsibility and exchange rate misalignment. These often led to large fiscal deficits, excessive monetary expansion and consequent inflation, excessive reliance on external sources of funding, overvalued currencies, and poor project profiles.

Fiscal irresponsibility in this case refers to the size of the government fiscal deficit allowed. Within a Keynesian model, fiscal policy is the main instrument used to shift the economy from one equilibrium position to another. This view is based on the concept that "it is feasible for the fiscal authority to control, at each point in time, the size of the fiscal balance so as to bring it close to what the government wants it to be" (Muns, 1984, p. 117). How the deficit is financed determines to a large extent the impact that it will have on the economy. In general, an increase in the deficit tends to raise domestic absorption and worsen the current account (Khan and Knight, 1983). When the deficit is financed by borrowing from abroad, external indebtedness is increased. Although this indebtedness may be beneficial, there can be problems when loans carry high interest rates, when loans are not used to finance productive expenditures, or when long-run projects are financed with short-term loans (Tanzi and Blejer, 1984).

Nigeria opted to undertake many projects and used its access to the capital market to support "white elephant" projects of doubtful viability. These are projects that have either no income streams to guarantee repayment of loans or a serious mismatch of loan maturities and expected profitability. Nigeria also borrowed funds to maintain consumption in the face of deteriorating export earnings.

In addition to expansionary fiscal policy and borrowing for consumption, Nigeria pursued policies that further weakened its external position in the first half of the 1970s. With growing fiscal deficits coupled with increasing private credit demand, there was a rapid expansion of the money supply, which contributed to higher inflation. Nigeria did not depreciate its currency during the period under consideration; the currency inevitably became overvalued. The extent of overvaluation has been variously put between 80 percent and 84 percent in the period 1970–84. Overvaluation can result from expansionary monetary and fiscal policies (aimed at maximizing growth) and from governmental industrial promotion strategies imposing high duties and quotas or bans on imports of industrial goods that compete with those produced by domestic industries (Ajayi, 1986). The behavior of the real exchange rate—the outcome of changes in the nominal exchange rate and the domestic and foreign rates of inflation—is a reflection of the way exchange rate policy and demand-management policies are coordinated (Khan and Knight, 1983). When the currency is overvalued, demand for imports is raised at the expense of exports. Thus, an appreciated currency, in addition to affecting the fiscal position, affects the current account balance and, ultimately, the magnitude of external borrowing required to finance the deficit on the current account.

Government policy (such as negative real interest rates) that deters saving not only encourages capital outflows, but also contributes to debt accumulation because external financing is needed to bridge the gap. All these domestic factors increase borrowing needs and lower the earnings from exports, and in the process reduce the ability to meet the rising debt-service obligations.

In summary, there were some changes in the international economy that could not have been anticipated by Nigeria's policymakers. These included the sharp increases in nominal and real interest rates, the duration and severity of the worldwide recession, and changes in the terms of trade resulting from the oil price increase of 1979, culminating in declines in commodity prices. Internal factors also played substantial roles. Nigeria had poor macroeconomic policy management in the early 1970s and particularly in the late 1970s, which would have resulted in problems even without the external surprises.

When it would have been appropriate to adjust, in the late 1970s and early 1980s, foreign exchange reserves were instead run down, and later heavy external borrowing took place, to avoid adjustment. The unrealistic nature of macroeconomic policy (resulting in overvaluation) and the inappropriateness of trade regimes discouraged export growth. The issue of the changed external environment was not properly addressed at the appropriate time, and domestic policy exacerbated the situation.

Empirical Estimates of the External and Internal Factors

The preceding section identified and analyzed the internal and external factors influencing Nigeria's debt accumulation. This section gives the analysis some empirical content, and this is done in two stages. The first stage follows the work of Krueger (1987), attempting a quantitative assessment of the following:

- the extent to which Nigeria borrowed in an unsustainable manner in the 1970s (this could be due to trade policy that did not support growth in export earnings to sustain additional debt, and/or to unsustainable macroeconomic policies);

- the extent to which the downturn of the early 1980s resulted in an altered world economic environment that fueled debt accumulation and the debt burden; and
- the extent to which Nigeria undertook policy reforms designed to avert imminent problems.

It should be emphasized here that although the contributory factors may be arbitrary, they nevertheless allow us to identify the origin of the debt crisis.

The analysis uses data on growth rates of export earnings and the deviation of export earnings from share-weighted world trade and debt. These figures are then used to estimate the unsustainable portion of the debt buildup for the 1970s and 1980s. The unsustainable portion is apportioned between deviations in country performance from average world trade performance and unsustainable macroeconomic policy. The shift in world conditions is added as an additional factor for the 1980s.

For the analysis, world exports are broken down into fuel and nonfuel exports in world markets. Constant share-weighted world trade was calculated on the basis of the 1976–78 shares of fuel and nonfuel exports in world markets. It is therefore possible to compare actual growth rates with constant-share growth. Thus, if actual growth performance is greater than the constant-share growth (represented by a minus sign), the impact of trade policy is positive. If the converse is true, that is, if constant-share growth is greater than actual performance, the country's trade policy was inadequate for it to maintain its share of world markets (see Krueger, 1987, p. 174). The results for 1970–79 and for 1979–82 are presented in Table 17.

Although Nigeria had a rising share of the petroleum market and fast growth in exports, the data show that, for the period 1970–79, the rate of growth of debt exceeded that of exports. This meant that Nigeria had macroeconomic policies that led to an accumulation of debt in excess of what was sustainable as judged by the export performance of the country. For the entire period, the net effect was 51.0 percent, indicating that macroeconomic policy coupled with inadequate trade policy led to a rate of borrowing that was not sustainable.

For the period 1979–82, the international economy deteriorated. There was a rapid decline in world export growth from 27.7 percent to 0.6 percent. Nigeria was not able to maintain the growth of debt to its exports, and neither trade performance nor macroeconomic policy offset the decline in the global economy. Thus, instead of adjusting to the changed international environment, the situation deteriorated because of it and was worsened by internal economic policies. By 1982 the debt-export ratio had risen significantly.

Table 17. Nigeria: Debt Buildup, 1970–82
(In percent)

	Average Annual Change	
	1970–79	1979–82
Growth of		
World exports[1]	27.9	0.6
Country's exports	48.6	–7.2
Country's debt	99.6	26.5
Excess debt from		
Unfavorable export performance	–20.7	–7.8
Macroeconomic policy	71.7	–1.4
Net	51.0	33.7
Debt-export ratio at end of period	34.3[2]	99.4[3]

Sources: Author's calculations from data in World Bank (1989b, 1990b); World Bank, *World Tables*, various issues, and Krueger (1987).

Notes: Growth rates are calculated on an end-point basis.

[1]Weighted by the 1976–78 fuel and nonfuel export shares for Nigeria.

[2]Refers to 1979.

[3]Refers to 1982.

The second method uses regression analysis to estimate the internal and external factors in the debt crisis.[4] The model has the following general form:

$$DSR_i = f(TOT, CGDP, FRRI, FPY, T, REER),$$

where

DSR_i = the debt-export ratio or the debt-GNP ratio

TOT = the terms of trade

$CGDP$ = the growth rate of income in industrial countries

$FRRI$ = the foreign real interest rate

FPY = the fiscal position of government, defined as revenue minus expenditure divided by GDP or GNP

T = a linear time trend

$REER$ = the real effective change rate index (developed in Appendix II).

In some regressions the growth rate of the terms of trade (*CTOT*) was used, and in others the fiscal balance itself (*FP*) rather than its

[4]This section has benefited immensely from a different but similar analysis by Khan and Knight (1983) and also subsequent discussion with Mohsin Khan. In what follows, we use DSR_8 and DSR_9, the debt-export ratio and the debt-GDP ratio, respectively.

ratio to GDP or GNP. Some regressions used logarithms of the terms of trade (*LTOT* and *LCTOT*) or real effective exchange rate (*LREER*) variables.

An improvement in the terms of trade or an increase in the growth rate of the industrial countries should lead to an improvement in the debt-export ratio. An increase in the foreign real interest rate would tend to worsen this ratio, just as an appreciation in terms of the real effective exchange rate would. The time trend variable, on the other hand, captures the influences of other external environmental factors such as trade barriers. Given the definition of the fiscal position, an increase in the ratio of government revenue minus expenditure to income means an improvement in the fiscal position. It is expected that a deterioration of the fiscal position will have a negative impact on these ratios.

In estimating the equations, various forms of the independent variables were used. In some cases the fiscal performance level was replaced with the fiscal surplus or deficit of the government (*FP*). The results of the estimations using the general equation incorporating both internal and external factors are shown in Tables 18 and 19.

From the tables we find in general that a worsening of the terms of trade worsens the debt-export ratio, as does a rise in the foreign real interest rate. A fall in the growth of industrial countries has the same effect. We would expect an improvement in the fiscal position to have a positive effect on this ratio. The significance of the time trend variable in all cases indicates that other variables not included in the regression analysis are very important. The goodness of fit of all the equations is good, however.

One cannot directly ascertain the relative importance of the variables included in the equations from their coefficients. Therefore beta coefficients are used, with the advantage that these measure the change in the explained variable (in standard deviation units) for a unit change in each explanatory variable (in standard units), holding other variables constant. These coefficients are presented in Table 20 for the debt-export ratio and in Table 21 for the debt-GNP ratio. The tables show (leaving out the time trend and constants) that the most important variables are the real effective exchange rate and the terms of trade, in all equations except one where fiscal performance is more important.

The results reported herein lend credence to the earlier findings that domestic policies have played an important role in the debt burden and other economic problems afflicting Nigeria. It should be emphasized that linkages exist between the domestic and external factors in

Table 18. Nigeria: Empirical Results for the Debt-Export Ratio

Variable	Regression 1	Regression 2	Regression 3	Regression 4
Constant	–3.140 (–0.413)	9.490 (6.296)*	–11.489 (–6.212)*	9.728 (8.291)*
LCTOT			–0.055 (–0.6941)	
TOT	–0.023 (–3.855)*	–0.045 (–4.848)*		–0.043 (–6.350)*
CGDP	–0.067 (–0.764)	–0.305 (2.531)*	0.122 (1.669)	–0.283 (2.680)*
FRRI	–0.004 (0.291)	–0.023 (–0.838)	0.007 (0.342)	–0.013 (–0.503)
T	0.319 (3.583)*		0.067 (8.990)*	
$REER_2$				–0.043 (–7.004)*
$LREER_1$	0.555 (0.411)			
$LREER_2$		–0.041 (–5.741)*		
FPY		1,293.28 (0.642)		
$REER_1$			0.053 (5.195)*	
FP			–0.053 (–1.289)	0.095 (1.721)
R^2	0.936	0.803	0.913	0.842
DW	1.728	1.435	1.767	1.546

Source: Author's calculations.
Note: *t*-statistics are in parentheses. Asterisked variables are significant above the 5 percent level.

the analysis, and that there is a very thin line between domestic and external variables.

Summary and Policy Implications

This chapter has analyzed the external debt of Nigeria within a general macroeconomic framework recognizing the specific nature of Nigeria's debt. A number of significant findings of this work can be highlighted:

Table 19. Nigeria: Empirical Results for the Debt-GNP Ratio

Variable	Regression 1	Regression 2	Regression 3	Regression 4
Constant	–5.579	–2.889	–6.830	–3.973
	(0.691)	(–5.502)	(–2.781)*	(–5.532)*
LCTOT		0.027	0.025	0.030
		(1.163)	(0.783)	(0.977)
TOT	–0.022			
	(–3.405)*			
CGDP	–0.040	0.027	0.040	0.054
	(–40.411)	(1.123)	(1.196)	(1.831)*
FRRI	–0.001	–0.003	–0.004	0.006
	(–0.101)	(–0.046)	(–0.447)	(0.735)
T	0.349	0.140	0.139	0.180
	(3.571)*	(7.005)*	(4.128)*	(6.926)*
$REER_2$				0.018
				(4.661)
$LREER_1$				
$LREER_2$	0.974		1.158	
	(0.691)		(2.551)*	
FPY		–1,463.19	–1,275.12	
		(–4.372)*	(–2.658)*	
$REER_1$		0.013		
		(4.515)*		
FP				–0.043
				(–2.637)*
R^2	0.938	0.899	0.808	–0.829
DW	1.653	1.964	1.529	1.951

Source: Author's calculations.
Note: *t*-statistics are in parentheses. Asterisked variables are significant above the 5 percent level.

- Structural changes took place in the composition of external debt outstanding. Whereas the preponderance of external debt outstanding came from official sources between 1970 and 1972, the share of private sources of external debt became important in the 1980s. By 1987 the share of external debt from private sources was 55 percent. Whereas less than 1 percent of total long-term debt was at floating rates between 1973 and 1975, that share stood at 49 percent in 1987. Thus the significant characteristics of Nigeria's debt structure are an increase in debt contracted at floating rates and a decrease in the share of official loans.

Table 20. Nigeria: Value of Beta Coefficients, Debt-Export Ratio

Variable	Regression 1	Regression 2	Regression 3	Regression 4
Constant	–2.323	7.021	–8.590	7.197
LCTOT			–0.070	
TOT	–0.440	–0.847	0.144	–0.819
CGDP	–0.079	–0.360	0.050	–0.333
FRRI	–0.029	0.167	3.115	–0.091
T	1.123			
$REER_2$				
$LREER_1$	0.150	–1.247		–1.281
$LREER_2$		0.116		
FPY			1.480	
$REER_1$			–0.144	
FP				0.259

Source: Author's calculations.

- Nigeria's debt-export ratio has been on the high side since the 1980s. That ratio was better than that of the rest of the subcontinent until the late 1980s, when the Nigerian situation worsened.
- Nigeria's accumulation of external debt can be directly traced to both domestic and external causes. The domestic causes include poor macroeconomic policies arising from fiscal irresponsibility, exchange rate misalignment (generally overvaluation), and economic mismanagement. The external causes include deteriorating terms of trade and rising real interest rates. It is difficult, however, to separate these factors into watertight compartments because of interlinkages.
- Empirical analyses demonstrate that Nigeria had macroeconomic policies that led to the accumulation of debt in excess of what was sustainable as judged by its export performance. It has been found that, for the entire period, macroeconomic policy coupled with inadequate trade policy led to a rate of borrowing that was not sustainable. When the international economy deteriorated in 1979–82, neither Nigeria's trade performance nor its macroeconomic policy offset the negative impact of the decline in the global economy.

The two main lessons to be drawn from this analysis are the need to pay off indebtedness and the need to restore the path of growth and

Table 21. Nigeria: Value of Beta Coefficients, Debt-GNP Ratio

Variable	Regression 1	Regression 2	Regression 3	Regression 4
Constant	–4.127	–7.754	–18.347	–10.672
LCTOT		0.127	0.199	0.140
TOT	–0.409			
CGDP	–0.409	0.116	0.170	0.229
FRRI	–0.011	–0.007	–0.099	0.153
T	1.230	1.784	1.779	2.305
$REER_2$				1.950
$LREER_1$				
$LREER_2$	0.282		1.219	
FPY		–0.478	–0.417	
$REER_1$			1.335	
FP				–0.424

Source: Author's calculations.

development. Paying off present debt is important, but the policy question is whether, given the existing level of debt and the payments arising from it, growth can be restored and sustained in the near future. Thus the issue of debt forgiveness, debt reduction, and interest rate reduction should be given serious consideration. Although the 1988 Toronto summit was important (even though the resulting cash flow relief has not been significant for the highly indebted countries), the initiatives are commendable, and further attempts in this direction can be beneficial.

The current solution to debt is said to rest on three pillars:

- a favorable international economic environment;
- strong and sustained adjustment efforts by countries that are heavily indebted; and
- an adequate flow of external financing.

It is generally believed that the restoration of sustained economic growth requires a proper mix of these three pillars. In the international economic environment, there is a need to eliminate trade restrictions, for example by decelerating or eliminating nontariff barriers. An open international trading system should be emphasized and action taken on the high real cost of external debt. High interest rates are likely to worsen the debt-servicing problems of highly indebted countries.

The extent, composition, and dimension of Nigeria's external debt raise a number of policy issues. The debt burden imposes a number of constraints on the country's growth prospects. The major macroeconomic problems are the need to earn foreign exchange and to find extra budget resources for debt service and adjust to a reduction in spendable resources.

To reduce the debt burden and increase debt-servicing capacity, an increase in exports and a reduction in world interest rates are required. Thus, two important external policy areas in this respect are real interest rates and protectionism.

Although the analyses above seem to emphasize the external sector, a larger role needs to be assigned to domestic policy. A cautious macroeconomic policy that avoids inflation and currency overvaluation should be adopted, and, in addition or as part of the package, borrowed funds must be used productively. The present structural adjustment program aims at expanding the productive base, removing infrastructural bottlenecks, and eliminating public sector inefficiency.

To restore investment to the levels needed for sustainable growth, the evolution of appropriate domestic policy to increase saving and promote investment will be required. Thus, policies that foster saving habits and remove impediments to investment will be necessary. Foreign investment, although beneficial, will only be forthcoming if the economic environment is suitable and if political stability exists. More reliance on domestic saving in the future will be needed, given the increasing stagnation in international capital flows to indebted countries.

Appendix I. The Debt Viability Model

The model used to estimate debt viability is the growth-cum-debt model described in the text (Solis and Zedillo, 1985).

The level of output is given by

$$Y = \sigma K. \tag{1}$$

Define

$$\Delta Y = \sigma(\Delta K) \tag{2}$$

$$\Delta K = I_t - \delta K_{t-1}. \tag{3}$$

Equation (1) becomes

$$Y_t = \sigma I_t + (1 - \delta)Y_{t-1}. \tag{4}$$

Given the following identities:

$$C_t + I_t + X_t - M_t = Y_t = C_t + S_t + r_t D_{t-1} \tag{5}$$

and

$$d_t = M_t - X_t + r_t D_{t-1}, \tag{6}$$

consequently, $I_t = S_t + d_t$. (7)

Let the saving function be

$$S_t = s\,(Y_t - r_t D_{t-1}). \tag{8}$$

Using Equation (4), investment can be expressed as

$$I_t = \left[\frac{s(1-\delta)}{1-s\sigma}\right] Y_{t-1} - \left(\frac{sr_t}{1-s\sigma}\right) D_{t-1} + \left(\frac{1}{1-s\sigma}\right) d_t \,\cdot \tag{9}$$

Equations (4) and (9) were solved for a number of possible paths of D and rt. The rule used for D_t is the dynamic equation

$$D_t = D_{t-1}\,(1+\gamma).$$

Appendix II. The Real Effective Exchange Rate

There are many methods of deriving the real effective exchange rate. One of the methods uses trade weights (exports plus imports), and it can use varying trade weights or specific-year trade weights. A specific year is chosen as the base in the latter case.

Another method uses import weights, which again can be done using varying import weights or specific-year import weights. Both of these methods capture the relationship between a country and its trading partners.

This chapter defines the real effective exchange rate as

$$\pi = \left(\frac{E_{it}}{E_{i0}} \bullet \frac{CPI_f}{CPI_d}\right)^{Wi},$$

where

E_{it} = price of domestic currency in terms of the ith trading partner at time t

E_{i0} = price of domestic currency in terms of the ith trading partner in the base period

CP_{If} = consumer price index of the foreign country at time t relative to the base period

CP_{Id} = consumer price index of the home country relative to the base period

W_i = weight of the trading partner included in the calculation of the index (the weights used are 1980 import weights) for seven of Nigeria's major trading partners.

We have two exchange rate measures defined as follows:

$$REER_1 = \left(\frac{E_{it}}{E_{i0}} \bullet \frac{CPI_f}{CPI_d}\right)^{W_i}$$

$$REER_2 = \left(\frac{E_{it}}{E_{i0}} \bullet \frac{WPI_f}{CPI_d}\right)^{W_i}.$$

The additional variable WPI_f is the wholesale price index of the foreign country.

References

Ajayi, S. Ibi, 1986, "Issues of Overvaluation and Exchange Rate Adjustment in Nigeria" (Washington: Economic Development Institute, World Bank).

———, 1989a, "Economic Survival: The Third World in the International Economy," inaugural lecture delivered at the University of Ibadan, March 30.

———, 1989b, "Exchange Rate Adjustment in Selected African Countries" (Washington: Economic Development Institute, World Bank).

Aliber, Rober Z., 1980, "A Conceptual Approach to the Analysis of External Debt of the Developing Countries," World Bank Staff Working Paper No. 421 (Washington: World Bank).

Bienen, Henry, 1983, "Oil Revenues and Policy Choice in Nigeria," World Bank Staff Working Paper No. 592 (Washington: World Bank).

Central Bank of Nigeria, *Annual Report and Statement of Accounts* (Lagos, various years).

———, *Economic and Financial Review* (Lagos, various issues).

Cline, W.R., 1985, "International Debt: Analysis, Experience and Prospects," *Journal of Development Planning*, Vol. 16.

Cohen, Daniel, 1985, "Reassessing Third World Debt," *Economic Policy*.

Conesa, E.R., 1987, "The Causes of Capital Flight from Latin America" (Washington: Inter-American Development Bank).

Corden, W. Max, 1990, "Macroeconomic Policy and Growth: Some Lessons of Experience," paper presented at the World Bank Annual Conference on Development Economics, Washington, April 26–27.

Cuddington, J.T., 1986, "Capital Flight: Estimates, Issues and Explanations," Princeton Studies in International Finance No. 58 (Princeton, New Jersey: Princeton University Press).

Dhonte, P., 1975, "Describing External Debt Situations: A Roll-Over Approach," *Staff Papers*, International Monetary Fund, Vol. 22 (March).

Dornbusch, R., 1985, "External Debt, Budget Deficits and Disequilibrium Exchange Rates," in *International Debt and the Developing Countries: A World Bank Symposium*, ed. by Gordon W. Smith and J.T. Cuddington (Washington: World Bank).

———, 1986a, "International Debt and Economic Instability," in *Debt, Financial Stability and Public Policy: A Symposium Sponsored by the Federal Reserve Bank of Kansas City, Jackson Hole, Wyoming, August 27–29, 1986* (Kansas City, Missouri: Federal Reserve Bank of Kansas City).

———, 1986b, "Third World," *Science*, Vol. 234.

———, 1986c, *Dollars, Debts and Deficits* (Cambridge, Massachusetts: MIT Press).

Dornbusch, R., and S. Fischer, 1985, "The World Debt Problem: Origin and Prospects," *Journal of Development Planning*, Vol. 16.

Dornbusch, R., and F.L.C.H. Helmers, eds., 1988, *The Open Economy: Tools for Policymakers in Developing Countries* (New York: Oxford University Press).

Eaton, J., and Lance Taylor, 1986, "Developing Country Finance and Debt," *Journal of Development Economics*.

Federal Republic of Nigeria, 1986, *Federal Republic of Nigeria Approved Budget* (Lagos).

Feeder, G., and R. Just, 1977, "A Study of Debt Servicing Capacity Applying Logit Analysis," *Journal of Development*, Vol. 4.

Filatove, V.S., and R.P. Mattione, 1985, "Latin America's Recovery from Debt Problems: An Assessment of Model Based Projections," *Journal of Policy Modelling*.

Fishlow, A., 1985, "The Debt Crisis: A Longer Perspective," *Journal of Development Planning*, Vol. 16.

Fleleke, N.S., 1984, "The Budget Deficit: Are the International Consequences Unfavorable?" *New England Economic Review*.

Frenkel, Jacob A., Michael P. Dooley, and Peter Wickham, eds., 1989, *Analytical Issues in Debt* (Washington: International Monetary Fund).

Frydl, Edward J., and Dorothy M. Sobol, 1988, "Prospects for LDC Debt Management: Debt Reduction Versus Debt Forgiveness," Research Paper No. 8826 (New York: Federal Reserve Bank of New York).

Greene, J.E., 1989, "External Debt Problem of Sub-Saharan Africa," in *Analytical Issues in Debt*, ed. by Jacob A. Frenkel, Michael P. Dooley, and Peter Wickham (Washington: International Monetary Fund).

Greene, J.E., and Mohsin S. Khan, 1989, "The African Debt Crisis," paper presented at the meeting of the African Economic Research Consortium, Nairobi, May 27–30.

Guttentag, Jack M., and Richard Herring, 1985, "Commercial Bank Lending to Developing Countries: From Overlending to Underlending to Structural Reform," in *International Debt and the Developing Countries: A World Bank Symposium*, ed. by Gordon W. Smith and John T. Cuddington (Washington: World Bank).

Helleiner, G.K., 1986a, "Balance of Payments Experience and Growth Prospects of Developing Countries: A Synthesis," *World Development*, Vol. 14, No. 8.

———, 1986b, "Outward Orientation, Import Instability and African Economic Growth: An Empirical Investigation," in *Theory and Reality in Development: Essays in Honor of Paul Streeten*, ed. by Sanjaya Lall and Frances Stewart (New York: Macmillan).

———, 1989, "The Sub-Saharan African Debt Problem: Issues for International Policy," paper presented at the Second World Scientific Banking Conference, Dubrovnik, June 7–10.

Husain, Ishrat, and I. Diwan, eds., 1989, *Dealing with the Debt Crisis: A World Bank Symposium* (Washington: World Bank).

International Monetary Fund, *International Financial Statistics Yearbook* (Washington, various issues).

———, 1986, *World Economic Outlook, May 1986: A Survey by the Staff of the International Monetary Fund,* World Economic and Financial Surveys (Washington).

Khan, Mohsin S., and Malcolm D. Knight, 1983, "Determinants of Current Account Balances of Non-Oil Developing Countries in the 1970s: An Empirical Analysis," *Staff Papers*, International Monetary Fund, Vol. 32, No. 4.

Khan, Mohsin S., and Peter J. Montiel, 1988, "Growth-Oriented Adjustment Programs: A Conceptual Framework," IMF Working Paper No. 88/64 (Washington: International Monetary Fund).

Khan, Mohsin S., and Nadeem Ul Haque, 1987, "Capital Flight from Developing Countries," *Finance & Development* (March).

Klein, Thomas, 1987, "Debt Relief for African Countries," *Finance & Development* (December).

Krueger, A.O., 1987, "Origins of the Developing Countries Debt Crisis," *Journal of Development Economics*, Vol. 27.

Krumm, K.L., 1985, "The External Debt of Sub-Saharan Africa: Origins, Magnitude and Implications for Action," World Bank Staff Working Paper No. 741 (Washington: World Bank).

Lessard, D.R., and John Williamson, eds., 1987, *Capital Flight and Third World Debt* (Washington: Institute for International Economics).

Maddala, G.S., 1977, *Econometrics* (Tokyo: McGraw-Hill and Kogakusha Ltd).

Mistry, Percy S., 1988, *African Debt: The Case for Relief for Sub-Saharan Africa* (Oxford: Oxford International Associates).

Muns, Joaquin, 1984, *Adjustment, Conditionality, and International Financing* (Washington: International Monetary Fund).

Nelson, Joan M., ed., 1990, *Economic Crisis and Policy Choice: The Politics of Adjustment in the Third World* (Princeton, New Jersey: Princeton University Press).

Officer, L.H., 1976, "The Purchasing Power Parity Theory of Exchange Rates," *Staff Papers*, International Monetary Fund, Vol. 22.

Ortiz, F., and J. Serra-Puche, 1986, "A Note on the Burden of the Mexican Foreign Debt," *Journal of Development Economics*, Vol. 21, No. 1.

Pfefferman, Guy, 1985, "Overvalued Exchange Rates and Development," *Finance & Development*, Vol. 22 (March).

Remolona, Eli M., and others, 1986, "Foreign Debt, Balance of Payments and the Philippines in 1983–84," *World Development*, Vol. 14, No. 8.

Rhomberg, R.F., 1976, "Indices of Effective Exchange Rates," *Staff Papers*, International Monetary Fund, Vol. 23.

Sachs, J., 1985, "Theoretical Issues in International Borrowing," Princeton Studies in International Finance No. 54 (Princeton, New Jersey: Princeton University Press).

———, 1988, "External Debt and Macroeconomic Performance in Latin America and East Asia," *Brookings Papers on Economic Activity: 2*, Brookings Institution.

———, ed., 1989, *Developing Country Debt and the World Economy* (Chicago: University of Chicago Press).

Selowsky, Marcello, and H.G. Van der Tak, 1986, "The Debt Problem and Growth," *World Development*, Vol. 14, No. 9.

Simonsen, Mario Henrique, 1985, "The Developing Country Debt Problem," in *International Debt and the Developing Countries: A World Bank Symposium*, ed. by Gordon W. Smith and J.T. Cuddington (Washington: World Bank).

Solis, Leopoldo, and Ernesto Zedillo, 1985, "The Foreign Debt of Mexico," in *International Debt and the Developing Countries: A World Bank Symposium*, ed. by Gordon W. Smith and J.T. Cuddington (Washington: World Bank).

Svedberg, P., 1990, "The Export Performance of Sub-Saharan Africa," *Economic Development and Cultural Change*, Vol. 38.

Sweet, L.M., 1987, "Currency Composition of Developing Country Debt: The Impact of Dollar Depreciation," Research Paper No. 8702 (New York: Federal Reserve Bank of New York).

Tallroth, Nills Borje, 1987, "Structural Adjustment in Nigeria," *Finance & Development*, Vol. 24 (December).

Tanzi, Vito, and Mario I. Blejer, 1984, "Fiscal Deficits and Balance of Payments Disequilibrium in IMF Adjustment Programs," in *Adjustment, Conditionality and International Financing*, ed. by Joaquin Muns (Washington: International Monetary Fund).

World Bank, *World Debt Tables* (Washington, various years).

———, 1986, *World Debt Tables, 1985–86* (Washington).

———, 1988, *World Debt Tables, 1987–88* (Washington).

———, 1989a, *World Development Report* (New York: Oxford University Press).

———, 1989b, *World Debt Tables, 1988–89* (Washington).

———, 1990a, *World Tables, 1989–90* (Washington).

———, 1990b, *World Debt Tables: External Debt of Developing Countries, 1989–90* (Washington).

World Bank and United Nations Development Program, 1989, *Africa's Adjustment and Growth in the 1980s* (Washington: World Bank).

Ghana: The Burden of Debt-Service Payment Under Structural Adjustment 3

Barfour Osei

Many sub-Saharan African countries face a serious external debt problem. The severity of the problem is seen from the size of the current debt relative to income, and from the high debt-service payments. From an estimated total of $6 billion at the end of 1970, the external debt of sub-Saharan African countries rose to an estimated $161 billion at the end of 1990 (World Bank, 1991b), representing over 110 percent of GNP. Debt service also rose from under $1 billion a year to over $10 billion, representing about 25 percent of export earnings. The huge expansion in the size of the debt relative to income not only can lead to capital flight but can also discourage future external funding for development in the region. High debt service means that a significant proportion of convertible currency is consumed by debt, thereby limiting countries' ability to import goods and services. Debt service also constitutes a considerable share of the budget in many countries and so imposes significant constraints on domestic investment.

The size of the current debt and of debt-service payments is compounded by the great poverty and serious structural weaknesses of sub-Saharan African economies. Structural weaknesses such as lack of a diversified export base make it more difficult for these countries to adjust to changing world economic conditions. Also, higher population growth in these countries makes achieving higher per capita income growth more difficult. These weaknesses prevent these countries from achieving the rapid economic growth necessary to escape from debt difficulties.

Beginning in the early 1980s, many sub-Saharan African countries embarked on structural adjustment. A dominant economic issue is how far the debt problem obstructs the drive toward rapid and sustainable growth. It is recognized that the debt problem varies not only between groups of countries, but also among countries within the same group. Therefore, proper understanding of the debt problem would necessarily require in-depth analysis of the situations in individual countries, followed by a synthesis of lessons from particular experiences. This chapter on Ghana intends to develop that understanding and synthesis.

The purpose of this chapter is to explore in detail the implications of Ghana's external indebtedness for sustained economic growth. The focus of the analysis is on debt in the 1983–90 period, during which Ghana pursued an Economic Recovery Program (ERP) and adopted structural adjustment policies. Where necessary, data are drawn from outside this period for comparative analysis. Specific issues addressed include

- the main features of the debt, including the size, type, sources, structure, and terms;
- the debt burden and the causes of the present debt difficulties;
- the sustainability of the debt; and
- the impact of the debt on economic growth.

The main objective is to provide a better understanding of Ghana's debt problem in order that adequate and effective debt management measures can be sought.

The chapter is divided into six sections. The section following this introduction provides background information. It examines Ghana's economic structure and performance and traces the accumulation of debt before the inception of the ERP. This section also discusses the dimensions of the debt. The next section assesses the debt burden and the causes of the current debt difficulties. The section after that tackles the issue of debt sustainability and fiscal stability. The impact of the debt on long-term economic growth is assessed in the final section before the conclusion.

Background

The Ghanaian Economy: Structure, Performance, and Debt Accumulation

A useful starting point in studying Ghana's present debt problems is to look at the economy's performance, its structural change, and past debt accumulation, since the present debt problems cannot be divorced from any of these.

The Ghanaian economy suffered a protracted decline in the three decades following independence in 1957, particularly in the 1970s and early 1980s. Output grew at a modest 2.2 percent a year between 1960 and 1970 (Table 1) but declined at a rate of 0.5 percent a year during the following decade. With a fast-growing population, Ghana moved from classification as a middle-income country in the 1960s to that of a low-income country by the end of the 1970s.

The economy has always been dominated by agriculture. An attempt to change this structure contributed to the poor economic performance during the first decade after independence. The government sought to stimulate social and economic development through industrialization, by establishing a number of import-substituting industries. Consequently, manufacturing grew rapidly, increasing its share of GDP from 2 percent to 9 percent between 1957 and 1960. Manufacturing also became an important contributor to exports, with a 14 percent share in 1969.

The industrialization attempt was biased against agriculture, however. The share of agriculture in GDP dropped from nearly 60 percent to 46 percent between 1957 and 1969. There was no clear policy for developing agriculture to feed the newly established industries, most of which relied on imported raw materials. Hence the attempt to make the country self-reliant through import substitution also made it foreign exchange dependent. Because of its neglect, agriculture, primarily cocoa, remained a relatively low productivity sector in the sense that, although it was the largest employer of labor, it contributed proportionately less to GDP. Cocoa, for example, employed 17 percent of the labor force to produce only 8 percent of GDP. As the nation's major foreign exchange earner and a major contributor to tax revenue, cocoa's neglect without an appropriate substitute contributed immensely to the decline in the economy.

The industrialization effort and the speed with which it was pursued dictated the pace of debt accumulation. As Ghana's first president Kwame Nkrumah said, "We need to do in ten years what has taken others a hundred years to do" (quoted in Killick, 1978).

In the haste to industrialize, heavy foreign borrowing became necessary, especially after 1961, because of a sharp shortfall in export earnings. Plants and equipment were financed largely by foreign supplier credits. These credits were of short maturity, and the heavy reliance on them caused debt problems to emerge early in the postindependence development effort. External debt rose sharply, from almost nothing at independence to nearly $600 million at the end of 1965; over 80 percent of this total consisted of suppliers' credits that had come due for repayment. However, because of the neglect of cocoa on the one hand, and external factors on the other hand, export earnings did not improve, as the debt rose and repayments came due. Hence, Ghana was by the end of 1965 facing a debt repayment crisis, which was resolved through debt-rescheduling agreements in 1966, 1968, and 1970.

The structure of the economy continued to be dominated by agriculture, and the neglect of the sector precipitated the economic decline of the 1970–82 period. By 1982 the share of agriculture had returned to 55 percent (Table 1), yet the nation was not producing enough to feed itself. The increase in the share of the agricultural sector was mainly

Table 1. Ghana: Selected Macroeconomic Indicators, 1960–70, 1975, and 1980–90

(In percent of GDP except as noted)

	1960–70	1975	1980	1981	1982	1983	1984	1985	1986	1987	1988	1989	1990
Growth rate of GDP													
(in percent a year)	2.2	–12.4	0.5	–3.5	–6.9	–4.6	8.6	5.1	5.2	4.8	5.6	5.1	3.0
Inflation (in percent a year)	2.0	29.8	50.2	116.5	22.3	122.8	39.7	10.3	24.6	39.8	31.4	25.0	37.1
National accounts													
Consumption	88	87	93	95	96	96	98	94	93.6	92.2	94.5	93.8	93.3
Gross domestic investment	. . .	12.7	5.6	4.6	3.4	3.7	6.9	9.6	9.4	10.4	10.3	13.5	15.1
Gross domestic saving	. . .	9.6	4.5	4.0	3.7	3.3	5.6	7.6	7.7	8.2	10.7	6.0	10.8
Sectoral distribution													
Agriculture	44	48	53	54	55	55	49	45	48	51	50	49	48
Industry	19	21	16	14	12	11	11	17	17	16	17	17	16
Services	37	31	31	32	33	34	40	39	35	33	34	33	34
Balance of payments													
Exports	20	20	9	5	3	6	8	10	16.6	19.7	18.5	16.9	16.0
Imports	24	19	9	5	3	6	8	12	–20.1	–26.2	–24.2	–24.4	–25.1
Current account balance	. . .	0.7	0.3	–3.3	–0.3	–2.4	–2.7	–4.5	–4.2	–4.9	–4.9	–5.8	–7.6
Overall balance	. . .	5.2	–1.6	–5.3	1.1	–2.1	–1.9	–1.8	–1.2	3.0	2.4	2.4	1.4
Export volume index													
(1980 =100)	222.6	142.8	100.0	103.1	116.5	84.0	85.7	103.7	114.9	123.8	139.0	166.6	176.6

Sources: Bank of Ghana, *Quarterly Digest of Statistics*, various issues; Ghana Statistical Service, *Economy Survey*, various issues; and World Bank (1992).

the statistical consequence of a decline in the industrial sector. Industry's share of GDP fell from 15 percent to 12 percent. The contribution of the service sector also dropped, from 49 percent in 1960 to 33 percent in 1982, since the hard economic conditions and struggle for survival reduced demand for services.

The decline in industry was a reflection of its dependence on imported inputs, which was hampered by a severe foreign exchange constraint. The foreign exchange constraint had two main causes. On the one hand, domestic production of the main export commodity—cocoa—fell drastically. On the other hand, Ghana's international credit rating was very low for the 1970–82 period, and the country was left far behind the rest of the developing world in the borrowing stampede of the 1970s. Capital inflows almost dried up. New commitments and disbursements of external funding remained modest throughout the period, as a result mainly of lack of action on macroeconomic adjustment. Commitments averaged between $45 million and $55 million per year in the first half of the decade and increased to an average of about $100 million per year during the second half (Table 2). Actual disbursements fell below these levels. The only significant jump in new debt was in 1980, following the short-lived optimism on the return of the country to civilian government (in 1979) after seven years of military rule. Consequently, external indebtedness remained low in both relative and absolute terms throughout the 1970s. Yet debt repayment problems persisted because of the foreign exchange constraint. The *yentua* policy of the government in 1972 (*yentua* is a local word that translates as "we shall not pay") reflected the desperation of the situation. This was followed by debt rescheduling in 1974.

The ERP was initiated in 1983 to reverse the decline in the economy, stabilize prices, and maintain a favorable balance of payments position. The program is roughly divided into two phases: the initial stabilization phase (1983–86) and the subsequent years of adjustment and growth. Since it began, the economy has shown signs of recovery: output growth has averaged about 5 percent per year since 1984 (Table 1), and the severe foreign exchange constraint seems to have eased. Even though agriculture still dominates the economy with a share in GDP of about 50 percent since 1983, the industrial sector has staged a remarkable recovery. The share of industry in GDP increased from 11 percent in 1983 to 17 percent by 1985, dropping only marginally thereafter to 16 percent in 1990. This growth is partly due to the rehabilitation of existing plant and equipment and the availability of imported raw materials made possible by an easing of the foreign exchange constraint.

Table 2. Ghana: External Debt and Its Growth, 1970–90

	In Current Dollars		In Constant Dollars[1]	
	In millions of U.S. dollars	Share of total (In percent)	In millions of U.S. dollars	Share of total (In percent)
1970	1,048.79		3,361.50	
1971	1,154.12	10.0	3,507.96	4.3
1972	1,167.01	1.1	3,287.35	–6.2
1973	1,277.11	9.4	2,922.44	–11.1
1974	1,290.82	1.1	2,112.63	–27.7
1975	1,315.75	1.9	1,957.96	–7.3
1976	1,340.68	1.9	1,971.59	0.7
1977	1,365.61	1.9	1,847.92	–6.3
1978	1,390.54	1.8	1,712.48	–7.3
1979	1,415.47	1.8	1,456.24	–14.9
1980	1,440.40	1.8	1,212.71	–16.1
1981	1,833.34	27.3	1,587.31	29.9
1982	1,907.00	4.0	1,739.96	9.6
1983	2,039.12	6.9	1,953.18	12.3
1984	2,431.00	19.2	2,388.02	22.3
1985	2,736.00	12.5	2,736.00	14.5
1986	2,669.00	–2.4	2,581.24	–5.6
1987	3,126.60	17.1	2,745.04	6.3
1988	3,133.22	0.2	2,635.17	–4.0
1989	3,223.60	2.9	2,681.03	1.7
1990	3,521.80	9.2	2,692.50	0.4

Source: World Bank, *World Debt Tables*, various issues.

[1]Calculated as the value of external debt deflated by the World Unit Import Value Index, 1985 = 100 (see Dornbusch and Helmers, 1988).

The constraint has eased as a result of the substantial external capital inflows that have backed the program. At the beginning of the ERP (1984–86), commitments of external funding averaged about $344 million (1984–86; Table 3). In 1990 total commitments were more than twice that level, reaching $850 million. Gross disbursements have also increased substantially, averaging at least $250 million a year since the inception of the program. The sustained high levels of commitments and disbursements suggest that the aid effort on the part of donors could be strong, given serious commitment on the part of the recipient to pursue economic reforms. The higher inflows, however, resulted in a sharp increase in the pace of debt accumulation. The situation is particularly problematic as the structure of the economy, in terms of its ability to earn foreign exchange to meet debt servicing, has not changed.

Table 3. Ghana: Commitments and Disbursements of External Funding, 1974–90
(In millions of U.S. dollars)

	Commitments			Disbursements		
	Official	Private	Total	Official	Private	Total
1974	45	. . .	45	13	18	31
1975	166	. . .	166	31	. . .	31
1976	116	22	138	41	. . .	41
1977	70	. . .	70	53	. . .	53
1978	92	. . .	113	84	28	112
1979	125	. . .	125	149	. . .	149
1980	194	. . .	194	182	. . .	182
1981	44	. . .	44	103	. . .	103
1982	48	. . .	48	94	. . .	94
1983	127	. . .	127	123	50	173
1984	196	33	230	98	19	118
1985	418	47	465	139	42	181
1986	210	128	338	256	109	366
1987	588	42	630	347	18	365
1988	486	0	486	390	. . .	391
1989	797	40	837	525	44	569
1990	808	42	850	535	38	573

Sources: World Bank, *World Debt Tables*, various issues; and External Debt Department, Bank of Ghana.

Dimensions of the Debt

Data Sources and Problems

The measurement of external debt is fraught with both conceptual and practical problems (see, for example, Krueger, 1987; Ajayi, 1991). A major practical problem is inadequacy of data. This problem extends to inconsistencies in published debt figures. Time series data from official Ghanaian sources are not consistent. Publications of the World Bank and the IMF often have the same defect, as the figures on debt sometimes depend on which World Bank or IMF publication is used.

Nonetheless, external debt data used in this study are largely drawn from World Bank publications. This data source has obvious advantages. To a large extent, statistics obtained from this source are not available from official Ghanaian sources. Also, the World Bank figures enable an easy and meaningful international comparison. However, where necessary the data have been supplemented with information obtained from the Bank of Ghana.

The following standard definitions, distinctions, and categorizations have been followed. External debt is defined by type. Long-term debt is debt that has an original or extended maturity of more than 12 years. Short-term debt is debt that has an original maturity of one year or less. Debt with an original or extended maturity of between 1 and 12 years is classified as medium-term debt. With regard to long-term debt, a distinction is also made between public and publicly guaranteed debt on the one hand, and private nonguaranteed debt on the other. Public and publicly guaranteed debt consists of obligations of the national government and autonomous public bodies, as well as obligations of private debtors that are guaranteed by the government. Private nonguaranteed debt consists of obligations of private debtors that are not guaranteed by the government or any public entity.

Creditors are categorized as either official or private. Debt from official creditors comprises loans and credits from international organizations (multilateral donors) and loans from governments (bilateral donors) and their agencies.

Total Debt

The total debt is the sum of long-term debt (public and publicly guaranteed debt and private nonguaranteed debt), medium-term debt (including IMF credits), and short-term debt. Table 2 shows Ghana's total external debt in both current and constant dollars since 1970. The growth rates of the debt are also shown. The trends in the total debt are depicted in Figure 1.

The stock of debt has increased sharply since the inception of the ERP, rising from $2 billion in 1983 to $3.5 billion (in current dollars) at the end of 1990. One reason behind the sharp increase is that Ghana's reported debt in the pre-ERP period was underestimated. The reported debt excluded payment arrears, which totaled over $232 million in 1984 by the Bank of Ghana's own estimates. However, the one significant factor that has influenced the level and growth of debt since the ERP is the government's determined effort at macroeconomic adjustment. As indicated elsewhere, the reforms have been supported with substantial loans and credits. The sharpest increase in the level of debt was experienced between 1983 and 1985, the stabilization and rehabilitation phase of the ERP. This is to be expected, as the shortages in the economy at the start of the program were such that Ghana needed massive injections of capital inflows if the re-

Figure 1. Ghana: Trends in Total Debt, 1970–90
(In billions of U.S. dollars)

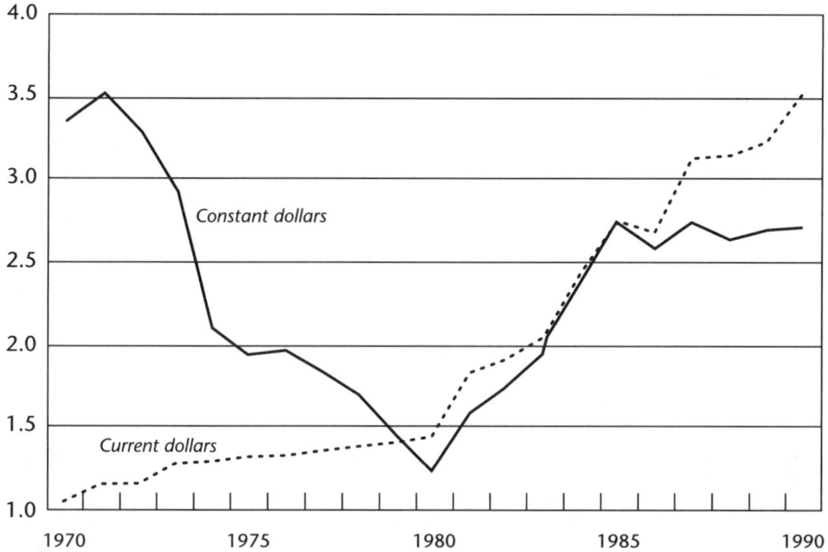

Source: World Bank, *World Debt Tables.*

forms were to take root. More significant, there were sizable shortfalls in export earnings between 1983 and 1985 (Table 1), which made increased borrowing a necessity. The level of debt actually fell in 1986, as a result of improvements in export receipts that year.

Structure, Source, Composition, and Type of Debt

Since 1983 some major changes have occurred within the total debt, with significant implications for how the debt affects the economy. Among these are important changes in the maturity structure of the debt. Compared with the pre-ERP period, the structure from 1986 reveals a shift toward long-term debt (Table 4).

Under the ERP, medium-term debt became significant during the stabilization period, as its share in total debt increased and the share of long-term debt decreased. In the initial stages of the ERP, the share of long-term debt fell somewhat, from 45 percent in 1982 to 33 percent in 1985. At the same time, the share of medium-term debt increased steadily, from 18 percent to 40 percent, largely because of the increased use Ghana made of IMF credits during the stabilization phase of the program. This is a reflection of existing practice in

Table 4. Ghana: Structure of Total Debt, 1970–90

(In millions of U.S. dollars except as noted)

		Long-Term Debt		Medium-Term Debt		Short-Term Debt	
	Total Debt	Amount	Share of Total (In percent)	Amount	Share of Total (In percent)	Amount	Share of Total (In percent)
1970	1,048.79	524.00	50	314.64	30	209.75	20
1971	1,154.12	555.82	48	325.09	28	273.21	23
1972	1,167.01	587.24	50	335.54	28	244.27	21
1973	1,277.11	618.66	48	345.99	27	312.46	24
1974	1,290.82	650.08	50	356.44	27	284.30	22
1975	1,315.75	681.50	51	366.89	27	267.36	20
1976	1,340.68	696.48	52	377.34	28	266.86	19
1977	1,365.61	711.46	52	387.79	28	266.36	19
1978	1,390.54	726.44	52	398.23	28	265.87	19
1979	1,415.47	741.42	52	408.65	29	265.40	18
1980	1,440.40	756.40	52	342.10	23	341.90	23
1981	1,833.34	887.84	48	365.10	20	580.40	31
1982	1,907.00	861.00	45	352.92	18	693.08	36
1983	2,039.12	869.33	42	655.19	32	514.60	25
1984	2,431.00	823.26	33	908.36	37	699.38	28
1985	2,736.00	909.88	33	1,087.81	40	738.31	27
1986	2,669.00	1,224.26	45	1,180.60	44	264.14	10
1987	3,126.60	1,611.00	51	1,257.80	40	257.80	8
1988	3,133.22	1,854.90	59	1,166.61	37	111.71	3
1989	3,223.60	1,998.63	62	1,116.11	34	108.86	3
1990	3,521.80	2,310.63	65	1,164.50	33	106.67	3

Sources: World Bank, *World Debt Tables*, various issues; and External Debt Department, Bank of Ghana.

Table 5. Ghana: Total External Debt by Type, 1970–90
(In millions of U.S. dollars except as noted)

	Long-Term Debt				Medium-Term Debt					
	Public and publicly guaranteed		Private nonguaranteed		IMF credits		Other		Short-Term Debt	
	Amount	Share (In percent)	Amount	Share (In percent)	Amount	Share (In percent)	Amount	Share (In percent)	Amount	Share (In percent)
1970	514	49.0	10	0.9	40	3.8	275	26.2	209	19.9
1971	545	47.2	10	0.8	20	1.7	305	26.4	273	23.6
1972	578	47.5	9	0.7	2	0.1	332	28.4	244	20.9
1973	610	47.7	8	0.6	0	0	345	27.0	312	24.4
1974	644	49.9	6	0.5	2	0.1	352	27.2	284	22.0
1975	670	50.9	10	0.7	45	3.4	321	24.4	267	20.3
1976	686	51.1	10	0.7	60	4.5	371	27.7	267	19.9
1977	701	51.3	10	0.7	63	4.6	324	23.7	266	19.4
1978	716	51.5	10	0.7	61	4.4	337	27.1	265	19.1
1979	732	51.7	9	0.6	74	5.2	334	23.6	265	18.7
1980	746	51.8	10	0.7	43	2.9	299	20.7	342	23.7
1981	877	47.8	10	0.5	28	1.5	337	18.4	580	31.6
1982	845	44.3	16	0.8	21	1.1	634	33.2	693	36.3
1983	848	41.5	21	1.0	280	13.7	628	30.8	514	25.2
1984	791	32.5	32	1.3	468	18.2	619	25.5	639	28.7
1985	866	31.6	40	1.5	658	24.0	522	19.0	753	26.9
1986	1,186	44.4	38	1.4	748	28.0	509	19.0	264	9.9
1987	1,581	50.6	30	0.9	748	23.9	517	16.5	257	8.2
1988	1,800	57.4	54	1.7	689	22.2	477	15.2	111	3.5
1989	1,940	60.2	58	1.7	680	21.0	436	13.5	108	3.3
1990	2,252	63.8	58	1.6	626	17.7	478	13.5	106	3.0

Sources: World Bank, *World Debt Tables*, various issues; and External Debt Department, Bank of Ghana.

Table 6. Ghana: Source Composition of External Debt, 1970–90

(In millions of U.S. dollars)

	1970	1971	1972	1973	1974	1975	1976	1977	1978	1979
Official	816	901	915	1,023	1,048	1,103	1,119	1,119	1,110	1,129
Bilateral	667	745	749	839	834	860	761	802	773	799
Multilateral	149	156	166	184	214	243	358	317	337	330
IMF	46	20	2	0	0	35	35	47	46	40
World Bank	74	74	78	72	117	204	226	256	278	293
Private	233	253	252	254	242	212	222	246	280	286
Guaranteed	223	243	243	246	236	202	212	236	270	277
Nonguaranteed	10	10	9	8	6	10	10	10	10	9

	1980	1981	1982	1983	1984	1985	1986	1987	1988	1989	1990
Official	1,325	1,736	1,800	1,891	2,283	2,543	2,404	2,836	2,880	2,935	3,356
Bilateral	966	954	981	994	1,050	1,297	1,177	1,147	1,181	1,148	1,244
Multilateral	359	782	819	897	1,233	1,246	1,227	1,689	1,699	1,787	2,112
IMF	43	85	75	280	468	656	686	767	762	737	745
World Bank	344	366	356	414	482	693	580	700	876	1,030	1,310
Private	115	97	107	142	148	193	265	290	252	188	165
Guaranteed	105	87	91	121	116	153	227	260	198	130	107
Nonguaranteed	10	10	16	21	32	40	38	30	54	58	58

Sources: World Bank, *World Debt Tables*, various issues; and External Debt Department, Bank of Ghana.

international development cooperation that requires developing countries undertaking economic adjustment to initially seek IMF funding. Most major donors only maintain sizable long-term lending programs if a country has an IMF-supported adjustment program. The problem is that this situation saddles the adjusting country with rapidly maturing debt, as the case of Ghana clearly illustrates. Since 1986, however, the shift has been toward long-term debt, whose share in total debt increased from 51 percent in 1987 to 65 percent in 1990. A significant feature since 1986 is the drastic reduction in short-term debt. This is the result of the conversion of some short-term debt into long-term debt, following restructuring agreements between Ghana and some of its creditors. This structural change has reduced the incidence of bunching together of repayments that creates severe pressures on the balance of payments.

The classification shown in Table 5 indicates that Ghana's long-term debt is overwhelmingly public and publicly guaranteed. Private nonguaranteed debt hovered around 1 percent of the total both before and during the ERP. This is a reflection of the dominant role of the public sector in the socioeconomic development of the country, and of the perceived low creditworthiness of private investment activity. This situation requires attention if the private sector is to play any meaningful role in the development process.

Important changes have also occurred in the source composition of the debt (Table 6). The source of debt is either private or official, and Table 5 reveals a steady decline of private debt in the total portfolio, from about 15 percent during 1974–82 to about 7 percent in 1983–90. This reveals an important difference between Ghana's debt structure and those of other severely indebted sub-Saharan African countries, such as Nigeria and Côte d'Ivoire, where debt from private sources has increased.

Official debt is divided into bilateral debt and multilateral debt. Both have increased steadily since 1983 (Table 6). The important feature of multilateral debt is the increased share of World Bank debt since 1986; by 1990 this debt made up over 60 percent of multilateral debt and nearly 40 percent of total official debt. The increased share of World Bank debt is largely responsible for improvements in the terms of debt, from an average maturity of 29 years with a 6.9-year grace period and a 4 percent annual rate of interest during 1970–82, to 31 years' maturity, with an eight-year grace period and a 2.6 percent annual rate of interest since the ERP (Table 7). On the other hand, the increased share has implications for debt relief; this type of debt is never forgiven and is rarely rescheduled.

The pattern of repayments (principal plus interest) has followed closely that of the total debt, rising sharply from the outset of the ERP

Table 7. Ghana: Average Terms of Debt, 1970–90

		Terms			
	Total Debt (In millions of U.S. dollars)	Interest rate (In percent a year)	Maturity period (In years)	Grace period (In years)	Grant element (In percent)
1970	1,048.79	2.0	36.7	9.7	66.8
1971	1,154.12	3.8	32.0	7.0	66.2
1972	1,167.01	3.0	35.0	8.0	68.4
1973	1,277.11	3.0	35.0	8.0	68.4
1974	1,290.82	5.2	26.6	6.8	36.8
1975	1,315.75	5.2	26.6	6.8	36.8
1976	1,340.68	5.0	30.0	6.0	49.8
1977	1,365.61	5.0	30.0	6.0	49.8
1978	1,390.54	4.4	25.0	6.0	54.9
1979	1,415.47	4.4	25.0	6.0	54.9
1980	1,440.40	1.6	38.7	9.1	68.5
1981	1,833.34	3.7	24.5	5.6	44.7
1982	1,907.00	5.9	17.8	4.3	26.5
1983	2,039.12	2.2	36.5	7.7	63.7
1984	2,431.00	1.9	39.1	8.5	69.8
1985	2,736.00	4.2	30.2	7.2	46.9
1986	2,669.00	4.7	26.0	6.0	39.2
1987	3,126.60	1.9	29.2	7.8	58.3
1988	3,133.22	2.0	30.0	8.0	64.0
1989	3,223.60	2.0	29.0	8.0	64.0
1990	3,521.80	2.0	29.0	8.0	64.0

Sources: World Bank, *World Debt Tables*, various issues; and External Debt Department, Bank of Ghana.

(Table 8). The sharp increase in repayments from 1983 on is due in part to pre-ERP factors. As indicated earlier, Ghana had accumulated a substantial amount of arrears by the start of the ERP. It was a requirement of the IMF that Ghana clear these arrears quickly in order to enhance its international creditworthiness. The arrears were scheduled to be cleared by the end of 1988. Moreover, debts that were rescheduled in 1974 had become due for repayment beginning in 1983, after the expiry of a 10-year grace period. Thus, the bulk of debt-service payments by the end of 1988 was due to accumulated arrears and rescheduled debt prior to the ERP. The retirement of these debts is reflected in the fall in repayments in 1989 and 1990. However, from 1985 on, debt-service payments to the IMF became more significant, reflecting the increased use Ghana made of IMF funds beginning in 1983.

Table 8. Ghana: Repayments of External Debt, 1970–90
(In millions of U.S. dollars)

	Principal	Interest	Total
1970	5.30	7.00	12.30
1971	8.20	8.00	16.20
1972	7.40	7.00	14.40
1973	10.75	9.90	20.65
1974	14.10	13.00	27.10
1975	24.20	16.30	40.50
1976	34.30	18.80	53.30
1977	8.30	15.50	33.80
1978	41.40	23.90	65.30
1979	39.50	26.30	65.80
1980	33.70	26.30	59.90
1981	40.30	30.10	70.40
1982	58.00	41.50	99.50
1983	136.40	67.10	203.50
1984	132.70	101.00	233.70
1985	252.30	102.80	355.10
1986	250.00	105.30	355.30
1987	161.80	121.50	283.30
1988	176.60	126.60	303.20
1989	142.50	111.90	254.40
1990	158.00	100.00	258.00

Sources: World Bank, *World Debt Tables*, various issues; and External Debt Department, Bank of Ghana.

The Debt Burden and Its Causes

The Debt Burden

Debt repayment inevitably imposes constraints on a debtor country's growth prospects since it involves the transfer of resources to other countries. Therefore, in order to adequately appreciate the problem of indebtedness, it is essential to relate the debt and its repayment to certain income resources generated by the debtor out of which repayments could be made.

A number of macroeconomic aggregates and debt ratios are often used to assess the debt burden of a country:

- total debt service to exports of goods and services;
- interest payments to exports of goods and services;
- debt outstanding and disbursed to GNP;

Table 9. Ghana: External Debt Outstanding and Selected Debt Burden Indicators, 1970, 1975, and 1980–90

	1970	1975	1980	1981	1982	1983	1984	1985	1986	1987	1988	1989	1990
Debt outstanding (In millions of U.S. dollars)	1,048.8	1,315.8	1,440.4	1,833.3	1,907.0	2,039.1	2,431.0	2,736.0	2,669.0	3,126.6	3,133.2	3,223.6	3,521.3
As share of GDP (In percent)	29.2	38	33	37	38	44	46	52	53	70	62	68	60
As share of exports of goods (In percent)	122	83	124	188	214	39	324	343	364	382	323	393	37
Debt-service ratio (In percent)	5.0	5.4	7.4	8.0	6.6	39	44	62	49	62	67	58	39

Source: World Bank, *World Debt Tables*, various issues.

- total debt service to GNP;
- interest payments to GNP;
- total external debt to exports of goods and services; and
- total external debt to GNP.

However, movements in the ratio of debt-service payments to exports of goods and services (the debt-service ratio) and in that of total external debt to income (the debt-GNP ratio) are the two most important indexes used to assess the debt burden; the higher these ratios, the greater the burden. These indexes for Ghana are shown in Table 9.

These trends have also been measured against a background of levels considered normal (see World Bank, 1989–90, Vol. 1) in Figures 2 through 4. A clear picture emerges from the table and figures: the debt problem has been critical since 1983, and Ghana is justifiably classified as a severely indebted low-income country. The debt-service ratio rose sharply, from 39 percent in 1983 to a peak of 67 percent in 1988, before falling back to about 39 percent in 1990.

It must be pointed out again that the sharp rise in the debt-service ratio from 1983 on was due largely to repayments of accumulated arrears and rescheduled debt prior to the ERP. Nonetheless, since 1983 the debt-service ratio has been above 30 percent—a reflection of a state of severe indebtedness. Likewise, the levels of both the debt-export ratio and the debt-GNP ratio (Figures 3 and 4) have remained above normal since 1983, also reflecting the critical nature of Ghana's debt. Although the outlook on the debt-service ratio should be for a moderation following the conclusion of repayments on accumulated arrears, the same cannot be said for the debt-export ratio and the debt-GNP ratio. It is obvious that Ghana's ability to generate faster growth in exports and income is crucial for any moderation in these ratios. It is common to use the debt-service ratio and the debt-GNP ratio as indexes of liquidity and solvency, respectively.[1] A liquidity problem refers to the inability of a country to service its debts now in the amount initially contracted. Lack of liquidity occurs when a country does not have enough cash on hand to pay current obligations (Ajayi, 1991). The solvency issue relates to whether the value of a country's liabilities exceeds the ability to pay at any time; a country is insolvent

[1]Liquidity and solvency may also be determined in a number of other ways. A simple rule for solvency is that the export growth rate be greater than the interest rate on the debt (Eaton and Taylor, 1986; Cohen, 1985). The difference between net debt (total indebtedness minus foreign reserves) and export earnings may also be used as an indicator of liquidity problems (Ajayi, 1991).

Figure 2. Ghana: Debt-Service Ratio, 1970–90
(In percent)

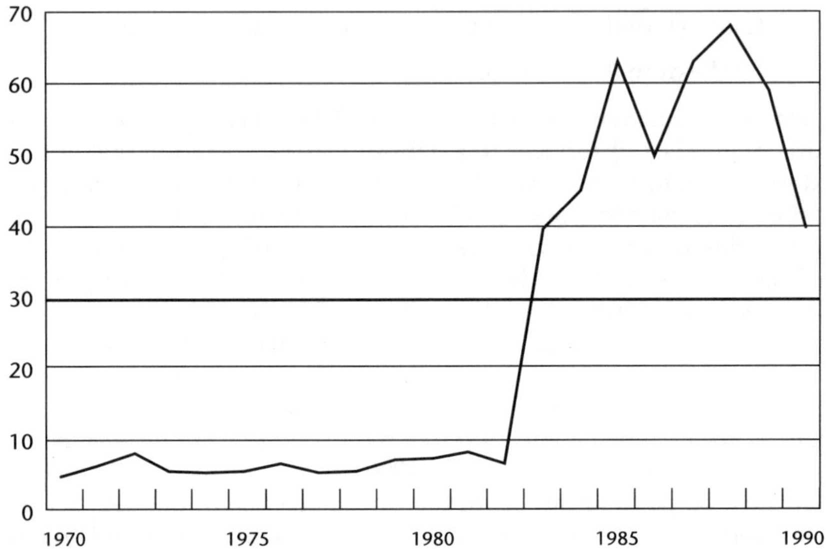

Source: World Bank, *World Debt Tables.*

Figure 3. Ghana: Debt-Export Ratio, 1970–90
(In percent)

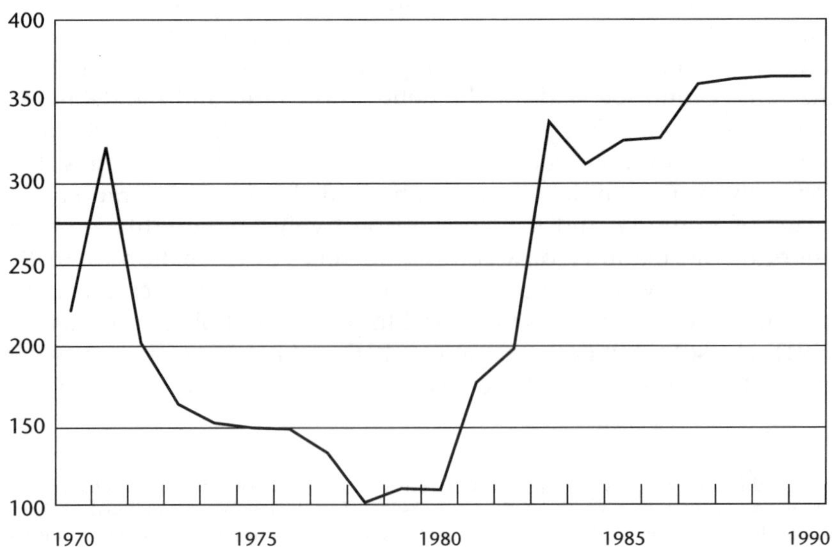

Source: World Bank, *World Debt Tables.*

Figure 4. Ghana: Debt-GNP Ratio, 1970–90
(In percent)

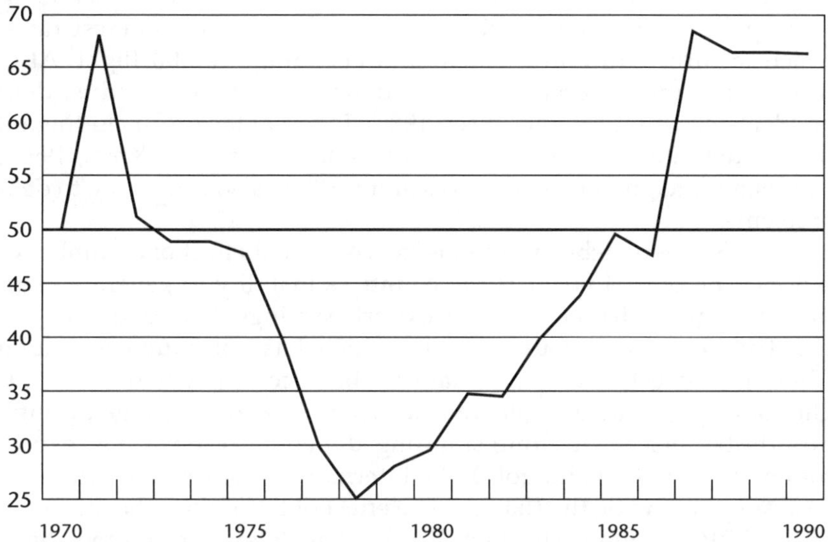

Source: World Bank, *World Debt Tables.*

when it is incapable of servicing its debt in the long run (Ajayi, 1991). With reference to the debt-service ratio and the debt-GNP ratio, it is apparent that Ghana has faced liquidity difficulties since 1983 and that its ability to remain solvent has also been impaired.

It is obvious that Ghana's creditworthiness over the past decade has been kept intact only by massive inflows of external grants, loans, and credits. The concern, however, is how long can Ghana expect to depend on such inflows.

Causes of the Debt Problem

The literature abounds with commentary on the causes of debt crises in developing countries. The underlying issue, emphasized by Dornbusch and Fischer (1985) as well as by Greene and Khan (1990), relates to the fundamental aim of borrowing: that the addition to the stock of external debt over time must contribute to growth and development and, in particular, to the country's ability to make payments to creditors. The argument is that a debtor country will face repayment difficulties if it is unable to generate a sufficient increase in output and export earnings. Many factors—domestic and external—are responsible for this outcome. The domestic factors often cited include wrong macroeconomic policies, such as fiscal irresponsibility and exchange rate misalignment (Khan and Knight, 1983). Other domestic factors include policies that deter saving, such as negative real interest rates, which in turn reduce investment and encourage capital flight. Also, when long-run projects are financed with short-term credits, debt problems occur (Tanzi and Blejer, 1984). External factors, including oil shocks, deteriorations in the terms of trade (Greene and Khan, 1990), and rising foreign interest rates (Krumm, 1985), also contribute to debt problems.

Ghana's severe debt situation is the combined effect of a number of factors. The crucial factor is the country's inability to generate sufficient foreign exchange through export earnings. Consequently, the country's current account deficit, which has continued to widen (Table 1), has been hard to sustain for balance of payments stability. The country is unable to generate sufficient foreign exchange through exports because of its long-standing dependence on a few export commodities (cocoa and gold), the international prices of which have been subject to wide fluctuation. The effect of these since the inception of the ERP is quite clear. Since 1983, Ghana's export volumes have more than doubled (see Table 1). Export values, however, have increased by a much smaller proportion. The less-than-proportionate increase in export values is due to the decline in the real prices of cocoa and gold. The real prices of both commodities decreased during the 1980s, with sharper and continuous declines since 1984. For example, taking 1980 as a base year, the index of the real cocoa price declined continuously from 113.2 in 1984 to 35 in 1990, and that for gold from 63.2 in 1984 to 48.2 in 1990. Indeed, there is a clear case for Ghana to reduce its long-standing dependence on so few primary commodities by widening and sustaining the base of its nontraditional exports.

Another factor behind Ghana's debt difficulties is the low rate of return on investment to which borrowed funds are applied. When capital inflows finance productive investments with rates of domestic and external return that are higher than the cost of borrowing, debt service should normally be met from the increased future stream of foreign exchange earnings and still leave a considerable net benefit for the recipient economy. In Ghana's case, much of the capital inflows went into infrastructural investments that have long gestation periods and/or large indivisibilities, so that returns are low, especially in their early years. Indeed, it is estimated that the average rate of return on investment in the major projects and programs to which foreign loans were applied is in the range of 0.8 per-

Figure 5. Ghana: Terms of Trade, 1970–90
(1975=100)

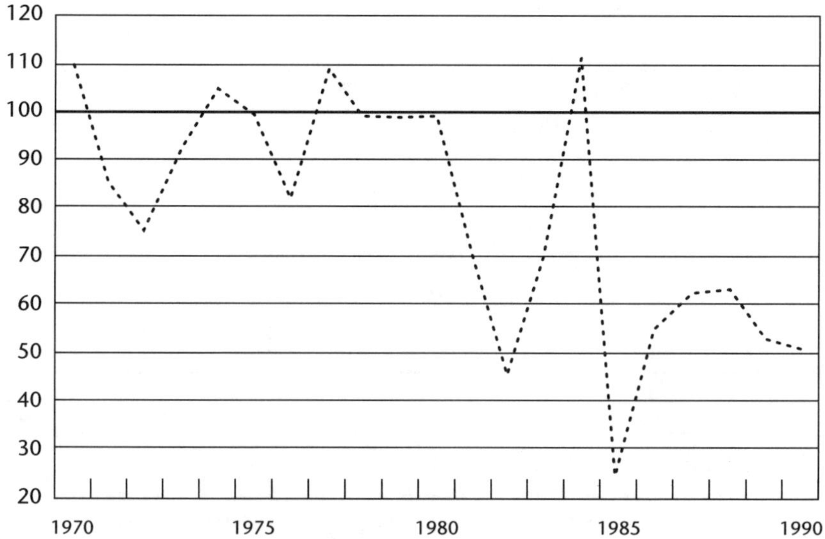

Source: International Monetary Fund, *International Financial Statistics.*

cent to 1.1 percent (Dordunoo, 1990), whereas the average rate of interest on debt during 1983–90 ranged between 1.9 and 4.7 percent (Table 7). As long as the rate of interest on a loan is above the rate of return on a given volume of investment from such a loan, there are bound to be debt difficulties. It certainly behooves Ghana to redirect borrowed funds into more productive investments to generate adequate returns.

Low saving is another factor contributing to Ghana's debt difficulty. Ghana has one of the lowest domestic saving rates in sub-Saharan Africa. In spite of major successes of the ERP, such as the lowering of inflation (Table 1) and reforms carried out in the financial sector, the domestic saving effort remains low. A major external factor that has contributed to the poor saving effort is the sharp deterioration in the country's terms of trade. Figure 5 indicates clearly the sharp deterioration in the terms of trade since 1984. This deterioration affects domestic saving through the so-called Harberger-Laursen-Metzler effect, which argues simply that a terms-of-trade deterioration decreases real income, and the decrease in real income reduces saving out of any given income.

The ratio of gross domestic saving to GDP, which averaged 6 percent between 1983 and 1990, was about one-third the 1970

Figure 6. Ghana: Investment-Debt Ratio, 1970–90
(In percent)

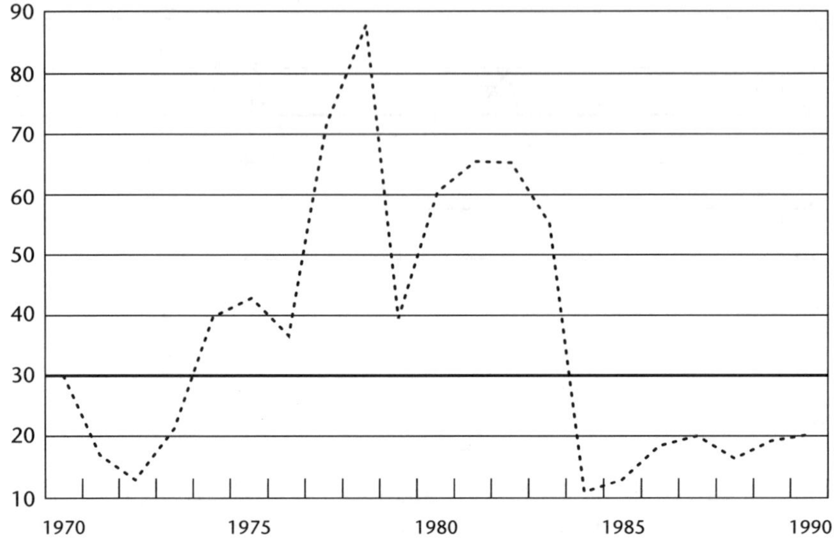

Sources: World Bank, *World Debt Tables*; and International Monetary Fund, *International Financial Statistics.*

level.[2] Consequently, the rate of domestic investment is also low. The average rate of domestic investment to GDP, at 9 percent between 1983 and 1990, was not even enough to replace depreciated capital, as the required minimum was estimated at about 13 percent. The investment-debt ratio (Figure 6) also shows the critical nature of the low investment effort.

It is essential that Ghana intensify its efforts to increase domestic saving. Major obstacles to the efficient functioning of the financial system, including lack of competition, lack of confidence of the saving public in the financial system, and discriminatory rules against privately owned financial institutions (see also Osei, 1992b), have to be addressed in an effort to expand the scope of business of the financial system to increase saving.

[2]Underlying the poor saving effort is low per capita income, which is still below pre-ERP levels. Also, the financial system still lacks depth. This is reflected in a low M2–GDP ratio, which in 1990 was 14 percent. This does not compare well with other sub-Saharan African countries like Kenya, Zambia, and Côte d'Ivoire, where rates of 30 percent are common.

A Paradox: Deteriorating Debt Profile, Low Saving and Investment, but Strong Economic Growth

It is paradoxical that in the face of a deteriorating debt profile and low saving and investment, Ghana has maintained strong economic growth since 1984. This derives from the state of the Ghanaian economy prior to the ERP and to reforms carried out under the ERP. However, a most significant factor behind the strong economic growth is the fortuitous return to normalcy in the weather. Adequate rains since 1984 have played a major part in restoring agricultural production. Output of food crops has risen, turning the severe food shortages of the pre-ERP era into surpluses. Production of cocoa has also recovered.

In addition, since 1983 there have been important changes in the foreign aid climate. Besides the sharp increases in inflows of foreign capital, the credit pipeline has been restructured, shifting available funds from slow-disbursing project aid to faster-moving program support. This has increased the pace of disbursement. In effect, even though the debt stock has also increased sharply, foreign credit has been available on time to enable Ghana to restore some momentum to its import program, which is so crucial to economic growth. Also, the timely availability of credits has quickly revived existing plant and machinery in the industrial sector, which now contributes appreciably to income growth.

Moreover, since the inception of the ERP there has been what may be termed "reversed public sector fungibility."[3] While acquiring debt, Ghana has overhauled its tax machinery, and the budgetary focus has been geared toward the elimination of subsidies. The result, as discussed in Osei (1992a), is that external credit over the ERP period supplements (rather than replaces, as was the case during 1970–82) productive state expenditure, contributing to the strong economic growth.

Certainly, the massive inflows of foreign capital since 1983 have propped up the economy and enabled some changes to be made. The problem remains the Ghanaian economy's low ability to repay the mounting debt. As we have already seen, the economy is still structurally weak in its dependence on a few primary commodities for foreign exchange earnings. In fact, the calculations in Table 10 indicate that the rate of growth of debt has exceeded the rate of growth of ex-

[3]"Public sector fungibility" may refer to a situation where there is replacement of productive state expenditure by external credit. This occurs when a country, in receiving credit, switches local resources into unproductive expenditure and/or into reductions in taxation.

Table 10. Ghana: Unsustainable Borrowing, 1971–90

	Growth Rate of Debt (In percent)	Growth Rate of Exports (In percent)	Unsustainable Borrowing[1]
1971	10.0	–18.2	–28.2
1972	1.1	13.7	12.6
1973	9.4	47.6	38.2
1974	1.1	14.2	13.1
1975	1.9	19.9	18.0
1976	1.9	–0.1	–2.0
1977	1.9	14.1	12.2
1978	1.8	–2.2	–4.0
1979	1.8	16.7	14.9
1980	1.8	4.2	2.4
1981	27.3	–31.4	–58.7
1982	4.0	–14.2	48.2
1983	6.9	–37.3	–44.2
1984	19.2	36.6	17.0
1985	12.5	10.5	–2.0
1986	–2.4	21.0	23.8
1987	17.1	10.7	–6.4
1988	0.2	5.8	5.6
1989	2.9	–7.3	–10.2
1990	9.2	10.6	1.4

Source: World Bank, *World Debt Tables*, various years.
[1]Unsustainable borrowing is defined as the excess of the percentage rate of growth of debt over the percentage rate of growth of exports.

ports for the greater part of the 1983–90 period.[4] As long as the rate of growth of debt exceeds the rate of growth of exports, difficulties in repayments are bound to occur.

Debt Sustainability and Fiscal Stability

There is no gainsaying that sustained economic growth is possible only within a sound macroeconomic framework. In such a framework, fiscal policy plays a key role; sound fiscal policy is crucial to macroeconomic stability. Essentially, there is a link between external debt

[4]The literature sometimes considers the excess of the percentage rate of growth of debt over the percentage rate of growth of exports of goods and services as the rate of unsustainable borrowing (see, e.g., Ajayi, 1991). In this sense, Ghana could be regarded as having undertaken unsustainable borrowing during alternate years, in 1983, 1985, 1987, and 1989. The growth rate of debt in these years was greater than the growth rate of exports (Table 10).

sustainability and fiscal stability, especially in a situation like Ghana's, where external debt is largely public sector debt (see, for example, Fischer and Easterly, 1990; van Wijnbergen, 1989).

The theoretical underpinning of the link between external debt and fiscal behavior is quite straightforward. Basically, there are four ways of financing a public sector deficit: printing money, running down foreign exchange reserves, borrowing abroad, and borrowing domestically. Each of these forms of finance can result in major macroeconomic imbalance: printing of money may lead to inflation; use of foreign reserves may be associated with the onset of exchange crises; foreign borrowing may lead to external debt crises; and domestic borrowing may be associated with higher real interest rates. Of course, there are links between and among these problems. For example, high transfers as a result of a debt crisis could cause government domestic borrowing to increase. This increase will reduce credit that otherwise would be available to the private sector, thereby putting pressure on domestic interest rates. Even where interest rates are controlled, high domestic borrowing may lead to credit rationing and crowding out of private sector investment.

The arithmetic of the relationship between external debt and fiscal behavior is as follows. The increase in the sum of domestic and external debt is equal to the government budget deficit, net of money creation. If only the government borrowed abroad, then the decrease in the government's external debt would be equal to the current account balance. Therefore, the current account balance is the sum of the increase in domestic government debt, the budget surplus, and money creation.

Decomposition of the 1983–90 data (Table 11) shows that the noninterest government surplus amounted to 41 percent of the current account balance, the seigniorage tax (defined as the variation in central bank liabilities in real terms) amounted to 28 percent, and the increase in domestic debt to 31 percent. However, if foreign grants are removed from government revenue, the decomposition shows that the share of the government surplus drops to 21 percent, that of the seigniorage tax increases to 41 percent, and that of the domestic debt increases to 38 percent.

These results are quite interesting. They point first to the high dependence of government revenues on foreign grants, and they highlight the need for increasing revenue generation by the government to achieve self-sustaining growth. As indicated elsewhere, fiscal reforms put in place under the ERP have to some extent overhauled the tax machinery and eliminated some subsidies. These, in addition to the effects of exchange rate reforms, have increased government revenue.

Table 11. Ghana: Current Account Counterparts, 1983–90

(In millions of cedis)

	1983	1984	1985	1986	1987	1988	1989	1990
Noninterest current account	–3,159	–684	1,850	12,792	30,463	42,647	65,870	69,154
Seigniorage	28,697	24,384	26,580	93,408	–24,980	192,957	123,034	73,170
Government surplus (with grants)	–4,934	–4,844	–7,580	299	4,059	8,911	9,894	12,874
Domestic debt	29,319	32,908	37,766	50,686	47,908	54,325	48,785	64,684
Bank of Ghana	16,778	19,881	21,634	23,954	23,954	21,841	13,686	13,691
Commercial banks	4,780	4,535	5,210	6,200	6,200	7,187	5,000	16,483
Secondary banks	1,241	1,481	3,482	6,074	6,074	. . .	. . .	. . .
SSNIT	1,951	2,388	2,898	7,326	7,326	14,754	11,936	18,046
Private sector (including institutions)	4,569	4,623	4,541	4,354	4,354	10,543	18,163	16,463

Sources: Ghana Statistical Service, *Economic Survey,* 1988; and Institute of Statistical, Social, and Economic Research (1993, Appendix Table B.7).

However, there is still a need for further measures and reforms to increase government revenue, especially since the government's overall budget deficit remains quite substantial.[5]

The decomposition also reveals the importance of the seigniorage tax in total government revenue. The literature is clear on the dangers of a high dependence on seigniorage. It is well known that rates of seigniorage of much more than 2.5 percent of GNP are not sustainable in developing countries (Fischer, 1982; Fischer and Easterly, 1990), and that even that rate would be tenable only in a very rapidly growing economy. Ghana has maintained rates of seigniorage to GNP more than three times that level since 1983, indicating the instability of the situation. The high dependence on this tax is a contributing factor to the government's inability to bring inflation down below the two-digit level or to target rates.

It is also apparent from the decomposition that the domestic debt accounted for a large share of the current account balance. Domestic borrowing is usually an act of expediency by a government that would prefer to finance the budget through taxation but finds it inconvenient to do so. Its use is more often advised as a temporary measure to meet emergencies that otherwise would require sharp increases in taxation. Contrary to the Ghanaian government's declared intention of reducing its domestic borrowing, the domestic debt has increased (see Table 11).[6] The implications of the increase in the domestic debt for interest rates and private investment are clear. The domestic debt increase is a major factor behind the substantial pressures on domestic interest rates, especially bank lending rates, which increased from 19 percent in 1983 to 33 percent in 1990. The high cost of borrowing is a major constraint on private investment. The rise in domestic interest rates may be thought of as a version of the transfer problem involved in foreign debt service, as the government is forced to repay its own domestic debt at higher interest rates.

These results indicate that there is a continuing fiscal problem in Ghana. The results require that Ghana take steps to ensure fiscal sta-

[5]The overall budget deficit, which stood at about 2.4 percent of GDP at the start of the ERP, fell considerably, to about 0.8 percent of GDP, in 1988–89. However, by 1990 it had risen again to 1.3 percent of GDP (see World Bank, 1991b, Table 1.6). The worsening fiscal performance, even as government expenditure continued to shrink, is due to a deterioration in revenue performance.

[6]It is noticeable from Table 11 that there has been a major shift away from the central bank as the principal source of deficit financing. Indeed, the nonbank private sector increased its share of domestic debt from 15.6 percent in 1983 to 25.5 percent in 1990. This is a positive development in the government's efforts at reducing inflationary pressures in the economy, notwithstanding the adverse consequences of the increase in the domestic debt.

bility as the country attempts to meet its external debt repayments. The literature cites many fiscal adjustment prescriptions that Ghana might take. These include the introduction of new taxes such as the value-added tax to increase government revenue; the elimination of waste in government expenditure; the intensification of diversification and privatization of state enterprises (see, e.g., Tsikata and Amuzu, 1992). Also, as pointed out by Fischer and Easterly (1990), sustainable fiscal policy depends on how fast an economy is growing.[7] The lesson here is that accelerated growth must be a target for Ghana to maintain fiscal stability and external debt servicing.

Debt and Economic Growth

The need for Ghana to pursue accelerated growth in order to reduce its debt problems and, more important, to break out of its low-income status makes it worthwhile to investigate how far external indebtedness would affect future growth. This section analyzes the effect of debt on medium-term growth.

Debt problems have been incorporated into models, commonly referred to as "growth-cum-debt" models, to address issues relating to debt sustainability. The focus is on how and how far debt affects the growth prospects of debtor countries. The literature on growth-cum-debt models has gone through two main phases. In the first phase, authors such as Avramovic and others (1964), King (1968), and Solomon (1977) were concerned with making judgments on the debt capacity of developing countries in the context of the Harrod-Domar growth model. The focus in the literature was on describing how debt situations evolve over time. Other authors, including Dhonte (1979), Loser (1977), and Feder and Just (1977), examined the circumstances under which countries experience debt-servicing difficulties. The attention here was on the external performance of the debtor's economy in relation to debt-service claims. Another set of authors focused on the supply side of the international financial market. Their studies, including those by Feder and Ross (1982) and Sachs and Cohen (1982), examined factors that influence lending behavior. The second phase, which represents more recent literature, includes studies by Cohen (1985, 1988), Solis and Zedillo (1985), and van Wijnbergen (1989). These studies provide a way to relate foreign indebtedness to long-run growth.

[7]This point is seen clearly from the following identity, which shows the determinants of the change in government debt: change in d = (primary deficit/GNP) – (seigniorage/GNP) + (real interest rate – growth rate) x d, where d is the ratio of government debt to GNP. A higher growth rate reduces the last term in the equation.

Debt and Economic Growth in Ghana

The issue of how far debt would affect growth in Ghana can be analyzed following some of the approaches developed in the second-phase literature. The model followed, as presented by Ajayi (1991), uses a level of output (Y) given by

$$Y = \sigma k, \tag{1}$$

where σ is the reciprocal of the incremental capital-output ratio, and k is the capital stock.
Let

$$\Delta Y = \sigma(\Delta k), \tag{2}$$

and

$$\Delta k = I_t - \delta k_{t-1}, \tag{3}$$

where I is investment and δ is the depreciation rate of capital. Equation (1) becomes

$$Y_t = \sigma I_t + (1 - \delta)Y_{t-1}. \tag{4}$$

Given the identities

$$C_t + I_t + X_t - M_t = Y_t = C_t + S_t + r_t D_{t-1}, \tag{5}$$

where X is exports, M is imports, S is saving, r is the rate of interest, D is debt, and

$$d_t = M_t - X_t + r_t D_{t-1}, \tag{6}$$

consequently,

$$I_t = S_t + d_t. \tag{7}$$

Let the saving function be

$$S_t = s(Y_t + r_t D_{t-1}). \tag{8}$$

Using Equation (4), investment can be expressed as

$$I_t = [s(1 - \delta)/(1 - s\sigma)]Y_{t-1} + [s/(1 - s\sigma)]r_t D_{t-1} + [1/(1 - s\sigma)]d_t. \tag{9}$$

Equations (4) and (9) are solved for a number of possible paths of D and r. The rule used for D_t is the dynamic equation

$$D_t = D_{t-1}(1 + \gamma), \tag{10}$$

where γ is a constant that is varied in each scenario. Equation (10) implies that

$$\Delta D_t = \gamma D_{t-1}, \tag{11}$$

Table 12. Ghana: Results of the Growth-cum-Debt Model

			Growth Prospects								
			$r = 0.01$ $\sigma = 0.25$			$r = 0.03$ $\sigma = 0.25$			$r = 0.06$ $\sigma = 0.25$		
γ	D_t	$M_t - X_t$	g	$\frac{D_t}{GDP}$	$\frac{M_t - X_t}{GDP}$	g	$\frac{D_t}{GDP}$	$\frac{M_t - X_t}{GDP}$	g	$\frac{D_t}{GDP}$	$\frac{M_t - X_t}{GDP}$
0.00	3,522	351	0.0465	0.606	0.059	0.0422	0.608	0.059	0.0399	0.610	0.059
0.01	3,557	359	0.0557	0.600	0.058	0.0456	0.599	0.061	0.0402	0.610	0.068
0.02	3,628	412	0.0557	0.585	0.064	0.0468	0.574	0.065	0.0402	0.591	0.068
0.03	3,736	551	0.0550	0.565	0.078	0.0492	0.555	0.078	0.0411	0.582	0.065
0.04	3,885	559	0.0542	0.551	0.075	0.0501	0.551	0.079	0.0456	0.566	0.062
0.05	4,079	585	0.0554	0.543	0.075	0.0542	0.542	0.078	0.0486	0.558	0.079
0.06	4,323	585	0.0463	0.546	0.075	0.0412	0.544	0.078	0.0401	0.599	0.078
0.07	4,626	588	0.0463	0.550	0.071	0.0412	0.551	0.072	0.0401	0.554	0.075
0.08	4,996	590	0.0445	0.556	0.069	0.0412	0.556	0.069	0.0401	0.571	0.072
0.07	5,446	605	0.0448	0.571	0.067	0.0400	0.570	0.069	0.0388	0.581	0.071
0.10	5,991	605	0.0437	0.591	0.068	0.0400	0.589	0.069	0.0388	0.670	0.071

Source: Author's calculations.

and since

$$\Delta D_t = d_t, \tag{12}$$

we have

$$d_t = \gamma D_{t-1}, \tag{13}$$

which implies that

$$(M_t - X_t) = (\gamma - r)D_{t-1}. \tag{14}$$

Thus, various scenarios of r and γ would allow an assessment not only of economic growth prospects, but also of the different paths of the trade balance $(M_t - X_t)$, as well as indications of the debt burden such as D_t/GDP.

Empirical Results

The value of γ is varied in the scenario from 0.00 to 0.10. The incremental capital-output ratio is calculated following its conventional definition as the ratio of capital formation in the current period to the increase in GDP over the previous period. Allowing for three possible values of the rate of interest (r = 0.01, 0.03, and 0.06), simulations were run for the period 1991–2000. The income growth prospects and the different paths of the trade balance and the debt burden under the various scenarios are summarized in Table 12.

In terms of the model, varying the rate of interest has very little impact on income growth, the trade balance, and the debt burden; little is lost in these indicators if the rate of interest is doubled from 3 percent to 6 percent.

The estimates indicate that, given the various scenarios, Ghana's trade balance would widen. As a share of GDP, the trade deficit would grow from about 5.9 percent to a peak of about 7.7 percent, before falling marginally to about 7.1 percent. Consequently, the debt burden would remain high. The debt-GDP ratio would stay above the critical 50 percent. These results reemphasize the necessity for Ghana to pursue export expansion for self-sustaining growth. The growth estimates indicate that Ghana would maintain a 4 to 5 percent growth rate for the next decade. This may be considered satisfactory, especially if viewed against the average for sub-Saharan Africa for the last 10 years of below 2 percent, which most analysts believe may not improve in the next decade. However, there may be little cause for optimism if the 4 to 5 percent growth rate is considered in relation to the accelerated growth Ghana needs to break out of its poverty trap. The World Bank (1992) estimates that at current rates of economic growth (5 percent a year) and population increase (about 3 percent a year), the average poor Ghanaian would not cross the poverty line for another half century. By contrast, if the pace of economic growth could be raised to 8 percent a year, this crossover time would be reduced to about 23 years.

Our earlier question of whether Ghana can achieve accelerated growth suggests that there may be preconditions for fast growth that do not yet exist in Ghana. The results here indicate that external debt is one factor that constrains rapid growth.

Conclusion

The basic conclusion reached in this chapter is that external debt represents a major constraint on Ghana's economic performance. The current debt situation requires that Ghana take steps to increase its ability to service foreign debt by vigorously pursuing export expansion. This draws attention to the long-standing dependence of the economy on a few traditional export commodities. Ghana should encourage more nondebt foreign exchange earnings, such as tourism, as well as take steps to widen and sustain the base of its nontraditional exports. Steps must also be taken to attract more foreign direct investment, which will bring in not only the external finance but also the skills and technology so essential for the rapid expansion of the economy. In addition, Ghana should pursue further internal reforms to increase domestic saving and fiscal reforms that would increase the government's revenue, so as to minimize dependence on types of financing that are detrimental to the economy's health.

Ghana can make a case for debt relief as it carries out its internal reforms. Creditors could grant debt reduction on a wider scale in order to reduce the debt stock and reduce repayments. Other remedial measures such as debt rescheduling should recognize the dependence of the Ghanaian economy on cocoa and incorporate built-in flexibility to correspond with international cocoa prices.

References

Ajayi, S.I., 1991, "Macroeconomic Approach to External Debt: The Case of Nigeria," African Economic Research Consortium Research Paper No. 8 (Nairobi: Initiative Publishers).

Allsopp, C., and V. Joshi, 1986, "The International Debt Crisis," *Oxford Review of Economic Policy*, Vol. 2, No. 1.

Alter, G.M., 1958, "Servicing of Foreign Capital Inflows by Underdeveloped Countries," in *Economic Development for Latin America* (New York: Macmillan).

Avramovic, D., and others, 1964, *Economic Growth and External Debt* (Baltimore: Johns Hopkins Press).

Bank of Ghana, *Quarterly Digest of Statistics* (Accra, various issues).

Berg, E.J., 1971, "Structural Transformation Versus Gradualism: Recent Economic Development in Ghana and Ivory Coast," in *Ghana and the Ivory Coast: Perspectives on Modernization*, ed. by P. Foster and A.R. Zolberg (Chicago: University of Chicago Press).

Claessens, S., and I. Diwan, 1990, "Investment Incentives: New Money, Debt Relief, and the Critical Role of Conditionality in the Debt Crises," *World Bank Economic Review*, Vol. 4, No. 1.

Cohen, D., 1985, "How to Evaluate the Solvency of an Indebted Nation," *Economic Policy*, Vol. 1, No. 1.

———, 1988, "The Management of the Developing Countries Debt: Guidelines and Applications to Brazil," *World Bank Economic Review*, Vol. 3, No. 1.

———, 1990, "Debt Relief: Implications of Secondary Market Discounts and Debt Overhang," *World Bank Economic Review*, Vol. 4, No. 1.

Corden, M.W., 1988, "International Debt Facility," *Staff Papers*, International Monetary Fund, Vol. 35, No. 3.

Dhonte, P., 1975, "Describing External Debt Situations: A Roll-Over Approach," *Staff Papers*, International Monetary Fund, Vol. 22 (March).

———, 1979, *Clockwork Debt, Trade and the External Debt of Developing Countries* (Lexington, Massachusetts: Lexington Books).

Dordunoo, C.K., 1990, "Ghana's Foreign Debt and Policy Recommendations: A Multiple Discriminant Analysis," *Nigerian Financial Review*, Vol. 3 (June).

Dornbusch, R., and S. Fischer, 1985, "The World Debt Problem: Origin and Prospects," *Journal of Development Planning*.

Dornbusch, R., and F.L.C.H. Helmers, eds., 1988, *The Open Economy: Tools for Policymakers in Developing Countries* (New York: Oxford University Press).

Eaton, J., M. Gersovitz, and J.E. Stiglitz, 1986, "The Pure Theory of Country Risk," *European Economic Review*, Vol. 30.

Eaton, J., and Lance Taylor, 1986, "Developing Country Finance and Debt," *Journal of Development Economics*.

Eshag, E., and R.J. Richards, 1967, "Comparison of Economic Development in Ghana and Ivory Coast," *Bulletin*, Oxford University Institute of Statistics, November.

Feder, G., 1980, "Economic Growth, Foreign Loans, and the Debt Servicing Capacity of Developing Countries," *Journal of Development Studies*, April.

———, and R. Just, 1977, "A Study of Debt Servicing Capacity: Applying Logit Analysis," *Journal of Development Economics*, Vol. 4.

Feder, G., and K. Ross, 1982, "Risk Assessment and Risk Premiums in the Euro-Dollar Market," *Journal of Finance*, Vol. 37 (June).

Fischer, S., 1982, "Seignorage and the Case for a National Money," *Journal of Political Economy*, Vol. 90 (April).

Fischer, S., and W. Easterly, 1990, "The Economics of the Government Budget Constraint," *World Bank Research Observer*, Vol. 5, No. 2.

Frank, C.R., and W.R. Cline, 1971, "Measurement of Debt Servicing Capacity: An Application of Discriminant Analysis," *Journal of International Economics*, Vol. 1.

Ghana Statistical Service, *Economic Survey* (Accra, various issues).

Greene, J.E., and M.S. Khan, 1990, "The African Debt Crisis," African Economic Research Consortium Special Paper No. 3 (Nairobi).

Hayes, H.P., 1964, "Long Run Growth and Debt Problems," in *Economic Growth and External Debt*, ed. by D. Avramovic and others (Baltimore: Johns Hopkins Press).

Institute of Statistical, Social, and Economic Research, University of Ghana, 1993, *The State of the Ghanaian Economy in 1992* (Accra).

Jebuni, C., and others, 1992, *Diversifying Exports: The Supply Response of Non-Traditional Export to Ghana's Economic Recovery Program*, ODI/University of Ghana.

Khan, Mohsin S., and M.D. Knight, 1983, "Determinants of Current Account Balances of Non-Oil Developing Countries in the 1970s: An Empirical Analysis," *Staff Papers*, International Monetary Fund, Vol. 30, No. 4.

Khan, Mohsin S., and P.J. Montiel, 1988, "Growth-Oriented Adjustment Programs: A Conceptual Framework," IMF Working Paper No. 88/64 (Washington: International Monetary Fund).

Killick, T., 1978, *Development Economics in Action* (Heinemann).

King, B.B., 1968, "Notes on the Mechanics of Growth Debt," World Bank Staff Occasional Paper No. 6 (Washington).

Krassowki, A., 1974, *Development and the Debt Trap* (London: Croom Helm).

Krueger, A.O., 1987, "Origins of the Developing Countries Debt Crisis," *Journal of Development Economics*, Vol. 27.

Krumm, K.L., 1985, "The External Debt of Sub-Saharan Africa: Origins, Magnitude and Implications for Action," World Bank Staff Working Paper No. 741 (Washington).

Loser, C.M., 1977, "External Debt Management and Balance of Payments Policies," *Staff Papers*, International Monetary Fund, Vol. 24 (March).

Manu, J.E.A., 1972, "Balance of Payments Constraints and Economic Development," *Economic Bulletin of Ghana*, Vol. 2, No. 2.

Organization for Economic Cooperation and Development, 1977, *Development Co-operation Review* (Paris).

———, 1985, *Twenty-Five Years of Development Co-operation* (Paris).

———, 1987, *Development Co-operation* (Paris).

Osei, B., 1992a, "The Effect of Foreign Aid on Domestic Savings in Ghana," *Journal of Management Studies*, Third Series, Vol. 8.

———, 1992b, "Monetary and Financial Developments," in *Policies and Options for Ghanaian Economic Development*, Institute of Statistical, Social, and Economic Research, University of Ghana (Accra: Wilco Publishers).

Sachs, J, and D. Cohen, 1982, "LDC Borrowing with Default Risk," NBER Working Paper No. 925 (Cambridge, Massachusetts: National Bureau of Economic Research).

Solis, L., and E. Zedillo, 1985, "The Foreign Debt of Mexico," in *International Debt and the Developing Countries*, ed. by Gordon Smith and J.T. Cuddington (Washington: World Bank).

Solomon, R., 1977, "A Perspective on Debt of Developing Countries," *Brookings Papers on Economic Activity: 2*, Brookings Institution.

Sowa, N.K., 1992, "Policy Consistency and Inflation in Ghana," African Economic Research Consortium Research Paper (Nairobi).

Steuer, M.D., 1973, "After the Crisis: Long-Term Prospects for the Economy of Ghana" (Accra: University of Ghana).

Sweet, L.M., 1987, "Currency Composition of Developing Country Debt: The Impact of Dollar Depreciation," Research Paper No. 8702 (New York: Federal Reserve Bank of New York).

Tanzi, V., 1985, "Fiscal Management and External Debt Problems," in *External Debt Management*, ed. by Hassanali Mehran (Washington: International Monetary Fund).

———, and M.I. Blejer, 1984, "Fiscal Deficits and Balance of Payments Disequilibrium in IMF Adjustment Programmes," in *Adjustment, Conditionality, and International Financing*, ed. by Joaquin Muns (Washington: International Monetary Fund).

Tsikata, G.K., and G.K. Amuzu, 1992, "Fiscal Development," in *Policies and Options for Ghanaian Economic Development*, Institute of Statistical, Social, and Economic Research, University of Ghana (Accra: Wilco Publishers).

van Wijnbergen, S., 1989, "External Debt, Inflation and the Public Sector: Towards Fiscal Policy for Sustainable Growth," *World Bank Economic Review*, Vol. 3, No. 3.

World Bank, 1983, *Ghana: Policies and Program for Adjustment* (Washington).

———, 1985, *Ghana: Towards Structural Adjustment*, Report No. 5854–GH (Washington).

———, 1989, *Ghana: Structural Adjustment for Growth*, Report No. 7515–GH (Washington).

———, 1991a, *Ghana: Progress on Adjustment, Report No. 9475–GH* (Washington).

———, 1991b, *World Debt Tables* (Washington).

———, 1992, *African Development Indicators* (Washington).

Growth and Foreign Debt: The Ugandan Experience 4

Barbara Mbire Barungi and Michael Atingi

During the last years of the 1980s, the external debt facing the sub-Saharan African countries received increasing attention. The immediate causes of the region's debt crisis during the decade were the economic slowdown and the sharp increases in international interest rates; the latter resulted from monetary contractions in some industrial countries and the fiscal policies being pursued by the United States. However, the roots of these difficulties lay in the oil price shocks and the resulting unprecedented increase in international lending to developing countries in the 1970s. The debt crisis decade of the 1980s was therefore almost the mirror image of the previous decade. The failure of many sub-Saharan African countries to adapt—especially in the area of their domestic policies—to the changed external environment aggravated the debt-servicing problem.

Many countries responded with structural adjustment programs supported by the World Bank and the IMF that aimed to induce growth, restore price stability, and reduce external imbalances. Despite attempts by donors to provide debt relief, and despite the continued provision of external assistance, the situation continued to deteriorate; by the turn of the 1990s the economic position of most of the countries in Africa had become precarious. As a result, most countries in sub-Saharan Africa now look back at almost a decade of lost growth. Uganda is no exception, and it is against this background of economic adjustment that Uganda's debt-service payment problems are analyzed here.

In the Ugandan case the decline in the foreign exchange earning capacity of the economy was aggravated by the decline of international coffee prices and hence receipts. This adversely affected Uganda's ability to service its debt and led to the rapid accumulation of arrears. The urgent need to rehabilitate the war-torn economy amid declining export receipts forced the government to resort to external financing, which led to a sharp rise in the stock of debt in 1987. By June 1993 the stock of debt outstanding and disbursed stood at $2.64 billion, with arrears of $253 million. This stock of arrears, which had been reduced from $586.3 million as of June 1982, had caused legal action against the government from some quarters and had greatly jeopardized the government's ability to manage its foreign reserves effectively. According to indicators, the debt outstanding and disbursed is estimated at 105 percent of GDP, with a debt-service ratio of nearly 80 percent, which constitutes a major bottleneck to Uganda's economic recovery and future development. There is a need to move the economy onto a growth path once again; on these grounds the government has developed an external debt strategy that involves prudent debt management.

Objectives

The major aim of this chapter is to provide an analysis of the debt crisis faced by Uganda and its implications for sustainable economic growth. This chapter therefore has the following objectives:

- to examine Uganda's external debt, including its size, structure, source, type, and composition;
- to assess empirically the internal and external factors influencing external debt accumulation;
- to analyze debt-servicing capacity and the sustainability of the debt (the Cohen model is used for debt sustainability analysis); and
- to draw policy implications for macroeconomic management.

Dimensions of the External Debt Problem

By the end of 1992 Uganda's total external debt was $2.6 billion. Over 60 percent was outstanding to multilateral institutions; debt service to multilaterals alone in 1991–92 was 31 percent of the total. Arrears stood at $253 million (117 percent of projected foreign exchange earnings). The debt-service ratio did not fall below 34 percent in the next five years.

Given this situation, it is likely that Uganda will find it difficult to service even its multilateral debt in the future without a substantial reduction in the debt-service obligations that it has to fund from its own resources. The Ugandan government has thus developed an external debt strategy with the aim of restructuring the country's debt. It is hoped that creditors and donors will adopt a flexible stance in recognition of Uganda's exceptional circumstances.

The decade of the 1970s witnessed average annual growth in the debt stock of 18.5 percent, whereas in the 1980s an average growth rate of 13.4 percent was recorded. The terms of trade over the same period averaged 176.11 and 107.56, respectively (1987 = 100), which also resulted in dwindling export receipts. Export growth was negative because of the decline of commodity prices in the world market. The arrears (part of the debt stock) position grew from $30 million in 1987 to $5.9 billion largely because of the persistently low level of foreign exchange inflows, which could not sustain the high debt-service ratio.

Since the External Loans Act (1962) gave powers to contract loans only to the minister of finance, all loans contracted for the public sector were government guaranteed. The Exchange Control Act did not until 1990 allow any agent except the central bank (the Bank of Uganda) to enter into external financial transactions; this meant that all external loans had a foreign currency guarantee by the Bank of Uganda. The nonguaranteed debt was contracted by the government on behalf of the private sector and is very small. By the end of June 1992 the stock of debt to the private sector was estimated at $52 million, which was just under 2 percent of all debt outstanding and disbursed. This rose to $75 million by the end of June 1993.

Size and Magnitude of Uganda's Debt

Table 1 shows the size of Uganda's external indebtedness in both current dollar and constant dollar values for the period 1970 to 1990. Growth of Uganda's external debt fell sharply in 1973. This was mainly due to the donor community's economic and financial retaliation after the declaration of economic war in 1972, which led to the expulsion of the Asian community (the backbone of the trade and commercial sector at the time) from Uganda. This resulted in both a slowing of disbursements and a freezing of commitments to Uganda. The steep rise of nominal debt by 22.1 percent in 1974 reflects a single disbursement from a multilateral creditor. The external debt in constant dollars fell between 1973 and 1975.

Most of the external financing from multilaterals during the 1970s came from the African Development Bank and the East African Development Bank. There was steady growth in nominal debt between 1975 and 1979. This was mainly debt from bilateral sources dominated by Arab creditors, who had a major influence on both political and economic trends in the country during that time. Between 1979 and 1987 a number of developments affected Uganda's level of indebtedness. The civilian regime that came to power in 1979 was quick to take advantage of reestablished ties with the donor community. The sharp declines in nominal debt (similar pattern of growth rate in constant terms) in 1984 and 1986 reflect the political and economic instability. In 1984 the stabilization program adopted in 1981 was abandoned in the midst of intense civil strife. The year 1986 saw the coming to power of the National Resistance Movement (NRM) government and the launching of the Economic Recovery Program. The government, in

Table 1. Uganda: External Debt, 1970–90

	In Current Dollars		In Constant Dollars	
	In millions of U.S. dollars	Change from previous year (In percent)	In millions of U.S. dollars[1]	Change from previous year (In percent)
1970	138.4		443.6	
1971	160.7	16.1	448.5	10.1
1972	183.1	13.9	515.8	5.6
1973	189.0	3.2	432.2	–16.2
1974	230.8	22.1	377.8	–12.6
1975	240.3	4.1	357.5	–5.4
1976	278.1	15.7	408.9	14.4
1977	354.1	27.3	479.1	17.2
1978	426.0	20.3	524.8	9.5
1979	574.2	34.8	591.0	12.6
1980	732.7	27.6	621.3	5.1
1981	793.9	8.4	687.3	10.6
1982	933.4	17.6	851.3	23.9
1983	1,016.1	8.9	973.2	14.3
1984	1,031.1	1.5	1,012.7	4.1
1985	1,171.3	13.6	1,171.3	15.7
1986	1,286.6	9.8	1,244.3	6.2
1987	1,659.0	28.9	1,456.4	17.1
1988	1,799.0	8.4	1,502.9	3.2
1989	1,809.0	0.6	1,493.8	–0.6
1990	2,200.0	21.6	1,656.6	10.9

Source: World Bank (1992).

[1]Computed by deflating the nominal external debt value by the World Unit Import Value Index, 1985 = 100.

order to implement this program, had to resort to external borrowing (albeit on concessionary terms), and this has resulted in the rise in debt since 1987.

Debt Profile

The financing of the debt was largely through official sources at both the multilateral and the bilateral levels (Table 2). Between 1970 and 1980, loans from multilateral institutions accounted for about 57 percent of the debt contracted, while the Paris Club share amounted to 4.9 percent; contributions of non–Paris Club bilateral and commercial creditors were 27.6 percent and 9.8 percent, respectively.

In the 1980s, the share contributed by the multilaterals increased to 67.6 percent, while that of Paris Club creditors rose to 9.5 percent; the

Table 2. Uganda: Outstanding Debt by Source, 1970–90
(In percent of total)

Source	1970–80	1981–90
Multilateral	57.1	67.6
Paris Club bilateral	4.9	9.5
Non–Paris Club bilateral	27.6	14.7
Commercial	9.8	8.2

Source: Bank of Uganda.

shares of non–Paris Club bilateral and commercial creditors declined to 14.7 percent and 8.2 percent, respectively. These changes are explained by the recent trend in the debt portfolio toward highly concessionary loans from the multilateral and Paris Club group of creditors. As a result of the prudent debt management policy being implemented by the government and the buildup of arrears to non–Paris Club and commercial creditors, less contracting of loans from the latter category is taking place.

External debt can further be broken down into public and publicly guaranteed, private nonguaranteed, and short-term debt. As can be seen from Table 3, public and publicly guaranteed debt has accounted for over 60 percent of Uganda's total external debt since 1980. Short-term debt has generally been below 10 percent.

Uganda's debt-export ratio was high—over 1,000 percent—between 1990 and 1993, as a result of adverse terms of trade and the fall in coffee prices, as shown in Table 4. Consequently, the debt-service ratio was also high over most of this period, at over 60 percent. This heavy debt burden further strains the weak balance of payments position and Uganda's quest for external viability. According to Sharer, De Zoysa, and McDonald (1995), given Uganda's initially weak external situation, its frequent inability to meet all contractual debt-service obligations, and the lack of access to commercial financing beyond normal trade credits, the traditional criterion of spontaneous access to commercial borrowing as an indicator of external viability is not relevant. Thus, under these circumstances, one can best assess Uganda's movement toward external viability in terms of the extent to which debt-service ratios and reliance on exceptional donor financing can be reduced.

We argue in this chapter that the composition and profile of Uganda's debt outstanding and disbursed and its debt-service obligations reveal an increasingly difficult external financial position, largely for the following reasons:

Table 3. Uganda: Total External Debt, 1980–90

	Total External Debt (In millions of U.S. dollars)	Long-Term Debt: Publicly guaranteed, In millions of U.S. dollars	Long-Term Debt: Publicly guaranteed, In percent of total	Long-Term Debt: Nonguaranteed, In millions of U.S. dollars	Long-Term Debt: Nonguaranteed, In percent of total	Short-Term Debt: In millions of U.S. dollars	Short-Term Debt: In percent of total
1980	732.7	578.0	78.9	9.7	1.3	65.7	9.0
1981	793.9	543.0	68.4	7.7	1.0	38.3	4.8
1982	933.4	593.0	63.5	7.3	0.8	51.5	5.5
1983	1,016.1	615.0	60.5	5.7	0.6	27.3	2.7
1984	1,031.1	652.0	63.2	6.0	0.6	42.4	4.1
1985	1,171.3	822.0	70.2	6.9	0.6	44.5	3.8
1986	1,286.6	966.0	75.1	8.0	0.6	72.1	5.6
1987	1,659.0	1,320.0	79.6	9.6	0.6	66.2	4.0
1988	1,799.0	1,455.0	80.9	9.1	0.5	235.2	13.1
1989	1,809.0	1,488.0	82.3	. . .	. . .	. . .	. . .
1990	2,200.0	. . .	. . .	. . .	. . .	. . .	. . .

Source: World Bank (1990, p. 579).

Table 4. Uganda: Debt Burden Indicators, 1980–92
(In percent)

	1980	1987	1988	1989	1990	1991	1992
Ratio of external debt to exports of goods and services	212.3	479.1	610.0	744.8	1,084.6	1,436.5	1,549.3
Ratio of external debt to GDP	55.7	31.4	30.7	43.6	63.3	87.9	109.6
Ratio of debt service to exports of goods and services	17.3	39.9	62.7	61.8	60.7	75.5	59.6

Source: World Bank (1996).

- the persistent low levels of foreign exchange inflows cannot sustain the high debt-service ratio;
- the preponderance of multilateral debt limits the benefits Uganda could obtain through traditional rescheduling;
- a large proportion of debt owed to the Paris Club group of creditors was contracted after the cutoff date (July 1, 1981) and is therefore not eligible for rescheduling;
- little precedent existed for rescheduling debt owed to non-OECD bilateral creditors, who account for the largest portion of nonmultilateral debt outstanding and disbursed; and
- of the uninsured commercial debt, 27 percent cannot be rescheduled on favorable terms, because a number of loans are owed to contractors with work in progress or were secured on specific terms.

Debt Management

Perhaps the most significant underlying factor in Uganda's debt crisis has been poor debt management. Debt management involves the deliberate and planned acquisition, deployment, and retirement of loans for the purpose of promoting economic growth and development. This entails articulation and formulation of external borrowing policy, control and surveillance of external borrowing, and the keeping of comprehensive and accurate data on external borrowing. These crucial aspects of debt management have not been well undertaken in Uganda's case.

Prior to 1982, very little information existed on Uganda's external debt, and there was no basic institution put in place to manage debt effectively through efficient data collection, assessment of sustainability, and advice on existing international resources. The Treasury Department in the Ministry of Finance and the Public Debt Section of the Accounts Department in the Bank of Uganda handled both the internal and the external debt; the composition, stock, and payment schedule were not clearly known.

Responsibilities for aid coordination and debt management were shared in varying degrees by the Aid Coordination Unit in the Ministry of Finance, the Commissioner/Treasury Officer of Accounts, the External Debt Management Office, the Foreign Exchange Operations in the Bank of Uganda, the Aid Coordination Unit in the Prime Minister's Office, and the Aid Coordination Unit in the former Ministry of Economic Planning. The exact role of each institution was not clearly defined or backed by full legislative authority. This led to a weakened flow of information among the units concerned, which in turn resulted in poor coordination and recordkeeping as well as inefficient verification and monitoring of debt.

The External Loan Act of 1962 and the Loans (Guarantee) Act of 1958 jointly vest legal authority for contracting and managing external debt with the minister of finance. The Aid Coordination Unit in the Ministry of Finance assists in the negotiation of new loans and facilitates the flow of aid-related funds into the country. The treasury, as stipulated by the Loans Act, authorizes all disbursement requests and all debt-service payments. It therefore has comparative advantage in keeping external debt-related information up to date. Nonetheless, the treasury is institutionally weak and does not have adequate capacity to perform its debt-reporting function. As a result, the External Debt Management Office in the Bank of Uganda has taken over this responsibility. Dependence on this office has been further increased by capacity constraints within the Ministry of Finance's Aid Coordination Unit and its apparent inability to take charge of the country's aid portfolio, as authorized by law.

As a result of insufficient information and poor coordination, the government has not been able to ensure that all new debt is contracted on terms compatible with the country's external debt burden and its ability to service and repay this debt in the future. In the mid-1980s the government succeeded in ensuring that the implementing ministries did not sign loans independently of the Ministry of Finance, although in some instances the implementing ministries have conducted negotiations with lenders and suppliers without earlier involvement of the ministry or the central bank. This has led to acceptance of financial commitments on unfavorable terms.

There had also been no clearly articulated policy defining the order of priority in which creditors should be paid, although maturities falling due to the IMF and the World Bank Group have always been serviced on time. As a result, creditors who have persistently pressured but who have not necessarily provided the maximum future benefits to Uganda have sometimes been paid in preference to other creditors. On some occasions the Bank of Uganda has had to resort to borrowing under the short-term commercial facility to make payments to key multilateral creditors.

Given the lack of coordination, it became almost impossible to keep accurate records of the volume and structure of Uganda's external debt and to determine the time profile of debt projections. Poor debt management created a problem of debt servicing for the country.

Owing to these weaknesses, the government in 1991 conducted an extensive debt management exercise within the Bank of Uganda; as a result, the total national stock of debt has been derived, verified with the creditors, and recorded centrally. The debt records have been computerized, and staff involved in debt management are being trained in the principles of debt management and the use of computer software related to debt.

Effective July 1992, the government centralized all functions of various units by creating a Central Debt Unit in the Ministry of Finance, although the External Debt Management Office in the Bank of Uganda maintains the duty of keeping all records pertaining to monitoring of disbursements, maturities, and all other data related to debt. This move has improved the control and coordination of policy, eliminated duplication of effort, and ensured efficient transfer of information.

External Debt Strategy

Given Uganda's debt crisis, the government decided to immediately develop and is currently implementing an external debt strategy to try to resolve the country's debt problem. In brief, the aims of the debt strategy include

- clearing the bulk of accumulated arrears, which were giving rise to legal actions against the government and threats to seize assets to satisfy claims, resulting in embargoes on disbursements and hence project disruptions;
- bringing a halt to increases in the accumulation of penalty and late interest charges; and
- reducing contractual debt service to a level commensurate with Uganda's ability to pay.

The components of the strategy include rescheduling, debt buyback and restructuring of uninsured commercial debt, implementation of the Fifth and Sixth Dimensions facilities, and possible cancellations. Our major focus will be on debt rescheduling, which forms an integral part of the debt strategy.

Paris Club Reschedulings

Uganda has benefited from a number of debt cancellations granted by the Paris Club creditors, in addition to reductions obtained under the 1989 rescheduling on Toronto terms and the 1992 rescheduling on enhanced Toronto terms. These include cancellations by France, Germany, the United Kingdom, and the United States of loans originally provided on concessionary terms.

As of the end of June 1992, approximately $279 million in debt was outstanding to the Paris Club creditors, of which $81 million represented arrears and penalty interest, and $26 million represented principal and interest falling due in 1991–92. The Paris Club does not reschedule or reduce any debt that was contracted after a particular date, which in the case of Uganda was set at July 1, 1981. Of the total amount outstanding to the Paris Club, 42 percent ($118 million) was contracted before this cutoff date. Consequently, only about $50 million in arrears and current maturities was eligible for rescheduling in the June 1992 agreement reached with the Paris Club.

Uganda was permitted to reschedule all arrears of principal, interest, and penalty interest coming due by the end of November 1993. This was exceptional in that the Paris Club usually grants rescheduling of maturities due during current IMF programs only (which in the case of Uganda was due to expire on November 30, 1992). The concession enabled Uganda to budget for fiscal year 1992/93 on the basis of this agreement. The amount rescheduled totaled nearly $50 million in arrears and maturities, of which $36 million was arrears and $14 million was current maturities. The impact was to reduce the debt service due in this category to only $2 million, the amount due, and moratorium interest. Under the enhanced Toronto terms granted to the least developed countries, penalty interest is not usually permitted to be rescheduled, but this was conceded for Uganda.

Debt Incurred After July 1, 1993

Since close to half the debt owed to Paris Club creditors was contracted after the cutoff date, a conventional rescheduling of pre-cutoff date debt would have a limited impact on the country's debt burden.

Uganda will therefore have to seek annually the maximum deferral of debt ineligible for the usual Paris Club rescheduling. The arrears on the post-cutoff date debt amounted to approximately $34 million. The Paris Club initially insisted that this be paid in full by November 1992, which was the guaranteed consolidation period. It was conceded that Uganda's domestic and foreign exchange budget would not permit this, but IMF assurances were made that at least half of this amount could be paid by November 1992. However, these deferrals are associated with terms that are stringent, with no grace periods, short repayment periods, and no reduction of principal or interest. The debt service that falls due is not deferred, and once deferred, arrears are not eligible for any future deferrals. This serves to intensify the debt overhang that the country is already experiencing, as it will not be possible to redefer these payments. It was also agreed that maturities up to November 30 could be restructured under this agreement. The year-by-year rescheduling approach adopted by creditors under these terms will require Uganda to return to the Paris Club on a regular basis for the foreseeable future.

Uganda benefited from the Toronto terms plan, which offered a menu of alternatives to choose from when the consolidated amount of $86 million was rescheduled in January 1989 (Table 5). One-third of the eligible debt was forgiven, and the maturity of the remaining debt was extended to 14 years, with an 8-year grace period. However, these terms have only partially addressed the problem, because the entire debt was not rescheduled at this single meeting, and because the burden of debt was postponed, which only intensified the overhang. In June 1992 the enhanced Toronto terms saw a write-off of debt worth 50 percent in terms of net present value. It included the exceptional element of rescheduling maturities outside the then-running IMF program and a rescheduling of penalty interest and 50 percent of the post-cutoff date arrears.

Non–Paris Club Bilateral Creditors

Non–Paris Club creditors are owed a significant amount of arrears and penalty charges, totaling $185.5 million as of the end of June 1992, with 1992–93 maturities totaling $47.3 million. In the course of the financial year 1992/93 the government entered into agreements with some of these creditors that saw the rescheduling of $17.6 million of arrears in that year.

This mainly resulted from the acceleration of maturities totaling nearly $17.6 million, while arrears amounting to $60 million were rescheduled. There was also a downward adjustment to the stock of arrears, totaling $14.7 million. The impact of these measures was to reduce the stock of debt outstanding and disbursed (including arrears)

Table 5. Uganda: History of Paris Club Debt Rescheduling

	Amount Consolidated (In millions of U.S. dollars	Maturity (In years)	Grace Period (In years)
November 1981	63	9	4.5
December 1983	16	9	4.5
June 1987	105	14	6.0
January 1989	86		Toronto terms: one-third write-off
June 1992	50		Enhanced Toronto terms: one-half write-off

Source: Bank of Uganda.

as of the end of June 1993. In the meantime, all the other creditors have been asked to reschedule their stock of arrears and maintain the concessional or semiconcessional interest rates that they apply to the underlying loans for rescheduling.

It should be noted that there are few precedents for rescheduling with some of these creditors, but it is proposed that the most favorable terms possible be requested from them.

Buyback and Restructuring of Uninsured Commercial Debt

A total of $242 million of debt was outstanding to uninsured commercial creditors as of June 30, 1992, of which $226 million represented obligations to nonbank commercial companies, mostly suppliers and creditors. Supervised under the debt reduction, a plan concluded on February 26, 1993, saw Uganda buy back $151.9 million of eligible debt out of its $2.6 billion debt outstanding and disbursed at 12 cents on the dollar, which represented 6 percent of the total debt, one-third of total arrears, and three-quarters of the commercial debt. The impact of this was debt forgiveness amounting to $133 million, using a grant provided by the International Development Association (IDA) under its debt reduction facility totaling $10 million. This deal provided some relief for the government to come up with longer-term debt restructuring strategies. It is also worth noting that Uganda became the fourth country to benefit from this facility, after Niger, Mozambique, and Guyana.

Given the relatively small stock of debt owed to commercial creditors, the London Club has not featured much in the restructuring of the Ugandan debt. The availability of the IDA debt restructuring facility and the bilateral grants made the buyback operation more significant for commercial debt.

The amounts to be converted into equity, approximately $13.1 million, mainly include arrears to private sector joint venture partners. The government has held discussions with these creditors to swap these arrears for government assets in accordance with the privatization program. East African Holdings and Shell are two companies with which the government has already concluded debt-equity swap agreements.

Multilateral Debt Service

The government has solicited bilateral donor assistance for servicing multilateral debt. Under the Fifth Dimension facility, Norway and Sweden have provided the government with resources equivalent to repayments due on the debt to the International Bank for Reconstruction and Development (IBRD), and the government has requested that these donors extend similar facilities for maturing African Development Bank (ADB) debt. The response has been positive: ADB maturities estimated at nearly $3.6 million of arrears and $1 million owed to the ADB were rescheduled. The government successfully negotiated with the East African Development Bank (EADB) a restructuring of amounts owed to it, and arrears guaranteed by the government as of June 30, 1993, are estimated at $15.3 million, down from $48.1 million a year earlier. The government had committed itself to a payment of nearly $6.8 million every financial year in order to clear these arrears over the next two and half years. It has divested itself of $33 million in arrears owed to EADB, and this is now to be paid by the private sector, which benefited from these loans. Other creditors that fall into this category of divestiture include Commonwealth Development Corporation, Commonwealth Technical Corporation, EXIM (India), and the International Finance Corporation (IFC), amounting to $51 million in arrears.

During the financial year 1992/93, $385 million in arrears was settled, of which exceptional financing accounted for $335 million (rescheduling alone contributed $141.3 million) and direct cash payments for $50 million. The maturities restructured through rescheduling are estimated at $45.7 million.

Impact of Debt Strategy

Although Uganda's debt strategy has assumed the maximum feasible rescheduling and accepts the accumulation of arrears to certain creditors, the minimum debt-service requirement remains high, at

Table 6. Uganda: External Financing Requirements, 1989/90–1993/94
(In millions of U.S. dollars)

	1989/90	1990/91	1991/92	1992/93	1993/94
Requirements	867	772	724	898	626
Imports (goods)	584	550	441	572	122
Services (net)	56	85	82	106	170
Scheduled debt service	197	185	249	1,786	80
Amortization	77	86	125	74	80
Interest (net)	77	62	90	84	10
IMF repurchases	43	37	34	18	19
Settlement of arrears	19	–65	–141	30	15
Reserves buildup	11	11	35	15	0
Other items (net)	0	6	58	–1	377
Own resources	337	260	286	325	262
Exports (goods)	210	177	173	196	168
Of which: Coffee	159	126	119	127	116
Private transfers	78	80	111	114	–1
Other items (net)	49	3	2	5	575
Financing gap	530	512	438	583	. . .
Foreign financing					
Existing commitments	530	512	438	466	375
IMF purchases	42	89	89	0	0
Project aid	249	236	236	236	240
Import support	196	186	186	180	135
Debt rescheduling	43	1	1	50	. . .
Disbursement from new sources	0	0	0	91	158
Individual financing gap	0	0	0	26	42

Source: Bank of Uganda.

over 60 percent of projected foreign exchange earnings. There is still a large financing gap, as shown in Table 6. The success of the debt strategy will therefore depend on limiting the extent to which the gap is financed through the accumulation of arrears. The financing gap has widened largely because foreign exchange earnings have fallen well below projected levels. Nonetheless, we hasten to mention the likely positive impacts of the debt strategy, mainly the reduction of arrears through rescheduling. Arrears could be reduced from \$585 million in June 1992 to \$76 million. This takes into account the debt buyback operation successfully executed in February 1993 and assumes that all rescheduling, restructuring, and cancellation in the various categories of debt are achieved in a timely manner. It is also estimated that the arrears buildup would be \$650 million to \$675 million at the end of the fiscal year 1992/93 and over $1 billion by the end of 1995 if the strategy were not implemented.

The impact of the debt strategy was largely realized during fiscal year 1992/93, which saw $385 million of arrears restructured, of which exceptional financing accounted for $335 million (rescheduling alone contributed $141.3 million) and direct cash payment for $50 million. The consequence of this was to reduce the stock of arrears by over 50 percent from the end-June 1992 level of $585.3 million to only $253.7 million a year later.

The maturities in financial year 1992/93 that were rescheduled are estimated at $45.7 million, whereas the impact of the debt strategy on maturities falling due between 1994 and 2000 is a reduction of interest and amortization amounting to $105.4 million (Table 7). Using the growth-cum-debt model described below, the impact of rescheduling on growth and debt indicators is shown in Table 8.

Although the impact of rescheduling of maturities falling due during this period is marginal, there is a savings on resource transfer amounting to an annual average of 0.06 percent of GDP and a reduction of the potential debt-GDP ratio by 2.5 percentage points; however, an increase in economic growth by 0.01 percent on a yearly basis is realized.

However, the cancellation of arrears during financial year 1992/93 had the fairly substantial effect of raising the estimated growth rate of GDP by 0.79 percentage point, lowering the debt-GDP ratio by 6.98 percentage points, and realizing a savings on resource transfer of 8.5 percent of GDP in calendar year 1993.

External Capital Requirements

Uganda's economic reform is highly dependent on external financing, given the collapse of the International Coffee Agreement (ICA) in July 1989 and the accompanying fall in coffee prices, which greatly affected the foreign exchange-earning capacity of the economy. Attempts to increase noncoffee exports may take time to increase export earnings sufficiently to cover the fall in coffee prices. At the same time, the economy needs a minimum level of imports to meet its growth and stabilization targets; this calls for considerable donor assistance together with the economic and structural reforms currently being implemented by the government. Although noncoffee export earnings are picking up, given the extremely small base of these exports the impact on the financing requirements has so far been marginal; a significant quantitative impact on the balance of payments can only be achieved over the medium term. Consequently, it may be that Uganda will continue for some time to be heavily dependent on donor support.

Table 7. Uganda: Impact of Debt Restructuring on Maturities Falling Due, 1994–2000

(In millions of U.S. dollars)

Creditor	1994	1995	1996	1997	1998	1999	2000	Total
Before restructuring								
Multilateral	72.02	85.05	102.15	120.05	117.99	110.99	96.95	705.16
Bilateral								
Paris Club								
Pre-cutoff date	17.39	16.81	16.24	18.01	22.93	21.89	22.63	135.90
Post-cutoff date	13.14	8.36	5.97	5.26	8.13	7.88	8.49	57.23
Non–Paris Club	26.5	39.89	41.11	39.95	46.66	40.06	37.23	271.40
Commercial nonbank	5.99	3.04	2.78	2.93	3.08	3.01	. . .	20.83
Other	8.23	11.15	6.82	3.6	2.94	2.73	2.42	37.89
Total	143.27	164.3	175.07	189.8	201.69	186.56	. . .	1,228.41
After restructuring								
Multilateral	73.32	84.58	99.71	109.54	102.96	94.82	82.16	647.07
Bilateral								
Paris Club								
Pre-cutoff date	17.15	16.49	15.83	17.61	22.72	21.47	20.23	131.50
Post-cutoff date	9.08	8.44	5.98	5.3	8.29	8.03	8.3	53.42
Non–Paris Club	22.69	35.07	31.81	32.61	31.2	30.52	27.95	211.85
Commercial nonbank	13.74	12.84	12.34	12.79	12.46	12.1	2.47	78.74
Other	0.131	0.122	0.113	0.053	. . .	. . .	. . .	0.42
Total	136.09	157.54	165.783	177.90	177.63	166.94	141.11	1,123.00
Reduction in debt service	7.18	6.76	9.29	11.90	24.06	19.62	26.61	

Source: External Debt Management Office, Bank of Uganda.

Table 8. Uganda: Impact of Rescheduling on Maturities Falling Due During 1994–2000
(In percent)

Variable	Before Rescheduling (Annual average)	After Rescheduling (Annual average)
Annual growth rate	5.73	5.74
Debt-GDP ratio	114.02	112.47
Resource transfer as share of GDP	0.16	0.22

Source: External Debt Management Office, Bank of Uganda.

As a result, Uganda continues to receive substantial disbursements from the donor community to cover the loss of coffee export earnings.

In addition to the increase in the level of external assistance, there has been a change in the pattern of aid allocation. Much of the 1980s saw project-related aid accounting for over 80 percent of gross disbursements; the trend in the 1990s is revealing a decline to less than 60 percent as donors increasingly seek to assist the government through import support aid, thereby providing not only much-needed balance of payments support but also the counterpart funding for the budget.

Causes of Uganda's Debt Crisis

The growing problem of debt accumulation in sub-Saharan Africa has received considerable attention in the literature and is now recognized as a serious global economic issue. Greene (1989) attributes this debt problem to both domestic policies and external factors. Besides expansionary fiscal policies and borrowing against exports to maintain consumption levels, many of these countries pursued other policies that weakened their external positions—for example, maintenance of high levels of imports, overvalued currencies, government subsidy policies, and external financing of overambitious development projects. Beginning in the late 1970s the shift in the terms of trade against African countries and a decline in export earnings have been a major external influence and have greatly hampered these countries' abilities to meet their debt obligations. Another factor that contributed to sub-Saharan debt burdens was the decline in net capital inflows. The rise in foreign interest rates, although less important because of the predominantly official character of sub-Saharan debt, may have affected a number of countries that made significant use of commercial borrowing.

The international economic environment has an important impact on sub-Saharan African economies. It drives the prices of African exports, the demand for those exports, and the effective interest rates countries pay. The terms of trade of developing countries are also indirectly affected by economic trends in the industrial countries.

A major external factor contributing to Uganda's debt crisis was the dramatic decline in export receipts due to declining coffee prices and unfavorable terms of trade. The price of coffee (the major export) declined steadily from 1985 to 1993, and Uganda suffered annual declines in its terms of trade every year from 1986 to 1992. The result was a sharp increase in Uganda's debt service to exports ratio, which between 1988 and 1993 was over 60 percent.

The high level of donor-financed development expenditures was another contributor. The reliance on external financing of the adjustment effort adopted in 1987 more than doubled Uganda's external debt during the adjustment period, from \$1.7 billion to \$2.9 billion as of June 1994. Most of this increase was attributable to credits obtained from multilateral institutions to support the balance of payments and to finance development projects. Multilateral debt as of June 1994 accounted for about 71 percent of the total debt stock, compared with about 43 percent in 1987.

Ajayi (1991) argues that the division of external and internal factors into two seemingly watertight compartments is quite misleading, since external factors do impinge crucially on domestic factors; for example, changes in the terms of trade may influence the real effective exchange rate. Hence the major factors contributing to Uganda's debt crisis can be thus summarized:

- price shocks throughout the world in the 1970s, mainly reflected through an increase in import prices due to oil price hikes;
- a deterioration in the terms of trade and a decline in export earnings, particularly in the 1980s, with a growth in arrears caused by the fall in coffee prices, which greatly affected not only the foreign exchange-earning capacity of the economy but also the ability to sustain the servicing of debt obligations;
- a buildup of interest on late payments to \$34.4 million as of the end of June 1992 (this is a contributory factor in the increase of the debt); and
- highly expansionary fiscal deficits.

Having identified the internal and external factors influencing Uganda's debt accumulation, we present an empirical assessment

Table 9. Uganda: Empirical Results for the Debt-Export Ratio

Variable	Regression 1	Regression 2
Constant	4.117 (7.880)*	4.082 (18.651)*
TOT	–0.535 (–3.256)*	–0.565 (–5.339)*
CGDP	–0.012 (–1.011)	–0.005 (–0.594)
FRRI	–0.071 (–1.038)	–0.073 (–1.346)
FP	–0.014 (–0.228)	
T	0.058 (4.322)*	0.053 (19.526)*
REER	–0.096 (–1.680)	–0.093 (–1.829)
$\bar{R}^2$	0.979	0.983
D-W	2.641	2.269

Source: Authors' calculations.

Note: All variables except *CGDP* are in logarithms; *t*-statistics are in parentheses. Asterisked values are significant above the 5 percent level.

using regression analysis to estimate these factors. The model (based on Ajayi, 1991) has the following general form:

$$DSR_i = f\,(TOT, CGDP, FRRI, FP, T, REER)$$

where

DSR_i = the debt-export ratio
TOT = terms of trade
CGDP = growth rate of income in the industrial countries
FRRI = foreign real interest rate
FP = fiscal performance (fiscal deficit)
T = linear time trend
REER = real effective exchange rate (developed in Appendix I).

Table 9 shows the regression results. We find that a worsening of the terms of trade significantly worsens the debt-export ratio. As in Ajayi (1991), an increase in the foreign interest rate would tend to worsen this ratio just as an appreciation in terms of the real effective exchange rate would. However, from our estimations the worsening of the terms of trade appears to have had the most significant impact, given that much of Uganda's experience over the period of study was characterized by a decline in its terms of trade. Despite the insignificant results for the fiscal performance variable, it is expected that a deterioration of the fiscal position will also have a negative impact on the debt-export ratio. The linear time trend variable is included to capture the likely influence of other external factors. The results in Table 9 (excluding the time trend and constants) show that the most important variables are the terms of trade and, to a lesser extent, the real effective exchange rate. This confirms that external factors have contributed significantly to Uganda's debt situation.

Debt and Economic Growth

Since 1981, stabilization and structural adjustment policies have been pursued in an attempt to stimulate recovery; these have attracted a substantial amount of foreign resources in the form of loans, because the required investment level could not be met by domestic saving. The reliance on foreign saving is justified by the fact that gross domestic saving as a percentage of GDP has for most of the sample period (between 1980 and 1995) been negative (Table 10). The saving rate is seen to lag behind the rate of investment—a pattern that is exhibited in both the public and the private sector. Beginning in 1989 the saving-GDP ratio did improve, however, largely because of high private unrequited transfers, reflected in the current account of the balance of payments.

An analysis of data on consumption and investment reveals that the economy absorbed more than it produced and saved, which may lead to the suggestion that external financing and the accumulation of arrears have sustained the Ugandan economy during the period under review.

This gloomy situation is largely attributed to the narrow tax base, which shrank during the years of economic decline and inefficient financial intermediation resulting from financial repression. A substantial percentage of the budget deficit was monetized, resulting in accelerated inflation; a fall in the real rate of interest on deposits in formal financial institutions reduced intermediation. At the same time an increasing proportion of the declining supply of real domestic credit was being expropriated by government to finance current expenditures. Consequently funds for both working capital and fixed capital investment, which had mainly been financed by the banking system, were doubly squeezed.

The stock of external debt doubled from $1.29 billion in 1986 to $2.65 billion in 1993. This is largely attributed to the implementation of the economic recovery program of rehabilitative investment and policy reforms that was adopted in 1987. The continuous rise in the debt was further aggravated by the accumulated effects of unpaid debt service, interest costs, and rescheduling. Economic liberalization and restructuring resulted in an average annual real GDP growth rate of 5 percent, with a 2 percent rise in per capita real incomes over the period 1987–93.

The question then arises as to the sustainability of this economic growth and the current stock of debt. In spite of more than 10 years of implementing economic recovery and structural adjustment, the economy remains fragile and the export sector is struggling to recover, and import capacity is largely sustained by the donor community.

A number of models have been constructed to illustrate the impact of capital imports on aggregate performance of the sub-Saharan African economies. The majority of these models deal with labor-surplus economies and emphasize growth of capital stocks. The model used for analytical purposes in this chapter emphasizes the incremental capital–output relationship, which suggests that the rate of economic growth increases if the ratio of investment to national income rises and further suggests that an increase in capital imports increases the investment ratio (Chenery, 1966).

We use the two-gap theory of Chenery and Bruno (1962), which suggests that growth is limited by two constraints: the saving gap, which constrains the country's ability to save and invest, and the foreign exchange gap accruing from limited export revenues—the targeted growth rate of the economy causes imports to exceed the economy's ability to finance them. We also use a Harrod growth equation of the type

$$g = sk,$$

where g is the real growth rate of national income, s is the ratio of saving to national income, and k is the incremental capital–output ratio.

It is observed that gross saving in Uganda has been negative for most of the latter part of the sample period; when gross domestic investment is taken into consideration, the saving gap is seen to be extremely large. This has in most cases been accompanied by positive real growth rates, and it therefore suggests that growth has been driven by aid, so that

$$g = (s + a)k,$$

where a is the ratio of aid to national income. If g^* is the targeted growth rate and k is the assumed constant over time, the rate of capital accumulation necessary to achieve the target growth rate is denoted by

Table 10. Uganda: Selected National Accounts Data, 1970–95
(In percent of GDP)

	Exports of Goods and Nonfactor Services	Imports of Goods and Nonfactor Services	Foreign Balance	Domestic Saving	Domestic Investment	Domestic Balance	Incremental Capital-Output Ratio
1970	24.62	21.10	–3.52	18.76	15.24	3.52	. . .
1971	20.75	24.90	4.15	12.45	16.60	–4.15	19.85
1972	20.77	17.80	–2.97	11.17	8.20	2.97	4.71
1973	17.19	13.75	–3.44	12.89	9.45	3.44	6.45
1974	17.37	17.37	0.00	13.42	13.42	0.00	–43.71
1975	8.68	11.09	2.41	5.78	8.19	–2.41	–5.46
1976	11.64	9.56	–2.08	8.32	6.24	2.08	10.30
1977	9.30	7.88	–1.41	7.48	6.06	1.41	3.14
1978	13.60	18.79	5.19	3.04	8.23	–5.19	–2.68
1979	19.35	17.49	–1.87	8.39	6.53	1.87	–0.50
1980	19.52	26.13	6.61	–0.40	6.21	–6.61	–1.35
1981	21.25	29.44	8.19	–0.74	7.45	–8.19	1.49
1982	21.51	33.25	7.73	1.43	9.17	–7.74	1.54
1983	18.97	24.65	5.68	4.26	9.94	–5.68	1.27
1984	9.75	30.95	21.20	–14.25	6.95	–21.20	–1.06
1985	9.60	30.40	20.80	–13.05	7.75	–20.80	3.90
1986	9.55	32.00	22.45	–12.50	10.00	–22.50	15.58
1987	8.40	35.20	26.80	–13.10	13.70	–26.80	2.04
1988	8.75	36.35	27.60	–14.85	12.70	–27.55	1.68
1989	9.15	32.35	23.20	–12.40	10.80	–23.20	1.48
1990	7.20	25.00	17.80	–5.75	12.00	–17.75	2.97
1991	6.90	21.50	14.60	–1.85	12.75	–14.60	3.08
1992	6.90	21.10	14.20	0.01	14.20	–14.19	2.04
1993	6.80	22.50	15.70	–1.10	14.55	–15.65	3.34
1994	7.05	22.00	14.95	–1.35	13.60	–14.95	3.20
1995	7.25	21.30	14.05	–1.05	13.00	–14.05	3.43

Sources: World Bank (1990); Ministries of Finance and Economic Planning; and Bank of Uganda.

$$g^* / k = s + a.$$

Let $s + a = c$; then $a = c - s$; hence, $c - s$ represents the saving gap.

This analogy seems to imply that aid inflows to Uganda should have the potential effects of supplementing domestic savings (and hence capital accumulation) and increasing the proportion of income saved. If this is the case, then aid increases the capacity for economic growth and should enable the country to reach a self-sustaining level that subsequently leads to a reduction of aid contracted. The assumption is that the increase in aid is greater than the increase in consumption.

With regard to the foreign exchange gap, the assumption is that the value and the volume of exports are given as exogenous ($X = X_o$), whereas the demand for imports largely depends on the targeted rate of economic growth. Imports of capital goods depend on the level of investment, and demand for intermediate goods derives from the capacity utilization rate. Since domestic inputs are an imperfect substitute for imported intermediate goods, the latter increase or decrease with an increase or decrease in production, respectively (Khan and Knight, 1983). The cost of financing such imports has in most cases exceeded the earnings of foreign exchange by exports, and a foreign exchange gap arises that, if not closed by aid resources, reduces targeted economic growth.

Given that $M = mY$, where m is the marginal propensity to import, and Y is national income, the size of the foreign exchange gap is then denoted as $mY - X_0$ and can be described in terms of aid (a) as

$$a = m - (X_0/Y).$$

The implication of the foreign exchange gap is that potential domestic saving is being frustrated because the capital goods necessary to undertake the desired investment are not produced locally, nor can they be acquired externally. Additional foreign exchange would raise the level of investment and subsequently the rate of economic growth; this would imply that aid not only raises investment but also permits an increase in domestic saving.

In the ex post accounting sense, the two gaps are exactly equal, so that:

$$a = c - s = m - (X_0/Y).$$

The changes in the domestic balance each year have a strong bearing on the changes in the external balance (see Table 10 for domestic and foreign imbalances). By linking the internal and external imbalances, the sources of financing for the domestic balance are seen to be changes in the external balance. Available data seem to identify the capital account of the balance of payments as the source of financing this overall domestic imbalance, and this is made up of medium- and long-term loans. This appears to justify the contracting of debt, particularly during the period of stabilization and structural adjustment of the Ugandan economy.

Debt Viability: Growth-cum-Debt Model Scenario

A growth-cum-debt model developed by Solis and Zedillo (1985) and used by Ajayi (1991) is adopted in this paper for the analysis of debt sustainability. It focuses on how debt affects the growth prospects of a debtor country. (Details of the model are presented in Appendix I of Chapter 2.)

Using a growth dynamic equation denoted by

$$D_t = D_{t-1}\,(1 + \tau),$$

where D_t is the total external debt, and its growth rate (τ) is varied for values between –0.03 and 0.07; interest rates of 2, 4, and 7 percent are used. These values are chosen in accordance with the external debt strategy implemented by the government of Uganda. This debt strategy calls for taking out highly concessionary loans and for the maximum possible reduction in the stock of debt. The rates of interest and of growth of the debt stock chosen for this analysis are therefore in line with the government debt strategy.

The incremental capital-output ratio (ICOR) of 2.375 is the average for the years 1987–95, the period under the Economic Recovery Program[1] (see Table 10); $s = 0.42$ (the reciprocal of ICOR).

Simulations using different rates of interest and amounts of external debt were run for the period 1993–2000. The following indicators were used:

g = growth rate of GDP

DB_1 = debt-GDP ratio

DB_2 = resource transfer.

The variables DB_1 and DB_2 are defined as

$$DB_1 = D/GDP$$

[1]The methodology used in computing ICOR in this chapter is derived from that of the Central Bank of Ecuador (FitzGerald and Vos, 1989). The impact of a foreign exchange boom (derived from exports) accompanied by average or lower growth rates of GDP is a high ICOR, and for Uganda the years 1976 and 1986 typify this. The ICOR is, of course, undermined or less meaningful when the economy is experiencing zero or negative growth.

$$DB_2 = [(D_t - D_{t-1}) - (r_t D_{t-1})]/GDP.$$

The results of the simulation, shown in Table 11, reveal that Uganda cannot at this time sustain debt that attracts interest rates of more than 7 percent a year with growth of more than 2 percent a year on average. This permits a real growth rate of only 2 percent a year; given a population growth rate of slightly more than 2 percent a year, there is zero or negative growth in real per capita incomes. Accompanying it are debt-GDP ratios that are seen to be high for every rate of growth of the debt stock; there is no positive resource transfer noted in this scenario. The scenario with interest rates of 4 percent shows that a zero growth rate in the debt stock is consistent with 4.42 percent annual growth in GDP, and a positive transfer of resources is only possible at a rate of growth of debt above 4 percent a year.

The simulation also shows that low interest rates (e.g., 2 percent) attract higher rates of economic growth, as greater resource transfer is permitted for every level of τ, and this is consistent with low and high DB_1 and DB_2, respectively.

The simulation results are compared with balance of payments projections for fiscal years 1993/94 through 2002/03 provided by the Ugandan authorities. The projections assume that all interest and amortization falling due are fully externalized, just as the model used here assumes. The projected average annual growth rate of external debt up to fiscal year 2000/01 is 3.44 percent, with a computed average interest rate of 1.64 percent a year. Table 12 gives the Ugandan authorities' projections, and these are compared with those simulated by the model used in this chapter.

The higher growth rate of 6.27 percent a year simulated by the model is based on the assumption that all foreign resources are fully used for investment. This is one major problem with the two-gap model: the model assumes that all foreign capital is used to complement domestic saving, thereby raising investment and economic growth. However, some of the foreign capital is used to finance consumption (Griffin, 1970), and capital inflows may affect relative prices by changing the sectoral balance of the economy (through changes in production patterns), and hence the income distribution and the domestic saving function.

The Ugandan authorities' projections appear to have allowed for current consumption because some of the foreign resources are actually used for budgetary support that ends up for current consumption.

Both scenarios (see Table 12) show that there will be a net transfer of resources to Uganda from the donor community averaging 2 percent of GDP annually for the period 1993–2000. This occurs largely on the

Table 11. Uganda: Simulation Results of the Growth-cum-Debt Model

τ	g	DB_1	DB_2
	$r = 0.02$		
0.07	0.0533	136.53	0.0638
0.06	0.0538	130.63	0.0493
0.05	0.0542	125.01	0.0357
0.04	0.0547	119.65	0.0230
0.03	0.0551	114.53	0.0111
0.02	0.0555	109.66	0.0000
0.01	0.0559	105.01	–0.0104
0.00	0.5562	100.57	–0.0201
–0.01	0.0666	96.33	–0.0292
–0.02	0.0570	92.29	–0.0377
–0.03	0.0573	88.44	–0.0456
	$r = 0.04$		
0.07	0.0377	145.78	0.0409
0.06	0.0387	139.14	0.0263
0.05	0.0398	132.84	0.0127
0.04	0.0407	126.86	0.0000
0.03	0.0416	121.19	–0.0180
0.02	0.0425	115.79	–0.0227
0.01	0.0434	110.67	–0.0329
0.00	0.0442	105.80	–0.0423
–0.01	0.0450	101.17	–0.0511
–0.02	0.0457	96.77	–0.0592
–0.03	0.0464	62.58	–0.0668
	$r = 0.07$		
0.07	0.0107	163.28	0.0000
0.06	0.0129	155.07	–0.0146
0.05	0.0150	147.36	–0.0281
0.04	0.0170	140.12	–0.0404
0.03	0.0189	133.30	–0.0510
0.02	0.0207	126.88	–0.0622
0.01	0.0207	120.83	–0.0718
0.00	0.0240	115.12	–0.0806
–0.01	0.0256	109.72	–0.0887
–0.02	0.0271	104.63	–0.0963
–0.03	0.0285	99.82	–0.1029

Source: Authors' calculations.
Note: Calculations are based on an incremental capital-output ratio (σ) of 0.42.

grounds that the rate of loan contracting is projected to be higher than the computed interest rate for this sample period. A simulation of economic growth rates and of debt-GDP and resource transfer ratios is carried out for the period 1993–2000, and this involves changing the

Table 12. Comparison of Ugandan Authorities' Projections with Simulated Variables Generated by the Growth-cum-Debt Model

Variable	Ugandan Authorities' Projections	Growth-cum-Debt Simulation
g	5.00	6.27
DB_1	121.13	112.94
DB_2 (as percentage)	2.1	2.0

Source: Authors' calculations.

domestic saving ratio and the ICOR used to generate the variables in Table 12. The numbers simulated for the different macroeconomic variables are then compared with their base values, that is, zero growth in the saving ratio and an ICOR of 2.375.

The results specifically reveal that policies designed to increase the efficiency of capital (i.e., lower the ICOR) for any given level of the domestic saving ratio do generally raise the rate of economic growth and lower the debt and resource transfer ratios expressed as a percentage of GDP. Any increase in the domestic saving ratio for any given level of ICOR has the same effect.

It is then suggested that the government pursue policies that increase utilization of the existing capital stock and increase the aggregate domestic saving ratio. These policies are analyzed elsewhere in this chapter.

A major problem of aid extended to Uganda is its fungibility. Even the World Bank,[2] which used to take pride in the soundness and high rate of economic return of its projects, has of late funded projects that could be ranked lowest on the list of economic priorities. To date, World Bank financing has not necessarily been geared to the most attractive projects. Bilateral aid has also tended to promote fungibility because of the sourcing conditions attached to these lines of credit. A good proportion of the raw materials and technical assistance, which is not always the most efficient, has to originate in the donor country.

Another impact of aid on Uganda's investment pattern is the extent to which it has stimulated the consumption of importables. To date, nearly 30 percent of tax revenue is generated from external trade sources, of which a good proportion is financed by the donor commu-

[2]The World Bank is the single largest source of credit to Uganda. In 1992 it accounted for 60.8 percent and 41.0 percent of total debt outstanding and disbursed from multilateral and all sources, respectively.

nity. Efforts to stimulate domestic saving through tax incentives have proved unsuitable for mobilizing domestically generated resources. It would then appear that Uganda can only continue recording positive growth rates with the funding of the donor community—a very discouraging situation.

An analysis of the types of investment funded by the donor community reveals that nearly 60 percent of it is allocated to social overhead capital and economic infrastructure (transport facilities, electric power, education, health, and road construction). Directly productive activities such as factory construction have only succeeded in attracting a relatively small proportion of total aid. Although infrastructure deserves priority, the general bias against directly productive activities has tended to lower the aggregate output of the economy. This point is important in relation to debt servicing, which is reaching crisis proportions in the country; because the gestation period of these projects exceeds the grace period, they add to the debt-servicing problem. The government borrows from bilateral sources in order to make payments to multilateral creditors, like the World Bank, that have financed such projects. Private investment, on the other hand, is relatively low and cannot on its own be relied on to make best use of the massive investment in overhead capital and economic infrastructure.

Ndulu (1991) suggests that in a situation where capacity underutilization obtains, a high investment growth rate could result in a low real economic growth rate; that is:

$$g = g_p + g_u,$$

where g_p is the sum of capacity growth driven by investment, g_u is the rate of capacity utilization, and g is the actual economic growth rate.

From this definition it is possible to observe that high investment (g_p) rates can coexist with declining or relatively low economic growth rates as long as capacity underutilization obtains. Capacity underutilization is prevalent in Uganda; in fact, the statistics from the index of industrial production indicate an average of less than 50 percent utilization of installed capacity.

It could then be argued that economic growth should influence not only capacity growth but also the rate of capacity utilization. One way to enhance growth, therefore, is to emphasize resource allocation between capacity expansion and utilization, given the fact that saving (and hence investment) ultimately depends on income growth.

An analysis of the components of investment reveals that foreign saving is the largest contributor and has a higher elasticity with respect to output than that of domestic saving. This is largely because domestic resource mobilization is inelastic to policies designed to mobilize it;

external capital may then be a key force propelling any growth that is accruing from investment.

The Cohen Model

The level at which debt sustainability can be attained is further investigated using an analytical framework adopted from Cohen (1985). Details of the model are provided in Appendix II.

If a country pays all interest falling due every period, the value of debt remains constant. If an indebted country neither repays its debt nor services the associated interest payments, the debt grows at the rate of interest. The interest rate exceeds the country's growth in exports. The central focus of Cohen's analysis is on that minimum level (b) of debt repayment that keeps the debt-export ratio constant. In Uganda's case we use the trade deficit as a proxy for b. What trade deficit is feasible if the debt-export ratio (defined as D/X, the debt stock–export ratio, where the debt stock is of the preceding year and exports are for the current year) is to be kept from rising? In other words, what trade deficit (b) gives us $D/X^0 = 0$?

Table 13 gives values for b and D/X; the 1982 D/X ratio is chosen as a starting point and D/X^0 is then kept constant. As an example, the economy would have had to have run a trade deficit of $29.1 million on its current account, instead of the recorded surplus of $114 million, in 1985 for D/X to have remained constant. The variable b^* compares with b in that b^* is the computed trade deficit that should have been run given D/X, the rate of growth of exports, and the interest rate on the stock of debt outstanding and disbursed; b is the actual trade deficit recorded (or expected to be recorded) for the period 1993–2000.

Table 13 suggests that the trade deficits recorded for the years 1983, 1984, 1987, 1988, and 1990–92 were not consistent with the stock of debt, and this therefore required the economy to run a surplus on its trade account through either exporting more or cutting down on imports, if D/X was to be held constant, so as to create an environment of debt sustainability. The rest of the sample period 1980–2000 suggests that a deficit could be run on the current account, not because of good performance in the export sector but rather on grounds that the computed rate of interest on the stock of debt happens to be lower than the growth in exports. It is sufficient that debt grows strictly less rapidly than the rate of interest. The years 1993–2000 permit the running of a deficit on the current account largely on the grounds of the implementation of the external debt strategy, which calls for contracting of highly concessionary loans, and a reduced stock of debt through restructuring of existing debt and reduced growth in the stock of debt.

Table 13. Uganda: Empirical Analysis Using the Cohen Model, 1981–2000

	D	*r*	*r**	*x*	*dx*	*m*	*d/x*	*b*	*b**
1981	793.9	13.2	. . .	345	. . .	293	. . .	–52	30.01
1982	933.4	26.3	0.03	396.86	15.03	379.69	2	–17.17	–18.75
1983	1,016.4	41	0.04	367.7	–7.35	421.1	2.54	60.4	–20.78
1984	1,031.1	65	0.06	342.2	–6.94	407.9	2.97	65.7	29.13
1985	1,171.3	53	0.05	379	10.75	264.1	2.72	–114.9	21.02
1986	1,286.6	43	0.03	406.8	7.34	438.2	2.88	31.4	–69.48
1987	1,659	36	0.02	333.6	–17.95	591.3	3.86	264.7	–125.8
1988	1,799	35	0.02	266.3	–20.17	658.2	6.23	391.9	27.57
1989	1,809	46	0.03	277.7	4.28	710	6.48	462.3	–366.2
1990	2,200	47.8	0.02	177.8	–35.97	617.6	10.17	439.8	–28.88
1991	2,300	73.8	0.03	173.8	–2.25	474.4	12.66	300.6	–208.5
1992	2,592	97.8	0.04	150.2	–13.58	512	15.31	361.8	236.6
1993	2,652	53.1	0.02	174.1	15.91	591.5	14.89	417.4	300.75
1994	2,783.1	52.8	0.02	218.4	25.45	629.3	12.14	410.9	199.73
1995	2,880.8	51.8	0.02	250.05	18.61	666.4	10.74	487.35	121.76
1996	2,969.9	51	0.02	290.95	12.31	707.3	9.9	416.35	85.06
1997	3,053	49.6	0.02	317.45	9.11	755.9	9.36	438.45	75.31
1998	3,143.5	47.4	0.02	344.5	8.52	808.4	8.86	463.9	71.41
1999	3,252.7	44.3	0.01	373.8	8.51	864	8.41	490.2	68.13
2000	3,395.8	40.7	0.01	405.6	8.51	925.1	8.02	519.5	. . .

Sources: World Bank (1990); Ministry of Finance, Uganda; Bank of Uganda; and authors' calculations.

Note: Definition of variables

D = debt stock
r = interest rate
*r** = computed interest rate
x = exports
dx = growth of exports
m = imports
d/x= debt-export ratio
b = trade deficit (actual and projected)
*b** = computed trade deficit

The Cohen and growth-cum-debt models can be compared for the period 1993–2000. With the Cohen model, the interest rate computed from Table 13 lies between 1 percent and 2 percent (the average is 1.75 percent for the sample period), with an average annual growth rate in debt outstanding and disbursed of 3.44 percent, which permits a net resource transfer as reflected by b^*.

The growth-cum-debt model, which uses interest rates of 1.64 percent and a growth in the debt stock of 3.44 percent, also suggests a positive net inflow of resources averaging 2 percent of GDP annually. The two models therefore seem to suggest that net resource inflows are possible—at least up to the year 2000—largely because of the external debt policy being pursued by the government.

Summary and Policy Implications

This chapter has analyzed the external debt burden of a severely indebted low-income country and raises the crucial issues of growth and debt sustainability. As of the end of June 1993, Uganda's total debt stock was estimated at $2.6 billion, with a debt-service ratio of over 80 percent.

Uganda's external debt since the 1970s has remained predominantly multilateral debt, with institutions such as the World Bank, the African Development Bank, and the IMF representing over 70 percent of the total debt stock. Uganda's debt-export ratio also remains high at over 1,000 percent. The fact that much of the debt accumulated is from multilateral creditors limits Uganda's flexibility in reducing its debt-service burden through traditional reschedulings.

Uganda's accumulation of external debt is due to both domestic and external influences. The external causes include the shift in the terms of trade and a resulting decline in coffee export earnings. The domestic causes include poor macroeconomic policies arising from fiscal indiscipline, exchange rate misalignment, overall economic mismanagement, and poor debt management.

The multilateral debt problem is one that has to be tackled specifically if any meaningful debt relief is to be experienced. The international financial institutions' main strategy for dealing with the huge debt claims has been concessional lending. Indeed, the international community has been generous in providing debt relief to Uganda, reflecting its adjustment record and its status as a severely indebted low-income country. However, the burden of its debt to multilateral creditors remains extremely heavy, and it is in view of this that a multilateral debt fund is to be set up specifically to address multilateral debt relief.

The accumulation of arrears compounds the problem. The successful implementation of the debt strategy depends on negotiating reschedulings in all categories of debt, on the achievement of a number of cancellations, and on the availability of funds to institute buybacks. Uganda is also receiving considerable concessional debt relief.

Debt relief is only part of the answer, however; continued government commitment to structural reforms and sound debt management is essential. The Ugandan government is currently implementing adjustment policies with the prime objective of restoring investment and economic growth. Increased domestic saving financed by resource mobilization through appropriate monetary policies could also raise the estimated growth rate, without any increase in aid inflows.

The two models used in this paper (the growth-cum-debt model and the Cohen model) show that Uganda is in a position to run a trade deficit between 1993 and 2000 of up to 6 percent of GDP on its current account while maintaining a constant debt-export ratio. This can be largely attributed to the debt strategy, which has greatly reduced the interest rate of loans contracted and further decreased the overall size of the debt through restructuring and debt reduction.

The target growth rate of 5 percent a year as estimated by the Ugandan authorities could be raised to 6.27 percent for the period 1993–2000. This is possible only if the resources devoted to current consumption funded by aid could be reduced. Any policy that limits estimated current consumption to domestically generated revenue while devoting external finance to investment could enable the achievement of faster economic growth.

Finally, Uganda has already made significant progress as a result of rescheduling agreements and more favorable lending terms, over and above recent improvements in export prices. The result has been a decline in its debt ratio. The overall increase in capital inflows has improved the prospects for less reliance on exceptional financing in the form of net accumulation of arrears, rescheduling, and gross use of IMF resources. The sustainability of a favorable balance of payments without exceptional financing depends very much on domestic performance. For growth to be sustained, strong and persistent adjustment efforts by the government have to be continuously maintained. These efforts should particularly address the productive base and reduce structural bottlenecks in the economy. At the same time, they should adopt appropriate macroeconomic policy to avoid the reemergence of uncontrollable inflation and encourage flexibility in the clearing of financial markets.

Appendix I. The Real Effective Exchange Rate

There are many methods of deriving the real effective exchange rate. The method used for this study is

$$REER = \lambda_i \, e_i \, (P_i/P_d),$$

where

λ_i = trade weight of Uganda's ith trading partner

e_i = nominal exchange rate between Ugandan shillings and the currencies of the major trading partners

P_i = consumer price index (CPI) of trading partner country i

P_d = Ugandan domestic CPI.

Appendix II. The Cohen Model

The stock of debt at the end of previous year is given by

$$(D/X^0) = d(D/X)/d \tag{1}$$

$$(D/X') = (D/X^0)/(D/X). \tag{2}$$

Equation (2) becomes

$$(D/X^0) = (D/X') * (D/X) = (D/X')d, \text{ where } d = D/X.$$

Given that

$$(D/X') = (D' - X')$$

$$(D/X^0) = (D' - x')d$$

$$= D'd - X'd, \tag{3}$$

where x = growth of exports,

$$(D/X^0) = (D^0/D)d - xd. \tag{3'}$$

If r is the world real interest rate, and B the trade deficit,

$$(R - X)d + B$$

$$(D/X^0) = (D^0/D)d - xd.$$

If

$$D^0/D = (rD + B)/D = r + (B/D),$$

then

$$(D/X^0) = (r - x)d + (B/D) * (D/X) \tag{4}$$

$$(D/X^0) = (r - x)d + B/X.$$

Let

$$B/X = b.$$

Equation (4) then becomes

$$(r - x)d + b.$$

For

$$(D/X^0) = 0$$

$$b = (r - x)d. \tag{5}$$

References

Ajayi, S. Ibi, 1991, "Macroeconomic Approach to External Debt: The Case of Nigeria," African Economic Research Consortium Research Paper No. 8 (Nairobi: Initiative Publishers).

Bank of Uganda, 1991, *External Debt Strategy* (Kampala).

———, *Quarterly Economic Reports* (Kampala), various issues.

Chenery, Hollis, 1966, "Foreign Assistance and Development," *American Economic Review*, Vol. 56, No. 4.

———, and M. Bruno, 1962, "Development Alternatives in an Open Economy: The Case of Israel," *Economic Journal*, Vol. 72, No. 285.

Cline, W.R., 1988, "International Debt: Progress and Strategy," *Finance & Development*, Vol. 25, No. 2.

Cohen, Daniel, 1985, "Reassessing Third World Debt," *Economic Policy*.

Fajana, Olufemi F., 1993, "Nigeria's Debt Crisis," UNECA Development Research Papers No. 5 (Addis Ababa: United Nations Economic Commission for Africa).

FitzGerald, E.V.K., and Rob Vos, 1989, *Financing Economic Development* (Brookfield, Vermont: Gower).

Greene, J., 1989, "The Debt Problem of Sub-Saharan Africa," *Finance & Development*, Vol. 2, No. 2.

———, and Mohsin S. Khan, 1990, "The African Debt Crisis," African Economic Research Consortium, Special Paper No. 3 (Nairobi: African Economic Research Consortium).

Griffin, K., 1970, "Foreign Capital, Domestic Savings and Economic Development," *Bulletin of the Institute of Economics and Statistics*, University of Oxford, Vol. 3, No. 2.

Husain, Ishrat, and J. Underwood, eds., 1991, *African External Finance in the 1990s* (Washington: World Bank).

Khan, Mohsin S., and M.D. Knight, 1983, "Determinants of Current Account Balances of Non-Oil Developing Countries in the 1970s:

An Empirical Analysis," *Staff Papers*, International Monetary Fund, Vol. 30, No. 4.

Lipumba, N., and E. Noni, 1992, "Foreign Debt and Economic Growth in Tanzania," Work in Progress Report (Nairobi: African Economic Research Consortium).

Ndulu, J. Benno, 1991, *Growth and Adjustment in Sub-Saharan Africa.*

Ng'eno, N.K., 1991, "The External Debt Problem of Kenya," paper presented to the African Economic Research Consortium, Nairobi.

Osei, Barfour, 1992, "Ghana: The Burden of Debt Service Payment Under Structural Adjustment," African Economic Research Consortium Research Paper No. 33 (Nairobi: African Economic Research Consortium).

Sharer, R.L., H.R. De Zoysa, and C.A. McDonald, 1995, *Uganda: Adjustment with Growth, 1987–94*, IMF Occasional Paper No. 121 (Washington: International Monetary Fund).

Solis, Leopoldo, and Ernesto Zedillo, 1985, "The Foreign Debt of Mexico," in *International Debt and the Developing Countries*, ed. by Gordon W. Smith and J.T. Cuddington (Washington: World Bank).

World Bank, 1990, *World Debt Tables, 1989–1990* (Washington).

———, 1992, *World Debt Tables, 1991–1992* (Washington).

———, 1996, *World Debt Tables: External Finance for Developing Countries* (Washington).

The External Debt Problem of Kenya 5

N.K. Ng'eno

Mexico's default on its debt in August 1982 set off a major global debt problem. The problem spread quickly from Latin America and soon reached crisis proportions in sub-Saharan Africa, where it has been more difficult to deal with than in the Latin American case. The high indebtedness of African countries led to the adoption by African leaders of the African Common Position on Africa's External Debt Crisis (Organization of African Unity, 1987).

The seriousness of the debt problem spawned numerous proposals to deal with it. The first of these was the Baker plan of October 1985, which was followed by the Toronto plan of June 1988 and the Brady initiative of March 1989. In May 1989 the World Bank and the IMF took initiatives to reduce the commercial debts of low-income countries.

The target of the Baker terms was a group of 15 highly indebted countries, whereas the Brady terms were intended for countries highly indebted to commercial creditors.[1] The Toronto facility targeted low-income African countries whose official debt could be rescheduled under the Paris Club arrangements, conditional on the implementation of IMF and World Bank structural adjustment programs. The Toronto terms were enhanced by the London terms of December 1991 and the Naples terms of December 1994.

These terms allowed for deeper reduction of the nonconcessional stock of bilateral debt for eligible poor countries. The Naples terms, which allows for relief of up to 67 percent of eligible debt in net present value terms, is accessible to low-income countries after they agree with the donors on debt-service programs that could be sustained over longer periods than is possible under the Toronto or London terms.

[1]The 15 countries were Argentina, Bolivia, Brazil, Chile, Colombia, Côte d'Ivoire, Ecuador, Mexico, Morocco, Nigeria, Peru, the Philippines, Uruguay, Venezuela, and Yugoslavia. The classifications of indebtedness and the number of countries considered to be overburdened with debt have varied over time. In 1996 the World Bank (World Bank, 1996, Vol. 1) listed some 41 countries as heavily indebted poor countries, of which 32 were classified as severely indebted. Twenty-five of the severely indebted countries are in sub-Saharan Africa, and the group includes Kenya.

The extent of the African debt crisis has been analyzed in various studies, including United Nations (1988), World Bank and United Nations Development Program (1989), Killick and Martin (1989), Krumm (1985), Mistry (1988, 1991), Greene and Khan (1990), Ajayi (1996), and Elbadawi, Ndulu, and Ndung'u (1996). However, individual country case studies are scanty. The few available include Degebe (1992), Ajayi (1991, 1996), Mbire and Atingi (1994), and Osei (1995).

The importance of country studies is that they highlight the differences in the causes of debt and debt management strategies among countries. Subregional studies do not take into account the differences in the structure of the economies of individual countries.[2] Debt relief or debt reduction programs, for example, are often linked to economic stabilization and structural adjustment programs. Since differences in economic structures across countries often lead to different policy responses, this would imply different debt strategies. Furthermore, differences in the degree of indebtedness imply differences in ability to service debt and in creditworthiness, which in turn determine debt management strategies and access to new money.

Differences in the sources of debt also imply different debt strategies among countries. For example, countries whose stocks of debt are mainly official would qualify for Toronto- or Naples-type debt relief, whereas those whose debts are predominantly commercial would go for market-based debt reduction strategies such as the Brady, IMF, and World Bank plans.

This chapter analyzes the extent of Kenya's debt problem, including the size, structure, and source of the stock of the debt. It also examines the causes of the problem and the strategies available to the authorities to manage the problem. Finally, the sustainability of Kenya's debt is assessed using a deterministic intertemporal model developed by Cohen (1985, 1988).

Debt and the Macroeconomy

This section reviews Kenya's macroeconomic performance since independence with the aim of highlighting the major events that have contributed to the external debt problem. Kenya's macroeconomic performance has been examined by Bevan and others (1987), Bevan, Collier, and Gunning (1990), Bevan and Karlstrom (1988), Killick (1984), Killick and Mwega (1990), Ng'eno (1991), Swamy (1994), and Mwega (1995).

---

[2]These points are emphasized by Cohen (1988), van Wijnbergen (1989), and Greene and Khan (1990).

The first decade (1964–73) of Kenya's independence was one of rapid economic growth and macroeconomic stability. The economy grew at an annual average rate of 6.5 percent between 1964 and 1971 (Republic of Kenya, 1989, Table 1.1) and by 5.8 percent in 1972, but growth declined to 5.2 percent in 1973 (Table 1). At the sectoral level, manufacturing, agriculture, and government services grew at 8.2 percent, 4.2 percent, and 9.8 percent, respectively, during 1964–71. The economy also maintained a manageable external balance during the first decade. Although the balance of trade was always in deficit, the current account deficit remained small, and the overall balance and the basic balance were for most years in surplus. Capital inflows were always sufficient to offset the current account deficits.

Excessively expansionary policies in 1970 and 1971 (Bevan, Collier, and Gunning, 1990) led to a balance of payments crisis in 1971. But the crisis was swiftly brought under control through credit, price, and exchange controls and by quantitative restrictions on imports. Although these policies were considered short-term measures at the time, they were used together or selectively to deal with macroeconomic imbalances for a long time thereafter.

The achievements made in dealing with the 1971 crisis were immediately reversed by the effects of the oil crisis of 1973–74, which led to a worldwide recession that contributed to Kenya's poor economic performance and worsened the terms of trade. The terms of trade declined by 24 percent during 1972–75, and the annual growth rate of real GDP declined from 5.8 percent in 1972 to 3.1 percent in 1974 and 1975. The decline in GDP growth was also due to the drought of 1974, which caused a 0.1 percent decline in the real growth of the agricultural sector.

The problems associated with the oil crisis were characteristically dealt with using import compression and credit, price, and exchange controls. But one of the policies used to deal with the problem this time was increased external borrowing, especially from the IMF, the World Bank, and commercial sources. Kenya was the first country to use the IMF Oil Facility in 1975.

The commodity boom of 1976–77 played a major role in halting the balance of payments problems and the economic decline occasioned by the oil crisis. Real GDP grew at an annual average rate of 8 percent in 1977–78. The boom also effectively led to a reduction in the level of protection. The volume of imports increased by 42 percent between 1976 and 1978, but because of strong export performance import liberalization had little impact on the balance of payments. Despite the apparent import liberalization, however, there was no radical change in the trade regime, as the control regime introduced in 1971 remained intact even though trade liberalization was a stated government policy.

The government's commitment to trade liberalization was stated in the 1974–78 Development Plan.

The government's failure to adjust to the oil shock led to increased private and public consumption, which contributed to a trade deficit of K Sh 355.5 million in 1978, the highest since independence at the time, and a decline in the terms of trade. These events once more triggered the use of credit and import controls, including an import deposit scheme introduced in December 1978. The government also ran down its foreign exchange reserves and borrowed to finance the deficits. Since most of the loans were obtained under harder terms, the cost of servicing the debt began to rise significantly. The debt-service ratio, which stood at about 14 percent in 1975, had almost doubled by 1982.

The overall state of the economy continued to worsen as real GDP growth declined from 8 percent in 1978 to 4 percent in 1980. As the structural weaknesses of the economy became evident, the government began stabilization and structural adjustment programs in 1980.[3] The performance of the economy remained poor (Table 1), however, as a result of poor export performance and deteriorating terms of trade, macroeconomic imbalances arising from public sector deficits, and structural rigidities in the economy. The inability of the government to carry through some of the adjustments agreed with the donors compounded the problems. The balance of payments and budget deficits, which began to run out of control in the late 1970s and continued into the 1980s, also began to be financed by increased external debt.

The second half of the 1980s started on a better note. Growth of real GDP averaged over 5 percent for the period. This favorable growth was stimulated by the coffee boom of 1986 and by lower oil prices. Despite reasonable economic growth, the period was characterized by serious balance of payments problems. The volume of exports stagnated after 1985, but the volume and prices of imports rose, causing serious deterioration in the terms of trade, which necessitated large capital inflows.

In 1986 new measures were introduced to deal with the structural weaknesses of the economy. These policies, initially outlined in Sessional Paper No. 1 of 1986 and subsequently in the 1989–93 Development Plan, emphasized sectoral reforms, of which the major programs were financed through World Bank loans. Twenty-two such projects were financed by the World Bank between 1989 and 1996. Balance of payments support was also obtained during the period under various

[3]No effort will be made here to examine specifics of the structural adjustment programs, stand-by arrangements, or any other agreement between the Kenyan government and donors or creditors on such issues as conditionalities or their success or failure. Some of these issues have been examined in Hecox (1988), Mosley (1986), Godfrey (1987), Bevan, Collier, and Gunning (1990), Swamy (1994), and Mwega (1995).

Table 1. Kenya: Selected Macroeconomic Indicators, 1970–95

	1970	1971	1972	1973	1974	1975	1976	1977	1978	1979	1980	1981	1982
							(In percent)						
Change in real GDP	5.9	4.2	5.8	5.2	3.1	3.1	4.2	8.2	7.9	5.9	3.8	6.0	4.8
Of which:													
Agriculture	3.4	1.2	7.2	2.1	–0.1	4.6	3.7	9.5	8.9	–0.3	0.9	6.1	11.2
Manufacturing	10.4	5.2	12.9	11.6	5.9	4.0	14.0	16.0	12.5	7.6	5.2	3.6	2.2
Government services	7.9	10.8	9.6	6.0	6.8	8.5	5.1	5.1	6.4	7.1	5.6	5.3	3.8
							(In millions of Kenya shillings)						
Balance of payments													
Balance of trade	–50.5	–91.4	–70.6	–51.2	–159.9	–82.2	–77.3	–61.3	–355.5	–299.4	–526.6	340.5	–290.9
Current account	17.5	–39.9	–38.4	–57.6	–126.1	–107.0	–64.3	–14.7	–284.2	–0.3	–373.3	–253.3	–159.7
Basic balance	13.4	23.2	44.7	58.9	82.9	80.5	38.8	96.3	–87.3	3.2	–125.6	–142.2	–124.0
Overall balance	15.2	–18.1	8.5	7.5	–31.5	–17.6	35.6	112.7	–77.6	70.6	–72.2	–90.2	–108.1
							(1990 = 100)						
External trade													
Export prices	43.0	42.0	43.0	51.0	66.0	74.0	87.0	125.0	113.0	125.0	152.0	136.0	124.0
Export volumes	75.0	57.0	86.0	100.0	95.0	87.0	92.0	96.0	88.0	87.0	89.0	84.0	82.0
Import prices	17.0	18.0	20.0	25.0	36.0	44.0	45.0	49.0	56.0	67.0	88.0	93.0	88.0
Import volumes	119.0	140.0	121.0	117.0	133.0	99.0	95.0	116.0	135.0	111.0	127.0	99.0	84.0
Terms of trade	84.0	86.0	112.0	109.0	96.0	90.0	112.0	117.0	108.0	106.0	109.0	103.0	100.0
Other indicators													
Consumer price index (1986 = 100)	17.1	18.0	18.6	20.3	23.8	28.3	31.3	39.8	41.3	44.5	50.4	56.5	68.7
Real exchange rate	69.7	74.1	75.2	75.5	100.5	94.6	95.8	92.5	87.1	99.3	114.8	121.3	109.4
Foreign exchange reserves	202.0	145.0	170.0	198.0	191.0	169.0	272.0	505.0	338.0	520.0	466.0	220.0	195.0
Budget deficit (in percent of GDP at current prices)	3.7	4.5	6.2	3.6	4.6	7.0	4.5	2.5	6.5	5.3	7.1	9.0	7.1

	1983	1984	1985	1986	1987	1988	1989	1990	1991	1992	1993	1994	1995
							(In percent)						
Change in real GDP	2.3	0.8	5.1	5.6	4.9	5.2	5	4.5	2.1	0.5	0.2	3	4.9
Of which:													
Agriculture	1.6	–3.9	3.7	4.9	3.8	4.4	3.9	3.4	–1.1	–3.7	–4.1	2.8	4.8
Manufacturing	4.5	4.3	4.5	5.8	5.7	6	5.9	5.2	3.8	1.2	1.8	1.9	3.9
Government services	4.2	2.9	5.1	6.3	4.8	5.8	5.5	4.6	3.6	2.4	2.1	1.1	1.8
							(In millions of Kenya shillings)						
Balance of payments													
Balance of trade	–180.6	–226.1	–270.7	–230.7	–587.4	–696.4	–1,067	–1,139.9	–885.5	–951.2	–890.8	–785.3	–1,964.8
Current account	–25.5	–86.3	–79.4	–31.1	–406.6	–403	–604.2	–595.9	–295.4	–157.3	287.8	291.1	–1,019.9
Basic balance	64.4	9.6	–121.6	54.2	–145.7	–124.5	23	–340.2	–107.3	–418.4	418.4	–432.6	–1,202.2
Overall balance	57.4	32.3	–94.2	73	–104.4	–67.7	80	–168.9	–143.3	–433	1,284.1	264.8	–368.9
							(1990 = 100)						
External trade													
Export prices	122	135	117	127	104	111	103	100	106	103	102	109	
Export volumes	79	78	81	93	90	95	94	100	103	103	121	137	
Import prices	93	88	91	87	87	89	93	100	93	92	82	76	
Import volumes	66	78	72	85	89	100	105	100	93	90	95	121	
Terms of trade	94	110	92	103	85	88	79	71	82	79	90	101	96
Other indicators													
Consumer price index (1986 = 100)	77.1	84.8	95.5	100	108.6	122.1	138.5	160.2	191.7	244	356.3	458.9	466.1
Real exchange rate	104.1	100.3	102.5	99.2	100.3	97.4	104.4	114.3	111.7	110.4	116.7	42.8	41.8
Foreign exchange reserves	349	377	376	386	222	247	257	184	98	35	388	539	335
Budget deficit (in percent of GDP at current prices)	4.5	5.8	4.5	8.6	4.7	4.5	4.7	4.5	1.9	3.6	5.6	3.6	0.9

Sources: Republic of Kenya, *Economic Surveys*, various issues, and *Statistical Abstracts*, various issues; and International Monetary Fund, *International Financial Statistics*, various issues.

IMF Enhanced Structural Adjustment Facility arrangements started in February 1988.

The policies introduced after 1986 were much deeper and wider ranging than those introduced earlier and were more successfully implemented. Prices were decontrolled in 1988, and interest rates were deregulated in 1991. Trade liberalization moved progressively from 1986, and by the end of 1991 all import and export controls had been abolished except for a small negative list. Tariff reform was also on track, with average import-weighted tariffs declining from 30 percent in 1984/85 to 20 percent in 1991/92 (Swamy, 1994). The effect of the trade reforms was to raise the trade balance to the highest levels from 1987 onward, but healthy capital flows negated any serious balance of payments problems. The shilling was relatively stable between 1985 and 1989 but appreciated slightly in 1990 and 1993. The liberalization of foreign exchange, which began toward the end of 1991, reached a climax in 1993 when exchange controls were removed; the shilling was effectively convertible by June 1994, when Kenya accepted the obligations of Article VIII of the IMF.

It has to be said, however, that despite the apparent success in policy reform, the first half of the 1990s was characterized by the worst economic performance since independence (Table 1). This state of affairs was a result of the lack of credibility of reforms due to inconsistency in implementation, financial mismanagement, the political turmoil leading to multiparty elections in December 1992, and the aid embargo by donors in November 1991. All these contributed to high inflation, low foreign capital inflows, unstable exchange rates, and high balance of payments deficits, which combined to depress the economy.

The Debt Situation

Kenya falls in the category of severely indebted low-income countries. With a ratio of the net present value of debt to exports in excess of 200 percent and a debt-service ratio higher than 25 percent, Kenya was considered to have not only a high liquidity problem but also a large debt overhang in 1991–93 (see World Bank, 1994, p. 40). It will be shown that this does not seem to have worried Kenyan policymakers.

Table 2 shows that turning points in Kenya's external indebtedness occurred in 1974, 1979, 1985, and 1993.[4] Kenya's external debt problem

[4]There are two sources of debt data: the *World Debt Tables* of the World Bank and CS-DRMS of the Debt Management Division of the Kenyan Ministry of Finance. The data from the two sources are more or less comparable. However, since CS-DRMS has five shorter series, World Bank data were used in this study. The data were obtained on diskette and used with the aid of the STARS system prepared by the International Economics Division of the World Bank.

is largely a problem of the 1980s, however. The total debt rose from less than \$0.5 billion in 1971 to \$1.3 billion in 1975 and then to \$3.4 billion in 1980. It stabilized between \$3.2 billion and \$3.6 billion during 1980–84 but rose again after 1985, reaching a high of \$5.8 billion in 1987. The debt stabilized again at \$5.8 billion to \$5.9 billion in 1988 and 1989, despite debt write-offs amounting to about \$627 million between 1987 and 1990 (Republic of Kenya, 1990). The total debt rose to \$7.5 billion in 1991 but declined to \$6.9 billion in 1992 as a result of the aid embargo by donors. The end of the embargo in December 1993 led to a rise in debt from \$7.1 billion in 1993 to \$7.3 billion in 1995.

A look at public and publicly guaranteed debt and private nonguaranteed debt, the two components of long-term outstanding debt, indicates that public and publicly guaranteed debt has been a major component, but private nonguaranteed debt was high during periods of crisis. This was true in 1975/76, 1979/80, and 1990/91, implying that as official credit declined, commercial sources became important (Table 2). Short-term debt has been relatively stable since 1978 but peaked in 1980, 1990, and 1993, implying greater reliance on this source during periods of crisis. The use of IMF credit has been stable since 1979/80. Private nonguaranteed debt not only has been low but has been rising relatively slowly over the years as well.

Total public and publicly guaranteed debt has been predominantly official (multilateral and bilateral) and concessional (Table 3). Official debt in 1995 made up 81 percent of total outstanding debt, and 76 percent of this debt was on concessional terms. A decomposition of official debt shows that multilateral debt constituted a major proportion of total outstanding debt. In 1995 this was 46 percent of the total, whereas bilateral debt was 37 percent. The major proportion of the multilateral loans are World Bank (IBRD and IDA) credits, which made up 57 percent and 28 percent of multilateral loans in 1997, respectively, but by 1995 the positions had reversed, with IDA contributing 68 percent of total multilateral loans while IBRD contributed 21 percent. It is also evident that bilateral credits began to rise after 1990 and were almost converging with multilateral credits by 1995.

The evolution of Kenya's debt problem can be illustrated further by changes in the volume and pattern of loan disbursements (Table 4). Although the pattern of total disbursements has not been consistent, it is clear that multilateral disbursements rose from 1986 on and peaked in 1989, when they represented 44 percent of total disbursements. Multilateral disbursements declined beginning in 1990 and only recovered in 1993. Disbursements of bilateral loans followed a similar pattern.

Table 2. Kenya: External Debt, 1970–95

(In millions of U.S. dollars)

	Total Debt	Long-Term Debt Outstanding and Disbursed	Publicly Guaranteed Debt	Private Nonguaranteed Debt	Short-Term Debt	Use of IMF Credit
1970	. . .	409	321	86	. . .	0
1971	498	426	345	81	72	0
1972	581	497	391	107	84	0
1973	845	723	517	206	122	0
1974	1,153	947	596	352	166	39
1975	1,290	1,023	631	392	187	80
1976	1,493	1,179	764	415	216	99
1977	1,658	1,291	1,021	271	303	64
1978	2,177	1,680	1,247	433	403	94
1979	2,727	2,110	1,673	438	429	188
1980	3,394	2,499	2,062	437	640	254
1981	3,234	2,505	2,139	366	470	259
1982	3,375	2,642	2,257	385	340	394
1983	3,638	2,765	2,268	497	408	464
1984	3,521	2,725	2,297	428	376	420
1985	4,201	3,209	2,690	519	470	522
1986	4,724	3,893	3,431	462	372	460
1987	5,755	4,762	4,169	593	592	401
1988	5,781	4,792	4,144	648	534	455
1989	5,862	4,836	4,166	670	610	415
1990	7,056	5,640	4,760	880	934	482
1991	7,455	6,254	5,267	987	708	493
1992	6,907	5,736	5,157	579	777	393
1993	7,118	5,852	5,252	600	903	363
1994	7,160	6,077	5,547	530	688	405
1995	7,312	6,372	5,927	445	630	310

Source: World Bank Debtor Reporting System.

Table 3. Kenya: Sources of Public and Publicly Guaranteed Debt, 1970–95

(In millions of U.S. dollars)

	Total	Official	Multilateral	Bilateral	Private	Multilateral Concessional	Bilateral Concessional
1970	321	237	38	199	84	35	138
1971	345	254	49	206	90	39	145
1972	391	294	79	215	97	49	156
1973	517	395	117	278	121	70	201
1974	596	472	142	330	124	82	245
1975	631	527	193	335	103	88	248
1976	764	628	274	354	135	105	276
1977	1,021	751	340	411	270	129	295
1978	1,247	826	419	407	420	163	280
1979	1,673	1,024	496	528	649	201	369
1980	2,062	1,203	630	572	860	293	414
1981	2,139	1,328	695	632	811	317	469
1982	2,257	1,565	867	698	692	412	539
1983	2,268	1,670	971	699	598	434	557
1984	2,297	1,858	1,078	780	438	472	645
1985	2,690	2,267	1,322	945	423	538	775
1986	3,431	2,804	1,594	1,209	627	612	985
1987	4,169	3,442	1,941	1,502	727	736	1,187
1988	4,144	3,448	1,912	1,536	696	860	1,228
1989	4,166	3,319	2,152	1,167	847	1,129	919
1990	4,760	3,737	2,487	1,250	1,023	1,479	1,014
1991	5,267	4,001	2,609	1,392	1,266	1,684	1,143
1992	5,157	3,982	2,507	1,475	1,176	1,721	1,178
1993	5,252	4,166	2,608	1,557	1,087	1,923	1,259
1994	5,547	4,801	2,755	2,046	746	2,129	343
1995	5,929	5,207	2,913	2,294	719	2,342	1,630

Source: World Bank Debtor Reporting System.

Table 4. Kenya: Debt Disbursements, 1970–95

(In millions of U.S. dollars)

	Total	Multilateral	Bilateral	Private Creditors	Total Private Nonguaranteed	Multilateral Concessional	Bilateral Concessional
1970	78	10	26	1	41	7	20
1971	66	11	32	12	11	4	29
1972	115	28	28	17	42	7	24
1973	222	34	54	14	121	16	42
1974	272	25	53	7	187	13	43
1975	210	53	47	10	111	7	35
1976	308	85	64	58	101	18	46
1977	317	68	72	128	50	25	36
1978	562	80	89	176	217	34	56
1979	549	82	131	245	91	38	95
1980	626	158	79	302	87	97	66
1981	407	98	139	154	16	33	102
1982	477	199	121	54	92	102	101
1983	535	147	96	103	189	37	84
1984	473	185	189	68	31	43	164
1985	457	134	90	64	169	47	56
1986	624	120	178	276	50	53	121
1987	650	159	194	207	90	83	96
1988	722	202	186	138	196	158	146
1989	840	366	173	282	20	283	108
1990	666	295	175	181	55	284	134
1991	902	228	234	380	60	207	190
1992	502	130	197	115	60	119	122
1993	404	238	80	22	65	236	65
1994	225	160	59	6	0	148	37
1995	695	221	345	130	0	194	345

Source: World Debtor Reporting System.

Table 5. Kenya: Debt Commitments, 1970–95
(In millions of U.S. dollars)

	Total	Official Creditors	Private Creditors
1970	49.9	48.5	1.1
1971	76.0	63.6	12.4
1972	135.3	107.4	27.9
1973	105.8	101.5	4.3
1974	157.7	151.3	6.4
1975	434.5	323.6	110.9
1976	264.1	87.7	176.4
1977	476.6	295.5	181.1
1978	551.1	401.5	149.6
1979	685.9	323.8	362.1
1980	518.0	514.0	4.0
1981	404.8	268.4	136.4
1982	638.8	504.8	134.0
1983	318.7	303.3	15.4
1984	584.0	423.8	160.2
1985	442.0	231.6	210.4
1986	427.6	232.6	195.0
1987	514.0	299.0	216.0
1988	640.0	421.0	219.0
1989	1,123.0	861.0	262.0
1990	825.0	606.0	219.0
1991	868.0	534.0	334.0
1992	227.0	197.0	30.0
1993	212.0	212.0	0.0
1994	98.0	98.0	0.0
1995	382.0	215.0	167.0

Source: World Bank Debtor Reporting System.

Disbursements from private creditors comprised a small proportion of guaranteed disbursements. Although these disbursements stood at $380 million in 1991, they declined consistently thereafter, reaching $6 million in 1994, their second-lowest ever, but then rose to $130 million in 1995. Similarly, except for a few years, private nonguaranteed debt represented a small percentage of gross disbursements. This emphasizes the point that Kenya's debt is predominantly official. The sharp decline in disbursements in 1992–94 confirms the downward trend in external debt flows. This is supported by the decline in commitments (Table 5) from $1.1 billion in 1989 to $98 million in 1994. There were no commitments by private creditors in 1993 and 1994, but a commitment of $167 million was made in 1995.

Total debt-service payments (Table 6) increased from $46 million in 1970 to $359 million in 1980 and then rose steadily, reaching $560 mil-

Table 6. Kenya: Debt-Service Payments, 1970–95
(In millions of U.S. dollars)

	Total	Multilateral	Bilateral	Private Creditors	Total Private Nonguaranteed	Multilateral Concessional	Bilateral Concessional
1970	46	2	13	16	16	1	7
1971	53	1	13	16	22	1	7
1972	48	2	15	10	22	1	8
1973	65	4	19	11	32	1	11
1974	98	6	20	12	60	2	11
1975	136	8	21	14	93	2	12
1976	157	16	21	18	102	2	12
1977	282	20	25	19	219	2	14
1978	212	29	27	76	81	3	11
1979	260	38	32	67	122	4	11
1980	359	49	35	148	127	5	13
1981	395	52	36	183	124	6	14
1982	413	56	38	214	105	6	17
1983	404	69	48	175	113	10	23
1984	441	88	53	165	134	11	26
1985	468	106	61	177	124	13	31
1986	493	140	66	153	134	15	35
1987	504	179	81	158	86	17	34
1988	560	203	94	153	110	21	46
1989	491	189	88	147	67	21	42
1990	576	226	86	189	75	30	39
1991	602	220	123	174	85	33	75
1992	524	219	66	123	116	38	41
1993	508	224	79	101	104	45	50
1994	820	230	180	294	116	52	81
1995	688	227	204	258	0	53	88

Source: World Bank Debtor Reporting System.

lion in 1988. After a decline in 1989, payments rose to $602 million in 1991, then declined in 1992 and 1993 before rising to a peak of $820 million in 1994. It is evident, however, that total debt-service payments for private and private nonguaranteed credit were comparable to debt service for official credit, despite the official debt being larger than private and private nonguaranteed debt. For example, private and private nonguaranteed debt constituted only 18 percent of long-term debt outstanding, which indicates that private credit and private nonguaranteed debt were contracted at high interest rates.

This pattern of debt service is evident from data on principal (Table 7) and interest (Table 8) repayments. The negative net transfers on debt from private creditors and on private nonguaranteed debt (Table 9) after 1981 (except for a few years) confirm that debt repayments for nonconcessional debt have been high. The negative transfers on multilateral debt are indicative of the large share of this debt in total debt. Moreover, since this debt does not provide scope for relief, its contribution to Kenya's future debt burden will be high.

Indicators of the debt burden (Table 10) show that the problem began to increase faster after 1980. Most of the indicators peaked in 1987, with a debt-service ratio of 40 percent, a debt-GNP ratio of 75 percent, an interest-export ratio of 17 percent, and a debt-export ratio of 339 percent. The indicators declined between 1988 and 1993, except for the debt-GNP ratio and the debt-export ratio, which had uneven trends. All the indicators were above the World Bank definitions of severe indebtedness (debt-export ratio of over 300 percent, debt-GNP ratio of 80 percent, and debt-service ratio of 25 percent) since 1990, implying that the government has made little headway in solving the debt crisis.

The terms of new debt commitments are good indicators of the future debt burden. The average terms for official debt became more favorable (Table 11) in the 1990s. Interest rates came down, while the maturity and grace periods rose and the grant element of the debt increased. These trends are comparable to those of the 1970s. The conditions for private debt, on the other hand, became harder from 1990 on. The increase in the share of public and publicly guaranteed debt from this source suggests a higher future debt burden.

Despite the high indebtedness, Kenya had not rescheduled its debts by the end of 1995, except for the $517 million in arrears restructured in January 1994. The reason behind the avoidance of restructuring debt has been to maintain the country's credit rating in the financial markets. The government has instead committed itself to a policy of debt reduction through the acquisition of concessional loans, debt write-offs, encouragement of foreign direct investment, and export promotion.

Table 7. Kenya: Repayments of Principal, 1970–95

(In millions of U.S. dollars)

	Total	Multilateral	Bilateral	Private Creditors	Total Private Nonguaranteed	Multilateral Concessional	Bilateral Concessional
1970	29	1	5	12	12	0.2	3
1971	35	0.2	5	12	18	0.2	3
1972	28	0.3	6	5	16	0.3	4
1973	36	0.3	9	5	21	0.3	6
1974	57	1	10	6	41	1	6
1975	90	1	11	8	70	1	7
1976	107	1	11	14	79	1	7
1977	223	1	13	12	194	1	8
1978	131	1	13	58	54	1	5
1979	151	1	16	41	87	1	5
1980	195	2	17	77	88	2	5
1981	235	16	19	11	87	2	7
1982	242	20	18	130	73	2	7
1983	253	26	26	124	77	5	11
1984	283	32	29	123	99	5	13
1985	304	45	35	139	86	7	17
1986	305	56	38	109	102	8	20
1987	278	82	43	101	53	9	16
1988	322	9	51	108	65	11	22
1989	293	99	55	105	34	12	27
1990	348	126	53	132	37	17	25
1991	356	127	62	127	40	16	32
1992	324	133	40	91	60	19	24
1993	301	140	38	73	50	28	24
1994	532	150	100	211	70	29	50
1995	469	150	116	204	0	32	46

Source: World Bank Debtor Reporting System.

Table 8. Kenya: Interest Payments, 1970–95
(In millions of U.S. dollars)

	Total	Multilateral	Bilateral	Private Creditors	Total Private Nonguaranteed	Multilateral Concessional	Bilateral Concessional
1970	17	1	8	5	4	0.3	4
1971	18	1	8	4	5	0.3	4
1972	21	2	9	5	6	0.4	4
1973	29	3	10	6	11	1	5
1974	41	5	10	6	19	1	5
1975	46	7	10	6	23	1	5
1976	51	13	10	4	24	1	5
1977	60	17	12	7	24	1	6
1978	92	24	14	18	27	2	6
1979	109	30	16	27	36	2	7
1980	163	36	18	70	39	3	7
1981	160	37	17	70	36	4	8
1982	171	36	20	84	32	4	10
1983	152	44	21	51	36	5	11
1984	158	57	24	42	35	6	13
1985	164	62	26	39	38	7	14
1986	188	85	28	44	31	7	15
1987	226	97	38	57	34	8	18
1988	238	105	43	45	45	10	24
1989	198	91	33	42	33	9	15
1990	228	100	34	57	38	13	14
1991	246	93	61	47	45	17	43
1992	200	85	26	32	56	19	17
1993	207	84	42	27	54	18	26
1994	289	80	80	82	46	22	31
1995	220	77	88	54	0	22	42

Source: Word Bank Debtor Reporting System.

Table 9. Kenya: Debt Net Transfers, 1970–95
(In millions of U.S. dollars)

	Total	Multilateral	Bilateral	Private Creditors	Total Private Nonguaranteed	Multilateral Concessional	Bilateral Concessional
1970	32	8	13	–15	25	7	13
1971	13	10	18	–4	–11	3	22
1972	66	26	13	8	20	6	15
1973	156	30	35	3	89	15	31
1974	174	20	33	–5	126	11	32
1975	73	44	26	–14	18	6	23
1976	150	69	43	40	–1	16	34
1977	35	48	47	109	–169	22	22
1978	349	51	62	100	136	31	46
1979	289	44	99	178	–31	34	84
1980	267	109	44	154	–41	92	53
1981	12	46	103	–30	–108	27	87
1982	64	143	83	–150	–13	96	84
1983	131	78	49	–72	97	28	61
1984	33	97	136	–97	–104	33	138
1985	–11	28	30	–113	45	33	26
1986	131	–19	112	123	–84	37	86
1987	146	–20	113	49	4	65	62
1988	162	–1	92	–15	86	137	100
1989	349	176	85	135	–47	262	67
1990	89	68	49	–8	–20	254	95
1991	299	8	110	206	–25	174	115
1992	–21	–88	131	–8	–56	81	82
1993	–102	14	0	–79	–39	190	15
1994	–501	–71	–121	–288	–110	96	–44
1995	7	–7	141	–128	0	141	257

Source: World Bank Debtor Reporting System.

Table 10. Kenya: Debt Indicators, 1971–95
(In percent)

	Debt-GNP Ratio	Debt-Service Ratio	Debt-Export Ratio	Interest-Export Ratio
1971	29	10	94	3
1972	28	8	100	4
1973	35	9	120	4
1974	40	10	119	4
1975	41	15	128	5
1976	45	15	131	4
1977	39	21	104	4
1978	43	14	141	5
1979	45	18	167	7
1980	48	20	154	10
1981	49	25	167	13
1982	55	28	190	13
1983	63	32	229	14
1984	59	34	209	14
1985	71	39	265	15
1986	68	36	249	14
1987	75	40	339	17
1988	71	39	306	17
1989	73	37	303	15
1990	87	36	316	15
1991	98	33	338	14
1992	91	31	321	12
1993	140	27	306	11
1994	110	32	268	12
1995	98	26	248	9

Source: World Bank Debtor Reporting System.

Efficient management of the existing stock of debt was also to be enhanced through the use of market-based instruments such as debt-equity swaps, debt buybacks, and discounting in the secondary markets. These policies have not been pursued aggressively, however.

The Causes of Debt

The literature is replete with explanations of the causes of external debt problems, which can be divided into internal and external factors. Mistry (1991), Humphreys and Underwood (1989), and Cline (1995) provide detailed accounts of the factors behind the sub-Saharan African debt crisis. Greene and Khan (1990) and Ajayi (1996) also discuss the major causes of the crisis in the region. The major external factors have been deteriorating terms of trade and rising world interest

Table 11. Kenya: Average Terms of New Commitments by Official Creditors, 1970–95

	Interest (In percent a year)	Maturity (In years)	Grace Period (In years)	Grant Element (In percent)	Private interest (In percent)	Creditors' Maturity (In years)	Grace Period (In years)	Grant Element (In years)
1970	2	38	8	64	7	11	2	12
1971	5	27	6	37	7	6	2	8
1972	3	36	8	55	7	8	3	13
1973	4	29	8	46	11	9	4	–10
1974	3	34	9	62	6	9	2	15
1975	7	28	7	27	8	13	6	11
1976	5	26	7	42	8	10	3	8
1977	5	27	7	41	8	11	2	10
1978	4	29	7	44	8	14	5	11
1979	4	33	8	50	11	8	1	–3
1980	4	32	8	54	8	6	0	5
1981	5	27	7	35	16	8	3	–25
1982	5	31	8	42	8	12	4	11
1983	6	31	8	36	9	14	4	5
1984	6	26	7	33	9	10	2	4
1985	6	20	5	27	9	13	2	2
1986	4	28	7	48	7	9	3	15
1987	3	35	8	60	8	8	3	8
1988	2	28	9	63	8	12	2	9
1989	2	33	9	65	7	9	3	10
1990	3	30	8	58	7	13	5	14
1991	2	35	9	67	8	12	2	8
1992	1	39	9	80	2	3	2	15
1993	2	32	9	64	0	0	0	0
1994	2	30	7	62	0	0	0	0
1995	2	35	10	67	8	6.3	1	0

Source: World Bank Debtor Reporting System.

rates. Other factors include increased protectionism in world markets, irresponsible lending by private and official creditors, poor advice by international financial institutions and official creditors, and reschedulings on punitive terms (Mistry, 1991). Cline (1983) emphasizes the role of external factors in the debts of the least developed countries. On the other hand, domestic factors are seen to arise mainly from economic mismanagement as manifested in unsustainable fiscal deficits, poor economic performance, and the maintenance of unrealistic exchange rates. Ajayi (1991) found that internal factors played a major role in the development of Nigeria's debt problem. Humphreys and Underwood (1989) list high population growth rates and poverty, commodity concentration, low saving and investment rates, low productivity of investments, and low export performance as the major factors behind the high indebtedness of sub-Saharan Africa.

The review of Kenya's macroeconomic conditions indicates that a deterioration in the terms of trade has been a major problem and could therefore be a major cause of the country's high indebtedness. Whereas interest rates could be hypothesized to have had less of an impact, because of Kenya's low commercial debt, the high interest payments on multilateral debt suggest that a large proportion of these debts were contracted at or close to market rates. Since this debt cannot be rescheduled, it is likely to have a significant impact on indebtedness.

The main internal factors that could be associated with high indebtedness are public sector deficits and exchange rate movements. Public sector deficits have been a major problem since the 1980s. The large fiscal and current account deficits were clearly behind increases in foreign borrowing in 1978–79 and in the second half of the 1980s.

Exchange rate movements can raise external indebtedness in several ways. First, an overvalued currency, by reducing the price of imports, can worsen the balance of payments, thus requiring higher capital inflows to finance imports. An overvalued currency can also raise expectations for devaluation, leading to capital flight. This was the major cause of increased indebtedness, especially in Latin America (Edwards and Larrain, 1989). Currency depreciation can also directly raise the stock of external debt. However, where depreciation leads to increased export earnings, it reduces the debt-export ratio and therefore improves creditworthiness.

This chapter models Kenya's long-term outstanding debt as a function of the terms of trade, the real effective exchange rate, real foreign interest rates, and budget deficits. The volume of exports is added as a proxy for export performance. The model equation to be estimated takes the following general form:

$$LDOD = f(BD, RER, INTR, TOT, EV), \qquad (1)$$

where

LDOD = long-term outstanding debt

BD = overall budget deficit

RER = real effective exchange rate

INTR = real foreign interest rate

TOT = terms of trade

EV = export volume.

It is hypothesized that higher budget deficits raise the stock of debt through increased foreign credit required to finance the deficits; hence its coefficient will be positive. If depreciation of the currency disproportionately increases the domestic currency value of exports, it reduces the debt, but it would lead to higher debt if the increase in exports is more than offset by the positive effect on the stock of debt. The coefficient of *RER*, therefore, cannot be established a priori. Higher world interest rates and a deterioration in the terms of trade would raise the stock of debt. Good export performance is expected to reduce external indebtedness.

Annual data from 1970 to 1995 are used. The real effective exchange rate is derived as the nominal exchange rate indexed by a ratio of the foreign price of tradable goods and the domestic price of nontradables. The foreign price of tradable goods is proxied by the wholesale price index of Kenya's major trading partners, while the domestic price of nontradables is proxied by the domestic consumer price index. The real world interest rate is determined as the six-month dollar London interbank offered rate (LIBOR) plus a 2 percent markup, deflated by the export price index for developing countries.

The properties of the data were first analyzed by performing unit root tests using weighted symmetric, Dickey-Fuller, and Phillips-Perron tests. The results (Table 12) indicate that all the variables have unit roots. Thus, the hypothesis of stationarity is rejected, implying that the variables can be stationary after first difference.

Co-integration was tested using the two-stage Engle-Granger procedure, and the result indicates that the stationarity hypothesis could not be rejected when the error correction term was added to the regression. Co-integration was therefore established. The equation was then estimated in first difference with the error correction term.

It should be noted first that the high frequency of the data could not allow for higher-order dynamic specification to avoid the loss of degrees of freedom. A dummy (*D78*) was introduced to account for the

Table 12. Unit Root Tests

Test	*LDOD*	*TOT*	*EV*	*BD*	*RER*	*INTR*
Weighted symmetric	–1.591	–2.016	–1.251	–1.463	–1.636	–1.136
	(0.862)	(0.677)	(0.945)	(0.901)	(0.845)	(0.961)
Dickey-Fuller	–1.326	–2.131	0.370	–1.401	–2.065	–2.399
	(0.881)	(0.529)	(0.997)	(0.861)	(0.565)	(0.380)
Phillips-Perron	–4.58	–8.928	–3.613	–16.769	–1.601	–8.882
	(0.850)	(0.512)	(0.908)	(0.133)	(0.979)	(0.516)

Source: Author's calculations.
Note: Figures in parentheses are the probability values for the null hypothesis.

1978 shock that led to high balance of payments deficits and a deterioration in the terms of trade, which triggered one of the largest increases in long-term debt. Another dummy (*D90*) was introduced to explain the unusually large increase in capital flows in 1990.

The estimated results (Table 13) indicate that the coefficients of all the independent variables, except the export volume variable, have the expected signs and are significant. The coefficient for export volume has the wrong sign and is significant. All the coefficients, however, are below unity. The positive coefficient of *RER* indicates that the effect of currency depreciation on the stock of external debt outweighs the positive effect on export performance. As is to be expected for annual data, the coefficient for the error correction term is low, implying slow adjustment.

To summarize, the model results indicate that the change in external debt is determined by the real effective exchange rate, the terms of trade, the budget deficit, and foreign interest rates. The impact, however, is moderated by low elasticities. The results indicate that the government can reduce indebtedness by maintaining realistic exchange rates and reducing the budget deficit. Despite the exogeneity of foreign interest rates, the government can minimize the impact of this variable on external debt by limiting access to external capital through commercial markets.

Debt Management

An effective debt management strategy should strive to reduce the current debt burden and hence the growth of future debt. Such a strategy would aim to reduce net transfers and, in the process, improve the country's creditworthiness. The strategy should also aim to increase

Table 13. Solved Static Long-Run Equation for Long-Term External Debt

Variable	Coefficient	Standard Error
Constant	0.103	0.101
RER	0.254	0.083
TOT	–0.235	0.147
EV	0.623	0.207
BD	0.144	0.035
INTR	0.113	0.065
D78	0.142	0.052
ECM1	–0.125	0.05
D90	–0.114	0.052

Note: The null hypothesis that the coefficients are zero is rejected. Wald test chi^2 (8) = 52.18 [0.0000]**.

capital inflows without necessarily increasing the future debt burden. The success of any debt strategy, however, will ultimately depend on the structure of the existing stock of debt and on sound macroeconomic policies.

Kenya's debt strategy has concentrated on efforts to increase access to concessional loans, reduce commercial loans and export credit, and request debt forgiveness from creditor governments. The country has not made use of the options available to the heavily indebted poor countries under debt-restructuring schemes such as the Naples terms or the market-based schemes such as debt-equity swaps and buybacks. Even when the country restructured its arrears in 1994, it did not request any write-offs or special concessional interest rates. Indeed, apart from the write-offs of the late 1980s, the country had not obtained any write-offs as of the end of 1996. An insignificant amount of debt was refinanced, and a debt swap on $10.3 million in debt was made in 1994 (World Bank, 1994).

Between 1980 and 1996, 31 sub-Saharan African countries, including South Africa, rescheduled their debts (Republic of Kenya, 1989). It therefore seems odd that Kenya has not rescheduled its debts despite having debt indicators that are higher than the average for sub-Saharan African countries. Moreover, Kenya was considered to have had a debt overhang and severe liquidity problems (World Bank, 1994) from as early as the late 1980s, making the fact that it had not rescheduled by 1996 seem paradoxical.

The truth of the matter is that Kenya has been able to avoid rescheduling its debt because it is not as highly stressed as many other sub-Saharan African countries, including those that rescheduled. Low commercial debt and relatively good performance of the export sector enabled the country to meet its debt obligations. Debt from private sources, which was 24 percent of total public and publicly guaranteed debt in 1991, had been reduced to 12 percent in 1995. The other reason for not rescheduling was the unfavorable political climate toward Kenya, especially on the part of bilateral donors. Since the aid embargo of 1991, Kenya has been viewed by donors to be a reluctant reformer in both economic and political affairs. This clearly played a role in discouraging the government from requesting debt restructuring, to avoid engaging donors on these issues.

Notwithstanding the past reasons for not rescheduling debt, there is no doubt that the economy would benefit from some form of rescheduling. Given that multilateral credits cannot be rescheduled or written off, and that only IDA loans are concessional, the recent shift toward increased IDA loans is a sensible debt strategy. Although private nonguaranteed debt is a small share of total outstanding debt, debt service on it is high. The government should aim to reduce this debt through the IDA debt reduction facility. The importance of using this facility is that it allows for reduction of debt to private creditors on better terms than those offered by Naples terms (Cline, 1996). This would directly improve the country's creditworthiness and therefore encourage new money on favorable terms and also encourage foreign direct investment. Kenya should also seek debt relief under the Naples terms, given that bilateral debt is rising faster than all other types of debt. This would require the government to be willing and ready to engage the donors in a more constructive dialogue on deeper economic and political reforms.

Sustainability of Kenya's Debt

Although Kenya has been able to meet all its debt repayments, the current low rate of economic growth and the decline in capital inflows suggest that this position may not be sustainable. The insistence on meeting external debt repayments at the expense of some other necessary expenditures, such as imports, development expenditures, and reduction of domestic debt, may hurt the economy in the short and the medium term. Moreover, if debt overhang is a problem in Kenya, as suggested by the World Bank (1994), then the associated negative impact on investment and private capital inflows will be a drag on economic growth. It is evident, therefore, that unless the problem of indebtedness is tackled through reduction of the growth of the stock of debt and increased access to concessional loans, the sustainability of Kenya's debt and hence the solvency of the economy may not be tenable in the long run.

The sustainability of a country's debt can be analyzed in either of two ways. The most common method follows the traditional Harrod-Domar (Harrod, 1948; Domar, 1946) growth model. This method was used by Greene and Khan (1990). The other method, associated with Cohen (1985, 1988), is a simple and deterministic intertemporal model. This model is discussed in Allsopp and Joshi (1985) and van Wijnbergen (1989). The model addresses the issue of debt sustainability more directly than the growth-cum-debt model and for this reason is preferred for our analysis.

Establishing the sustainability of a country's debt normally involves picking a time horizon and then projecting the growth rate of selected macroeconomic variables for the horizon. The level of indebtedness at the end of the period is compared with some indicators of indebtedness to determine whether the level is sufficient to avoid future debt-service problems. For example, Cohen (1985) divided the future into two subperiods, 1983–85 and 1996 onward, and projected future growth of exports using past export growth rates and an assumed future rate of interest inclusive of spread plus fees to calculate a solvency index.

This chapter analyzes the sustainability of Kenya's debt a posteriori. Since Kenya's debt has been sustainable, the aim is to determine why that has been the case. This is done by calculating Cohen's solvency index and then deducing from the results why the solvency conditions have been met. This approach is useful in delineating what it would take for the country's debt to remain sustainable into the foreseeable future.

Following Cohen (1985), the model used in this study is specified as:

$$b = \frac{(r - x)d}{(1 + x)}, \tag{2}$$

where

d = the debt-export ratio or the debt-GNP ratio

x = real growth of exports

r = real foreign interest rates.

A simple solvency condition compares the rate of growth of the real interest rate (r) and the rate of growth of exports (x). A country is said to be insolvent if $(r - x) < 0$, so that insolvency can be attributed to rising real interest rates and declining growth of exports. Cohen suggests that this is a simplistic and inadequate method of determining insolvency, because a country is not necessarily insolvent when $r > x$ as long as b satisfies the condition that the present value of future debt tends toward zero in the long term. A country therefore need not repay the principal or the interest due to remain solvent as long as the condition holds.

This model assumes that a debtor country is interested in maintaining the variable *d* at some constant level in order to be creditworthy. For example, highly indebted countries have tried to maintain their creditworthiness by generating trade surpluses through import compression and/or export promotion. The amount of trade surplus (transfers) necessary to maintain a given level of *d* is represented by the index *b*, and this has led Cohen (1985, 1988) to define *b* as the level of trade surplus or maximum proportion of resources above which a country would rather default than remain solvent. Cohen (1988) established that, on average, debtor countries should not devote more than 15 percent of their exports to service debts. In terms of Equation (2), *b* is therefore the level of minimum debt to be repaid when the interest rate exceeds a country's growth of exports.

Two solvency indexes (*bx* and *by*) are calculated where *d* is defined as the debt-export ratio and the debt-GNP ratio, respectively. The averages for the two indexes are 1.0 and 0.3, reflecting a higher debt-export ratio compared with the debt-GNP ratio (Table 14). The trends for the ratios are the same, however. The indexes are positive for most years, reflecting insolvency under the simple solvency criteria. Negative indexes imply $r < x$, a condition under which the country is perfectly solvent (Cohen, 1985).

Concentrating on the index based on the debt-export ratio, for comparison with Cohen's results, the value *bx* for the periods 1970–80, 1981–90, and 1991–94 was 4.1, 3.0, and –11.5, respectively. These indexes, like the whole-period average, are below Cohen's critical value of 15.0. The relatively high indexes for 1970–80 and 1981–90 were a result of high interest rates and poor export performance. On the other hand, despite the relatively high interest rates, the negative index during 1991–95 was a result of good export performance.

It can be concluded that, over the period covered by the study, Kenya has neither defaulted nor rescheduled its debt because the solvency index has been well below the critical level. Moreover, moderate interest rates and good export performance have kept the level of the index down. The policy implications of these results are that the government, in its efforts to remain solvent, should carry out policies to improve export performance. The government should also take steps to lower the debt stock and avoid contracting debt that pays high interest rates.

Conclusion

This chapter has established that Kenya's economic reforms took about two decades to implement and were marked by a stop-and-go

Table 14. Kenya: Solvency Indexes, 1971–95

	Real Interest Rate (In percent)	Export Growth (In percent)	b_x	b_y
1971	1.4	–31.5	45.1	13.9
1972	1.3	33.7	–24.2	6.8
1973	1.3	14.0	–13.3	-3.9
1974	1.0	–5.3	8.0	2.7
1975	0.8	-9.2	14.1	4.5
1976	0.8	5.4	–5.8	-2.0
1977	0.9	7.2	–3.3	–1.2
1978	1.3	-9.1	16.1	4.9
1979	1.5	–1.1	4.3	1.2
1980	1.5	2.2	–1.1	–0.3
1981	1.9	–6.0	14.0	4.1
1982	1.9	–2.4	8.4	2.4
1983	2.1	–3.8	14.0	3.8
1984	2.7	–1.3	8.6	2.4
1985	2.5	3.7	–3.2	–0.9
1986	2.3	12.9	23.4	–6.4
1987	2.9	–3.3	21.5	4.8
1988	2.6	5.6	–9.5	–2.2
1989	2.5	–1.1	10.9	2.6
1990	2.3	6.0	–11.1	–3.0
1991	1.8	2.9	–3.7	–1.2
1992	2.2	0	7.1	2.0
1993	2.4	14.9	–33.5	–15.3
1994	2.0	11.7	–23.3	-9.6
1995	3.3	5.0	–4.0	–1.6
Averages:				
1971–95			0.55	0.34
1971–80			4.1	2.7
1981–90			3.0	0.076
1991–95			–11.5	–5.1

Source: Author's calculations.

pace with a few cases of reversals. The reforms began to be implemented in earnest during the early 1990s, yielding low inflation, stable exchange rates, and declining budget deficits. Economic growth, although rising, continues to be below the expected level, as are foreign direct investment and domestic investment. These results reflect the low credibility of economic reforms arising from high domestic debt, which continues to crowd out the private sector, and a high and rising stock of external debt accompanied by high debt repayments.

Kenya's stock of debt is mostly official, and although it was earlier dominated by multilateral debt, bilateral debt has been rising and has almost equaled multilateral debt in recent years. Debt-service payments have also been high in recent years.

The structure and volume of Kenya's debt have important implications for debt management. First, multilateral debt, which consists mainly of IDA loans, although concessional, cannot be written off. Second, although bilateral debt can be written off, the price to pay in terms of conditionality may be high. This is especially true, given Kenya's poor image abroad. Last, although private debt has been a small proportion of total external debt, debt-service payments on this debt have been almost as high as those on official debt. Moreover, the terms of payment have become increasingly hard, suggesting that debt-service payments will rise in the future.

On the basis of these observations, Kenya's debt management should concentrate on removing the possible debt overhang by reducing the debt burden through market-based instruments, available restructuring schemes, and appeals for write-offs. The use of all available avenues for debt reduction would lead to maximizing the level of reduction. The most immediate objective, however, would be to reduce commercial debt using the IDA debt reduction facility. This would be a follow-up to the restructuring of arrears in 1994. This step is important to reduce the heavy burden that repayment of private debt imposes on the economy. The government should also make a better case for write-offs by bilateral creditors. This would require greater flexibility on the part of the government toward donors concerned about deeper economic and political reforms. The government should also evaluate whether it is not possible to reduce the burden of debt through the Heavily Indebted Poor Countries debt initiative. This again would require greater commitment by the government to economic reforms and greater understanding and cooperation from creditors.

This chapter establishes that depreciation in terms of the real effective exchange rate, higher budget deficits, and higher foreign interest rates raise external debt, whereas improvement in the terms of trade reduces debt. It is also established that the solvency index for Kenya has been low primarily because of moderate world interest rates and good export performance.

The implication of these results is that maintenance of macroeconomic stability is important in dealing with the debt crisis. It is important to ensure that economic reforms are credible to sustain low inflation and stable exchange rates and to encourage inflows of new money at favorable rates and increased foreign direct investment. Credible reforms would also lower capital flight and encourage domestic investment, leading to more rapid economic growth. Most important, credible economic reforms would facilitate negotiations toward debt restructuring and/or appeals for debt write-offs.

To summarize, the high and rising stock of external debt and debt-service payments mean that the Kenyan government has to take serious steps to resolve the problem. This would involve exploring and using all available channels for debt reduction. The government should also undertake the economic reforms necessary to move the economy into sustainable growth, thus providing a favorable climate for debt reduction in the long run.

References

Ajayi, S.I., 1991, "Macroeconomic Approach to External Debt: The Case of Nigeria," African Economic Research Consortium Research Paper No. 8 (Nairobi: Initiative Publishers).

———, 1996, "An Analysis of External Debt and Capital Flight in Severely Indebted Low Income Countries in Sub-Saharan Africa," paper presented to the IMF/World Bank Conference on External Financing for Low Income Countries, Washington, December 10–11.

Allsopp, C., and V. Joshi, 1995, "The International Debt Crisis," *Oxford Review of Economic Policy*, Vol. 2, No. 1.

Bevan, D.L., A. Bigsten, P. Collier, and J.W. Gunning, 1987, *East African Lessons on Economic Liberalization* (Gower: Aldershot).

Bevan, D.L., P. Collier, and J.W. Gunning, 1990, *Controlled Open Economies* (Oxford: Clarendon Press).

Bevan, D.L., and Bo Karlstrom, 1988, "Kenya: Macroeconomic Events 1966–86" (unpublished: Oxford University).

Cline, W.R., 1983, *International Debt and the Stability of the World Economy* (Washington: Institute for International Economics).

———, 1995, *International Debt Reexamined* (Washington: Institute for International Economics).

———, 1996, "Debt Relief for the Highly Indebted Poor Countries: Lessons from the 1980s Debt Crisis," paper presented to the IMF/World Bank Conference on External Financing for Low Income Countries, Washington, December 10–11.

Cohen, D., 1985, "How to Evaluate the Solvency of an Indebted Nation," *Economic Policy*, Vol. 1, No. 1.

———, 1988, "The Management of the Developing Countries' Debt: Guidelines and Application to Brazil," *World Bank Economic Review*, Vol. 2, No. 1.

Degebe, B., 1992, "Growth and Foreign Debt: The Ethiopian Experience 1964–1986," African Economic Research Consortium Research Paper No. 14 (Nairobi: Initiative Publishers).

Dickey, D.A., and W.A. Fuller, 1981, "Likelihood Ratio Statistics for Autoregressive Time Series with Unit Root," *Econometrica*, Vol. 4.

Domar, E.D., 1946, "Capital Expansion Rate of Growth and Employment," *Econometrica* (April).

Edwards, S., and F. Larrain, eds., 1989, *Debt, Adjustment and Recovery* (Oxford: Basil Blackwell).

Elbadawi, I.A., B.J. Ndulu, and N. Ndung'u, 1996, "Debt Overhang and Economic Growth in Sub-Saharan Africa," paper presented to the IMF/World Bank Conference on External Financing for Low Income Countries, Washington, December 10–11.

Engle, R.F., and C.W.J. Granger, 1987, "Co-Integration and Error Correction: Representation, Estimation and Testing," *Econometrica*, Vol. 55, No. 2.

Godfrey, M., 1987, "Stabilization and Structural Adjustment of Kenya's Economy, 1985–98: An Assessment of Performance," *Development and Change*, Vol. 8.

Greene, J.E. and M.S. Khan, 1990, "The African Debt Crisis," African Economic Research Consortium Special Paper No. 3 (Nairobi: Initiative Publishers).

Harrod, R.F., 1948, *Towards a Dynamic Economics: Some Recent Developments of Economic Theory and Their Applications to Policy* (London: Macmillan).

Hecox, W.E., 1988, "Structural Adjustment, Donor Conditionality, and Industrialization in Kenya," in *Industrialization in Kenya: In Search of Strategy*, ed. by P. Coughlin and G.K. Ikiara (Nairobi: Heinemann Kenya).

Humphreys, C., and J. Underwood, 1989, "The External Debt Difficulties of Low-Income Africa," in *Dealing with the Debt Crisis*, ed. by I. Husain and I. Diwan (Washington: World Bank).

Killick, T., 1984, *The IMF and Stabilization: Developing Country Experiences* (London: Heinemann).

———, and M. Martin, 1989, "African Debt: The Search for Solutions," United Nations Africa Recovery Program Briefing Paper No. l.

Killick, T., and F.M. Mwega, 1990, "Monetary Policy in Kenya, 1967–88," *Eastern African Economic Review*, Vol. 6, No. 2.

Krumm, K.L., 1985, "The External Debt of Sub-Saharan Africa: Origins, Magnitude and the Implications for Action," World Bank Staff Working Paper No. 471 (Washington: World Bank).

Mbire, B., and M. Atingi, 1994, "Growth and Foreign Debt: The Ugandan Experience," paper presented at a workshop of the African Economic Research Consortium, Nairobi.

Mistry, P.S., 1988, "African Debt: The Case for Relief for Sub-Saharan Africa" (Oxford, England: Oxford International Associates).

———, 1991, *African Debt Revisited: Procrastination or Progress?* (The Hague: FONDAD).

Mosley, P., 1986, "The Politics of Economic Liberalization: USAID and World Bank in Kenya, 1980–84," *African Affairs*, Vol. 85.

Mwega, F.M., 1995, "Trade Liberalization, Credibility and Impacts: A Case Study of Kenya, 1972–94," final report prepared for the African Economic Research Consortium Collaborative Project on Trade Liberalization and Regional Integration in Sub-Saharan Africa, September.

Ng'eno, N.K., 1991, "Kenya's Export Performance," in *Trade and Development in Sub-Saharan Africa*, ed. by J.H. Frimpong-Ansah, S.M. Ravi Kanbur, and P. Svedberg (Manchester, England: Manchester University Press).

Organization of African Unity, 1987, *African Common Position on Africa's External Debt Crisis* (Addis Ababa).

Osei, B., 1995, "Ghana: The Burden of Debt Service Payment Under Structural Adjustment," African Economic Research Consortium Research Paper No. 33 (Nairobi: Initiative Publishers).

Perron, P., 1988, "Trends and Random Walks in Macroeconomic Time Series: Further Evidence from a New Approach," *Journal of Economic Dynamic and Control*, Vol. 12.

Phillips, P.C., 1987, "Time Series Regression with a Unit Root," *Econometrica*, Vol. 55.

Republic of Kenya, 1974, *Development Plan for 1974/78* (Nairobi: Government Printer).

———, 1984, *Development Plan for 1984/88* (Nairobi: Government Printer).

———, 1986, *Sessional Paper No. 1 of 1986, Economic Management for Renewed Growth* (Nairobi: Government Printer).

———, 1989, *Development Plan for 1989/93* (Nairobi: Government Printer).

———, 1990, *Budget Speech, 1990/91* (Nairobi).

———, *Economic Surveys*, various issues (Nairobi: Government Printer).

———, *Statistical Abstract*, various issues (Nairobi: Government Printer).

———, Ministry of Finance, 1994, *Annual Report on Debt Management in Kenya* (Nairobi: Government Printer).

Swamy, G., 1994, "Kenya: Patchy, Intermittent Commitment," in *Adjustment in Africa: Lessons from Country Case Studies*, ed. by I. Husain and R. Faruqee (Washington: World Bank).

United Nations, 1988, *Financing Africa's Recovery: Report and Recommendations of the Advisory Group on Financial Flows for Africa* (New York).

van Wijnbergen, S., 1989, "External Debt, Inflation, and the Public Sector: Towards Fiscal Policy for Sustainable Growth," *World Bank Economic Review,* Vol. 3, No. 3.

World Bank, 1983, *Kenya: Growth and Structural Change* (Washington).

———, 1994, *World Debt Tables,* Vol. 1 (Washington).

———, 1996, *World Debt Tables,* Vols. l and 2 (Washington).

World Bank and United Nations Development Program, 1989, *Africa's Adjustment and Growth in the 1980s* (Washington).

An Econometric Analysis of External Debt and Economic Growth in Sub-Saharan African Countries

6

Milton A. Iyoha

Socioeconomic conditions in African countries deteriorated sharply during the 1980s, a decade that is widely regarded as Africa's "lost decade" of development opportunities. Available empirical evidence shows that per capita income in sub-Saharan Africa declined at an average annual rate of 2.2 percent; per capita private consumption fell by 14.8 percent; export volume was stagnant while import volume plummeted at an average annual rate of 4.3 percent; and the terms of trade fell by 9.1 percent (see Tables 1–3 and Figure 1).

Using data on GDP instead of GNP improves the picture marginally, but the situation is still nothing short of catastrophic. An analysis of Tables 4 and 5 confirms that, between 1981 and 1990, the average annual growth rate of real GDP in sub-Saharan Africa was 1.7 percent. However, given the region's high population growth rate, the average annual growth rate of real GDP per capita between 1981 and 1990 was –0.9 percent. Among all developing regions, sub-Saharan Africa's performance on the latter measure was the poorest, with the exception of the Middle East and North Africa region. Indeed, sub-Saharan Africa's negative growth rate contrasts sharply with East Asia's impressive real per capita GDP growth rate of 6.3 percent and China's fantastic growth rate of 8.2 percent during the decade.

Nor did the economic performance of sub-Saharan Africa improve in the early 1990s. Table 5 confirms that, between 1991 and 1993, the region's growth rate of real per capita GDP was negative, averaging –2.3 percent annually. In 1994, real per capita GDP remained negative at –0.7 percent. Only in 1995 did the growth rate become positive, reaching 1.1 percent. This, of course, still fell well short of the 8.0 percent growth rate posted by East Asia and the 9.2 percent growth rate of real GDP per capita achieved by China.

The bottom line is that the 600 million people inhabiting the roughly 50 countries in sub-Saharan Africa are among the poorest in the world. The World Bank classifies 74 percent of these countries as low-income economies, and the United Nations Development Program classifies 79 percent of them as low-human-development countries. Finally, of the 41 countries in the world classified as Heavily In-

Figure 1. Sub-Saharan Africa: GNP Per Capita, 1970–94
(In U.S. dollars)

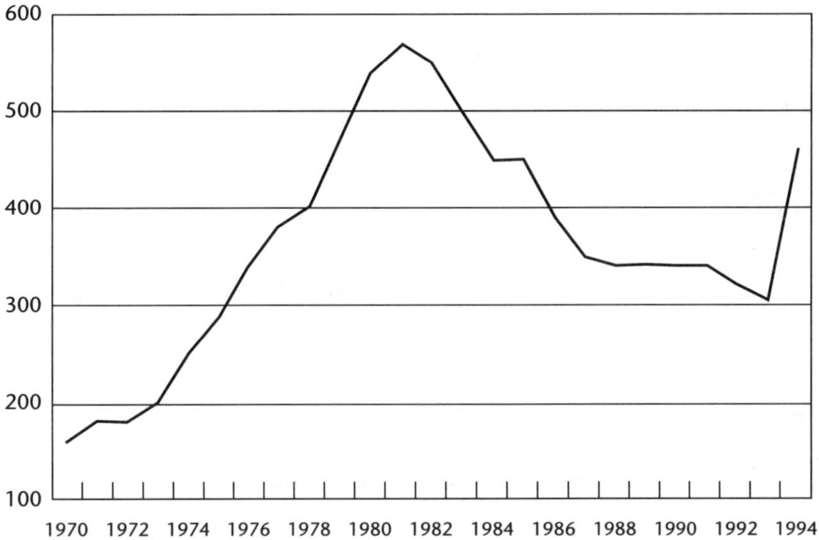

Sources: World Bank (1992a, 1992c, 1996b).

debted Poor Countries by the World Bank and the IMF, 33 (80 percent) are in sub-Saharan Africa. Thus, the great majority of countries in sub-Saharan Africa not only are poor (by any standard of evaluation) but also report low or negative rates of growth of per capita income. The conclusion is therefore inescapable that the income gap between sub-Saharan African countries and the rest of the world is continuing to widen.

A close examination of Table 5 shows that the relative position of sub-Saharan African countries started to deteriorate significantly in the 1980s, when the region found itself in a quagmire of economic problems. The acute economic crisis of the last 15 years—which has led to extremely poor growth performance—is attributable to a host of factors, both internal and external. The internal factors are connected with domestic macroeconomic policy weaknesses that have led to inflation, unemployment, rising fiscal deficits, and capital flight. The effects of domestic macroeconomic policy mistakes have been exacerbated by structural weaknesses in the economies, and in particular by a narrow and technologically backward production base and heavy dependence on exports of a narrow range of primary products. The external factors reflect an increasingly hostile interna-

Table 1. Sub-Saharan Africa: GNP Per Capita, 1970–94

	U.S. Dollars[1]		U.S. Dollars[1]
1970	160	1983	500
1971	180	1984	450
1972	180	1985	450
1973	200	1986	390
1974	250	1987	350
1975	290	1988	340
1976	340	1989	340
1977	380	1990	340
1978	400	1991	340
1979	470	1992	321
1980	540	1993	306
1981	570	1994	460
1982	550		

Sources: World Bank (1992a, 1992c, 1996b).
[1]Calculated according to the World Bank Atlas methodology.

Table 2. Sub-Saharan Africa: GDP, 1970–94

	In Millions of U.S. Dollars	Growth Rate (In percent)
1970	138,913	8.3
1971	150,442	7.7
1972	162,027	2.7
1973	165,000	2.6
1974	170,727	7.6
1975	183,703	1.2
1976	185,908	7.0
1977	198,921	4.0
1978	206,878	–0.2
1979	206,465	2.4
1980	211,420	3.2
1981	212,426	0.7
1982	213,913	2.7
1983	219,689	0.05
1984	219,799	0.2
1985	223,763	3.4
1986	228,821	3.6
1987	232,577	0.9
1988	241,765	4.4
1989	249,466	3.1
1990	251,969	1.1
1991	254,205	2.5
1992	253,863	1.8
1993	256,154	0.9
1994	258,460	2.2

Sources: World Bank (1992c, 1995).

Table 3. Comparative Economic Indicators
(In percent except as noted)

	Sub-Saharan Africa	Low-Income Economies	High-Income Economies
Growth of per capita GNP, 1980–89	–2.2	2.3	2.5
Change in per capita private consumption, 1980–90	–14.8	31.3	24.0
Gross domestic saving as a share of GDP, 1990	16.0	28.0	22.0
Gross domestic investment as a share of GDP, 1990	19.0	31.0	22.0
Growth of export volume, 1980–90 (annual)	0.2	5.4	4.3
Growth of import volume, 1980–90 (annual)	–4.3	2.8	5.3
Change in terms of trade, 1985–90	–9.1	–6.5	3.1
Gross international reserves, 1990 (in months of import coverage)	2.3	3.4	3.1

Source: International Monetary Fund, *World Economic Outlook,* various issues.

tional economic environment characterized by low and falling primary commodity prices, declining terms of trade, soaring global interest rates, rising protectionism in the industrial countries, dwindling capital flows into African countries that have resulted in mounting current account and balance of payments deficits, and an escalating external debt stock. The total external debt stock,[1] which was $84 billion in 1980, had jumped to $165 billion in 1988 and $190 billion in 1990. By 1995 the external debt stock amounted to $223 billion (World Bank data). Between 1980 and 1995 the debt stock increased by $139 million, for an average annual rate of 6.7 percent. Associated with the rising external debt stock has been a crushing debt-service burden. From a level of $6.4 billion in 1980, total debt service on long-term debt[2] rose to $12.3 billion in 1990 and then

[1]The total external debt stock consists of public and publicly guaranteed long-term debt, private nonguaranteed long-term debt, the use of IMF credit, and estimated short-term debt. This is to be distinguished from debt outstanding and disbursed, which is defined as the total debt outstanding and disbursed of long-term official concessional, official nonconcessional, and private loans. Long-term external debt is defined as debt that has an original or extended maturity of over one year that is owed to nonresidents and repayable in foreign currency, goods, and services.

[2]Total debt service measures debt-service payments on long-term debt (public, publicly guaranteed, and private nonguaranteed), use of IMF credit, and interest on short-term debt.

Table 4. Growth of Real GDP by World Region, 1966–95
(Annual averages, in percent)

	1966–73	1974–80	1981–90	1991–93	1994	1995
World total	5.1	3.4	3.2	1.2	2.9	2.8
Industrial countries	4.8	3.0	3.2	1.3	3.0	2.5
Developing countries[1]	6.9	5.0	3.3	4.6	4.6	4.9
East Asia	7.9	6.8	7.6	8.7	9.3	9.2
China	8.5	6.3	9.9	12.3	12.2	10.2
South Asia	3.7	4.0	5.7	3.2	4.7	5.5
Sub-Saharan Africa	4.7	3.4	1.7	0.6	2.2	3.8
Latin America and the Caribbean	6.4	4.8	1.7	3.2	3.9	0.9
Middle East and North Africa	8.5	4.7	0.2	3.4	0.3	2.5

Source: International Labor Organization (1996).
[1]Excludes Eastern Europe and the former Soviet Union.

dipped to $8.8 billion in 1995, largely because of reschedulings and some amount of debt forgiveness. The debt-service ratio (the ratio of actual debt-service payments to exports of goods and services), which was a mere 5.4 percent in 1970, had jumped to 21.3 percent in 1985 before falling to 14.7 percent in 1995 (Table 6).

One disturbing aspect of the macroeconomic management of sub-Saharan African economies in the 1980s was the failure of these economies to respond favorably to the ministrations of structural adjustment programs. These programs were recommended by the World Bank and the IMF as an antidote to the economic crisis brought on by the debt crisis, among other reasons. Structural adjustment programs were presented as programs that would restore stabilization in the short term and sustainable growth in the medium to long term. A majority of sub-Saharan African countries adopted structural adjustment programs in the 1980s, but unfortunately, in virtually all of them structural adjustment has meant a period of austerity, declining income and living standards, mounting unemployment, and increasing poverty (International Labor Organization, 1996, p. 1). Table 7 compares labor force with population in sub-Saharan Africa. Devaluation, which featured in virtually all structural adjustment programs, led to an increase in total debt and debt-service payments denominated in domestic currency. The deflation required by the structural adjustment programs led to a fall in domestic product and a reduction in national income available for

Table 5. Growth of Real Per Capita GDP by World Region, 1981–95
(Annual averages, in percent)

	1981–90	1991–93	1994	1995
World total	1.2	–0.4	1.2	1.4
Industrial countries	2.2	0.7	2.4	1.8
Developing countries	1.2	2.6	2.7	3.2
East Asia	6.3	7.2	7.6	8.0
China	8.2	11.0	10.5	9.2
South Asia	3.1	1.1	2.7	3.6
Sub-Saharan Africa	–0.9	–2.3	–0.7	1.1
Latin America and the Caribbean	–0.5	1.3	2.0	–0.7
Middle East and North Africa	–3.0	0.7	–2.2	0.1

Source: International Labor Organization (1996).

consumption, provision of public services, and investment. A reduction in investment meant a fall in economic growth. Meanwhile, increased inflows of foreign capital expected on the adoption of structural adjustment programs failed to materialize, because of a lethal combination of political instability, poor macroeconomic policies, weak economic performance, and the debt overhang syndrome. In addition, heavy debt-service payments have tended to crowd out foreign investment (Tables 8 and 9). Indeed, aid and foreign investment were routinely diverted into debt-service payments mainly to pay the World Bank and the IMF, because debt owed to these multilateral institutions cannot be rescheduled or written off (Kapijimpanga, 1996). Besides, debt rescheduling by bilateral donors does not constitute true debt relief; rather it leads to a further buildup of the debt stock, as rescheduled debt often attracts higher interest rates, and the interest accumulated is capitalized (Tables 10 and 11). "So, rescheduling has not solved the African debt problem but rather intensified it" (Kapijimpanga, 1996, p. 14).

With the rapid buildup of external debt and poor economic performance, sub-Saharan Africa's debt crisis has deepened, and the debt burden has become even more crushing. Indeed, relative to exports and economic activity (as measured by GNP),[3] sub-Saharan Africa's debt is the highest of any region in the world (Klein, 1987; Iyoha and

[3]According to the World Bank (1996b), sub-Saharan Africa's net present value of external debt amounted to 50 percent of GNP in 1994. This compares unfavorably with the ratios for the other low- and middle-income regions of the world, namely, Latin America and the Caribbean (39 percent), Middle East and North Africa (32 percent), East Asia and the Pacific (28 percent), South Asia (26 percent), and Europe and Central Asia (25 percent).

Table 6. Sub-Saharan Africa: Debt Indicators, 1970–95

(In percent except as noted)

	EDT/XGS	DOD/XGS	EDT/GNP	DOD/GNP	TDS/XGS	RES/MGS (In months)	RES (In millions of U.S. dollars)
1970	91.0	63.2	20.5	14.3	5.4	2.5	2,028
1971	105.8	73.5	24.2	16.8	6.2	2.2	1,899
1972	113.0	76.2	20.0	13.5	7.0	2.3	2,139
1973	106.9	70.0	22.6	14.8	8.8	2.5	3,027
1974	77.6	50.4	23.8	15.5	4.5	4.7	8,167
1975	93.7	61.6	24.3	16.0	5.8	3.4	7,908
1976	98.1	64.7	24.5	16.2	5.8	3.1	7,696
1977	98.6	64.3	25.6	16.7	4.8	2.4	7,475
1978	138.4	92.4	28.9	19.3	7.1	1.6	5,407
1979	129.8	85.2	30.7	20.2	7.1	3.0	10,215
1980	119.7	78.6	30.6	20.1	7.8	3.4	22,249
1981	143.4	108.4	28.7	21.7	10.3	1.7	7,870
1982	199.7	152.9	32.0	24.5	15.0	1.4	5,335
1983	259.2	197.2	42.2	32.1	20.3	1.5	4,713
1984	203.3	155.7	47.9	36.7	18.3	1.5	5,127
1985	227.9	173.3	55.1	41.9	21.3	1.7	6,519
1986	223.7	183.2	56.2	46.0	22.0	1.8	7,075
1987	244.1	199.7	64.3	52.6	18.4	1.9	8,090
1988	242.9	198.9	67.2	55.2	20.7	1.5	10,378
1989	237.7	195.4	69.1	56.8	17.9	1.7	12,129
1990	225.7	183.9	70.8	57.7	17.8	2.0	15,597
1991	239.4	195.8	70.6	57.7	16.4	2.3	18,054
1992	235.6	188.7	69.8	55.9	15.7	1.8	14,280
1993	251.9	195.2	73.2	56.7	14.9	1.9	15,310
1994	265.7	206.4	78.7	61.1	14.0	2.1	20,107
1995	269.8	210.5	74.1	57.8	14.7	. . .	. . .

Source: Author's calculations based on data from World Bank, *World Debt Tables,* various issues.

Note: Indicators are defined as follows: EDT = total external debt stock; XGS = exports of goods and services; DOD = total debt outstanding and disbursed; TDS = total debt service; RES = international reserves; MGS = imports of goods and services.

Table 7. Sub-Saharan Africa: Labor Force and Population, 1970–95
(In millions)

	Labor Force	Population		Labor Force	Population
1970	130.0	287	1983	185.8	415
1971	133.5	295	1984	191.0	427
1972	137.4	303	1985	196.4	440
1973	141.2	311	1986	201.8	453
1974	145.2	320	1987	207.5	467
1975	149.3	329	1988	213.4	481
1976	153.7	339	1989	220.0	496
1977	157.8	349	1990	226.0	511
1978	162.1	359	1991	232.0	526
1979	166.5	370	1992	238.0	542
1980	171.0	380	1993	244.4	558
1981	175.8	391	1994	251.0	575
1982	180.7	403	1995	257.8	592

Sources: World Bank (1994b, 1995, 1996b).

Iyare, 1994; International Labor Organization, 1995). According to the International Labor Organization (1995, p. 3),

> Africa's external debt is the highest in the world as a proportion of GDP; some countries in the region are spending more than half of their export earnings to service foreign debts. The debts of many African countries are so large in relation to their foreign exchange earnings potential that it would be impossible to pay them off even if growth resumed and was sustained at unrealistically high levels. Largely as a consequence of debt servicing, flow of capital *from* Africa is significantly more than flow of new capital to the region.

As a result of a deterioration in the terms and conditions of sub-Saharan Africa's debt in the 1980s, the region's debt-export ratio (measured as the ratio of debt outstanding and disbursed to exports of goods and services) doubled between 1980 and 1985, from 78.6 percent to 173.3 percent, and almost doubled again between 1985 and 1991, to 329.4 percent (Figure 2). The ratio of actual to scheduled debt-service payments deteriorated during the 1980s—falling from 66 percent in 1983 to 63 percent in 1989. Between 1989 and 1995 the average ratio of actual to scheduled debt service was 58.9 percent (Table 12 and Figure 3). Further evidence of debt distress is found in the fact that, in 1986, 27 of the 44 countries in Africa had payments arrears. Also, between 1986 and 1987, 23 sub-Saharan African countries renegotiated their official bilateral debt through the Paris Club. In the mid-1980s, 30 countries were officially classified as "debt dis-

Table 8. Sub-Saharan Africa: Investment and Saving, 1970–94

	Gross Domestic Investment Per Capita (In 1987 U.S. dollars)	Investment (In percent of GDP)	Saving (In percent of GDP)
1970	70	16.7	15.5
1971	80	18.8	15.1
1972	80	19.5	16.8
1973	80	19.8	18.4
1974	100	19.6	21.9
1975	110	23.3	16.6
1976	120	25.9	20.5
1977	130	26.0	19.5
1978	100	23.5	15.1
1979	90	21.0	16.7
1980	100	21.9	19.7
1981	100	22.0	13.0
1982	90	19.9	11.5
1983	80	15.8	10.8
1984	60	12.8	12.3
1985	60	13.1	13.1
1986	70	16.7	12.5
1987	50	15.9	12.6
1988	50	15.7	11.5
1989	50	15.9	13.4
1990	50	16.1	15.5
1991	50	15.9	12.7
1992	60	16.0	14.0
1993	60	15.7	14.8
1994	. . .	17.0	. . .

Sources: World Bank (1992c, 1995, 1996b).

tressed" (Klein, 1987). In the 1990s, 33 countries have been classified as Heavily Indebted Poor Countries (World Bank, 1996a). Finally, the huge burden of sub-Saharan African debt constitutes a serious obstacle to employment creation and growth, as "investment resources for productive pursuits are consistently used to meet external debt service obligations" (International Labor Organization, 1995, p. 3).

These two issues—debt and lack of growth—are clearly interrelated. Indeed, all indications are that the excessive stock of external debt is retarding the growth and hampering the socioeconomic development of sub-Saharan Africa. It seems apparent that, given the structural weakness of most of these economies, their low income, and their low saving and low investment, the current high levels of debt and debt servicing would militate against rapid economic growth and development. Today, analysts and international policy-

Table 9. Sub-Saharan Africa: Capital Stock and Marginal Product of Capital, 1970–93

	Capital Stock[1] (In billions of U.S. dollars)	Marginal Product of Capital
1970	457.7	0.22809
1971	446.6	0.24140
1972	441.3	0.25243
1973	439.8	0.25159
1974	439.5	0.25482
1975	440.0	0.26677
1976	449.8	0.26456
1977	464.2	0.27571
1978	481.1	0.28132
1979	493.7	0.27380
1980	500.0	0.27350
1981	508.8	0.26829
1982	517.4	0.26394
1983	521.1	0.26348
1984	516.8	0.25781
1985	506.1	0.25548
1986	497.5	0.25572
1987	498.4	0.25334
1988	498.0	0.25680
1989	498.6	0.25855
1990	500.8	0.25495
1991	503.9	0.25007
1992	506.5	0.24415
1993	509.1	0.23988

Source: Author's calculations.
[1]A 5 percent depreciation rate is assumed.

makers appear to have reached a consensus that a satisfactory recovery of investment and output growth in indebted sub-Saharan African countries will remain difficult, perhaps unattainable, as long as they are saddled with a burden of debt servicing that requires a sizable net transfer of resources abroad. Stated simply, there is no way in which many of these countries can service their debt and still have adequate resources left for development finance. Thus, many now believe that a necessary condition for economic growth and development in sub-Saharan Africa is debt relief. This must go beyond debt reschedulings and even beyond the Naples terms of 1994. It could be a policy package that combines debt reduction with a significant amount of debt forgiveness.

This econometric study uses a simulation approach to investigate the impact of external debt on economic growth in sub-Saharan African

Table 10. Sub-Saharan Africa: External Debt Stock, Debt Outstanding and Disbursed, and Debt Service, 1970–95

(In millions of U.S. dollars)

	External Debt Stock	Debt Outstanding and Disbursed	Debt Service
1970	8,296.0	5,761.4	522.9
1971	9,772.0	6,769.3	516.7
1972	11,235.0	7,571.0	648.8
1973	15,168.0	9,928.5	1,165.5
1974	19,340.0	12,558.1	1,046.5
1975	22,721.0	14,879.7	1,300.9
1976	26,996.0	17,807.5	1,476.2
1977	33,705.0	21,968.3	1,554.0
1978	43,655.0	29,142.7	2,103.3
1979	55,485.0	36,422.8	2,853.3
1980	84,049.0	58,208.0	3,977.7
1981	75,668.0	57,190.0	4,576.6
1982	81,946.0	62,393.0	5,235.0
1983	88,233.0	67,164.0	6,411.1
1984	88,866.0	68,046.0	7,885.1
1985	96,396.0	75,979.0	8,918.9
1986	127,145.0	104,116.0	8,975.0
1987	162,629.0	133,135.0	8,296.0
1988	164,981.0	135,476.0	10,974.0
1989	171,236.0	140,735.0	9,761.0
1990	190,260.0	155,088.0	12,264.0
1991	194,779.0	159,364.0	11,176.0
1992	192,781.0	154,439.0	10,862.0
1993	197,886.0	153,372.0	9,890.0
1994	212,416.0	165,048.0	9,315.0
1995	223,298.0	174,281.0	8,784.0

Sources: World Bank, *World Debt Tables*, various issues; and World Bank (1995).

countries. In particular, it undertakes policy simulations (using alternative debt stock reduction scenarios) to analyze the effect of debt on investment and output in these countries between 1987 and 1994.

Following this introduction, the next section offers a discussion of the scope, nature, and severity of the debt crisis in sub-Saharan Africa. The section that follows presents a specification, estimation, and discussion of an econometric model of external debt and economic growth for the region. The basic model consists of two stochastic equations explaining output and investment, and two identities (a capital accumulation identity and a debt accumulation identity). The simultaneous-equations model is estimated by the two-stage least-squares technique. The model is dynamically simu-

Table 11. Sub-Saharan Africa: Average Terms of New Commitments and Commercial Bank Lending Rate, 1970–93
(In percent)

	Average Terms of New Commitments[1]	Commercial Bank Lending Rate		Average Terms of New Commitments[1]	Commercial Bank Lending Rate
1970	3.6	6.7	1982	8.5	13.7
1971	4.2	6.8	1983	8.2	14.6
1972	4.4	7.0	1984	6.3	14.5
1973	5.5	6.9	1985	5.9	14.5
1974	5.2	7.1	1986	5.1	13.5
1975	5.6	7.5	1987	4.5	13.5
1976	5.5	8.6	1988	4.0	13.6
1977	5.5	8.0	1989	4.1	15.1
1978	6.6	10.1	1990	4.3	16.0
1979	8.1	10.8	1991	4.1	16.2
1980	7.3	12.0	1992	3.3	16.8
1981	10.1	13.4	1993	3.3	18.0

Sources: World Bank, *World Debt Tables*, various issues; and World Bank, *Annual Report*, various issues.
[1]Averages are for all creditors.

Table 12. Sub-Saharan Africa: Indicators of Debt Distress, 1989–95
(In millions of U.S. dollars except as noted)

	Actual Debt Service	Scheduled Debt Service	Ratio of Actual to Scheduled Debt Service
1989	12,880	20,551	62.7
1990	14,999	25,618	58.5
1991	13,376	20,999	63.7
1992	12,843	21,191	60.6
1993	11,710	21,225	55.2
1994	11,212	21,776	51.5
1995	12,207	20,154	60.6
Average	12,747	21,645	58.9

Source: World Bank (1996a).

lated in the penultimate section, which also includes a discussion of the results of a historical simulation carried out for the 1971–94 period and policy simulations for 1987–94. The policy simulations involved assessing the impact of alternative debt stock reduction scenarios (effective in 1986) on investment and output in the subsequent years. The last section contains policy recommendations, a summary, and some concluding remarks.

Figure 2. Sub-Saharan Africa: Debt Indicators, 1970–95
(In percent)

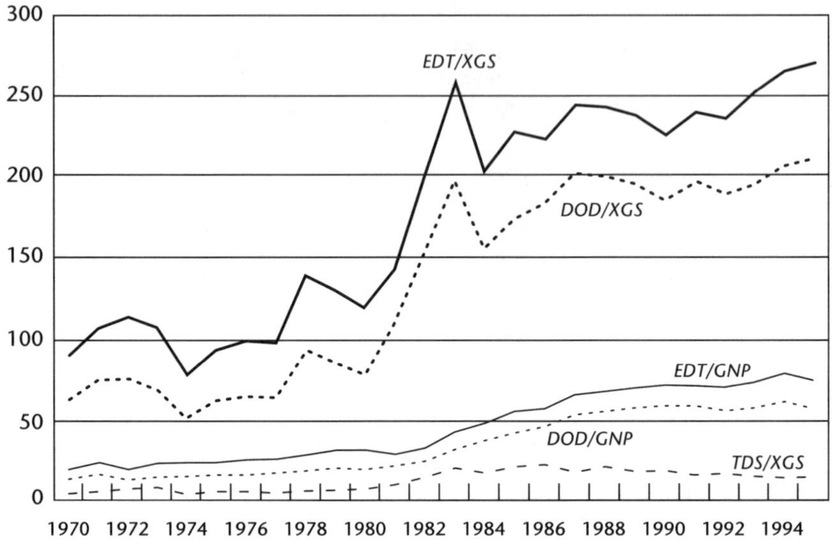

Source: Author's calculations based on data from World Bank, *World Debt Tables.*

Figure 3. Sub-Saharan Africa: Ratio of Debt Service Paid to Debt Service Due, 1989–95
(In percent)

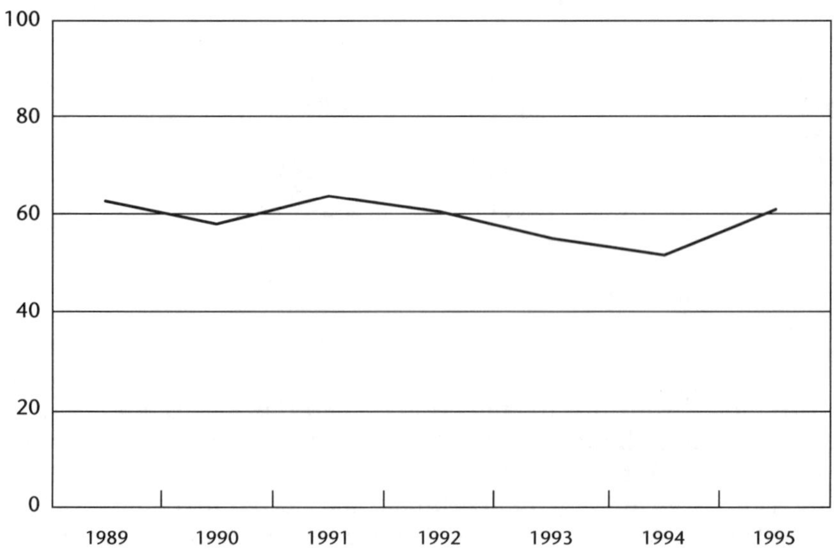

Source: World Bank (1996a).

External Debt of Sub-Saharan African Countries: Scope, Nature, and Severity

The external debt crisis of sub-Saharan Africa is best understood as an integral part of the global debt crisis that emerged in 1982. This crisis arose as a result of

- overborrowing by the developing countries and reckless lending by international commercial banks in the 1970s;
- the collapse of world commodity prices (especially petroleum) in the early 1980s; and
- the sharp increase in international interest (lending) rates in 1982.

The phenomenal increase in foreign borrowing that preceded the debt crisis was triggered by the oil price shocks of 1973 and 1979, which resulted in acute current account deficits in most non-oil-producing developing countries. These countries resorted to foreign borrowing to tide them over the problems raised by the internationally generated shocks to their balance of payments. At the same time, during the period following the oil price hike of November 1973, the international commercial banks were awash with "petrodollars," which they were anxious to recycle. Thus the needs of the cash-strapped developing countries and the excessively liquid international banks seemed to complement each other, and loans were liberally, if not recklessly, approved. Things appeared to go on smoothly for some years as the debts of developing countries were rolled over as they fell due.

The era of easy availability of credit came to a sudden end with the global financial crisis of 1982. The crisis was precipitated by the collapse of oil prices and the sharp increase in interest rates that led to the Mexican debt default. The immediate effect of the crisis was that developing country debt could no longer be rolled over. Henceforth, debtor countries could only service their debts by increasing exports or reducing imports. Many debtor countries in the developing world were ill prepared for the required belt tightening. Nor were world trade conditions conducive to any significant increase in export earnings by developing countries. The crisis was further aggravated by the actions of the international banks, which belatedly scrambled to cover dangerously exposed positions. This was the genesis of the global debt crisis, which saw a real fear of a domino effect resulting in massive defaults by the highly indebted countries of Latin America. Such an eventuality would certainly have shaken the international financial system to its very foundations and could have led to a global depression.

The external debt of the sub-Saharan African countries witnessed a rapid buildup during the period immediately following the global

Table 13. Sub-Saharan Africa: Total External Debt, 1970–95

	In Millions of U.S. Dollars	Change from Previous Year (In percent)
1970	8,296	—
1971	9,772	17.79
1972	11,235	14.97
1973	15,168	35.01
1974	19,340	27.51
1975	22,721	17.48
1976	26,996	18.82
1977	33,705	24.85
1978	43,655	29.52
1979	55,485	27.10
1980	84,049	51.48
1981	75,668	-9.97
1982	81,946	8.30
1983	88,233	7.67
1984	83,866	0.72
1985	96,396	8.47
1986	127,145	31.90
1987	162,629	27.91
1988	164,981	1.45
1989	171,236	3.79
1990	190,260	11.11
1991	194,779	2.38
1992	192,781	–1.03
1993	197,886	2.65
1994	212,416	7.34
1995	223,298	5.12

Source: World Bank (1996a).

debt crisis, with external debt obligations skyrocketing from $84 billion in 1980 to $223 billion in 1995 (Table 13). Thus, the region's external debt stock increased by 165.5 percent in 15 years, for an annual average growth rate of 6.7 percent.

The sharp external debt buildup in the post-1982 period is attributable to several factors, including

- continued decline in the terms of trade;
- uncontrolled fluctuations in export earnings;
- higher interest rates;
- realignment of exchange rates; and
- rescheduling and refinancing of external debt, which only served to increase the debt stock.

Thus, it would be erroneous to attribute the current debt crisis in sub-Saharan Africa to purely wasteful and unproductive expenditures by these countries. The fact is that a significant proportion of the increase in the region's external debt since 1982 can be attributed to exogenous factors. Indeed, the doubling of sub-Saharan Africa's external debt stock in the 1980s took place during a period when the countries borrowed virtually no additional money for productive investment, and the meager borrowings were directed mainly to debt service and occasionally to the maintenance of minimal import requirements.[4] Many analysts have pointed out that the rapid buildup in external debt in the 1980s occurred notwithstanding the sharp cutback made in their expenditures and the tenacious implementation of socially debilitating IMF- and World Bank-inspired structural adjustment programs. Despite the widespread adoption of structural adjustment programs, there was a sharp fall in real net resource flows, especially from the IMF and the International Bank for Reconstruction and Development (World Bank) during the 1980s (Table 14). Moreover, the implementation of structural adjustment programs has led to the sacrifice of medium- to long-term growth objectives in these countries (Iyoha, 1991b; United Nations Economic Commission for Africa, 1989).

Several factors have brought the issue of external debt to the forefront of the problems facing the sub-Saharan African countries. They include

- the rapid rise of the stock of external debt, especially since 1982;
- the deterioration in the terms and conditions of debt, caused partly by changes in the composition of debt but mainly by the rise in interest rates;
- the rapid increase in debt-servicing obligations arising from the first two factors;
- the emergence of debt servicing problems, including risk of default and loss of creditworthiness;
- the stubborn problem of debt overhang; and
- the adverse effects of all these factors on the growth prospects of the countries in the region.

It is now generally agreed that the combined effects of these factors and a sharp fall in real net resource flows since the early 1980s have

[4]In other words, external borrowing by sub-Saharan African countries in the 1980s was not "purposive" but "reactive." The foreign borrowing was not undertaken to boost investment and the rate of development. Rather, borrowing was undertaken to finance unexpected and unmanageable current account deficits and to finance burdensome debt-service payments (see Iyoha, 1991b).

Table 14. Sub-Saharan Africa: IMF, World Bank, and External Transfers, 1980–89

	1980	1983	1984	1985	1986	1987	1988	1989
IMF								
Gross disbursements[1]	1,217	1,618	952	738	735	678	1,033	865
Repayments and interest[2]	487	739	993	1,172	1,689	1,541	1,495	1,593
Net transfer	730	879	–41	–434	–954	–863	–462	–728
IDA								
Disbursements	424	637	778	881	1,400	1,681	1,697	1,700
Repayments and interest	21	44	56	79	94	111	128	126
Net transfer	403	593	722	802	1,306	1,570	1,569	1,574
IBRD								
Disbursements	400	708	832	647	898	998	581	835
Repayments and interest	328	438	527	616	865	1,073	1,306	1,226
Net transfer	72	270	305	31	33	–75	–725	–391
Total net transfers by IMF, IDA, and IBRD	1,205	1,742	986	399	385	632	382	455
Other net transfers								
Multilateral[3]	707	664	442	487	650	709	672	607
Bilateral[3]	1,657	2,295	1,925	472	1,210	1,194	630	945
Private[4]	2,818	270	–1,667	–2,648	–1,132	–213	–434	–428
Total debt-related net transfers	5,657	4,092	1,727	–856	2,067	3,185	1,712	2,307
Total net transfers, including grants and foreign direct investment	5,843	6,606	4,460	3,213	6,163	7,626	7,973	9,420

Source: Author's calculations from data in World Bank (1991, pp. 130–33).
[1]Purchases.
[2]Repurchases and charges.
[3]Excluding grants.
[4]Publicly guaranteed and unguaranteed, excluding foreign direct investment.

had a debilitating impact on the economies of sub-Saharan African countries. Most of these economies have shrunk during this period and there has been a significant decline in the standard of living. Real per capita incomes were on average lower at the end of the 1980s than at the beginning (Figures 1 and 4). In addition, consequent on the collapse of investment, a large part of the region's infrastructure has disappeared, and gains made in education, health, and nutrition during previous decades were dissipated.

Since 1970 there has been a pronounced upward trend in the external debt stock of sub-Saharan Africa. Table 13 provided data on the

Figure 4. Sub-Saharan Africa: Growth of Real GDP, 1970–95
(In percent)

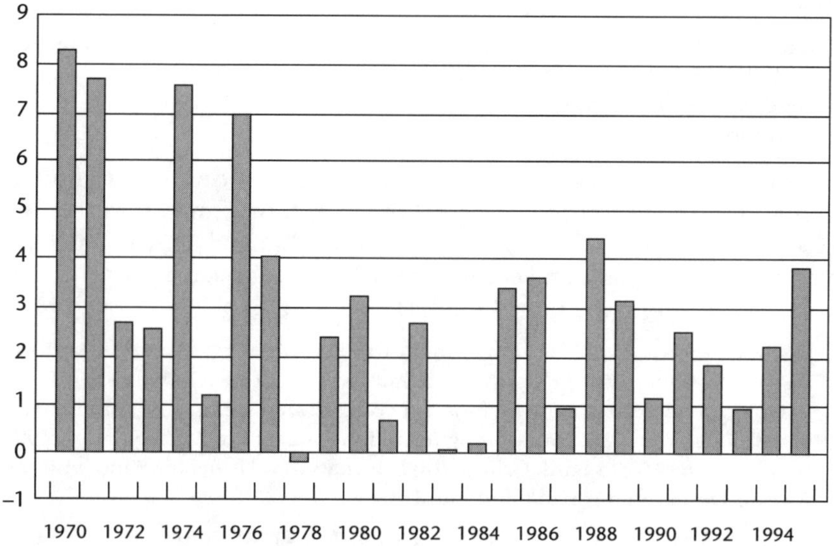

Source: World Bank (1992c, 1995).

level and growth of the region's external debt from 1970 to 1995. From $8.3 billion in 1970, sub-Saharan Africa's total external debt stock increased rapidly to $22.7 billion in 1975. During this period, external debt grew at an average annual rate of 22.55 percent. The growth in external debt was even more rapid during the next five years: between 1976 and 1980 the average annual rate of growth of total external debt amounted to 30.4 percent. The highest annual growth rate during this period was 51.5 percent, reported in 1980. With total external debt at a worrisome $84 billion in 1980, its rate of growth moderated. Thus, between 1981 and 1985 the average annual growth rate of external debt was a mere 3 percent. The next two years, however, witnessed a renewed upsurge in the growth of external debt, at rates of 32 percent in 1986 and 28 percent in 1987. In 1987 the total external debt stock stood at the alarming level of $162.6 billion. Since 1988 the annual growth rate of external debt has been 7 percent or less, except in 1990 when it jumped to 11.1 percent. However, despite the moderate growth rate in the 1990s, by 1995 sub-Saharan Africa's total external debt was astronomical at over $223 billion. During the decade of the 1980s, despite a reduction in the tempo of its growth, the region's external debt increased faster than that of the developing world as a whole (Iyoha and Iyare, 1994).

Compared with Latin America, Africa depends more on official borrowing and less on commercial borrowing from international banks. According to Klein (1987, p. 12),

> Official debt dominates the external obligations of most African countries. Only five Sub-Saharan African countries—Congo, Côte d'Ivoire, Gabon, Nigeria, and Zimbabwe—owe more to commercial banks than to official creditors.

However, while available empirical evidence shows that there has been a shift in the source of North Africa's external finance during the 1980s, that of sub-Saharan Africa has hardly changed. Official bilateral and multilateral loans still account for the bulk of the region's external debt. According to the World Bank (1996a, p. 170),

> Seventy percent of outstanding debt at the end of 1995 was owed to official creditors—90 percent if Nigeria and South Africa are excluded. The region is a major recipient of inflows, most on concessional terms, from multilateral institutions. Thirty percent of long-term debt outstanding at the end of 1995 is owed to the World Bank Group, the International Monetary Fund, and the African Development Bank and Fund.

Available World Bank data also show that sub-Saharan Africa, as a region, receives the largest share of official development assistance. Indeed in 1994 official development assistance equaled 12.4 percent of the region's GNP. This percentage is greater than that of other low- and middle-income regions, which are invariably less than 2 percent. In quantitative terms, official development assistance flows to sub-Saharan Africa reached $16.9 billion in 1995, up from $15.4 billion in 1994 (World Bank, 1996a, p. 170). Nevertheless, since the outbreak of the debt crisis there has been a tendency for the middle-income countries in sub-Saharan Africa to depend slightly more on commercial (private) external finance than was hitherto the case. Table 15 gives data on the structure and composition of sub-Saharan Africa's external debt by maturity and type of creditor, while Figures 5 and 6 provide graphical illustrations. In the second half of the 1980s, loans from the multilateral agencies, particularly the IMF, began to dry up. By 1989, net transfers from both the IMF and the World Bank had become negative. This means that sub-Saharan African countries were, on a net basis, transferring resources to the Bretton Woods institutions (Table 14). Since many sub-Saharan African countries are low-income countries, disbursements from the International Development Association have remained relatively buoyant, actually rising from $424 million in 1980 to $1.7 billion in 1989.

From 58.4 percent in 1980, the share of long-term debt rose to a peak of 82.2 percent in 1989 and thereafter declined slightly but

Table 15. Sub-Saharan Africa: Composition of External Debt, 1980–95

		Long-Term Debt				Use of IMF Credit		Short-Term Debt	
	Total External Debt	PPG	PNG	Total	Share of total debt (In percent)	Amount	Share of total debt (In percent)	Amount	Share of total debt (In percent)
1980	84.0	53.8	4.6	58.4	69.5	3.0	3.6	22.6	26.9
1988	165.0	130.7	4.8	135.5	82.1	7.0	4.3	22.5	13.6
1989	171.2	135.7	5.0	140.7	82.2	6.4	3.7	24.1	14.1
1990	190.3	149.8	5.3	155.1	81.5	6.6	3.5	28.6	15.0
1991	194.8	154.0	5.4	159.4	81.8	6.6	3.4	28.8	14.8
1992	192.8	149.3	5.1	154.4	80.1	6.4	3.3	32.0	16.6
1993	197.9	148.3	5.1	153.4	77.5	7.0	3.5	37.5	19.0
1994	212.4	159.5	5.6	165.1	77.7	7.9	3.7	39.4	18.6
1995	223.3	167.5	6.8	174.3	78.1	7.2	3.2	41.8	18.7

Source: World Bank, *World Debt Tables*, various issues.
Note: PPG, public and publicly guaranteed debt; PNG, private nonguaranteed debt.

Figure 5. Sub-Saharan Africa: Maturity Composition of External Debt, 1988–95
(In percent)

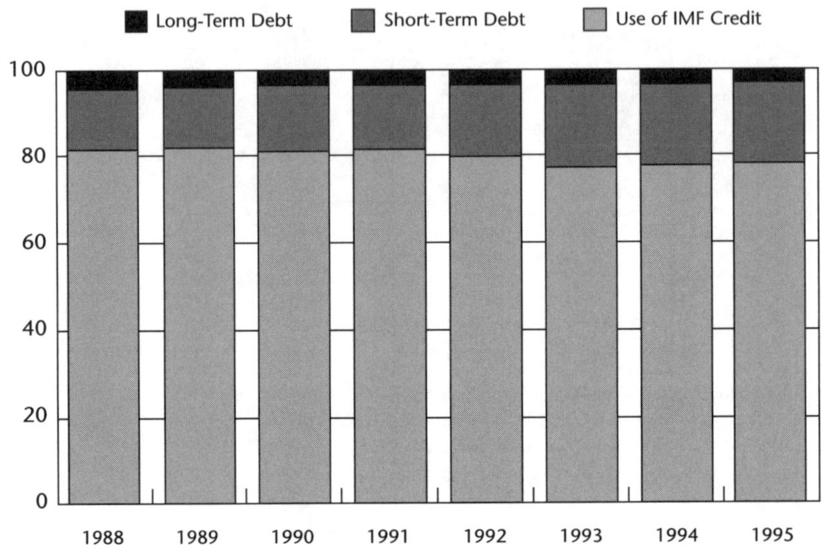

Source: World Bank, *World Debt Tables.*

steadily, reaching 81.8 percent in 1991. The share of short-term credit in total external debt fell from 26.9 percent in 1980 to 14.8 percent in 1991, while the share of IMF finance in the total debt declined from 3.6 percent in 1980 to only 3.4 percent in 1991. See Figure 5 for an illustration.

The severity of sub-Saharan Africa's problems is best appreciated by undertaking a comprehensive analysis of debt indicators. Debt indicators or debt ratios are measures of the debt burden. They can be used as analytical tools or for policy purposes; they may also be used for descriptive or predictive purposes (Nowzad and others, 1981). As a descriptive measure, external debt indicators provide in an understandable and functional way a history of the terms, structure, and scale of past borrowing. They may therefore be used in intertemporal analysis to examine the level and rate of change in debt capacity and debt-service capability.

In the analysis that follows, primary emphasis is given to an examination of the two most important debt indicators, the debt ratio and the debt-service ratio. Table 6 presented data concerning the key debt indicators for sub-Saharan Africa during the 1970–95 period, while Figure 2 provided a graphic illustration. The debt ratio is con-

Figure 6. Sub-Saharan Africa: Creditor Composition of External Debt, 1988–95
(In percent)

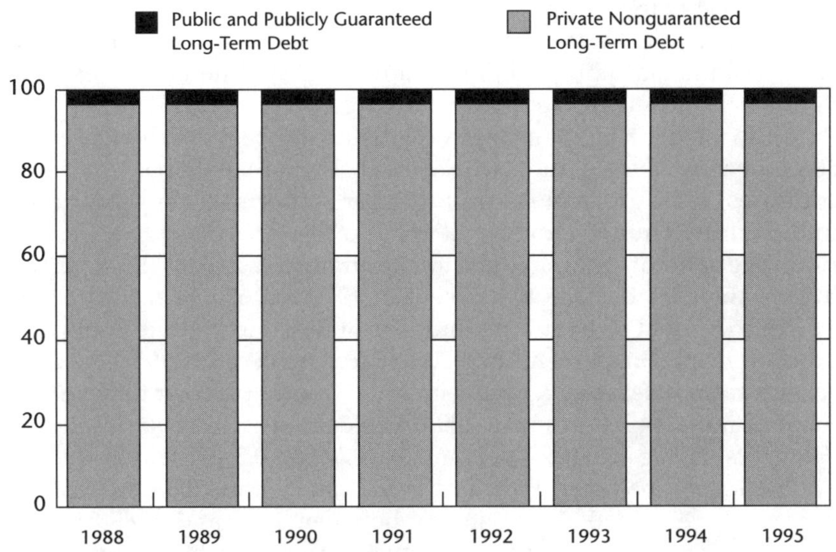

Source: World Bank, *World Debt Tables.*

ventionally measured by the ratio of total external debt to GDP, or of total external debt to export earnings of goods and services.[5] The debt-service ratio is conventionally measured by the ratio of debt-service payments to exports of goods and services. Table 6 shows that the ratio of external debt to GNP increased by half, from 20.5 percent to 30.7 percent, between 1970 and 1979. In the 1980s, Africa's "lost decade" of development opportunities, GNP declined. With external debt growing faster than GNP, the ratio of external debt to GNP increased sharply. Sub-Saharan Africa's debt-income ratio doubled in five years, rising from 28.7 percent in 1981 to 56.2 percent in 1986.

[5]There is some debate as to what variable should be used for normalization, that is, as the denominator of total external debt and debt-service payments. Taking a short-term view, exports of goods and services would appear to be the more appropriate scalar, as they are the main source of the foreign exchange resources that can be used to service debt. However, taking a longer-term view, GDP seems to be the appropriate scalar, since the foreign exchange constraint may be lessened by growth in the nontraded sector, provided prices are flexible (Nowzad and others, 1981). Iyoha (1991b) argues for using different scalars for total external debt and debt service: GDP should be used to normalize total external debt, and exports of goods and services as the denominator for debt-service payments. Thus the external debt–GDP ratio may be interpreted as a measure of debt capacity or debt burden and the debt-export ratio as a measure of debt-service capacity or debt-service burden.

The debt-income ratio then moderated but continued to rise in the late 1980s, reaching 70.8 percent in 1990. The 1990s witnessed a continued increase in the debt-income ratio, which peaked at 78.7 percent in 1994 before dipping to 74.1 percent in 1995.

The story told by the ratio of debt outstanding and disbursed to GNP is similar, although slightly more serious. Whereas the external debt–GNP ratio increased by 261.5 percent between 1970 and 1995, the ratio of debt outstanding and disbursed to GNP increased by 304.2 percent during the same period. In the sub-Saharan African countries, debt grew more rapidly than exports during the period under study. Thus, the debt-export ratio rose sharply during the period. The ratio of external debt to exports increased by 196.5 percent during the period, from 91 percent in 1970 to 269.8 percent in 1995. The ratio of debt outstanding and disbursed to exports rose by 233.1 percent, from 63.2 percent in 1970 to 210.5 percent in 1995. The debt-service ratio rose from 5.4 percent in 1970 to 22.0 percent in 1986 before falling to 14.7 percent in 1995. The debt-service ratio doubled in the 1970s, rising from 5.4 percent in 1970 to 10.3 percent in 1981. It doubled again between 1981 and 1986, rising from 10.3 percent to 22 percent. It remained rather steady between 1986 and 1988 and has fallen ever since (as a result of debt restructuring, debt reschedulings, and forgiveness of debt or interest), reaching a level of 14.7 percent in 1995.

This decline in debt-service payments hides more than it reveals. For many countries in the region, which are poor, highly indebted, and deficient in export earnings, there is often a wide divergence between actual and scheduled debt-service payments. Thus, there is generally a significant difference between the ratio of actual debt service to export earnings and that of scheduled debt service to export earnings (Table 17). Yet it is the ratio of scheduled debt to export earnings that is the more accurate measure of the pressure of debt service on export earnings and on the economy. According to Kapijimpanga (1996, p. 12),

> The external debt burden reflects itself in the inability of a country to meet its debt service obligations (scheduled debt service) in relation to its foreign currency earnings. In Eastern and Southern Africa, the respective figures for this ratio during 1994 were Ethiopia 53 percent; Kenya 51 percent; Madagascar 53 percent; Mozambique 91 percent; Tanzania 64 percent; Uganda 50 percent; Zambia 51 percent; and Zimbabwe 26 percent. It is evident from these figures that debt is a serious problem for many of these countries. Mozambique was supposed to pay 91 percent of its foreign exchange earnings to service its external debt. In reality, simply because of lack of resources, Mozambique only paid 23 percent during the year.

Thus, for sub-Saharan African countries at least, the actual ratio of debt service to exports grossly underestimates the true nature of the debt burden and the debt crisis.[6]

Without exception, there was a deterioration in all the debt indicators during the period under study. The debt burden increased while the debt-service capacity deteriorated. Klein (1987) has further pointed out that some low-income African countries have been unable to repay debt rescheduled with a standard ten-year maturity, even with a five-year grace period. Increasingly, many countries are being compelled to reschedule already rescheduled debt, and being forced to borrow to pay interest on past borrowing, thus escalating total debt and falling deeper into the debt trap.

The severity of the debt crisis in sub-Saharan Africa may be better appreciated when it is realized that, since 1982, external debt has been escalating at a time of massive decline in export revenues and dwindling capital inflows. According to Drouin (1989, p. 3), "over the last decade, the foreign debt burden of the region grew worse than that of any other category of country facing debt servicing problems." Also, Gonçalves asserts (1996, p. 5), that

> the devastating impact of debt on the fragile African economies can easily be illustrated by revelations that Uganda, for example, spends only US$3 per person on health compared to US$17 per person on debt payments. From 1990 to 1993, Zambia spent 35 times more on debt payments than it did on primary school education.

Indeed, relative to exports and economic activity, sub-Saharan Africa's debt is among the highest of any region in the world (Iyoha and Iyare, 1994). Table 16 presents data on debt indicators for developing countries by region. It is easily verified that, in the early 1990s, sub-Saharan Africa's debt-export ratio was higher than that of any region except Latin America and the Caribbean. By 1995, its debt-export ratio, at 269.8 percent, was the highest of any region.

The fiscal dimension of the debt burden also needs to be highlighted. Given that the composition of debt is heavily tilted to the public domain, responsibility for debt service also falls heavily on the public sector. The heavy debt-service payments have inevitably put great pressure on the budget, leading to rising fiscal deficits in the highly indebted countries. This leads to several problems. The

---

[6]The ratio of international reserves to total external debt, which reached 27.3 percent in 1980, collapsed during the period—falling to a low of 6.3 percent in 1988—but recovered slightly to 8.2 percent in 1994. The reserves-import ratio deteriorated during the period, falling from 3 months in 1980 to a low of 1.5 months in 1988 before recovering to 2.1 months in 1994.

Table 16. Comparative Debt Indicators by Developing Region, 1990–95
(In percent)

	Share of Total Debt,	Debt-Export Ratio					
	1995	1990	1991	1992	1993	1994	1995[1]
All developing countries	100	161.6	175.3	166.7	168.6	162.8	150.0
Sub-Saharan Africa	11	225.7	239.4	235.6	251.9	265.7	269.8
East Asia and the Pacific	23	106.6	106.0	101.6	101.3	93.3	83.3
South Asia	8	315.9	311.7	319.4	287.9	271.6	245.7
Europe and Central Asia	18	120.2	157.8	143.6	151.5	153.7	144.6
Latin America and the Caribbean	29	277.4	282.0	276.2	274.6	258.6	254.2
Middle East and North Africa	11	109.8	129.2	126.1	134.5	148.5	136.9

Source: World Bank (1996a).
Note: Data are based on nominal debt stock at end of year.
[1]Preliminary.

first is that taxes need to be increased in order to raise the resources (in domestic currency) to service the debt. One of the consequences of the anticipated tax burden is to depress investment—the debt overhang effect. Second, it is necessary to transform the domestic resources into foreign exchange, in which debt service must be paid. The desperate demand for foreign exchange to service debt often results in aid resources being routinely diverted to finance debt-service payments. Third, the stiff demand of high debt-service payments on the budget results in forced reductions in public investment and reduced spending on education and health. The diversion of resources from public investment to debt service is related to the crowding out hypothesis. Thus, pressures of debt service have relevance for the fiscal sustainability of debt in addition to the sustainability of high investment, as demonstrated in the debt overhang and crowding out of investment. Certainly, the brutal pressure of debt service on the budget explains not only the escalating budget deficits but also the increasingly large discrepancy between actual and scheduled debt-service payments in many sub-Saharan African countries. Growth is bound to be retarded because of the depressing effect on investment of heavy debt-service payments and the reduction of growth-supporting government expenditures.

As matters now stand, sub-Saharan African countries are constrained to use approximately 20 percent of their export earnings for debt servicing. Since the foreign exchange earnings of many of these countries are inadequate to begin with, it is apparent that reducing the already insufficient amount by 20 percent leaves grossly inadequate resources for financing development.[7] This is why a study by the United Nations Economic Commission for Africa (1991, p. 10) concluded that

> It is increasingly clear that very little progress, if any, can be made in Africa without the resolution of the debt crisis; and that there is no way in which Africa can service its existing debt and still have resources left for development financing.

There is a growing consensus among analysts on the need to go beyond traditional debt relief mechanisms (which consist mainly of IMF and World Bank loans and Paris Club[8] reschedulings). Indeed, it is increasingly clear that for highly indebted low-income countries in sub-Saharan Africa, even the full use of traditional debt relief mechanisms would continue to prove insufficient in helping them achieve debt sustainability. As a result, many now believe that it is necessary to go beyond traditional debt relief mechanisms if many sub-Saharan African countries are to achieve sustainable debt levels within reasonable time horizons. In particular, because of the inadequate relief offered by debt reschedulings, some analysts now consider debt forgiveness or debt cancellation as the most appropriate way of reducing the debt burden of heavily indebted low-income countries. According to Ogbe (1992, p. 29),

> Debt forgiveness or cancellation is, no doubt, the most complete and effective strategy of debt relief. The principal debt is not only extinguished but also the steady accumulation of debt that comes from repeated debt rescheduling and the resulting capitalization of interest and arrears are eradicated. Moreover, the sizeable administrative and financial burdens associated with periodic debt rescheduling are also eliminated.

---

[7]This is why Goran Ohlin (1966) maintains that a poor country has no debt-servicing capacity at all. According to Ohlin, for low-income developing countries, debt service competes with essential imports for foreign exchange earnings, which are insufficient to begin with, and with the investment needs of the country for savings, which are often deficient and inadequate. Besides, high debt-service ratios make a country extremely vulnerable to pressures on its balance of payments, further hampering the development effort.

[8]The Paris Club of creditors represents only government-guaranteed creditors. Its membership includes Canada, Germany, France, the United Kingdom, and the United States. These governments guarantee the export activities of their nationals through their official export credit agencies. The first Paris Club meeting was held in 1956. Meetings are held to discuss repayment problems and negotiate debt relief agreements for debtor nations. The London Club of creditors deals with uninsured and unguaranteed debts extended by commercial banks to nationals of debtor countries. Thus, the members are commercial banks based in the industrial countries. The first London Club meeting was held in 1976. Meetings are called to discuss repayment problems and conclude restructuring agreements with debtor nations.

A Model of External Debt and Growth in Sub-Saharan Africa

This section presents a small macroeconometric model that permits simulation of the effect of external debt on economic growth in sub-Saharan African countries. The basic macroeconometric simulation model consists of four equations, of which two are stochastic and two are identities. The two stochastic equations relate to the production function (output equation) and an investment demand equation incorporating a debt overhang variable and a variable designed to capture the crowding-out effect of debt-service payments. The third equation is a capital accumulation identity, and the fourth equation is a debt accumulation identity.

The Output Equation

The inspiration for the output equation used in this study is neoclassical, tracing its roots to Solow (1957), who hypothesized that output depended on capital and labor inputs and on disembodied technical change. It also owes much to the modifications introduced by development economists, particularly Chenery and his associates (for example, Chenery and Strout, 1966), who emphasized the role of investment and the investment-income ratio. This combination is now becoming standard in the development literature, and variations of the model have been used by Oseghale and Amenkhienan (1987), Ram (1985), Mjema (1996), Iyoha (1995, 1997), Khan and Kumar (1993), and Pindyck and Solimano (1993). In this study it is hypothesized that output depends on labor and investment per capita (used as a proxy for the capital stock). Thus, the output equation to be estimated econometrically using time series data is

$$\ln GDP = a_0 + a_1 \ln L + a_2 \ln PCI + e_t, \tag{1}$$

where GDP is gross domestic product, L the labor force, and PCI per capita gross domestic investment; ln stands for the natural logarithm, e_t is the random error term (assumed to be Gaussian white noise), $a_1 > 0$ is the elasticity of output with respect to labor, and $a_2 > 0$ is the elasticity of output with respect to investment per head.

Equation (1) was estimated using the ordinary least-squares regression method for the period 1970–94. From preliminary calculations it was found that the one-period lagged value of PCI gave better and more consistent results than its contemporaneous value. It was therefore decided to use PCI_{t-1} in place of PCI_t. The estimated output equation obtained is

$$\ln GDP = 6.32 + 1.04\ln L + 0.13\ln PCI_{t-1} \quad (2)$$
$$(16.6)\ (19.5)\qquad (4.2)$$

$R^2 = 0.964$ $\bar{R}^2 = 0.96$ $F(2, 21) = 279$

SEE = 0.03

Mean of dependent variable = 12.266

D-W statistic = 0.58

where t-values are reported in parentheses below the coefficients. Given the value of the R^2, it can be concluded that the two independent variables (labor and per capita investment) together explain over 96 percent of the systematic variations in output during the period being studied. The F value of 279 passes the significance test at the 1 percent level. Thus, the hypothesis of a significant linear relationship between output and the two independent variables is validated. The signs of both coefficients are correct, and the t-values of the two independent variables are highly significant; both pass the two-tailed test of significance at the 1 percent level. The high significance of $\ln PCI_{t-1}$ suggests the existence of a distributed lag relationship. In other words, investment affects output with a lag. However, the Durbin-Watson statistic is very low, indicating positive first-order serial correlation.

In an attempt to correct for autocorrelation, we experimented with both first-order and second-order autoregressive schemes using both the Cochrane-Orcutt method and the Newton-Raphson iterative inverse interpolation method (Pesaran and Pesaran, 1991). The most satisfactory results were obtained with a first-order autoregressive scheme using the Newton-Raphson method. It converged after only seven iterations. The estimated regression set of equation is

$$\ln GDP = 6.97 + 0.97\ln L + 0.05\ln PCI_{t-1} \quad (3)$$
$$(11.1)\ (8.5)\qquad (1.62)$$

$$U_t = 0.89U_{t-1} \quad (4)$$
$$(9.6)$$

$R^2 = 0.984$ $\bar{R}^2 = 0.98 F(3, 20) = 408$

SEE = 0.02

Mean of dependent variable = 12.266

D-W statistic = 1.73

where, as before, t-values are reported below the coefficients. An examination of Equations (3) and (4) confirms that we have improved on Equation (2). The serial correlation has been eliminated, as indicated by a Durbin-Watson statistic of 1.73. The first-order autoregressive parameter, $\hat{\rho}$, lies between zero and unity in absolute value. Its t-value is

Figure 7. Sub-Saharan Africa: Actual and Fitted Values of GDP, 1971–94
(In logarithmic values)

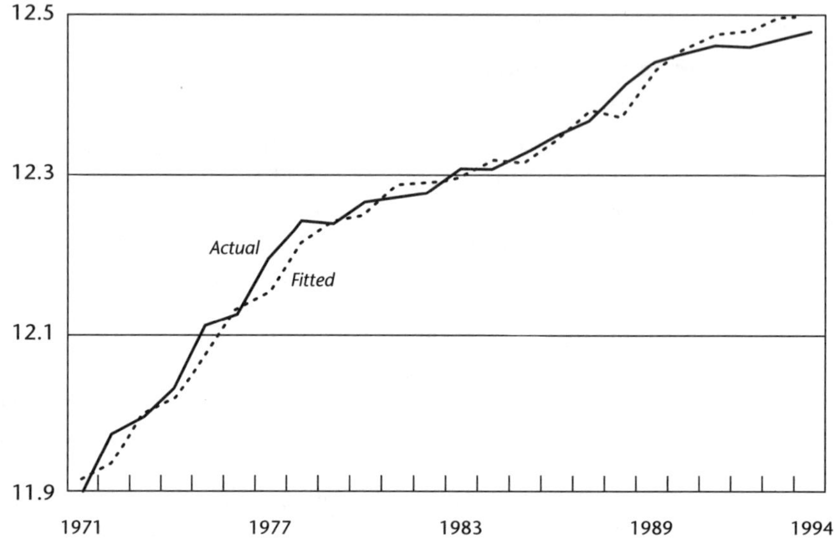

Source: Author's calculations.

significantly different from zero at the 1 percent level. With an R^2 of 0.984, it is apparent that we are able to explain over 98 percent of the systematic variation in GDP by the two independent variables. Both variables are correctly signed. The labor force variable passes the significance test at the 1 percent level, but investment fails the significance test at the usual 5 percent level. It nevertheless passes the test at the 10 percent level. The *F*-statistic of 408 is significant at the 1 percent level. Thus the hypothesis of a significant linear relationship between GDP and the two regressors is validated. A plot of actual and fitted values of ln*GDP* is given in Figure 7.

The Investment Equation

Gross domestic investment collapsed in sub-Saharan Africa in the 1980s, especially starting from 1983. According to World Bank data, from a level of $44 billion in 1981, gross domestic investment rapidly fell to a low of $23 billion in 1984. From that level it rose slowly, reaching $37.6 billion in 1991. According to the World Bank (1994b), the average annual growth rate of gross domestic investment was 5.1 percent over 1970–80 but was –3 percent between 1980 and 1992.

As may be expected, the investment-GDP ratio also declined sharply. In analyzing the movement of the investment-GDP ratio, the World Bank (1992a) shows that while the annual average ratio was 21.5 percent in 1975–79, it collapsed to 15.6 percent during 1980–85. Indeed, if the period 1983–86 is considered, it is found that the average investment-GDP ratio was only 13 percent. In fact, from a ratio of 26 percent of GDP in 1977, the investment ratio had fallen to a catastrophic 12.8 percent in 1984. No doubt a fall in gross domestic saving partly accounts for this. World Bank (1992a) statistics show that the ratio of gross domestic saving to GDP, which averaged 18.9 percent between 1975 and 1979, had fallen to 13.4 percent between 1980 and 1985. Many analysts believe that the poor investment and growth performance of many highly indebted developing countries (including those in sub-Saharan Africa) since the onset of the global debt crisis in 1982 can be attributed in part to the disincentive effect of their external debt burden. This phenomenon is often referred to as the debt overhang problem. The debt overhang hypothesis posits that the accumulated external debt of these countries acts as a tax on future output and thus discourages private investment. The theoretical case for the debt overhang effect has been made by several authors, including Dooley (1986), Krugman (1988), Sachs (1989), Froot (1989), and Calvo (1989). Some attempts have also been made to test the hypothesis empirically. Among these are Sachs (1989), Claessens (1990), Borensztein (1990, 1991), Cohen (1990), Warner (1992), Degefe (1992), Savvides (1992), Chhibber and Pahwa (1994), and Iyoha (1997). Researchers like Sachs (1989) and Krugman (1988) have also analyzed the crowding-out effect of debt-service payments. This arises from the fact that many highly indebted poor countries frequently divert resources, including foreign aid and other foreign exchange resources, to take care of pressing debt-service obligations, particularly debt owed to the multilateral financial institutions, which are deemed nonreschedulable.

Borensztein (1990) provided a major and interesting attempt to empirically test the debt overhang effect. Using data for the Philippines, he found that the debt overhang hypothesis was largely valid. Specifically, he found that the debt overhang had an adverse effect on private investment, which was strongest when private debt, rather than total debt, was used as a measure of debt overhang.

Following Sachs (1989), Krugman (1988), Borensztein (1990), Chhibber and Pahwa (1994), and Iyoha (1995, 1997), we specify an investment demand function that has its roots in neoclassical optimization theory. We also make allowance for the potential existence of both a debt overhang effect and a crowding-out effect of external debt. Finally, we allow for the possible existence of an investment accelerator effect. In the specification, investment per capita is hypothesized to depend negatively on domestic interest rates, positively on the marginal product of capital, negatively on the price of investment goods, positively on growth in real GDP, negatively on the external debt-income ratio, and negatively on the ratio of debt service to exports. Thus, the basic specification of the investment demand function is given by

$$PCI = b_0 + b_1 r + b_2 MPK + b_3 P_I + b_4 GDPGR + b_5(D/Y) + b_6(DS/X) + u. \tag{5}$$

The a priori signs for the coefficients are $b_1 < 0$, $b_2 > 0$, $b_3 < 0$, $b_4 > 0$, $b_5 < 0$, and $b_6 < 0$. *PCI* is per capita gross domestic investment; *r* is the interest rate (the commercial lending rate); *MPK* is the marginal product of capital;[9] P^I is the price of investment goods; *GDPGR* is the growth rate of real output, which is expected to capture the investment accelerator effect; *D/Y* is the ratio of the external debt stock to GNP, which is the usual measure of debt overhang; *DS/X* is the ratio of total debt-service payments to exports of goods and services, which is expected to capture the crowding-out effect of external debt; and *u* is a stochastic error term assumed to be Gaussian white noise.

Some researchers, including Borensztein (1990), have suggested that the debt overhang effect should be particularly strong when considering private investment and private debt. This hypothesis could not be tested in this study for lack of the requisite data.[10]

From preliminary ordinary least-squares regression calculations, it was found that the partial regression coefficient of the price of investment goods (P^I) in Equation (5) was not statistically significant, and the variable was therefore dropped in the final equation. The one-period-lagged values of the interest rate and the debt-GNP ratio were also found to give better and more consistent results than their contemporaneous values. It was therefore decided to use r_{t-1} in place of r_t and D/Y_{t-1} in place of D/Y_t. The amended equation was then estimated by the ordinary least-squares technique, and the following results were obtained:[11]

[9]Following Borensztein (1990), we approximate *MPK* by the real average product of capital multiplied by the relative share of capital in output. The capital stock and *MPK* series used are available on request.

[10]Iyoha (1997) also finds econometric evidence of a private debt overhang for Nigeria: there is both a debt overhang and a crowding-out effect with respect to private investment. Thus, the evidence is that heavy debt-service payments do crowd out (that is, reduce) not only public investment but also private investment.

[11]The following alternative estimate was obtained using *D/XGS* instead of *D/Y* as a measure of the debt overhang:

$$\begin{aligned} PCI = &-101.9 + 3.3r_{t-1} + 403.6MPK \\ &(-1.58)(2.36) \qquad (3.53) \\ &+ 1.69GDPGR - 0.303\,(D/XGS)_{t-1} - 1.19(DS/X) \\ &(1.52) \qquad (-3.1) \qquad (-1.66) \end{aligned}$$

$$PCI = -122.9 + 3.5r_{t-1} + 406.6MPK + 2.1GDPGR \qquad (6)$$
$$(-1.8)\ (2.4) \qquad (3.6) \qquad (1.9)$$
$$-0.7(D/Y)_{t-1} - 2.5(DS/X)$$
$$(-3.1) \qquad (-4.3)$$

$R^2 = 0.88$ $\qquad \bar{R}^2 = 0.84$ $\qquad F(5, 18) = 26$

SEE = 9.49

Mean of dependent variable = 78.33

D-W statistic = 1.4.

In Equation (6), t-values are again given in parentheses below each coefficient. Judging from the value of R^2, it can be concluded that the independent variables in this equation explain over 87 percent of the systematic variations in per capita gross domestic investment during the period under study. The F-value of 26 is significant at the 1 percent level, indicating that there is a significant linear relationship between the independent variables taken together and per capita investment. All the signs are correct except that of the interest rate. Of the four correctly signed independent variables, three (*MPK*, the debt-income ratio, and the debt-service ratio) pass the significance test at the 1 percent level. The fourth variable, the growth rate of real GDP, misses the two-tailed test of significance at the traditional 5 percent level. It nevertheless passes the significance test at the 8 percent level. Thus, there is some evidence of an investment accelerator effect, but it is not very strong. Since the debt overhang variable (D/Y) and the crowding-out effect variable (DS/X) are highly significant, there is clear evidence of both effects. Since their signs are negative, as postulated, their effect is to depress the level of investment. However, the D-W statistic shows evidence of serial correlation.

In an attempt to correct for autocorrelation, we experimented with both first-order and second-order autoregressive schemes using both the Cochrane-Orcutt method and the Newton-Raphson iterative method. The most satisfactory results were obtained with a second-order autoregressive scheme using the Newton-Raphson iterative method.

$R^2 = 0.878$ $\qquad \bar{R}^2 = 0.84$ $\qquad F(5, 18) = 25.9$
SEE = 9.5
Mean of dependent variable = 78.33
D-W statistic = 1.35.

A comparison of the two equations shows that the fits are similar, although the equation with D/Y is slightly better since both the debt overhang variable and the crowding-out variable are significantly different from zero. Therefore, the equation in the text, using D/Y as the debt overhang variable, is preferred.

It converged after only nine iterations. The estimated regression equation was

$$\begin{aligned} PCI = &-120 + 2.3r_{t-1} + 450MPK + 1.4GDPGR \\ &(-1.8)\ (1.5)\qquad (3.4)\qquad (1.7) \\ &-0.6(D/Y)_{t-1} - 2.0(DS/X) \\ &(-2.2)\qquad\quad (-3.2) \end{aligned} \tag{7}$$

$$\begin{aligned} U_t = &\ 0.49U_{t-1} - 0.32U_{t-2} \\ &(2.5)\qquad (-1.6) \end{aligned} \tag{8}$$

$R^2 = 0.9$ $\bar{R}^2 = 0.86$ $F(7, 16) = 20.7$

SEE = 9.11

Mean of dependent variable = 78.33

D-W statistic = 2.09

where t-values are reported in parentheses below the coefficients. An examination of Equations (7) and (8) confirms that we have improved upon Equation (6). The serial correlation has been removed as indicated by a D-W statistic of 2.09. The second-order autoregressive parameters, $\hat{\rho}_1$ and $\hat{\rho}_2$, lie between zero and unity in absolute value. Their t-values are significantly different from zero at the 2 percent and the 12 percent level, respectively. With an R^2 of 0.9, it is clear that we are able to explain 90 percent of the systematic variation in per capita gross domestic investment by the five independent variables. All the variables except the interest rate have the correct signs, but only three are significantly different from zero, at traditional levels of significance. *MPK* passes the significance test at the 1 percent level. The debt-service ratio is also significantly different from zero, using a two-tailed test, at the 1 percent level. The debt overhang variable (D/Y) passes the significance test at the 5 percent level. The investment accelerator variable (*GDPGR*) only passes the two-tailed significance test at the 10 percent level. The F-statistic of 20.7 is significant at the 1 percent level. Thus, the hypothesis of a significant linear relationship between per capita investment and the five independent variables is validated. A plot of actual and fitted values of per capita investment is given in Figure 8.

The results offer a confirmation of the debt overhang hypothesis for the sub-Saharan African countries. The debt overhang variable, proxied by the ratio of external debt to GNP, is negative and highly significant. The elasticity[12] of investment with respect to the debt overhang

[12]Since this is a linear equation, the elasticity-at-the-mean of a given independent variable is obtained as the coefficient of that variable multiplied by its mean and divided by the mean of the dependent variable.

Figure 8. Sub-Saharan Africa: Actual and Fitted Values of Per Capita Investment, 1971–94
(In 1987 U.S. dollars)

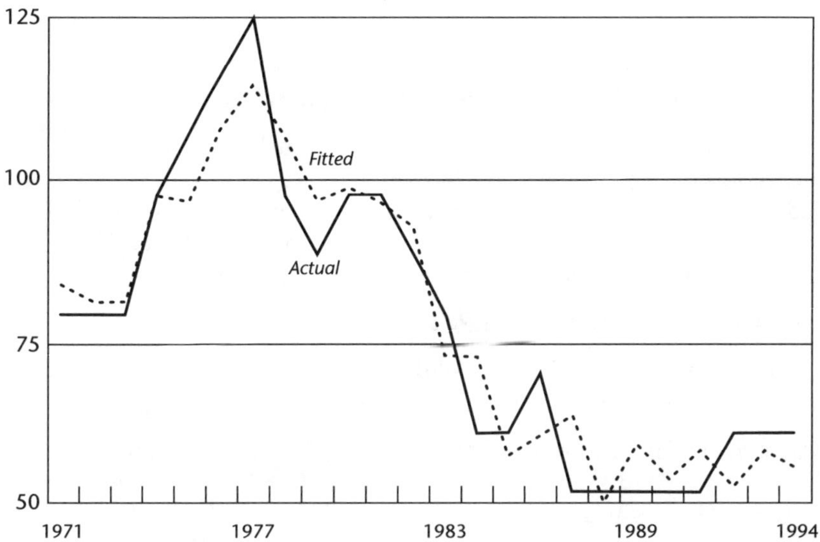

Source: Author's calculations.

variable is –0.337. Thus, a 10 percent decrease in the debt-GNP ratio will lead to approximately a 3 percent increase in investment per capita. Notice that the debt-income ratio affects investment with a lag. The effect of the combination of this lagged response of investment to changes in the debt level and the lagged response of output to changes in investment (arising inter alia from gestation lags) means that the impact of a reduction in the debt stock on output will not be instantaneous. Rather, it will manifest after some time lag.

The results also provide confirmation of a crowding-out effect in sub-Saharan African countries. The coefficient of the crowding-out effect variable, proxied by the ratio of total debt-service payments to exports of goods and services, is negative and significantly different from zero at the 1 percent level. The elasticity of investment with respect to the crowding-out variable is –0.335. Thus, a 10 percent reduction in the debt-service ratio would increase investment by approximately 3 percent.

To summarize, we find, using econometric techniques, that sub-Saharan Africa's heavy external debt stock and debt-service payments act to reduce investment through both the debt overhang effect and the crowding-out effect. There is evidence of a distributed lagged response of investment to changes in the debt-income ratio (and of a distributed lagged response of output to changes in investment). Thus, reductions in debt stock will affect investment and output after some lag in time (rather than instantaneously).

A Simultaneous-Equations Model of External Debt and Economic Growth in Sub-Saharan Africa

To make explicit allowance for interaction between external debt and economic growth, a simultaneous-equations model is now specified. In particular, the output equation and investment demand function are considered as a system of simultaneous equations. The simultaneous-equations system is given by these modified equations:

$$\ln GDP = a_0 + a_1 \ln L + a_2 \ln PCI + u_{1t} \quad (9)$$

$$PCI = b_0 + b_1 r_{t-1} + b_2 MPK + b_3 \ln GDP + b_4 GDPGR + b_5 (D/Y)_{t-1} + b_6 (DS/X) + u_{2t}, \quad (10)$$

where u_{1t} and u_{2t} are stochastic error terms. In this system of equations, there are two endogenous variables, ln*GDP* and *PCI*. There are seven predetermined variables: ln*L*, ln*PCI*, r_{t-1}, *MPK*, *GDPGR*, $(D/Y)_{t-1}$, and *DS*/*X*. Using the order condition of identification, it can be ascertained that both equations are overidentified. The two-stage least-squares regression method can therefore be used to estimate the equations of the model. Given the identification status of the equations, econometric theory assures us that the resulting estimates of the structural coefficients will be consistent and asymptotically efficient.

Using the two-stage least-squares technique, the following estimates were obtained, with *t*-values reported in parentheses below the coefficients:

$$\underset{}{\ln GDP} = \underset{(13.1)}{6.86} + \underset{(13.8)}{0.93 \ln L} + \underset{(2.72)}{0.13 \ln PCI} \quad (11)$$

$R^2 = 0.943$ $\bar{R}^2 = 0.938$ $F(2, 21) = 173$

SEE = 0.039

Mean of dependent variable = 12.26

D-W statistic = 1.02

$$PCI = \underset{(-1.7)}{-1993} - \underset{(-0.37)}{1.22 r_{t-1}} - \underset{(-0.29)}{96 MPK} + \underset{(1.61)}{101 \ln GDP} + \underset{(2.22)}{2.38 GDPGR} - \underset{(-2.66)}{2.38 (D/Y)_{t-1}} - \underset{(-3.2)}{2.0 (DS/X)} \quad (12)$$

$R^2 = 0.9$ $\bar{R}^2 = 0.86$ $F(6, 17) = 25$

SEE = 8.96

Mean of dependent variable = 78.33

D-W statistic = 1.85.

To test whether it makes much difference empirically which definition of debt is used—total external debt stock (*EDT*) or debt outstanding and disbursed (*DOD*)—the system of equations was reestimated using *DOD*/*GNP* instead of *EDT*/*GNP* as the measure of debt overhang. The estimated results using *DOD* instead of *EDT* (with *t*-values in parentheses under the coefficients) were

$$\underset{}{\ln GDP} = \underset{(22.3)}{7.34} + \underset{(19.7)}{0.87\ln L} + \underset{(3.2)}{0.91\ln PCI} \qquad (13)$$

$R^2 = 0.96$ $\bar{R}^2 = 0.956$ $F(2, 21) = 250$

SEE = 0.03

Mean of dependent variable = 12.26

D-W statistic = 0.78.

$$PCI = \underset{(-2.1)}{-2373} \underset{(-0.88)}{- 2.92r_{t-1}} \underset{(-0.71)}{- 232.2MPK} + \underset{(2.0)}{218.7\ln GDP}$$

$$+ \underset{(2.31)}{2.33GDPGR} \underset{(-3.1)}{- 2.0\,(DOD/Y)_{t-1}} \underset{(-2.34)}{- 1.53(DS/X)} \qquad (14)$$

$R^2 = 0.909$ $\bar{R}^2 = 0.876$ $F(6, 17) = 28.2$

SEE = 8.465

Mean of dependent variable = 78.33

D-W statistic = 1.84.

A comparison of Equations (12) and (14) shows that the overall fits are about the same.[13] Also, the same variables—*GDPGR*, the debt-income ratio, and the debt-service ratio—are significant in both. Thus, there is little difference as to whether we use *EDT* or *DOD* as our measure of debt. However, we choose to use *EDT* since it is a broader and more comprehensive measure of external debt.

Capital Accumulation Identity

This is one of the two identities used to close the model. This study uses the basic empirical relationship between the capital stock and investment: abstracting from depreciation, change in the capital stock is

[13]The estimated coefficients for the output equation in the two sets are identical because the system is recursive.

equal to investment. After including depreciation, which has the effect of reducing the capital stock, the capital accumulation identity is specified as

$$KSTOCK = (1 - \delta)\ KSTOCK\ (-1) + INV, \quad (15)$$

where δ is the average rate of depreciation of capital in sub-Saharan Africa,[14] *KSTOCK* is the capital stock, and *INV* is investment.

Debt Accumulation Identity

The model is closed with a second identity, a debt accumulation identity. Given knowledge of the debt situation in sub-Saharan Africa, it was decided to use the following identity:

$$DTOTAL = (1 + AVINT)\ DTOTAL\ (-1) - DSPAY, \quad (16)$$

where *DTOTAL* is total debt, *DSPAY* is total debt-service payments, and *AVINT* is average interest paid on debt.

Simulation Results

In the course of this econometric study, both a historical simulation and a policy simulation were undertaken. These are discussed in turn.

Historical Simulation

A historical simulation, also called an ex post simulation, is performed over the estimation period of a macroeconometric model. The main reasons for historical simulation are model validation and evaluation. A comparison of the actual or historical series for the endogenous variables with the simulated series for the same variables is often used to test the validity of a macroeconometric model. Such a comparison allows an analyst or policymaker to determine how well a macroeconometric model tracks the economy and, specifically, how well each simulated data series tracks or approximates the corresponding actual series. Measures used to test how closely a simulated series of an endogenous variable tracks its corresponding historical series include

- the root-mean-square (rms) simulation error;
- the root-mean-square percent error; and

[14]In the empirical work, a depreciation rate of 7 percent was found to give satisfactory results.

• Theil's inequality coefficient, U.[15]

In this study, the root-mean-square simulation error and Theil's inequality coefficient (Theil, 1978, p. 368) are used in addition to the correlation coefficient between the actual and simulated data series. To achieve a more efficient simulation and obtain richer results, the number of endogenous variables was increased to seven by specifying identities for the logarithm of per capita investment, the debt-GNP ratio, and the debt-service ratio.

Dynamic simulation was then undertaken. Simulations were done for the seven endogenous variables: the logarithm of GDP, per capita investment, total external debt, the debt-GNP ratio, the debt-service ratio, the logarithm of per capita investment, and the capital stock. Graphical representations of the historical simulations for output and investment are shown in Figures 9 and 10, respectively. Table 17 contains summary statistics for the historical simulations—the correlation coefficient, root-mean-square error, and Theil's inequality coefficient—for five key endogenous variables. Notice that the values for Theil's inequality coefficient for output and investment are close to zero, signifying a close fit between the simulated and actual series of the two variables. Also, the correlation coefficients between their simulated and actual series are 97 percent and 85 percent, respectively.

Policy Simulation

Policy simulation is the term applied to experimentation with a macro econometric model using alternative policy scenarios. In this study the main objective of the policy simulation exercise was to examine the effect of debt stock reduction on the endogenous variables, particularly investment and output. Results of this type of simulation for Nigeria were recently reported by Chhibber and Pahwa (1994) and by Iyoha (1997). As

[15]The three measures are defined thus:

$$\text{rms error} = \sqrt{\frac{1}{T}\sum_{t=1}^{T}(Y_t^s - Y_t^a)^2}$$

$$\text{rms percent error} = \sqrt{\frac{1}{T}\sum_{t=1}^{T}\left(\frac{Y_t^s - Y_t^a}{Y_t^a}\right)^2}$$

$$U = \frac{\sqrt{\frac{1}{T}\sum_{t=1}^{T}(Y_t^s - Y_t^a)^2}}{\sqrt{\frac{1}{T}\sum_{1-t}^{T}(Y_t^s)^2} + \sqrt{\frac{1}{T}\sum_{1-t}^{T}(Y_t^a)^2}}$$

Table 17. Historical Simulation: Summary Statistics

Variable	Correlation Coefficient	Root-Mean-Square Error	Theil's Inequality Coefficient 1961	Theil's Inequality Coefficient 1966
GDP	0.97	0.04	0.0016	0.003
Investment	0.85	13.09	0.081	0.160
Debt	0.94	30.58	0.132	0.254
Debt-GNP ratio	0.91	12.93	0.138	0.261
Debt-service ratio	0.78	3.73	0.132	0.264

Source: Author's calculations.

an illustrative example, this study considers policy scenarios of a reduction of 40 percent, 50 percent, and 75 percent in the external debt stock effective from 1986. Dynamic simulations for the 1987–94 period were then undertaken to investigate the effects of the various packages of debt stock reduction on key endogenous variables. In the simulations, it was assumed that a given debt stock reduction led to a corresponding reduction in the debt-service ratio after a one-year lag.

Figure 9. Sub-Saharan Africa: Actual and Dynamically Simulated Values of GDP, 1971–94
(In logarithmic values)

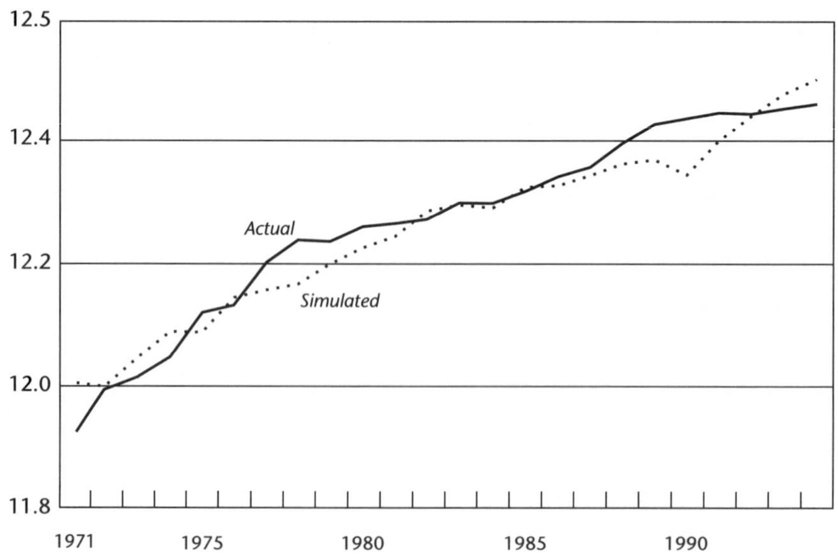

Source: Author's calculations.

Figure 10. Sub-Saharan Africa: Actual and Dynamically Simulated Values of Per Capita Investment, 1971–94
(In 1987 U.S. dollars)

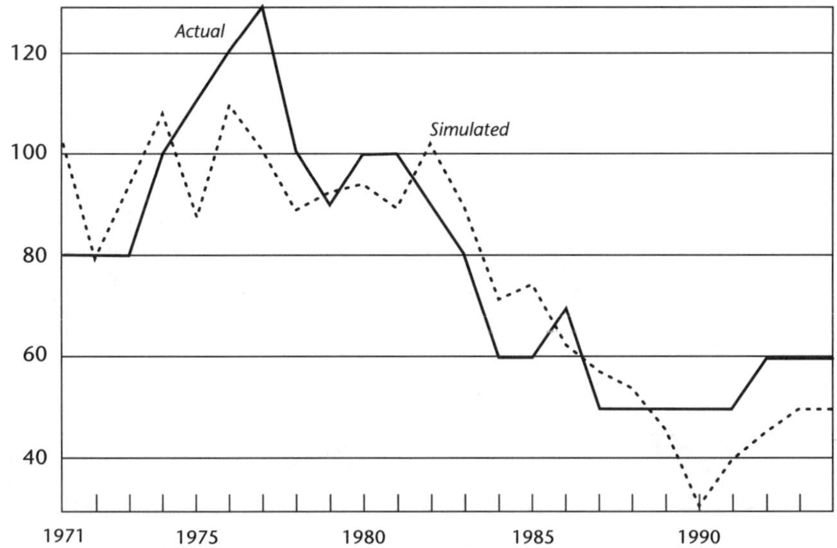

Source: Author's calculations.

The simulation results came out as expected. A reduction in the debt stock led to a rise in per capita investment, an increase in GDP, a fall in total external debt, a fall in the debt GNP ratio, and a fall in the debt-service ratio. The results of the policy simulations are summarized in Tables 18, 19 and 20, and graphs of the simulations of output and investment with a 75 percent debt reduction are presented in Figures 11 and 12, respectively.

An analysis of the results reported in Table 18 shows that, between 1987 and 1994, simulated average per capita investment without a debt stock reduction was $53.57. We may then compare this outcome with an average per capita investment of $58.88 if the debt stock is reduced by 40 percent; $67.23 if the debt stock is reduced by 50 percent; and $86.12 if the debt stock is reduced by 75 percent. Thus, a 75 percent[16] reduction in the debt stock in 1986 would have increased per capita investment during the 1987–94 period by 60 percent, on average.

An examination of Table 19 indicates that the simulated average level of ln*GDP* without debt stock reduction was 12.42. If the external debt

[16]A 75 percent reduction in the debt stock is close to the effective debt reduction for which low-income highly indebted countries are eligible under the Naples terms of December 1994 (Central Bank of Nigeria, 1996, p. 10).

Figure 11. Sub-Saharan Africa: Simulation of GDP With and Without a 75 Percent Debt Stock Reduction, 1971–94
(In logarithmic values)

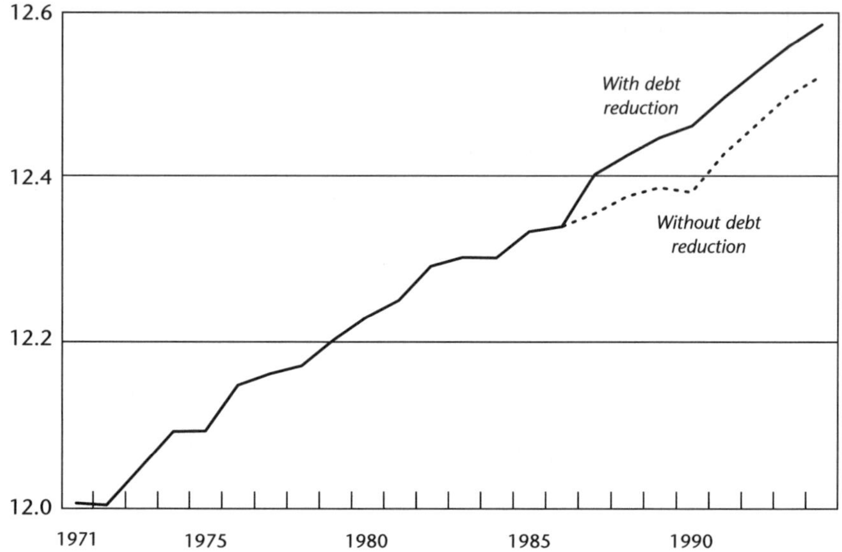

Source: Author's calculations.

stock had been reduced by 40 percent in 1986, the average level of ln*GDP* during 1987–94 would have risen to 12.44. If the external debt stock had been reduced by 50 percent, the average level of ln*GDP* would have increased to 12.45, and if the external debt stock had been reduced by 75 percent, the average level of ln*GDP* during the subsequent eight-year period would have risen to 12.48. Thus, a 75 percent reduction in the external debt stock would have raised the logarithm of GDP from 12.42 to 12.48, or by 6 percent. Note that between 1987 and 1994 the average recorded growth rate of real GDP in sub-Saharan Africa was 2.1 percent. Adding 6.0 percent to this figure, we get 8.1 percent. Therefore, the implication of our results is that if there had been a 75 percent debt stock reduction in 1986, the average growth rate of real GDP during 1987–94 would have been a healthy 8.1 percent instead of the anemic 2.1 percent actually achieved.[17] Results obtained in this study are similar to those ob-

[17]Note that the small macroeconometric model used in this study permits debt (or debt stock reduction) to affect growth only via investment. A larger model would, in addition, allow for a direct transmission channel from debt to growth. These direct effects are linked to the impact of debt on growth-supporting expenditures such as human capital and on expenditures that enhance investment productivity. In such a case, debt stock reduction would increase growth

Figure 12. Sub-Saharan Africa: Simulation of Per Capita Investment With and Without a 75 Percent Debt Stock Reduction, 1971–94
(In 1987 U.S. dollars)

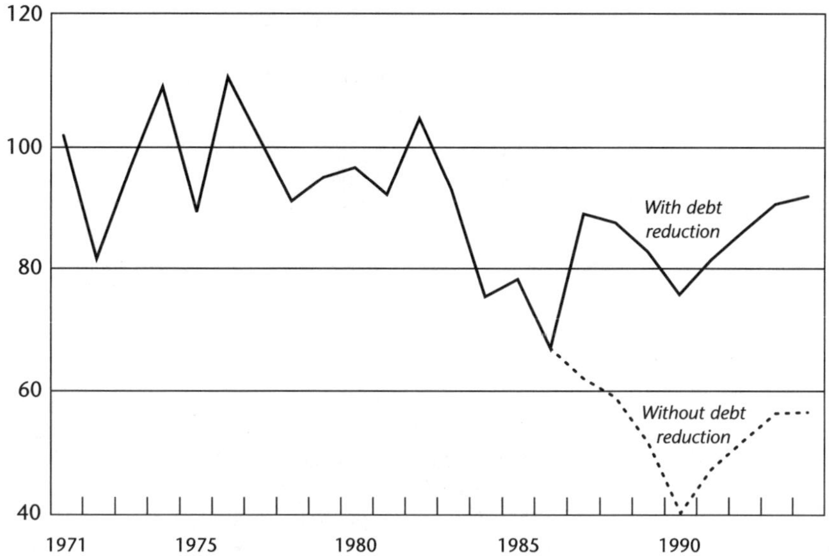

Source: Author's calculations.

tained by Chhibber and Pahwa (1994) for Nigeria. They simulated a 50 percent debt reduction for Nigeria, also starting in 1986; they found that during the 1987–91 period GDP growth would have averaged more than 2 percent higher. Thus, with a 50 percent debt stock reduction, Nigeria's average GDP growth during 1987–91 would have been 7.28 percent instead of the recorded 5.18 percent (Chhibber and Pahwa, 1994, p. 132).

It is necessary to point out that, mainly because of the operation of the debt overhang effect and the crowding-out effect, there would have been a significant recovery of investment and an increase in growth of real output as a result of the hypothesized reductions in debt stock. There would also have been corresponding improvements in debt indicators. An analysis of Table 20 confirms that a 75 percent debt stock reduction would, by 1994, have reduced the debt-income ratio by 65 percent. Similarly, the debt-service ratio would have declined by approximately 62 percent as a result of a 75 percent debt stock reduction.

via a rise in investment and directly by inducing increased growth promotion expenditures. Conceivably, then, such a specification would increase the impact of debt stock reduction on economic growth.

Table 18. Policy Simulations: Per Capita Investment Under Alternative Debt Reduction Scenarios, 1987–94
(In U.S. dollars)

	Debt Reduction			
	None (Baseline)	40 percent	50 percent	75 percent
1987	62.28	66.46	73.29	89.28
1988	59.42	63.87	71.10	87.88
1989	52.07	57.09	65.04	83.06
1990	40.54	46.92	56.25	76.13
1991	47.68	53.46	62.39	82.18
1992	52.58	58.15	66.94	86.83
1993	56.84	62.32	71.09	91.18
1994	57.14	62.78	71.80	92.46

Source: Author's calculations.

Table 19. Policy Simulations: Logarithm of Output Under Alternative Debt Reduction Scenarios, 1987–94
(In billions of U.S. dollars)

	Debt Reduction			
	None (Baseline)	40 percent	50 percent	75 percent
1987	12.35	12.36	12.37	12.40
1988	12.37	12.38	12.40	12.42
1989	12.39	12.40	12.41	12.44
1990	12.38	12.40	12.42	12.46
1991	12.42	12.44	12.46	12.49
1992	12.46	12.47	12.49	12.52
1993	12.49	12.51	12.52	12.55
1994	12.52	12.53	12.55	12.58

Source: Author's calculations.

Summary and Conclusions

This study presented a small macroeconometric model that facilitated simulations of the impact of external debt on economic growth in sub-Saharan Africa. The complete simultaneous-equation model consisted of two stochastic equations (for output and investment demand) and five identities. The five identities in the dynamic simulation were for debt accumulation, capital stock, the debt-GNP ratio, the debt-service ratio, and the logarithm of per capita investment. The simultaneous-equation model was estimated by two-stage least squares for the 1971–94 period. It was found that there is a significant debt overhang effect as well as a crowding-out effect. In other words, the large stock of external debt and heavy debt-service payments have had a depressing effect on investment in the region.

Historical simulation was undertaken in order to assess the validity of the model. On the whole, the model performed well, with the simulated values of the two key endogenous variables (investment and output) closely tracking their corresponding actual data series. In this respect, Theil's inequality coefficient (1961 version) of less than 0.002 was obtained for both investment and output.

Policy simulation was also carried out. In particular, the effect of alternative debt stock reduction packages effective in 1986 was simulated. It was found that hypothesized debt reductions of 40 percent, 50 percent, and 75 percent, assumed effective in 1986, would have significantly increased investment and GDP during the subsequent period. Similarly, the various debt stock reduction scenarios would have reduced, to corresponding degrees, total external debt stock, the debt-GNP ratio, and the debt-service ratio. The policy simulations showed that a 75 percent debt stock reduction would have raised per capita gross domestic investment by about 60 percent and increased GDP growth by 6 percentage points, on average, during the 1987–94 period. These results largely mimic those obtained for Nigeria by Chhibber and Pahwa (1994) and Iyoha (1997).

Results obtained in this study confirm that an excessively high stock of external debt depresses investment and lowers the rate of economic growth. Thus, heavily indebted countries in sub-Saharan Africa need to articulate creative strategies for bringing about debt reduction so that the high debt stock and associated crushing debt-service burden do not have such a negative impact on economic growth. Traditional debt relief mechanisms currently being used by these countries include debt restructuring, debt rescheduling, reduced debt servicing, debt buybacks, interest rate options, and various debt conversion schemes such as debt-equity swaps. Overall, the effectiveness of these techniques in reducing the debt stock has been rather limited (Ogbe, 1992). New steps that could be taken to effectively reduce the region's external debt stock include, inter alia,

- adoption and implementation of macroeconomic policies that would encourage repatriation of flight capital;
- adoption of a medium-term economic program approved by the IMF and the World Bank in order to qualify for debt reduction under the enhanced Toronto terms, the Naples terms, and the IDA reduction facility; and

Table 20. Policy Simulations: Effect of a 75 Percent Debt Stock Reduction on External Debt Stock, Debt-GNP Ratio, and Debt-Service Ratio, 1987–94

	Total Debt (In billions of U.S. dollars)		Debt-GNP ratio (In percent)		Debt-Service Ratio (In percent)	
	Without reduction	With reduction	Without reduction	With reduction	Without reduction	With reduction
1987	99.44	36.51	39.32	14.44	15.14	5.75
1988	115.59	41.94	47.08	17.08	15.75	6.00
1989	133.33	47.94	53.82	19.35	16.39	6.22
1990	153.83	54.82	57.26	20.41	17.10	6.49
1991	176.30	62.40	63.89	22.62	17.80	6.76
1992	201.31	70.85	72.88	25.65	18.39	7.00
1993	228.98	80.23	84.69	29.68	18.99	7.21
1994	259.81	90.70	96.27	33.61	19.62	7.45

Source: Author's calculations.

- pressing for debt forgiveness or debt cancellation through diplomatic action.

Given the potential beneficial effects of debt stock reduction on investment and GDP in sub-Saharan Africa, it is recommended that the international community make a greater effort to provide debt reduction, preferably through debt forgiveness, as a matter of priority. It seems clear that, provided appropriate domestic macroeconomic policies are adopted and implemented along with debt reduction packages, debt reduction would provide a much-needed stimulus to investment recovery and growth in sub-Saharan African countries in the years ahead.

Although plausible, the results obtained in this chapter by the use of two stochastic equations and five identities should be considered preliminary. It is expected that more robust results would be obtained by carrying out the simulations with a larger macroeconometric model of sub-Saharan Africa.

References

Ajayi, S.I., 1991, "Macroeconomic Approach to External Debt: The Case of Nigeria," African Economic Research Consortium Research Paper No. 8 (Nairobi: Initiative Publishers).

———, 1995, "Capital Flight and External Debt in Nigeria" African Economic Research Consortium Research Paper No. 35 (Nairobi: Initiative Publishers).

Avramovic, D., 1991, "Africa's Debt and Economic Recovery," *African Development Review*, Vol. 2, No. 2, December.

Boorman, J., and A. Chopra, 1991, "Discussion Paper on Africa's Adjustment and External Debt Problems: Issues and Options," paper presented at an IMF/AACB Symposium on Structural Adjustment, External Debt and Growth in Africa, Gaborone, Botswana.

Borensztein, E., 1990, "Debt Overhang, Debt Reduction, and Investment: The Case of the Philippines," IMF Working Paper No. 90/77 (Washington: International Monetary Fund).

———, 1991, "Will Debt Reduction Increase Investment?" *Finance & Development*, Vol. 28, No. 1.

Calvo, G., 1989, "A Delicate Equilibrium: Debt Relief and Default Penalties in an International Context," in *Analytical Issues in Debt*, ed. by J.A. Frenkel, M.F. Dooley, and P. Wickham (Washington: International Monetary Fund).

Central Bank of Nigeria, 1996, "Management of Nigeria's Public Debt," CBN Briefs No. 96/09 (Lagos).

Chenery, H.B., and A.M. Strout, 1966, "Foreign Assistance and Economic Development," *American Economic Review*, Vol. 56, No. 4.

Chhibber, A., and S. Pahwa, 1994, "Investment Recovery and Growth in Nigeria: The Case for Debt Relief," in *African Debt Burden and Economic Development: Selected Papers for the 1994 Annual Conference of the Nigerian Economic Society*, ed. by F.E. Onah.

Claessens, S., 1990, "Debt Laffer Curve: Some Estimates," *World Development*, Vol. 18.

Cline, W.R., 1988, "International Debt: Progress and Strategy," *Finance & Development*, Vol. 25, No. 2.

Cohen, D., 1990, "Slow Growth and Large LDC Debt in the Eighties: An Empirical Analysis," CEPREMAP Working Paper No. 9002 (Paris: CEPREMAP).

Degefe, B., 1992, "Growth and Foreign Debt: The Ethiopian Experience: 1964–1986," African Economic Research Consortium Research Paper No. 13 (Nairobi: Initiative Publishers).

Dooley, M.P., 1986, *An Analysis of the Debt Crisis*, IMF Working Paper No. 86/14 (Washington: International Monetary Fund).

Drouin, M., 1989, "Africa's Debt" (unpublished).

Froot, K., 1989, "Buybacks, Exit Bonds, and the Optimality of Debt and Liquidity Relief," *International Economic Review*, Vol. 30.

Gonçalves, F., 1996, "Entangled in the Adjustment Web," *Southern Africa Political and Economic Monthly*, Vol. 9, No. 12, September.

Green, R.H., and S. Griffith-Jones, 1986, "Sub-Saharan Africa's External Debt Crisis," *Third World Affairs* (London).

Greene, J., 1989, "The Debt Problem of Sub-Saharan Africa," *Finance & Development*, Vol. 26 (June).

Greene, J.E., and M.S. Khan, 1990, "The African Debt Crisis," African Economic Research Consortium Special Paper No. 3 (Nairobi: Initiative Publishers).

Griffin, K., 1996, "Macroeconomic Reform and Employment: An Investment-Led Strategy of Structural Adjustment in Sub-Saharan Africa" (unpublished).

Hall, B.H., 1995, *Times Series Processor Version 4.3 Reference Manual* (Palo Alto, California: TSP International).

Helleiner, G.K., 1989, "The Sub-Saharan African Debt Problem: Issues for International Policy," paper presented at the Second World Scientific Banking Conference, Dubrovnik, June 7–10.

———, 1991, "Alternative Approaches to Africa's Adjustment and External Debt Problem," paper presented at an IMF/AACB Symposium on Structural Adjustment, External Debt and Growth in Africa, Gaborone, Botswana.

Heller, H., and E. Frenkel, 1982, "Determinants of LDC Indebtedness," *Columbia Journal of World Business*, Vol. 17, No. 1.

Husain, I., and J. Underwood, 1991, "The Debt of Sub-Saharan Africa: Problems and Solutions" (Washington: World Bank).

International Labor Organization, 1995, *African Employment Report 1995* (Abidjan, Côte d'Ivoire: ILO Regional Office for Africa).

———, 1996, *World Employment 1996* (Geneva).

International Monetary Fund, *World Economic Outlook* (Washington, various issues).

Iyoha, M.A., 1991a, "Macroeconomic Management and Planning in African Countries," working paper (Benin City, Nigeria: Department of Economics and Statistics, University of Benin).

———, 1991b, "Debt, Commodities and Resource Flows," in *Development Economics: An African Perspective*, ed. by S. Rasheed and S. Tomori (Addis Ababa: United Nations Economic Commission for Africa).

———, 1995, "Debt Overhang, Debt Reduction, and Investment: The Case of Nigeria," working paper (Benin City, Nigeria: Department of Economics and Statistics, University of Benin).

———, 1997, "An Econometric Study of Debt Overhang, Debt Reduction, Investment and Economic Growth in Nigeria," working paper (Benin City, Nigeria: Department of Economics and Statistics, University of Benin).

———, and S.O. Iyare, 1994, "Africa's Debt Problems," in *African Debt Burden and Economic Development: Selected Papers for the 1994 Annual Conference of the Nigerian Economic Society*, ed. by F.E. Onah.

Kapijimpanga, O., 1996, "SAPs and Debt," *Southern Africa Political and Economic Monthly*, Vol. 9, No. 12, September.

Khan, M.S., and M. Kumar, 1993, "Public and Private Investment and the Convergence of Per Capita Incomes in Developing Countries," IMF Working Paper No. 93/51 (Washington: International Monetary Fund).

Killick, T., and M. Martin, 1989, "African Debt: The Search for Solutions," United Nations Africa Recovery Program, Briefing Paper No. 1.

Klein, T., 1987, "Debt Relief for African Countries," *Finance & Development*, Vol. 24 (December).

Krugman, P., 1988, "Financing vs. Forgiving a Debt Overhang: Some Analytical Notes," *Journal of Development Economics*, Vol. 29 (November).

Looney, R.E., 1987, "Determinants of Third World Mineral-Oil Economies' External Debt," *Journal of Economic Development*, Vol. 12, No. 2.

Lyakurwa, W., 1990, "External Debt Problems of Sub-Saharan Africa in the Context of Structural Adjustment," *Tanzania Journal of Economics*, Vol. 2.

Martens, A., 1987, "Structural Adjustment in the Sahel: Beyond the Point of No Return?" (unpublished).

Mistry, P.S., 1988, "African Debt: The Case for Relief for Sub-Saharan Africa," paper presented at a symposium on Swedish Development Cooperation with Sub-Saharan Africa in the 1990s, in Saltsjobaden, Sweden, September.

Mjema, G.D., 1996, "The Impact of Foreign Debt and Debt Servicing in the Economy of Tanzania: A Simultaneous Equation Approach," *African Journal of Economic Policy*, Vol. 3, No. 1 (June).

Nowzad, B., and others, 1981, *External Indebtedness of Developing Countries*, IMF Occasional Paper No. 3 (Washington: International Monetary Fund).

Ogbe, N.E., 1992, "Evaluation of Nigeria's Debt-Relief Experience (1985–1990)," Technical Paper No. 55 (Paris: Organization for Economic Cooperation and Development).

Ohlin, G., 1966, *Foreign Aid Policy Reconsidered* (Paris: Organization for Economic Cooperation and Development).

Oseghale, B.D., and F.E. Amenkhienan, 1987, "Foreign Debt, Oil Exports, Direct Foreign Investment and Economic Performance in Nigeria (1960–1984)," *Nigerian Journal of Economic and Social Studies*, Vol. 29.

Pesaran, M.H., and B. Pesaran, 1991, *Microfit 386 Version 3.21* (Oxford, England: Oxford University Press).

Pindyck, R.S., and D.L. Rubinfeld, 1976, *Econometric Models and Econometric Forecasts* (New York: McGraw-Hill).

Pindyck, R.S., and A. Solimano, 1993, "Economic Instability and Aggregate Investment," in *NBER Macroeconomic Annual*, ed. by O. Blanchard and S. Fischer (Cambridge, Massachusetts: MIT Press).

Ram, Rati, 1985, "Exports and Economic Growth: Some Additional Evidence," *Economic Development and Cultural Change*, Vol. 32 (January).

Sachs, J., 1980, "A Strategy for Efficient Debt Reduction," *Journal of Economic Perspectives*, Vol. 4, No. 1.

———, 1989, "The Debt Overhang of Developing Countries," in *Debt, Stabilization, and Development*, ed. by G. Calvo, R. Findlay, P. Kouri, and J. Macedo (Oxford: Basil Blackwell).

Savvides, A., 1992, "Investment Slowdown in Developing Countries During the 1980s: Debt Overhang or Foreign Capital Inflows?" *Kyklos*, Vol. 45.

Serven, L., and A. Solimano, 1993, "Debt Crisis, Adjustment Policies and Capital Formation in Developing Countries: Where Do We Stand?" *World Development*, Vol. 21.

Singer, H.W., 1989, "The 1980s: A Lost Decade—Development in Reverse?" in *Growth and External Debt Management*, ed. by H.W. Singer and S. Sharma (London: Macmillan).

Solow, R.M., 1957, "Technical Change and the Aggregate Productive Function," *Review of Economics and Statistics*.

Stanovnik, J., 1985, "The Impact of External Indebtedness on Economic Development Prospects," *Development and South-South Cooperation*, Vol. 1, No. 1.

Theil, H., 1978, *Introduction to Econometrics* (Englewood, New Jersey: Prentice-Hall).

United Nations Economic Commission for Africa, 1989, *African Alternative Framework to Structural Adjustment Program for Socio-Economic Recovery and Transformation* (Addis Ababa).

———, 1991, "Financing Growth and Development in Africa: Outlook and Issues—A View from ECA," paper presented at an IMF/AACB Symposium on Structural Adjustment, External Debt and Growth in Africa, Gaborone, Botswana.

van Wijnbergen, S., 1991, "Debt Relief and Economic Growth in Mexico," *World Bank Economic Review*, Vol. 5, No. 3.

Warner, A.M., 1992, "Did the Debt Crisis Cause the Investment Crisis?" *Quarterly Journal of Economics*, Vol. 107, No. 4, November.

World Bank, 1989a, *African Economic and Financial Data* (Washington).

———, 1989b, *Sub-Saharan Africa: From Crisis to Sustainable Growth* (Washington).

———, 1991, *World Debt Tables, 1990–91* (Washington).

———, 1992a, *African Development Indicators* (Washington).

———, 1992b, *World Debt Tables, 1992–1993, External Finance for Developing Countries, Vol. 1: Analysis and Summary Tables* (Washington).

———, 1992c, *World Tables 1992* (Baltimore: Johns Hopkins University Press).

———, 1994a, "Nigeria: Structural Adjustment Program: Policies, Implementation, and Impact," Report No. 13053–UNI (Washington).

———, 1994b, *World Development Report, 1994* (New York: Oxford University Press).

———, 1995, *African Development Indicators, 1994–1995* (Washington).

———, 1996a, *World Debt Tables: External Finance for Developing Countries, Vol. 1: Analysis and Summary Tables* (Washington).

———, 1996b, *World Development Report, 1996* (New York: Oxford University Press).

———, *World Debt Tables* (Washington, various issues).

Wynn, R.P., and K. Holden, 1974, *An Introduction to Applied Econometric Analysis* (London: Macmillan).

Part II

Capital Flight

Capital Flight and External Debt in Nigeria

7

S. Ibi Ajayi

Over the last few years, many heavily indebted countries have experienced heavy capital outflows or capital flight, and capital flight has become an important topic for detailed study in some of these countries. This interest arises, among other reasons, because of the role that external assets stored away in foreign lands could play if left in the domestic economy, to augment the dwindling resources from international creditors.

It is widely believed that the study of capital flight from highly indebted countries is important because of the economic problems such flight can create (see Khan, 1989). The outflow of capital can cause a shortage of liquidity in the economy and lead to upward pressure on the interest rate. Similarly, the shortage of liquidity can cause a depreciation of the domestic currency if the authorities are operating a floating exchange rate system. If the government is defending a particular exchange rate, a loss of reserves will ensue.

The loss of resources has several long-term effects. The first is that the availability of resources for domestic investment is reduced. The rate of capital formation is reduced by capital flight, and this adversely affects the country's current and future prospects. Income that is generated abroad as well as wealth held abroad are outside the purview of relevant authorities and cannot be taxed. The effects are a reduction in government revenue and government debt-servicing capacity. Capital flight can exacerbate a balance of payments crisis if, at the time the balance of payments difficulty is being experienced, capital outflows are taking place. Capital flight can also compound the foreign finance problems of heavily indebted countries if creditors are reluctant to give further assistance as a result of capital outflows.

The link between capital flight and growth is expressed vividly in the literature. Two of the relevant works are Deppler and Williamson (1987) and Lessard and Williamson (1987). The linkage is expressed as follows by Deppler and Williamson (1987, p. 52):

> the fundamental economic concern about capital flight, however, is that it reduces welfare in the sense that it leads to a net loss in the total real resources available to an economy for investment and growth. That is, capital flight is viewed as a diversion of domestic savings away from financing domestic real

investment and in favor of foreign financial investment. As a result, the pace of growth and development of the economy is retarded from what it otherwise would have been.

The linkage is expressed by Lessard and Williamson (1987, p. 224) in the same vein:

> The best case involves a reduction in the savings to finance domestic investment of a magnitude essentially equal to the size of the capital flight. Future growth will in consequence be lower. The worst case involves a reduction not just in future growth possibilities but also in the current level of output by some multiple of the size of capital flights.

A brief critique of the views expressed is given later.

Many reasons are often adduced for capital flight. The preponderant causes are economic, but the economic aspects are inextricably interwoven with political causes and favorable foreign economic incentives. Domestic macroeconomic policy distortions are a main factor. These distortions manifest themselves in large public sector deficits, exchange rate misalignment, and financial repression. Apart from these, there are also the incentives provided by foreign banks and governments. Part of the explanation for capital flight is also political. This is predicated on corruption and access to foreign funds by political leaders. It has been alleged that some political leaders, through the perquisites of their offices, siphon funds to foreign countries.[1]

Nigeria is one of the heavily indebted countries where the issue of capital flight has been regarded as important. There is, however, no comprehensive study on the causes, measurement, magnitude, and consequences of capital flight in Nigeria.[2] Given the magnitude of Nigeria's external debt and the possible impact of capital flight on the country's real debt-service capacity, a study of capital flight and external debt is essential.

This chapter intends to take up that challenge.[3] It focuses on the definition, magnitude, determinants, mechanisms, and consequences of capital flight. The analysis also explores possible measurements of assets in which the money is held once it arrives abroad. The emphasis

[1]For the developing countries, examples often cited included the late Ferdinand Marcos, president of the Philippines, and former leaders of Haiti and Zaïre (now the Democratic Republic of the Congo). In Nigeria, some powerful politicians who fled the country after the military coup of 1983 are alleged to belong to the same category.

[2]The available studies that refer to Nigeria are limited. The comprehensive study by Rojas-Suárez (1991) lumped Nigeria in the group of heavily indebted countries. The study did not estimate capital flight for each country.

[3]A survey of the various methods undertaken by Deppler and Williamson (1987) lists only four of the methods discussed here.

is on the macroeconomic effects of capital flight within the context of economic, socioeconomic, and other functions.

Specifically, the chapter

- examines the magnitude of capital flight for the period 1970–88 and a number of alternative methods of its measurement;
- analyzes the economic (mainly macroeconomic) and other factors responsible for capital flight;
- examines the conduits through which capital flight takes place
- identifies the major consequences of capital flight for the domestic economy; and
- examines the linkages between capital flight and external debt and draws policy conclusions.

The Definition of Capital Flight

This section surveys and analyzes the various definitions and measures of capital flight in the existing literature. The approach adopted is twofold. First is a discussion at the conceptual level, exploring the rationale or basis for classifying domestic outflows as capital flight instead of normal flows. The second approach is strictly empirical. The objective is to compute and analyze alternative measures (estimates) of capital flight. The measurements are derived from a common database for the period 1970–88 to show the variation in the estimates under alternative definitions.

The use of the term *capital flight* arouses strong emotions. Some analysts view capital flight as a symptom of a sick society. Some observers see it as the cause of the heavily indebted countries' inability to recover from their problems. Capital flight is regarded by others as an unnecessarily pejorative description of natural, economically rational responses to the portfolio choices that have confronted wealthy residents of some debtor countries in recent years (Lessard and Williamson, 1987, p. 201). The controversy surrounding the term is due partly to the absence of a precise and universally accepted definition for it, and partly due to the way the term is used between developed and developing countries. It is usual among some economists to refer to capital outflows from developed countries as foreign investment, whereas the same activity undertaken by the residents of a developing country is referred to as capital flight.

One of the reasons for this dichotomy is the belief that investors from the developed economies are responding to better opportunities abroad. The investors from developing countries, on the other hand, are said to be escaping the high risks they perceive at home. This interpretation makes it obvious why a lot of economists are ill at ease with this definition of capital flight. In general, it is believed that investors from all countries, whether developed or developing, will base their decisions on the relative returns and risks of investments at home and abroad.

A distinction is also often made between legal and illegal transactions in distinguishing between capital flight and so-called normal capital outflows. Since illegal transactions are not reported to the compilers of the balance of payments statistics, it is difficult to know the extent to which they therefore constitute capital flight. Capital flight is capital that flees (Walter, 1986; Kindleberger, 1987). Alternatively, capital outflows in response to economic or political crises are capital flight (Husted and Melvin, 1990). Normal capital flows, on the other hand, refer to flows that correspond to ordinary portfolio diversification on the part of domestic residents.

According to Cuddington (1986, p. 2), capital flight refers to short-term capital outflows. It involves hot money that responds to political or financial crises, heavier taxes, a prospective tightening of capital controls, a major devaluation of the domestic currency, or actual or incipient hyperinflation. Morgan Guaranty Trust Company (1986, p. 13) defines capital flight as the reported or unreported acquisition of foreign assets by the nonbank private sector and elements of the public sector.

To classify our thoughts on capital flows, Table 1 presents a taxonomy of factors explaining international capital flows used by Lessard and Williamson (1987). The upper left section of the table identifies various factors based on differences in economic returns across countries. In the upper right section are those additional factors that deal with two-way flows, or normal portfolio diversification. Most theoretical and empirical studies of capital flight have emphasized the lower left and right sections. The factors emphasized are those that create a wedge between economic and financial returns, regardless of whether they operate across the board or asymmetrically between residents and nonresidents (Lessard and Williamson, 1987).

From Table 1 it can be seen that normal capital outflows are those that seek to maximize economic returns and opportunities between countries. Normal portfolio diversification takes place on the basis of differentials in economic returns. Capital flight, on the other hand, as seen from this analysis, is that subset of capital outflows that is propelled by source country policies (Lessard and Williamson, 1987, p. 217).

Table 1. Taxonomy of Factors Explaining International Capital Flows

	One-Way Flows	Two-Way Flows
Economic risks and returns	Natural resource endowments Terms of trade Technological changes Demographic shifts General economic management	Differences in absolute riskiness of economies Low correlation of risky outcomes across countries Differences in investor risk preferences
Financial risks and returns	Taxes (deviations from world levels) Inflation Default on government obligations Devaluation Financial repression Taxes on financial intermediation Political instability, potential confiscation	Differences in taxes and their incidence between residents and nonresidents Differences in nature and incidence of country risk Asymmetric application of guarantees Different interest ceilings for residents and nonresidents Different access to foreign exchange–denominated claims

Source: Lessard and Williamson (1987, p. 216).

A Review of the Measures and Estimates of Capital Flight

A number of estimates of capital flight have been made over the last several years. The preponderance of these studies focuses on Argentina, Brazil, Chile, Korea, Mexico, Peru, the Philippines, and Venezuela. A study by Rojas-Suárez (1991) covers Argentina, Bolivia, Chile, Colombia, Ecuador, Gabon, Jamaica, Mexico, Nigeria, Peru, the Philippines, Venezuela, and the former Yugoslavia. These studies differ from one another in terms of methodology, country coverage, data sources, and time span. The most significant of the studies on capital flight that have made an impact are those by Dooley (1986), Dooley and others (1986), World Bank (1985), Morgan Guaranty Trust Company (1986), Cuddington (1986), Cumby and Levich (1987), Gulati (1985), Lessard and Williamson (1987), Khan and Ul Haque (1985), and Khan (1989).

In the World Bank (1985) study, capital flight is defined as the sum of gross capital outflows and the current account deficit less increases in official foreign reserves. Cuddington (1986) takes a different approach. Capital flight is defined as short-term speculative outflows; according to him, this is the typical meaning of capital flight, and the term therefore refers to short-term external assets held by the nonbank private sector plus errors and omissions in the balance of payments. Cuddington's (1986) approach is concentrated on so-called hot money funds, because these funds respond quickly to changes in expected returns or to changes in risk. Variations in economic conditions are likely to affect the flow of these funds, which are expected to return very quickly to the home country when economic conditions improve.

Khan and Ul Haque (1985) calculated capital flight for eight highly indebted developing countries for the period 1974–82. Capital flight is defined in two ways. First, it is defined simply as gross private short-term capital flows plus net errors and omissions in the country's balance of payments accounts. This is the same as Cuddington's definition. The second method tries to take account of normal capital flows. Capital flight is defined as that part of the increase in external claims that yields no recorded investment income (see Dooley, 1986).

The Dooley (1986) study does attempt to tease out the normality of capital flows by specifically separating normal and abnormal capital flows. The Dooley method seeks to measure the stock of privately held foreign assets that do not generate income reported to the domestic authorities. The identified capital outflows in the balance of payments accounts are cumulated, and three adjustments are then made to capture the unreported capital flows. First, errors and omissions are added. Second, a comparison is made between the stock of external debt as reported in the World Bank data and those reported in the balance of payments statistics. The difference between the two is added to the estimate of the increase in private sector foreign assets. The third adjustment involves the calculation of the stock of external assets needed to give the observed amount of investment income in the balance of payments at international market rates, for example the U.S. treasury bill rate.

In the Morgan Guaranty Trust Company (1986, p. 13) study, capital flight is defined as the reported or unreported acquisition of foreign assets by the nonbank private sector and some elements of the public sector. Capital flight is therefore net investment inflows plus changes in gross external debt plus the current account balance and changes in selected gross foreign assets. Cline (1986) critiques this definition. He argues that income from tourism and border transactions should be subtracted, since these earnings are beyond the control of the relevant foreign exchange authorities. He also argues that reinvested investment income should not be considered as capital flight, since this also is beyond the control of the authorities.

Table 2. Alternative Measures of Capital Flight

Definition	Methodology	Authors
Narrow measure	Net short-term capital outflows plus errors and omissions	Cuddington (1986)
Derived measure[1]	Part of the increase in external claims that yields no recorded investment income	Dooley (1986)
Residual measure or sources-and-uses approach	Change in debt plus net foreign and direct investment minus current account deficit plus change in reserves	Chang and Cumby (1991), World Bank (1985), Pastor (1990)
Private claims measure	Acquisition of external claims by the private sector, including deposit banks and the nonbank sector, plus recorded errors and omissions in the balance of payments	Conesa (1987)
Mirror stock statistics method	Cross-border bank deposits by residence of depositor	Khan and Ul Haque (1985)
Change in private foreign assets[2]	The counterpart of the sum of net direct investment inflows, the change in gross external debt, the current account balance, and the change in selected gross foreign assets	Morgan Guaranty Trust Company (1986)

[1]Also called the stock of unreported foreign assets measure.
[2]Also often seen as another aspect of the residual measure.

In what are referred to as "mirror stock statistics," capital flight is measured as the recorded cross-border bank deposits of nonbanks by residence of depositor. These figures can be found in the statistics published by the IMF.

Apart from these various measures, it is also possible to take cognizance of the misinvoicing of exports and imports in international trade. The derived results from trade misinvoicing can be added to any of the measures to derive another set of data on capital flight.

A schematic summary of the different definitions (or types of measure), the methodology, and the authors is presented for easy reference in Table 2. It should be emphasized that the different methods will yield different results, not only because the definitions are different but also because of differences in data sources. The results may therefore conflict, and comparisons are difficult to make.

Alternative Measures of Capital Flight for Nigeria

There are a number of objectives behind the calculation of the various alternative measures of capital flight for Nigeria. The primary objective, which is modest, is to show the range of capital flight estimates implied by the alternative definitions of capital flight that are offered. The additional objectives are to examine the extent to which capital flight is continuous or episodic. In other words, do heavy outflows tend to concentrate in certain years, and small flows in others? That finding in itself may suggest that capital flight is associated with particular economic or political events. In this realm, capital flight may be associated with poor macroeconomic management, large inflows of foreign exchange from exports (an export boom), changes between civilian and military governance, and so on.

As mentioned earlier, there is no precise and universally acceptable way of measuring capital flight. Some judgment is required, taking due cognizance of the objectives for measuring capital flight and the economic and social environment of the country for which capital flight is being measured. In this chapter a number of approaches are taken. The first recognizes that capital flight is speculative capital: it is hot money on the wing and can be expected to respond to the various forms of distortion mentioned earlier. Taking this approach, of course, means that capital flight refers essentially to capital exports by the private nonbank sector, although in some cases banks and official entities may also engage in it (Cuddington, 1986). Since capital flight is essentially concealed, it shows up in the errors and omissions of the balance of payments entry. Thus, capital flight is defined as the sum of short-term private capital flows plus errors and omissions in the balance of payments statistics. The results of the calculations are shown in Table 3.

As can be seen, some of the figures are negative. The intuitive explanation is that the negative signs cannot connote capital flight. As explained in the Cuddington study (1986, p. 5), the figures reflect capital flight net of unrecorded capital inflows.

Essentially, however, the years with negative signs are better perceived as years of capital repatriation, capital flight reversal, or capital inflows. Thus, in the period 1972–89, Nigeria's total capital inflow was $7.6 billion. Out of this total, $7.4 billion (97 percent) came in between 1972 and 1978, the period of Nigeria's oil boom. During the political era, that is, the period in which a civilian government was in power, the capital inflow was $270 million. Thus, using this technique of calculation, one can see the episodic nature of capital flight. As a result of

Table 3. Nigeria: Capital Flight, 1970–89
(In millions of U.S. dollars)

	Capital Flight
1970	134.0
1971	205.0
1972	119.0
1973	–177.0
1974	48.0
1975	–42.0
1976	5.0
1977	–231.0
1978	43.0
1979	211.0
1980	–673.0
1981	106.0
1982	149.0
1983	–63.0
1984	–642.0
1985	–2,014.0
1986	–249.0
1987	–953.0
1988	–1,315.0
1989	–1,895.0
Totals	
1972–78	–7,362.0
1972–89	–7,573.0
1979–83	–270.0

Source: Author's calculations from data in International Monetary Fund (1990).

the buoyant economy associated with the oil boom years, the macroeconomic environment can be said to be favorable to capital inflows.

Using approaches by Cumby and Levich (1987), Varman (1989), and Varman-Schneider (1991), we calculate from the balance of payments statistics a number of capital flight estimates for Nigeria using various methods shown in Table 4. The data are drawn mainly from the IMF's *International Financial Statistics Yearbook* and *Balance of Payments Statistics Yearbook* and from the World Bank's *World Debt Tables*. The result of the calculation is shown in Table 5. This is the first time that this has been done for Nigeria; there has been no similar calculation elsewhere using the different definitions shown in Table 4.

The differences in the magnitudes of the results using various definitions of capital flight are not surprising given the differences in definitions. The similarities and differences can be classified according to different periods. In 1970–73, for example, the World Bank (1985)

Table 4. Notations of Estimating Capital Flight

Notations	
A.	Current account balance
B.	Net foreign direct investment
C.	Private short-term capital outflows
D.	Portfolio investment
E.	Foreign assets of the banking system
F.	Changes in reserves
G.	Errors and omissions
H.	Changes in debt
I.	IMF credit
J.	Travel credit
K.	Reinvested income from foreign direct investment
L.	Other investment income
M.	Counterpart items

Capital Flight Estimates		
World Bank	=	(H + B + A + F)
Erbe	=	(H + B + A + F)
Morgan	=	(H + B + A + E + F)
Cline	=	(H + B + A + E) – (J + K + L)
Duwendag	=	(H + B + A + F + G + I + M)

Source: Lessard and Williamson (1987), p. 38.

and Erbe (1985) estimates were generally lower than the other three estimates. The amplitudes of capital flight for the period 1985–87, however, were not too different in the four measures. What is important is the cumulative sums of capital flight for given specific years.

Of the four approaches, the Duwendag (1987) approach consistently gave the lowest estimates. A line graph of the approaches reveals that the Erbe, World Bank, and Duwendag approaches are close, as shown by the variations of these figures, just as the Morgan Guaranty and Cline estimates are very close in terms of the amplitude of the figures.

It is clear that the different results obtained derive from the choice of elements that go into the calculation of capital flight. It is also clear that all the approaches yield significant amounts of capital flight over the period covered.

Table 5. Nigeria: Alternative Estimates of Capital Flight, 1972–89
(In millions of U.S. dollars)

	Erbe (1985) and World Bank (1985)	Morgan Guaranty (1986)	Cline (1986)	Duwendag (1987)
1972	106.40	477.28	453.37	127.70
1973	636.10	1,265.38	1,228.03	551.75
1974	325.00	5,995.00	5,824.27	450.88
1975	119.80	5,988.60	5,474.48	148.04
1976	124.80	5,524.44	5,044.21	187.40
1977	2,490.00	7,021.86	6,554.79	2,111.95
1978	508.40	2,695.20	2,309.07	235.23
1979	–86.30	5,659.54	5,370.07	601.59
1980	2,713.30	12,974.11	12,234.36	2,590.79
1981	2,132.30	6,145.22	5,267.31	1,345.14
1982	–3,805.80	–2,230.87	–2,230.87	–3,812.09
1983	2,016.10	3,098.82	2,893.61	1,991.64
1984	–169.80	1,594.72	1,494.72	182.81
1985	3,569.40	5,385.40	5,272.14	2,994.58
1986	5,502.90	6,841.80	6,592.39	5,138.37
1987	5,874.60	7,522.20	7,368.83	5,462.11
1988	1,043.80	2,479.12	2,385.12	902.80
1989	–299.70	2,212.46	2,102.46	–369.70
Totals				
1972–79	4,224.2	34,627.3	32,258.7	4,414.5
1972–89	22,801.3	80,650.3	75,330.3	20,841.0
1979–83	2,969.6	25,646.8	23,196.0	2,717.7

Source: Author's calculations.

In the period 1972–89, the amount of capital flight varied from $20.8 billion by the Duwendag method to a high of $80.7 billion by the Morgan Guaranty method. It is not surprising that the Duwendag measure is exceedingly low because of the variables used. Given the relative importance of capital in capital-scarce economies like Nigeria, the most relevant definition of capital flight, which uses the sources-and-uses approach, is more appropriate, because it implicitly assumes that any outflow is abnormal because of the scarcity value of capital in developing countries. Concentrating on the World Bank definition, which is the more appropriate, implies that during the period 1972–79 total capital flight from Nigeria was $22.8 billion. This figure will be used later in this chapter for purposes of comparison with the increases in external debt.

According to the World Bank approach, the years 1979, 1982, 1984, and 1989 were years of capital inflows. As to whether capital flight is

Table 6. Nigeria: Cross-Border Deposits of Nonbanks by Residence of Depositor, 1981–89

	Stock of Deposits	Change in Deposits	Ratio of Deposits to External Debt	Ratio of Deposits to GNP
	(In millions of U.S. dollars)		*(In percent)*	
1981	1,540		0.128	0.016
1982	1,380	150	0.108	0.015
1983	1,380	0	0.075	0.016
1984	1,170	–210	0.063	0.013
1985	1,500	230	0.078	0.017
1986	1,680	180	0.073	0.037
1987	2,300	620	0.077	0.096
1988	1,960	–350	0.063	0.068
1989	2,790	840	0.085	0.101
Total 1981–89	15,700	1,460		

Sources: IMF (1989, 1990); World Bank (1990).

episodic, it can be seen that during the period 1972–78, cumulative capital flight was $4.3 billion. This was a period of military rule and one that coincided essentially with the peak in Nigeria's oil wealth syndrome. The total amount of capital flight during the civilian regime (1979–83) was $3.0 billion, that is, 69 percent of that under the military regime. It is difficult, however, to come to any conclusion as to whether more capital flight actually occurred under the military regime than under the civilian regime, because the economic fortunes of Nigeria were not the same in the two periods.

The third approach is what was referred to earlier as the mirror stock statistics method. This method draws on international banking statistics to evaluate the amount of assets held abroad by residents of developing countries. This method of estimating capital flight has been used by Khan and Ul Haque (1987). It is particularly useful, as we shall see, in determining the minimum level of assets held abroad. For this method, the statistics recorded by the IMF are the cross-border bank deposits of nonbanks by residence of depositors, which for Nigeria are shown in Table 6. The statistics for Nigeria start in 1981. When capital flight is defined as the increase in this stock over the previous year, we find that the amount is relatively small. In all cases it is the lowest of all the estimates.

There are a number of reasons why this cannot be an adequate measure of capital flight. First, some funds are held in deposits outside the major financial centers. Indeed, the nationality of depositors in some foreign banks is never revealed. The example most often cited is that of Swiss bank accounts, where secret codes are maintained to conceal not only the identity but also the nationality of the depositor. Second, substantial amounts that are not revealed are held in financial assets other than bank deposits, such as equities, bonds, or treasury bills, and in physical assets. As a result, the figures underestimate capital flight.

In a larger sense, however, these amounts are indicative of money that could have been used domestically. Such deposits are better seen within the context of other macroeconomic variables such as external debt and GNP (Table 6), where we find that the ratio of cross-border deposits to external debt varied from 6.3 percent to 12.8 percent. The ratio of cross-border deposits to GNP varied from 1.3 percent to about 10 percent for the period shown.

Causes of Capital Flight

The causes of capital flight as discussed in the literature are many. The various economic factors can be grouped under relative risks, exchange rate misalignment, financial sector constraints, fiscal deficits, and external incentives (Khan, 1989) and disbursements of new loans to developing countries (Cuddington, 1987). There are also other, noneconomic factors that, although important, are often ignored. These include corruption of political leaders and extraordinary access to government funds. These factors are now discussed.

In deciding where to invest, wealth holders look at the various risks of each prospective investment. There are certain inherent characteristics of developing countries that make risk attached to investments there larger than those of developed countries. Using the concept of expropriation risk within the context of an intertemporal optimizing model, Khan and Ul Haque (1985) show that any increase in risk in a rational expectations setting would tend to increase the outflow of private capital from the domestic economy into foreign countries where investments are less risky. This expropriation risk could include a variety of distortions, such as differences in taxes and political instability resulting in possible destruction of private property. Eaton (1987) builds on the Khan–Ul Haque model by relating the risk of expropriation of capital owned domestically, which is defined (especially in this case) as higher taxation, to public and publicly guaranteed foreign debt. The tax obligation arising from an increase in external debt can lead to capital flight. The flight of one investor leads to a rise in the potential tax obligations of the remaining investors. This also may create an incentive for other investors to move their assets abroad.

It is generally agreed that one of the principal causes of capital flight is exchange rate misalignment. It has been amply demonstrated in the empirical analysis of several studies (Dornbusch, 1985; Cuddington, 1986; Lessard and Williamson, 1987; Pastor, 1989, 1990) that the real exchange rate plays a significant role in the direction and magnitude of capital flight from highly indebted countries. Under normal circumstances, if a currency depreciation is expected, domestic wealth owners will shift out of domestic assets into foreign assets. In general, it is difficult to measure exchange rate expectations precisely. It is safe to assume, however, that if a currency is overvalued, economic agents will expect the currency to be devalued in the future. Holding firm to this expectation would cause residents to avoid the potential capital loss by converting domestic into foreign claims.

Financial sector constraints can lead to capital flight. It is well known that narrowness of capital and money markets is a feature of developing economies. These markets therefore provide only a limited variety of financial instruments in which wealth can be held. Many developing countries also lack full or credible deposit insurance on assets held in the domestic banking sector. As a result of these constraints, residents of developing countries look abroad to invest their wealth.

Additionally, there are extensive controls on interest rates and other aspects of financial market behavior in developing countries. Government policies in the financial sector have resulted in nominal interest rates that are far below the rates on comparable foreign financial instruments. In such situations it is expected that investors will seek alternative assets that will yield not only positive but higher returns.

Dornbusch (1985) has shown that capital flight is typically accompanied by a fiscal deficit. When a rising fiscal deficit is financed through the printing of money, this leads to inflationary pressure. To prevent the erosion of their monetary balances by inflation, investors move out of domestic assets as one way of avoiding the inflation tax. When a fiscal deficit is financed through bond sales, domestic residents may expect that at some future date their tax liabilities may increase to pay for the national debt. This would encourage domestic investors to move their assets to foreign countries to avoid potential tax liabilities.

Ize and Ortiz (1987) formalized the link between deficit financing and capital flight. In the Ize-Ortiz model, capital flight is related to the overall financial solvency of government. Insolvency and default risks created by a fiscal deficit appear explicitly as the determinants of capital flight.

A number of external factors influence the flight of capital, generally in terms of the opportunities available outside the country, including the attractiveness of interest rates and the range of financial instruments in which wealth can be held. This is aptly put by Walter (1986, p. 20):

> flight implies havens, and havens take the form of national status that provide an attractive range of real and financial assets to foreign based investors, political and economic stability, a favorable tax climate for nonresidents and various other attributes that generally are the obverse of conditions triggering capital flight in the first place.

Withholding taxes are not imposed on some types of nonresident deposits. Certain countries allow secret accounts, which are attractive to some wealth owners and can facilitate illegal transactions and tax evasion.

Under the principle of national sovereignty, it is difficult for foreigners to have inside information on asset holdings abroad. One safeguard is the domestic bank secrecy law, which bars both national and foreign authorities alike. The other is the blocking statute, which effectively prevents the disclosure, copying, inspection, or removal of documents located in the host country unless there is an order from or by foreign authorities.

Some authors argue that capital inflows in the form of disbursements to developing countries are a major cause of capital flight. In the case of public sector borrowing, the availability of foreign exchange increases the potential for graft and corruption. It is, therefore, logical to assert that for many developing countries (Nigeria included), abuse of official power can lead to capital flight. There is anecdotal evidence that highly placed public officials using the perquisites of their office siphon some of the money under their care to foreign countries solely for their private use.

In Nigeria's case it is difficult to rank the various causes of capital flight in any order of importance. However, a poor macroeconomic policy stance there has resulted in all kinds of distortions. At the same time, the role played by other factors such as access to foreign exchange through various perquisites of office and consequent possible abuse cannot be underestimated.

The Mechanisms of Capital Flight

There are many ways in which capital flight can occur. The conduits are varied, and it is almost impossible to develop an exhaustive inventory of channels. This section discusses the most significant channels for Nigeria.

First, transfers can take place through cash or monetary instruments. These are usually in the form of either foreign or domestic currency, traveler's checks, or other checks. In the early 1970s, stories abounded about Nigerian currency being carried out of the country to major financial centers such as London and New York to be exchanged legally for other currencies at current market rates. In spite of the present economic predicament, there are still some African countries where the naira is exchanged for other currencies in the course of trade.

Second, capital flight can take place through bank transfers from a local affiliate of a foreign institution to a designated recipient abroad. This is possible at the market rate where no constraints or restrictions are in place. Transfers can still be possible in the face of exchange controls, but possibly at a less favorable rate. The history of the development of banking institutions in Nigeria shows the existence of local affiliates of foreign banks. That transfers of the type mentioned have been taking place in Nigeria cannot be in doubt. It is reasonable to claim, however, that such transfers may not be available for incomes that are illegally generated.

Another method of transfer is through precious metals and collectibles, including works of art. Local currency is converted into gold and silver or other precious metals, precious stones, jewelry, and similar assets that not only can be held abroad but will also retain their value. The sale value of these items is usually high in foreign currency, and governments generally tend to restrict or prohibit their import and export. Such international transfers therefore usually involve smuggling, with its inherent risks.

The fourth mechanism of transfer is through false invoicing of trade transactions, where export and import invoices issued differ from agreed prices. Estimates of this type of transfer have been undertaken by Bhagwati (1964), Naya and Morgan (1974), and Bhagwati, Krueger, and Welbulswasdi (1974). An analysis by Gulati (1987) shows that there can be systematic overinvoicing and underinvoicing of exports or imports. The expectation in the case of capital flight is that exporters will systematically engage in underinvoicing, whereas importers overinvoice, and in the process derive foreign exchange that is outside the control of the foreign exchange authority. The procedure is as follows: the foreign supplier issues an invoice that is greater than the agreed price of the product. The importer on receipt of the necessary foreign exchange remits it to the foreign supplier, who then keeps the difference in a bank for the use of the importer. On the export side, the invoice issued is for an amount in foreign currency that is less than the agreed price. The foreign buyer places the difference between the invoice price and the agreed price in a foreign bank account in the exporter's name and remits the invoice amount. It is this amount of money that is surrendered to the central bank for local currency at the prevailing official exchange rate. To measure the magnitude of misinvoicing, partner country analysis is generally undertaken.

Capital flight through false trade invoicing generally involves the local affiliates of multinational companies and owners of businesses engaged in international trade. It is known in some cases that misinvoiced transactions are used to effect capital flight. This activity, in effect, arbitrages official and parallel-market exchange rates (Walter, 1986, p. 113).

A fifth method of transferring money abroad is through the black market, until recently a thriving source of such funds. The amount of money transferred in this way is difficult to estimate. Capital can also be transferred overseas through commissions and agents' fees, which are paid by foreign contractors into the foreign bank accounts of residents.

The Link Between Capital Flight and External Debt

Several authors have pointed out the link between capital flight and debt accumulation in developing countries. Indeed, some studies have shown that the ease with which capital flight takes place is related to the availability of foreign exchange. It is more appropriate, however, to examine the macroeconomic relationship between external debt and capital flight.

Within this context, the discussion can be along two lines. The first analyzes the relationship strictly in terms of causality between external debt and capital flight, whereas the second considers the various macroeconomic issues related to external indebtedness and capital flight. The literature indicates two kinds of linkages between external debt and capital flight. The first linkage runs from external debt to capital flight, and the second from capital flight to external debt. Each of these linkages can also be subdivided into two. Thus, the direct linkage can be divided into four major groups on the basis of whether the direction of causality runs from debt to capital flight or vice versa, and whether one simply provides the motive for the other or provides the means as well. The debt-to-flight mechanisms can be characterized as

- *Debt-driven capital flight.* If, consequent to external borrowing, residents of a country are motivated to move their assets to foreign countries, debt-driven capital flight is the result. Capital flees the country in response to attendant economic circumstances directly attributable to the external debt itself. The attendant economic circumstances leading to debt-driven capital flight are expectations of currency devaluation, fiscal crisis, possible crowding out of domestic capital, and avoidance of taxes and the risk of expropriation.

- *Debt-fueled capital flight*. In this case the inflow of capital provides both the motive and the resources for capital flight. In the case of debt-fueled capital flight, borrowed funds are themselves transferred abroad. There are two processes through which money can be transferred. First, government can borrow money and sell it to domestic residents, who then transfer the money abroad through legal or illegal means. In this case government is the provider of foreign exchange. Second, government can on-lend funds to private borrowers through a national bank, and the borrowers in turn transfer part or all the capital abroad. In this case the external borrowing provides the necessary fuel (the resources) for capital flight.

We now turn to an examination of causation in the other direction. There is, on the one hand, a case that is purely motivational, and on the other hand, a case where capital flight provides resources that reenter the country. These are referred to as flight-driven external borrowing and flight-fueled external borrowing, respectively:

- *Flight-driven external borrowing*. This situation develops when, as a result of capital that has left the country, there is a gap that needs to be filled in the domestic economy. Consequently, there is a demand for replacement on the part of both the government and the private sector. External creditors' willingness to meet this demand can be attributed to different risks and returns facing resident and nonresident capital.
- *Flight-fueled external borrowing*. In this situation domestic currency leaves the country but reenters in the guise of foreign currency. What happens is that the

  > flight capitalist seeks to arbitrage the yield and risk differentials between resident and external capital, by engaging in a series of transactions sometimes known as "round tripping" or "back to back loans." Resident capital is dollarized and deposited in an overseas bank, and the depositor then takes out a "loan" from the same bank (for which the deposit may serve as collateral) (Boyce, 1990, pp. 68–69).

The second set of arguments in this connection state that, when capital flees a country, the amount of money lost is equal to the potential investment in productive domestic activity. This investment would have earned foreign exchange if it had been made in the tradables sector of the economy. One popular argument calls for either an incentive to return funds held abroad by domestic residents or a significant reduction in the outflow of such funds. Accordingly, the heavily indebted countries would be in a better position for at least two reasons. The first is that the funds so returned can be used to boost domestic investment and thereby enhance debt-servicing capacity. Thus, the issue of capital flight is germane to the issue of real debt-servicing capacity. This is very important in the case of Nigeria because of its high debt-service ratio.

Second, a heavily indebted country that restricts capital flight would be in a better position to adjust to any subsequent fall in external funding. These two arguments are no doubt overstatements of the issues involved in capital flight. The impression is given that economic opportunities are equal between countries (which is not the case) and that the adoption of appropriate macroeconomic policies can release more funds domestically for investment purposes. Most of the arguments in the area are being increasingly linked to the issues of stabilization and growth (see, for example, Dornbusch, 1990). What is often ignored in the argument, however, is that it is possible for resources to be returned to the domestic economy in the form of financial holdings (fixed deposits, etc.), and not as machines and equipment for production or investment in the tradables sector.

There are other linkages between capital flight and external debt. One of the most popular hypotheses is the debt overhang argument, which states that large external debt discourages domestic investment. This is based on the fear that the tax liability of domestic investors will rise in the future.

Another relationship is that of internal transfer, where resources are transferred from the private to the public sector to finance government expenditure. As foreign debt increases, the internal transfer problem will also increase in magnitude, fostering capital flight.

A large external debt is a source of instability if for no other reason than that the outcome of the debtor-creditor position is hard to predict. As the fiscal burden of high external debt increases, a potentially unhealthy struggle for scarce resources within the economy is put in motion.

A better understanding of the relationship between capital flight and external debt can be gained by looking at some important statistics (Table 7). Using the capital flight figures derived earlier, we find the cumulative sum for the period 1972–89 is $32.8 billion. The cumulative sum of the change in debt for the same period is $32.2 billion. Thus, the ratio of capital flight to the change in external debt is about 79 percent for the entire period. For a year-by-year analysis, some selected periods have been chosen: in 1977, 1980, 1985, and 1986, capital outflows exceeded foreign debt accumulation, indicating the depletion of domestic resources.

Table 7. Nigeria: External Debt, Capital Flight, and Growth in GNP, 1972–89

	External Debt	Capital Flight	Change in External Debt	Ratio of Capital Flight to External Debt	Growth in GNP	Ratio of Gross Investment to GDP	Ratio of Capital Flight to Change in Debt
	(In millions of U.S. dollars)			(In percent)			
1972	732	106.4	81	14.5	15.0	18.3	131.4
1973	1,205	636.1	473	52.8	12.2	19.4	134.4
1974	1,274	325.0	69	25.5	74.1	14.6	471.0
1975	1,143	119.8	–131	10.5	20.8	21.8	–71.5
1976	906	124.8	–237	13.8	22.8	27.1	52.6
1977	3,146	2,490	2,240	79.1	13.7	26.7	111.2
1978	5,091	508.4	1,945	10.0	9.2	24.8	26.1
1979	6,235	–86.3	1,144	–1.4	25.5	20.1	–7.5
1980	8,934	2,713.3	2,699	30.4	29.0	20.5	100.5
1981	12,018	2,132.3	3,084	17.7	–5.6	21.4	69.2
1982	12,954	–3,805.8	936	29.4	–2.4	15.4	–406.6
1983	18,539	2,016.1	5,585	10.9	–3.5	11.4	36.1
1984	18,537	–169.8	–2.0	0.09	3.5	6.4	
1985	19,551	3,569.4	1,014	18.3	–3.7	7.5	352.0
1986	24,043	5,502.9	4,492	22.9	–48.2	11.4	122.5
1987	31,193	5,814.6	7,150	18.8	–49.2	12.3	81.4
1988	31,947	1,043.8	754	3.2	20.7	12.5	138.4
1989	32,832	–2,997.0	885	0.9	–1.2		
Total 1972–89		32,801.3	32,181				

Sources: International Monetary Fund, *International Financial Statistics Yearbook*, various issues; World Bank, *World Debt Tables*; various issues; and World Bank (1990).

It is significant that when the ratio of capital flight to the change in external debt was as high as 352 percent in 1985, the year preceding the adoption of the structural adjustment program in Nigeria, the investment-GDP ratio was 7.5 percent.

Important insights can be gained by looking at the changes in external debt and in investment and growth. In periods of rapid growth in external indebtedness, as in 1977–81, gross investment as a percentage of GNP was at the high end of its range of 20 to 27 percent for the entire period. Thus, increases in debt accumulation had an impact on investment. But the effect it could have had on growth in GDP was counteracted by capital flight. In 1981, 1983, 1985, and 1986, when the ratio of capital flight to the change in debt was 69 percent, 36 percent, 352 percent, and 122.5 percent, respectively, growth rates were negative 6 percent, 4 percent, 4 percent, and 48 percent.

These findings seem to lend credence to the general belief that capital flight has deterrent effects on the growth of the economy. The validity of such a statement and its definitiveness can only be based on rigorous empirical analysis beyond the scope of this study.

Conclusions

This chapter has addressed several general issues relating to capital flight. The magnitude of capital flight has been estimated using a number of alternative methods. The chapter has also discussed the causes and the mechanisms of capital flight and the link between capital flight and external debt, among other issues.

A number of conclusions can be drawn. The first is that there is no generally accepted definition of capital flight. Given the institutional framework and the nature of the economy, we have been able to adopt a definition and a measure of capital flight. Second, a significant proportion of total capital flight is recorded in the balance of payments and debt statistics. The implication of that, however, is that the adequacy of the measure depends on the accuracy of the items in the balance of payments statistics and the debt data. To the extent that these statistics are not accurate, their usefulness is in doubt.

Other important vehicles of capital flight are left out of the present estimates. Such vehicles include smuggling, currency movements, and misinvoicing. There are indications that a lot of money is transferred through trade misinvoicing. In general, since both the underinvoicing of exports and the overinvoicing of imports add to capital flight, the two should be added to estimate the net effect of trade misinvoicing on capital flight. To the extent that underinvoicing and overinvoicing exist in Nigeria, capital flight is underestimated. A third conclusion is that if a large amount of domestically owned wealth resides abroad, tax revenues are adversely affected, and policy variables cease to be representative of the real situation.

Fourth, even though domestic policy distortions can lead to capital flight, the role of access to political office and the perquisites of office cannot be ignored. Indeed, many people who have transferred money abroad, and who belong to this category, do so not in the course of business but as a result of access to foreign exchange. The extent to which the provision of domestic incentives and the elimination of policy distortions will bring a reversal of capital flows is not precisely known. What is certain, however, is that political and macroeconomic stability plays an important role in the flow of capital. A suitable and stable macroeconomic environment that minimizes domestic macroeconomic policy errors will ensure that the economic distortions that bring about capital flight are eliminated.

Of significance in the area of policy errors that propel capital flight are inflation, exchange rate misalignment, fiscal deficit, and financial repression. The issue of corruption is more difficult for prescriptive purposes. The only safe thing that can be said is that there is a need for attitude changes, which require serious commitment to honest government on the part of political office holders.

Nigerians may own domiciliary accounts in which foreign currencies can be kept. The availability of this avenue may be important in the repatriation of some foreign funds. Its usefulness in attracting large sums of money to the country under the present system is limited, however.

References

Ajayi, S. Ibi, 1991, "Macroeconomic Approach to External Debt: The Case of Nigeria," African Economic Research Consortium Paper No. 8 (Nairobi: Initiative Publishers).

———, 1992, "An Economic Analysis of Capital Flight from Nigeria," World Bank Working Paper Series No. 993 (Washington: World Bank).

Alesina, Alberto, and Guido Tabellini, 1989, "External Debt, Capital Flight and Political Risk," *Journal of International Economics*, Vol. 27, No. 3/4.

Bhagwati, Jagdish, 1964, "On the Underinvoicing of Imports," *Bulletin of the Oxford University Institute of Statistics*, Vol. 26.

———, Anne Krueger, and Chaiyawat Webulswasdi, 1974, "Capital Flight from LDCs: A Statistical Analysis," in *Illegal Transactions in International Trade*, ed. by J.N. Bhagwati (Amsterdam: North-Holland).

Boyce, James K., 1990, *The Political Economy of External Indebtedness: A Case Study of the Philippines* (Manila: Institute of Development Studies).

Chang, P.H. Kevin, and Robert E. Cumby, 1991, "Capital Flight in Sub-Saharan African Countries," in *African External Finance in the 1990s*, ed. by Ishrat Husain and John Underwood (Washington: World Bank).

Cline, William R., 1986, "Capital Flight Estimates" (unpublished).

Conesa, E.R., 1987, *The Causes of Capital Flight from Latin America* (Washington: Inter-American Development Bank).

Cuddington, J.T., 1986, *Capital Flight: Estimates, Issues and Explanations*, Princeton Studies in International Finance No. 58 (Princeton, New Jersey: Princeton University Press).

———, 1987, "Macroeconomic Determinants of Capital Flight: An Econometric Investigation," in *Capital Flight and Third World Debt*, ed. by D.R. Lessard and J. Williamson (Washington: Institute for International Economics).

Cumby, R., and R.M. Levich, 1987, "On the Definition and Magnitude of Recent Capital Flight," NBER Working Paper No. 2275 (Cambridge, Massachusetts: National Bureau of Economic Research).

Deppler, Michael, and Martin Williamson, 1987, "Capital Flight: Concepts, Measurement and Issues," *Staff Studies for the World Economic Outlook*, World Economic and Financial Surveys (Washington: International Monetary Fund).

Dooley, Michael P., 1986, "Country Specific Risk Premiums, Capital Flight and Net Investment Income Payments in Selected Developing Countries" (unpublished; Washington: International Monetary Fund).

———, 1988, "Buy-Backs and the Market Valuation of External Debt," *Staff Papers*, International Monetary Fund, Vol. 35 (June).

———, William Helkie, Ralph Tryon, and John Underwood, 1986, "An Analysis of External Debt Positions of Eight Developing Countries through 1990," *Journal of Development Economics*, Vol. 21, No. 2.

Dornbusch, Rudiger, 1985, "External Debt, Budget Deficit and Disequilibrium Exchange Rates," in *International Debt and the Developing Countries*, ed. by G.W. Smith and J.T. Cuddington (Washington: World Bank).

———, 1990, "Policies to Move from Stabilization to Growth," in *Proceedings of the World Bank Annual Conference on Development Economics* (Washington: World Bank).

Duwendag, D., 1987, "Capital Flight from Developing Countries: Estimates and Determinants for 25 Major Borrowers," SUERF Series

No. 52A (Tilburg, Netherlands: Societé Universitaire Européenne de Recherches Financières).

Eaton, Jonathan, 1987, "Public Debt Guarantees and Private Capital Flight," *World Bank Economic Review*, Vol. 1, No. 3 (May).

el Hadj, Elie, 1971, "The Economics of an Offshore Banking Centre," *Euromoney*.

Erbe, S., 1985, "The Flight of Capital from Developing Countries," *Intereconomics*, Vol. 20.

Froot, K., 1989, "Buybacks, Exit Bonds, and Optionality of Debt and Liquidity Relief," *International Economic Review*, Vol. 30.

Gordon, D.B., and Ross Levine, 1989, "The `Problem' of Capital Flight—A Cautionary Note," *World Economy*, Vol. 12.

Gulati, S.K., 1985, "Capital Flight through Faked Invoices: 1977–1983: A Statistical Note" (unpublished; New York: Columbia University).

———, 1987, "A Note on Trade Misinvoicing," in *Capital Flight and Third World Debt*, ed. by D.R. Lessard and J. Williamson (Washington: Institute for International Economics).

Husted, Steven, and Michael Melvin, 1990, *International Economics* (New York: Harper & Row).

International Monetary Fund, 1989, *International Financial Statistics Yearbook* (Washington).

———, 1990, *International Financial Statistics Yearbook* (Washington).

———, *International Financial Statistics Yearbook* (Washington, various years).

International Monetary Fund Research Department, 1991, *Determinants and Systemic Consequences of International Capital Flows*, IMF Occasional Paper No. 77 (Washington).

Ize, A., and G. Ortiz, 1987, "Fiscal Rigidities, Public Debt and Capital Flight," *Staff Papers*, International Monetary Fund, Vol. 32, No. 4.

Khan, Mohsin, 1989, "Flight of Capital from Pakistan," *Pakistan and Gulf Economist*, January 21–27.

———, and Nadeem Ul Haque, 1985, "Foreign Borrowing and Capital Flight: A Formal Analysis," *Staff Papers*, International Monetary Fund, Vol. 32, No. 4.

———, 1987, "Capital Flight from Developing Countries," *Finance & Development*, Vol. 24.

Kindleberger, C.F., 1987, "Capital Flight—A Historical Perspective," in *Capital Flight and Third World Debt*, ed. by D.R. Lessard and J. Williamson (Washington: Institute for International Economics).

Krugman, Paul, 1988, "Financing vs. Forgiving a Debt Overhang: Some Analytical Notes," *Journal of Development Economics*, Vol. 29.

Lessard, D.R., and John Williamson, eds., 1987, *Capital Flight and Third World Debt* (Washington: Institute for International Economics).

Morgan Guaranty Trust Company, 1986, "LDC Capital Flight," *World Financial Markets* (March).

Naya, Seji, and Theodore Morgan, 1974, "The Accuracy of International Trade Data: The Case of Southeast Asian Economies," in *Illegal Transactions in International Trade,* ed. by J.N. Bhagwati (Amsterdam: North-Holland).

Pastor, Manuel, Jr., 1989, *Capital Flight and the Latin American Debt Crisis* (Washington: Economic Policy Institute).

———, 1990, "Capital Flight from Latin America," *World Development,* Vol. 18.

Rojas-Suárez, L., 1991, "Risk and Capital Flight in Developing Countries," in *Determinants and Systemic Consequences of International Capital Flows,* IMF Occasional Paper No. 77 (Washington: International Monetary Fund).

Sachs, Jeffrey, 1989, "The Debt Overhang of Developing Countries," in *Debt, Stabilization and Development: Essays in Memory of Carlos Diaz Alejandro,* ed. by G. Calvo and others (Oxford: Basil Blackwell).

Varman, Benu, 1989, *Capital Flight—A Critique of Concepts* (Hamburg: Verlag Weltarchiv).

Varman-Schneider, S., 1991, *Capital Flight from Developing Countries* (Boulder, Colorado: Westview Press).

Walter, I., 1986, "The Mechanism of Capital Flight," paper presented at a conference on Capital Flight and Third World Debt, Institute for International Economics, October 2–4.

World Bank, 1985, *World Development Report 1985* (New York: Oxford University Press).

———, 1990, *World Development Report 1990* (New York: Oxford University Press).

———, *World Debt Tables* (Washington, various years).

Capital Flight from Uganda, 1971–94: Estimates, Causes, and Consequences 8

Razaq A. Olopoenia

One of the major characteristics of the economic crisis in Africa in the past two decades is external disequilibrium, manifested in persistent current account deficits in virtually all sub-Saharan African economies currently implementing structural adjustment programs. These programs usually require capital inflows from abroad as a precondition for success. Yet little attention has been given to one aspect of external flows that may play a significant role in the external sector disequilibrium. Capital outflows, in the form of flight capital from Africa, have received less attention in the analysis of the continent's external debt problems. Exceptions to this general omission are the studies by Ajayi (1990) on capital flight from Nigeria, Ng'eno (1992) on Kenya, and Chang and Cumby (1991) on a number of African countries.

This chapter attempts to contribute to our understanding of capital flight from Africa by providing some estimates of capital flight from Uganda. Like many countries in sub-Saharan Africa, Uganda has experienced a fairly long period of macroeconomic disequilibrium. The country's macroeconomic situation in the past two decades has been marked by high inflation, currency overvaluation, and negative real GDP growth. Although policy reforms have succeeded in controlling inflation, reducing the overvaluation of the currency, and reversing the trend of real output growth, the problems of fiscal imbalance, reduced export earnings, and a large current account deficit have persisted. Until recently, the macroeconomic and political environment in the country was characterized by many of the features identified in the literature as likely to encourage capital outflows (see Dooley and others, 1986; Lessard and Williamson, 1987; Khan and Ul Haque, 1985; and Pastor, 1990). It is therefore reasonable to expect that Uganda has experienced some capital flight in the recent past.

This paper attempts to assess the extent of capital flight from Uganda during 1971–94. In this period, the country experienced economic and political crises as well as regime changes. It is likely that the behavior of capital outflows would be different for some of these episodes of economic and political change. In particular, the degree of capital outflow was more likely to have been different before 1990 than after. The years between 1971 and 1990 were marked by either economic distortions or political instability, or both. Although political stability was, by and large, restored by 1990, economic reforms had not yet established a firm base. Since 1991, many elements of the reform package have been steadily implemented; by 1993, these had started to show positive results. One would therefore expect both political stability and economic reform to have significant effects on the nature of capital flows into and out of the country.

This chapter first reviews the various definitions and the implied measures of capital flight in the literature and then attempts to estimate capital flight from Uganda using those definitions and measures that can be applied within the constraints of the available data. In addition, it investigates the causes and consequences of capital flight out of Uganda during 1971–94. The chapter also reviews the theoretical explanations of capital flight in the literature. This is followed by a discussion of developments in the Ugandan economy, particularly those that suggest the likelihood of capital flight. Estimates of capital flight from Uganda are also reported. The chapter then discusses the significance of capital outflows from Uganda, as well as the results of some tests of hypotheses about capital flight with Ugandan data. The chapter concludes with a summary of the findings and their policy implications.

Definitions, Measurement, and Causes of Capital Flight

Definitions and Measurement of Capital Flight

The recent literature on capital flight recognizes the diversity of definitions and related measures of the phenomenon (Khan and Ul Haque, 1985; Ajayi, 1990; Pastor, 1990; and Ng'eno, 1992). The question "what is capital flight?" leads to different concepts and measurements. Some analysts prefer a narrow definition of capital flight as a short-term speculative outflow of funds, which Cuddington (1986) identifies as the prototypical form of capital flight. Others define capital flight as all outflows of capital that represent that part of a country's total wealth that is not available for servicing a country's external debt or for development financing because residents acquire assets abroad (Khan and Ul Haque, 1985; and Chang and Cumby, 1991).

The variety of definitions of capital flight arises because in a world of varying country-specific risks, optimal portfolio selection rules suggest that rational agents prefer assets with low risk and high returns in an attempt to protect the value of their wealth. Thus, if the risk of holding a domestic asset is high in a developing country, owners will prefer to hold foreign rather than domestic assets. Hence, the outflow of capital from developing to developed countries would be the normal response. Thus, it has been suggested that the term *capital flight* is a "pejorative description of natural, economically rational responses to the portfolio choices that have confronted wealthy residents of some debtor countries in recent years" (Lessard and Williamson, 1987, p. 201).

A contrary view is that, as far as capital outflows from developing countries are concerned, all such outflows that are not in response to national needs should be treated as capital flight. This position is usually justified on the basis of the scarcity of capital, especially in the form of foreign exchange, in these countries. Given this scarcity, it is presumed that the rate-of-return differential on investment between developing and developed countries would suggest that the flow of capital should be from the latter to the former. Also, the likely consequences of capital outflows from the developing countries have been invoked in support of this definition of capital flight. Among these are the negative domestic growth effect of the diversion of investment abroad, and the "perverse" combination of external debt accumulation and private asset acquisition abroad, the earnings from which are often not available for servicing the country's external debt. In addition, such private foreign asset accumulation is likely to undermine the rationale for resolving the debt problem either through the provision of new credit or through debt relief, because new resources made available in the process of resolving the debt problem might be used to finance private acquisition of foreign assets by domestic residents (Pastor, 1990).

Cumby and Levich (1987) pragmatically suggest that "any specification of capital flight ought to be consistent with the economic or policy question under consideration" (p. 49). Given the economic problems confronting many debt-burdened developing countries, this guideline would support the broader definition of capital flight, which is based on the difference between the sources and uses of foreign exchange. This definition is adopted in Dooley and others (1986), Morgan Guaranty Trust Company (1986), Lessard and Williamson (1987), and Pastor (1990). It is also one of the definitions used in Ajayi (1990).

At least two definitions of capital flight attempt to reflect this broader development perspective. The first attempts to distinguish between "normal" capital flows and capital flight. Normal capital outflows are defined as that portion of private residents' acquisitions of external claims associated with repatriated interest earnings. Capital flight is then defined as the difference between total private capital outflows and the part of those outflows for which interest income is identified and reported in the balance of payments (Khan and Ul Haque, 1985). A similar definition is found in Dooley (1986).

While focusing broadly on the same development-related implications of capital flight, Pastor (1990) adopts a wider concept of capital flight. His concept embraces all nonrepatriated external claims by domestic residents. The two approaches start from a common base of private capital outflows, but Pastor (1990) attempts to capture all nonrepatriated foreign assets of domestic residents. Thus, capital flight in this context is defined as the stock of gross capital outflows over some period (as in Khan and Ul Haque, 1985), plus the difference between the implied earnings on this stock and the reported income of residents from foreign investment. This approach views capital flight as that part of the stock of domestic residents' claims on foreigners that is not available for use in the domestic economy. This definition embraces both recorded and unrecorded private capital outflows.

Cuddington's narrow (1986) definition of capital flight, which focuses on speculative short-term capital while accepting the "normality" of capital outflows, differs from the Khan and Ul Haque (1987) definition. It defines capital flight as the sum of short-term capital outflows and net errors and omissions as reported in the balance of payments. The justification is that this measures transactions that are unaccounted for through the normal channels. This introduces a legal dimension to the concept of capital flight. Yet another approach to the measurement of capital flight from developing countries is based on nonbank cross-border deposits by residents of the country. It is suggested that this measure is more reliable because the deposits are directly and openly reported. Their use thus avoids the problems inherent in indirect estimates (Khan and Ul Haque, 1985, p. 611).

Each of these definitions of capital flight has its shortcomings. The narrow definition, which restricts capital flight to short-term capital movements plus net errors and omissions, suffers from two limitations. First, it focuses too narrowly on the legality of capital outflows. Even then it fails to embrace all illegal outflows. It neglects the problems of trade misinvoicing, which would normally be considered illegal. Neglecting such activities would either underestimate a surplus or overestimate a deficit in the current account. These "errors" in the recorded current account would be reflected in reserve movements. Thus, this approach, which attempts to measure discrepancies between the recorded current account balance and changes in reserves as part of capital flight, would underestimate such outflows by relying on reported net errors and omissions, whose estimate would be distorted by trade misinvoicing. It also ignores the long-term components of capital outflows by focusing on short-term capital movements. Yet in the circumstances of many African countries, the long-term dimension of capital flight is as important an economic and policy question as the short-term one, if not more so. One of the major problems facing these countries is that of a low rate of investment, and one of the common policy issues is how to attract foreign investment into these economies.

The definition based on the distinction between normal and abnormal private capital outflows may not be the most appropriate from the perspective of the relevant policy issues for most developing countries. This is particularly true of most African countries, whose needs involve the resolution of the growth-cum-debt problem. For such economies a broader definition of capital flight would seem more germane. The nonbank cross-border deposit approach is an inadequate concept of capital flight for a number of reasons. Even though such flows are openly reported, the measure may not provide a reliable estimate of such deposits. Some deposits may be held in nonreporting institutions (Vos, 1990), or the nationalities of the depositors may be hidden by "arm's-length transactions." Domestic residents of a country may hold foreign assets in the form of real estate, bonds, equities, and other business investments in foreign countries that would be excluded from cross-border bank deposits (Khan and Ul Haque, 1987).

The broader definition may be appropriate for the economic and policy questions facing most developing countries, but like the others it does not take trade misinvoicing into account. Chang and Cumby (1991), using a similar definition, attempt to adjust their estimates for trade misinvoicing. But their estimates result in a distribution that makes it hard to conclude whether or not this has been a consistent channel of capital flight in these countries (p. 167).

Associated with each of the definitions of capital flight surveyed thus far is a particular approach to its measurement, and the difficulty of defining capital flight renders its measurement even more difficult. One characteristic of capital flight is the multiplicity of channels through which it can occur, and these are mostly difficult to identify. Even when some can be identified, transactions through them are unrecorded, which makes accurate direct measurement impossible. Hence, attempts to estimate capital flight usually rely on indirect methods.

With the exception of the definition that focuses on private nonbank cross-border deposits, all the definitions lead to indirect measurements based on estimates from the balance of payments accounts. The cross-border bank deposits approach, because of its shortcomings, can only provide a baseline indicator of capital flight, as it is likely to give the lowest estimate for most developing countries.

Reference to the relevant balance of payments items for the estimation of capital flight facilitates a discussion of the various alternative measures of the phenomenon commonly used in the literature. The re-

Table 1. External Debt and Balance of Payments Items for Capital Flight Estimation

	External debt
A	Change in long-term debt
B	Change in short-term debt
	Balance of payments
C	Current account balance
D	Net foreign direct investment
E	Portfolio investment
F	Change in private banks' net foreign assets
G	Private nonbank short-term capital (net)
H	Change in reserves
I	Errors and omissions

view of the methods of estimating capital flight that follows is based on the list of possible elements of capital flight in Table 1.

Cuddington (1986) measures capital flight as the sum of all short-term private capital outflows and net errors and omissions in the balance of payments accounts. This gives a measure of capital flight (*KF*) from the entries in Table 1 as follows:

$$KF = F + G + I. \tag{1}$$

Although this method corresponds to the hot money definition of capital flight, it is narrower than a more logical definition of hot money as "capital that flees" a country. The logic behind the hot money concept of capital flight would suggest that its measurement should include movements of portfolio capital. This view is, in particular, supported by recent developments in international capital markets. Witness the outflow of portfolio investment from Mexico during the first quarter of 1995 in response to economic policy failure (*The Economist*, March 11–17, 1995). Thus, this estimate of capital flight, apart from the conceptual issues mentioned above, does not in fact capture all outflows that may qualify as capital flight even under the hot money definition. In addition, it does not adjust for the distortions that trade misinvoicing may introduce into the reported net errors and omissions in the balance of payments accounts. There are also the measurement problems that arise when cross-border smuggling and parallel markets in foreign exchange are used as channels for capital flight. Khan and Ul Haque (1987) identify the particular case of the "Hundi" market in the Middle East.

Estimates of capital flight based on the concept of normal capital outflows define such outflows as all private acquisitions of foreign assets that generate reported interest earnings for residents. The measurement of normal private capital outflows is derived indirectly, by estimating the stock of external claims that would have earned the interest income on foreign investment recorded in the balance of payments. The measurement of capital flight under this approach involves two steps: First, gross private capital outflows are estimated on the basis of the sources and uses of foreign exchange. This approach measures gross private capital outflows as the difference between the sum of changes in external debt and net foreign direct investment on the one hand, and that of the current account balance, changes in official international reserves, and the net foreign asset position of domestic banks on the other. Thus gross private capital outflow (*GPCX*) for each period is estimated, using the entries in Table 1, as follows:

$$GPCX = A + B + D + C + F + H. \qquad (2)$$

In the second stage of the estimation, gross private capital outflows are cumulated over some period. The difference between this stock of external claims and the stock of external claims on which interest income is reported is considered capital flight. This represents the difference between gross private capital flows and normal capital flows. The estimate of the stock of normal capital requires the use of some measure of the foreign interest rate in the estimate of normal capital outflows from the foreign interest earnings of residents.

Some estimates of gross private capital outflow (for example, those of Khan and Ul Haque, 1987) do not include net foreign direct investment as a source of foreign exchange. Others, such as the World Bank (1985), Erbe (1985), Morgan Guaranty Trust Company (1986), and Chang and Cumby (1991), do. The estimates of capital flight in these studies, however, differ from those based on the concept of normal capital outflows. They do not subtract an estimate of normal capital outflows from the gross estimates derived on the basis of the sources-and-uses approach. The estimate of capital flight under that approach is simply the difference between inflows of funds and their uses through current account deficit financing and official and private banks' foreign asset accumulation.

Pastor (1990) measures capital flight by first estimating gross outflows, using the sources-and-uses approach. He then estimates the stock of external claims of residents over some period using the following formula:

$$CS_t = \Sigma(CS_{t-1} + GPCX_t + r^*CS_{t-1} - FII_t), \qquad (3)$$

where CS_t is the stock of private residents' external claims at time t, $GPCX_t$ is gross private capital outflows at time t, measured by Equation (2) above, r^* is an appropriate foreign interest rate, CS_{t-1} is the stock of private external claims in the previous period, and FII_t is foreign investment income inflows at time t.

This formula does not just measure just the stock of external claims arising from private capital outflows by taking the existing stock of such claims and current outflows. It also adds estimates of potential interest income to the stock of capital outflows. The difference between this value over a given period and the reported repatriated investment income is then taken as an estimate of capital flight over the period. This approach requires the choice of an initial value of the stock of external claims, to which is added each year's outflow of capital derived by the residual approach in order to obtain an estimate of the stock of private residents' external claims at any given time. The initial stock is simply assumed to be equal to the external assets implied by the reported interest income and some measure of the international interest rate for the initial year.

This leads to an underestimation of the initial stock of capital outflows. It assumes that the reported private investment income from abroad reflects all such incomes. Even if the interest earnings in the first year are fully reported, the interest rate proxy may be different from the actual rate of interest. The underestimation of the initial stock may lead to a situation in which the reported repatriated income exceeds the estimated potential earnings. This would lead to an underestimation of capital flight as defined under this method. Pastor (1990) suggests an adjustment that either uses a reinitialization of the previous year's stock or simply sets the earnings differential to zero and adds the current year's capital outflow estimate. Whereas the second method preserves the initial downward bias, the first involves a process that may lead to an overestimation.

The estimate of the sources of funds requires care in the measurement of changes in external debt (Chang and Cumby, 1991). There is a need to decide what to include in external debt. Should the measurement be based on long-term obligations alone, or should it include short-term debt? Should long-term debt include public and publicly guaranteed debt as well as private nonguaranteed debt? The addition of the latter would lead to an estimate of the change in gross private sector foreign assets. This would normally be matched by a corresponding increase in private liabilities. If such liabilities are expected to be serviced and repaid by the private sector, the corresponding acquisition of assets should not be counted as capital flight (Chang and Cumby, 1991). However, if the public sector ultimately assumes the responsibility for the servicing and repayment of such liabilities, the asset acquisition associated with them would properly be considered capital flight.

If short-term debts are obligations of the public sector, they should be included in the measure of the stock of external debt. Also, the use of the debt stock would include significant currency revaluation effects if a large proportion of the debt is in currencies other than the U.S. dollar, in which the debt data are reported.

The problems of debt discovery, interest rescheduling, and the transfer of private sector obligations to the public sector have been suggested as reasons for preferring the use of the stock rather than the flow of external debt to obtain the change in debt. The estimates of sources of foreign exchange used in the measurement of capital flight in this study are therefore based on the stock of external debt.

Determinants of Capital Flight

A number of factors have been suggested in the literature as the major theoretical explanation for capital flight. Major contributions to the discussion include Khan and Ul Haque (1985), Cuddington (1987), Lessard and Williamson (1987), and Pastor (1990). The discussion that follows relies mainly on the work of Khan and Ul Haque and that of Pastor. The theoretical explanation for capital flight focuses on the motives for the substitution of foreign for domestic assets in a resident's wealth portfolio. Such asset substitutions are influenced by the overall domestic investment climate as well as the external position of the economy. The profitability of domestic investment and the performance of the external sector depend on developments in the macroeconomy. These are in turn determined by both internal and external factors. Accelerating domestic inflation imposes an implicit inflation tax on domestic currency assets. The choice between foreign assets and domestic real investment or financial assets would depend on the rate of return on foreign assets (adjusted for expected currency devaluation) relative to that on the alternative domestic assets. If the domestic currency is perceived to be overvalued in terms of the real exchange rate, there would be a strong expectation of future depreciation. This would encourage movement out of domestic assets into foreign ones, even in the absence of inflationary pressure.

Both the monetary and the fiscal policy stance of the government will, to a large extent, determine the inflation trends. A growing fiscal deficit financed by money creation, or the possibility of its being monetized in the near future, would precipitate inflationary expectations, with a resultant movement of assets out of domestic currency. An expansionary monetary policy independent of the public sector deficit would have similar consequences for inflation.

Financial repression in an inflationary environment often leads to low or even negative real interest rates. This reduces the attractiveness of domestic financial assets. The control of interest rates may make domestic nominal rates lower than those on foreign financial assets. The underdevelopment of domestic capital markets reduces the opportunity to protect private wealth against domestic inflation. In such an environment the incentive to acquire foreign assets will be strong. The external position of a country can be a major source of the motive for capital flight. When a country suffers a persistent balance of payments deficit, failure to take corrective policy actions leads to a loss of confidence in the economy. Balance of payments problems may be due to external shocks (such as a deterioration in the terms of trade) or inappropriate macroeconomic policies. The external imbalance will be exacerbated by the need to meet foreign debt obligations. The deficits would lead to external debt accumulation while constraining the economy's capacity to service existing debt. Sooner or later, policymakers would be forced to adopt corrective measures. The expectation of such policies would encourage domestic residents to move their wealth into foreign assets in an attempt to protect their value against the expected devaluation.

The attempt to avoid domestic taxation is one of the motivations identified in the literature as a cause of capital flight (Khan and Ul Haque, 1987; Pastor, 1990). If the tax system is based on taxation by origin rather than by residence, both the foreign assets held by domestic residents and the incomes therefrom would be outside the jurisdiction of domestic fiscal authorities. Hence, expectation of tax increases would be a powerful incentive for the export of capital. A persistent public sector fiscal imbalance would be a strong indicator of future tax hikes and therefore a likely cause of capital flight.

In the analysis of the causes of the capital flight, the phenomenon of two-way flows has recently attracted attention. The determinants of capital flight identified above cannot provide a convincing rationale for the phenomenon of "simultaneous foreign borrowing and investment at home and abroad" (Khan and Ul Haque, 1985, p. 607). Some authors assume an agent separation framework, with the government borrowing abroad to finance its budget while private agents acquire foreign assets. Khan and Ul Haque have argued that unless the government's fiscal position is independent of developments in the economy (which cannot be the case), this approach cannot provide a valid rationale for the two-way flow of capital between developed and developing countries. They propose an explanation based on the assumption of unequal uncertainty associated with domestic and foreign investment. The degree of uncertainty (which they label "expropriation risk") associated with domestic investment is higher because of the inadequacy of institutions to facilitate market transactions and the instability of political and economic regimes—both of which raise transaction or insurance costs, or both, in developing countries.

Pastor (1990) emphasizes two dimensions of external loans that, he argues, encourage the two-way flow. First, foreign loans receive favored treatment from local authorities through the implicit or explicit public guarantee of such loans. Domestic investment is not protected by the public sector against failure. In addition, a portion of the resident investors' domestic assets may be acquired through direct or inflation taxes in the event of a debt crisis. The public guarantee of private external debts makes the two-way flow profitable to the private investor, especially in a regime of currency overvaluation. Investors can finance domestic investment with external loans while simultaneously acquiring foreign assets with their own domestic resources. The domestic resource costs of both transactions are reduced by overvaluation.

Success of the domestic investment (which implies that investors would pay back the foreign loan) would only involve a loss equal to the differential between the rate of interest on the external loan and the deposit rate abroad. This would, however, be compensated for by the profitability of the domestic investment. If the domestic investment fails, external debt repayment could be avoided either through declaration of bankruptcy or assumption of the external obligation by the government. In either case the private external liabilities are transferred to the society. The availability of foreign loans provides the liquidity that facilitates this hedging operation by the private sector. A similar argument is advanced by Cuddington (1987), which emphasizes the liquidity aspect, and by Lessard and Williamson (1987), in which both the "discriminatory treatment" and the "possibility of a crisis" arguments are articulated. The possibility of a crisis arises from the fact that foreign credit availability, by encouraging private hedging, raises external debt, which may eventually lead to currency devaluation, higher taxes, and domestic inflation. The analysis presented above on the determinants of capital flight suggests that an understanding of the phenomenon requires exploring the role of both internal and external factors.

The basic model used to explain capital flight in this study draws mainly from the model presented in Pastor (1990). The model emphasizes two groups of determinants of capital flight: the overall domestic investment climate (Pastor, 1990, p. 7) and external factors. However, the model is designed to be parsimonious in view of the likely problem of degrees of freedom in estimating the model. The following key variables are considered as the determinants of capital flight in the econometric analysis:

- the domestic inflation rate;
- a measure of financial incentives in the domestic economy;
- a measure of domestic currency overvaluation; and
- the growth rate of the domestic economy relative to that of the likely destination of exiting residents' capital.

Macroeconomic Developments in Uganda from 1970 to 1993

From the early 1970s until recently, the Ugandan economy experienced traumatic developments as a result of political instability and economic mismanagement. Although Uganda was one of the most vibrant economies in Africa during the early post-independence years, the country's GDP declined during most of the 1970s and the first half of the 1980s. Plagued by distortions arising from government intervention in the economy—exchange and price controls, financial repression, public sector monopoly in the marketing of major export commodities, and the like—the economy experienced persistent macroeconomic disequilibrium between 1973 and 1986. This disequilibrium was marked by excessive money financing of public sector deficits, a high rate of growth of the money supply, and one of the highest inflation rates on the continent, reaching over 100 percent in some years. During the period export revenue fell to nearly 50 percent of its 1970 level (World Bank and United Nations Development Program, 1990). Parallel-market activities dominated foreign exchange transactions. For a while during this period, the country could only import goods and services on a cash-and-carry basis—declining export earnings meant that import volume was limited to what foreign exchange earnings could finance. Lack of imports of capital and intermediate goods led to declining output. The economic situation was further compounded by several shocks: the expulsion of Asians, the war to overthrow Idi Amin, and the civil war during the early 1980s.

These developments would no doubt have created a strong motivation for capital flight out of Uganda. Although the ongoing adjustment programs have reversed most of the negative trends of the recent past, the economy still experiences persistent balance of payments disequilibria. This has been aggravated by the adverse trend in the terms of trade of the last several years. This has exacerbated the incipient debt crisis, which is currently obscured by the favorable attitude of international donors toward the country (see Mbire and Atingi, 1994; see also Table 5 and the Appendix to this chapter for the trend in Uganda's external debt accumulation). Although investment picked up from a low of about 6 percent of GDP on average for 1976–80 to an average of about 13 percent over 1987–93, gross domestic saving was negative from 1984 up to 1993, resulting in a domestic saving gap averaging a little over 20 percent of GDP between 1984 and 1993 (Mbire and Atingi, 1994; see also Table 7 below).

The low levels of domestic saving and investment, the persistent balance of payments deficits, and the heavy reliance on external financing as the basis of the economic turnaround that Uganda is currently experiencing provide the rationale for an exploration of capital flight from the country. It is hoped that such an exploration will reveal the extent of the problem, its causes, and the effects on the economy. An understanding of the phenomenon will permit the design of appropriate policies that may succeed in permitting Uganda to ameliorate the flow and explore the possibilities of tapping domestic residents' accumulated assets abroad, to help resolve the country's debt-growth conflict.

Capital Flight from Uganda

Estimates of Capital Flight

The estimates of capital flight reported in this section are based on the following four approaches:

- the "normal" capital flow method;
- the Pastor (1990) method;
- the hot money approach; and
- the cross-border deposit approach.

The steps followed in the application of each of these methods are described below.

The cross-border deposit approach simply measures capital flight as the change in such deposits over a given period. The hot money approach measures capital flight as the sum of net private short-term capital movements and net errors and omissions in the balance of payments. Two variants of the hot money approach are reported in Table 2. The first is based on Equation (1) in the text; it adds both private nonbank and banking sector short-term capital movements to net errors and omissions. The second excludes commercial banks' net foreign asset movements from the computation of private net short-term movements; these are reported in the last two columns of Table 2.

Table 2. Uganda: Alternative Estimates of Capital Flight, 1971–94
(In millions of U.S. dollars)

	Normal External Claim Basis				Pastor (1990) Unrepatriated External Claim Basis				Hot Money Approach	
	I	II	III	IV	I	II	III	IV	I	II
1971	–30.5	–27.9	–30.5	–27.9	–19.0	–14.4	–19.0	–14.4	–2.9	–7.5
1972	31.6	34.1	31.8	34.1	4.0	6.8	4.2	7.0	44.8	42.3
1973	36.9	35.3	36.9	35.3	47.8	46.8	47.8	46.8	50.9	52.5
1974	22.1	21.5	22.4	21.8	19.7	19.9	20.1	20.2	20.7	21.3
1975	–67.5	–74.2	–66.1	–73.2	–54.3	–60.4	–53.3	–59.4	–30.1	–23.4
1976	81.0	70.2	82.0	81.6	67.0	66.3	68.5	67.8	32.9	33.7
1977	93.6	83.7	129.0	119.1	131.5	121.6	167.2	157.3	19.5	29.4
1978	–28.6	–12.9	–36.5	–20.8	–4.3	11.0	–8.8	6.1	–47.5	–31.8
1979	287.4	298.8	301.9	313.3	224.8	236.9	243.8	255.8	209.3	197.9
1980	–185.0	–148.0	–166.1	–166.1	–66.5	–60.4	–36.2	–33.7	64.8	64.6
1981	35.1	38.7	3.2	6.8	49.4	95.1	67.5	73.6	59.8	56.2
1982	52.8	44.7	61.9	53.8	100.3	100.3	121.2	116.0	16.6	24.7
1983	25.5	24.5	14.3	13.3	83.9	89.1	84.1	85.0	35.6	36.6
1984	182.8	103.0	195.3	195.5	241.4	248.1	264.9	267.0	–24.7	–24.9
1985	167.0	258.5	169.8	181.3	279.1	299.6	298.4	312.7	–8.8	–20.3
1986	189.0	183.0	213.0	207.0	307.4	311.5	348.2	345.9	–93.5	87.5
1987	425.5	415.3	426.4	416.2	517.3	516.5	536.9	530.0	49.8	60.0
1988	–207.9	–192.7	–190.1	–174.9	13.2	38.3	52.8	70.8	–110.0	–125.0
1989	3.1	3.1	28.2	28.2	262.5	279.0	321.7	327.7	79.4	79.0
1990	112.7	109.0	149.5	145.8	429.5	445.9	511.6	515.2	6.3	10.0
1991	–38.8	–55.8	–3.2	–20.2	277.6	278.6	357.4	346.5	3.8	20.8
1992	12.5	–8.3	–10.7	–31.5	268.4	261.2	287.6	270.9	–20.3	0.5
1993	–441.8	–457.1	–471.1	–486.4	–244.4	–231.7	–227.4	–241.2	. . .	. . .
1994	223.0	. . .	190.9	. . .	454.5	. . .	472.8	. . .	. . .	. . .

Source: Author's calculations.

Table 3. Uganda: Alternative Estimates of Private Capital Outflows, 1971–94
(In millions of U.S. dollars)

	Gross Private Capital Outflows (GPCX Residual Method)				Hot Money Approach	
	GPCX I	GPCX II	GPCX III	GPCX IV	I	II
1971	–18.2	–13.6	–18.2	–13.6	–2.9	–7.5
1972	5.2	7.7	5.4	7.9	44.8	42.3
1973	49.4	47.8	49.4	47.8	50.9	52.5
1974	15.6	15.0	15.9	15.3	20.7	21.3
1975	–59.9	–66.6	–58.9	–65.6	–30.1	–23.4
1976	65.4	64.6	66.8	66.0	32.9	33.7
1977	126.8	116.9	162.2	152.3	19.5	29.4
1978	–16.7	–1.0	–24.6	–8.9	–47.5	–31.8
1979	196.5	207.9	211.0	222.4	209.3	197.9
1980	–131.3	–131.1	–112.4	–112.4	64.8	64.6
1981	38.2	41.8	6.3	9.9	59.8	56.2
1982	49.8	41.7	58.9	50.8	16.6	24.7
1983	31.6	30.6	20.4	19.4	35.6	36.6
1984	182.8	183.0	195.3	195.5	–24.7	–24.9
1985	180.0	191.5	182.8	194.3	–8.8	–20.3
1986	191.0	185.0	215.0	209.0	–93.5	87.5
1987	382.5	372.3	383.4	373.2	49.8	60.0
1988	–179.9	–164.7	–162.1	–146.9	–110.0	–125.0
1989	3.1	3.1	28.2	28.2	79.4	79.4
1990	112.7	109.0	149.5	145.8	6.3	10.0
1991	–13.3	–30.3	22.3	5.3	3.8	20.8
1992	7.4	–13.4	–15.8	–36.6	–20.3	0.5
1993	–386.7	–402.0	–416.0	–431.3	. . .	. . .
1994	165.4	. . .	–133.3	. . .	. . .	. . .

Source: Author's calculations.

The estimates based on the normal capital flow concept and on Pastor's method involve two steps. First, total private gross capital outflows (GPCX) are estimated using the sources-and-uses method. Four different estimates of private gross capital outflows are shown in Table 3. These are based on different definitions of the sources and uses of foreign exchange. GPCX I estimates the sources of foreign exchange as the change in long-term external debt and net foreign direct investment inflow, and counts only current account deficit financing and changes in official foreign exchange reserves as the uses of foreign exchange. GPCX II uses the same definition of sources of foreign exchange as GPCX I but adds commercial banks' net acquisition of foreign assets as part of the uses of foreign exchange. GPCX III is based on the same definition of the uses of foreign exchange as GPCX I but adds changes in short-term external debt to the sources of foreign exchange. GPCX IV uses the same definition of the sources of foreign exchange as GPCX III; its definition of the uses is the same as that used in the computation of GPCX II.

The computation of the four variants of private gross capital outflow can be derived from the entries in Table 1 as follows:

$$\text{GPCX I} = A + D + C + H \tag{4}$$

$$\text{GPCX II} = A + D + C + H - F \tag{5}$$

$$\text{GPCX III} = A + B + D + C + H \tag{6}$$

$$\text{GPCX III} = A + B + D + C + H - F. \tag{7}$$

The data used in the derivation of all four variants of private gross capital outflows of Table 3 are found in Table 4.

To estimate capital flight as defined under the normal capital flow concept, the GPCX series are cumulated over a given period to obtain the total stock of external claims by Ugandan residents. These are reported in Table A2 in the Appendix. The columns in that table under "gross private capital outflows" are the stock of total external claims derived on the basis of the four variants of the GPCX series defined in Equations (4) through (7), respectively. From each of these the changes in the stock of external claims implied by the interest income inflow in the balance of payments is deducted to obtain the adjusted stock of the normal capital flow. The adjusted stock of external claims corresponding to the different measures of private gross capital outflow is reported in the first four data columns of Table 5.

The estimation of the stock of external claims based on Pastor's (1990) framework uses Equation (3). The series was initialized using the 1970 implied stock of external claims derived from the inflow of interest income reported in the balance of payments. The four variants of the adjusted stock of external claims are derived from the Pastor (1990) basis gross capital outflow of Equations (4) through (7) above.

Both procedures for deriving the adjusted stock of external claims described above require the use of an "appropriate" foreign interest rate. Ideally, the interest rate used should be a weighted average of the interest rates of the countries in which the residents' external claims that generated the reported interest income are located. In the absence of information about the geographical sources and the distribution of Uganda's inflows of interest income from abroad, U.K. treasury bill rates (IMF, *International Financial Statistics*, line 60C) were used as a proxy. To the extent that this proxy is different from the actual rates of return generating the reported interest income, the estimates of the normal stock of external claims in Table A2 in the Appendix will be incorrect. When the normal stock of external claims is underestimated,

Table 4. Uganda: External Debt and Balance of Payments Flows Used in Capital Flight Estimations, 1971–94

(In millions of U.S. dollars)

	Change in Long-Term External Debt	Change in Total External Debt	Net Foreign Direct Investment Balance	Current Account Balance	Change in Reserves[1]	Change in Private Banks' Net Foreign Assets	Private Short-Term Capital Flow (net)	Net Errors and Omissions	Foreign Investment and Income Inflow
1971	34.4	34.4	–1.2	–85.8	34.4	–4.6	0.6	6.9	3.1
1972	5.1	5.3	–11.9	16.4	–4.4	–2.5	–2.3	–40.0	2.4
1973	–0.8	–0.8	–1.4	43.0	8.6	1.6	–11.4	–41.1	4.1
1974	25.8	26.1	1.7	–24.1	12.2	0.6	1.2	–22.5	4.3
1975	5.6	6.6	2.1	–56.1	–11.5	6.7	–1.6	29.3	4.0
1976	33.4	34.8	1.2	43.2	–12.4	0.8	–11.9	21.8	2.8
1977	58.4	93.8	0.8	68.1	–0.5	9.9	–7.5	–21.9	2.8
1978	121.7	113.8	1.1	–137.4	2.1	15.7	–44.0	75.8	3.4
1979	118.9	133.4	–166.4	39.5	36.5	–11.4	–26.4	171.5	5.9
1980	92.2	111.1	0.0	–88.2	26.1	–0.2	0.0	64.5	2.0
1981	65.1	33.2	0.0	7.7	–34.6	–3.6	–18.0	–38.2	1.4
1982	154.2	163.3	0.0	–69.9	–34.5	8.1	0.0	–24.7	0.8
1983	132.4	121.2	0.0	–72.2	–28.6	1.0	0.0	–36.6	0.0
1984	52.8	65.3	0.0	103.5	26.5	–0.2	3.3	21.6	0.0
1985	158.1	160.9	0.0	4.6	17.3	–11.5	72.5	–52.2	0.0
1986	158.6	182.6	0.0	–3.8	36.2	6.0	117.6	–40.1	1.5
1987	514.8	515.7	0.0	–112.0	–20.3	10.2	–86.4	26.4	2.9
1988	12.9	30.7	0.0	–195.2	2.4	–15.2	–29.9	154.9	0.0
1989	260.8	285.9	0.0	–259.5	1.8	0.0	–41.4	–38.0	0.0
1990	370.8	407.5	1.0	–263.3	5.2	3.7	–19.5	9.5	0.0
1991	169.2	203.8	1.0	–169.8	–12.7	17.0	–21.4	0.6	2.8
1992	157.6	131.4	3.0	–99.6	–50.6	20.8	–9.5	9.0	4.1
1993	–197.5	–226.3	3.4	–135.7	–57.4	. . .	. . .	5.1	6.4
1994	356.3	324.2	4.5	–27.7	–167.7	. . .	. . .	–33.6	14.0

Source: Author's calculations based on data in Appendix Table A1.

[1]A positive entry indicates a decrease in reserves, that is, the use of reserve assets to finance the balance of payments, and a negative entry indicates an increase in reserves, that is, the use of foreign exchange inflows to acquire reserve assets.

Table 5. Uganda: Adjusted Stock of External Claims, 1971–94
(In millions of U.S. dollars)

	"Normal" Capital Flow Basis				Pastor (1990) Basis			
	I	II	III	IV	I	II	III	IV
1971	8.8	13.4	8.8	13.4	22.3	26.9	22.3	26.9
1972	40.4	47.5	40.6	47.7	26.3	33.7	26.5	33.9
1973	77.3	82.8	77.5	83.0	74.1	80.5	74.3	80.7
1974	99.4	104.3	99.9	104.8	93.8	100.4	94.4	100.9
1975	31.9	30.1	33.8	31.6	39.5	40.0	41.1	41.5
1976	112.9	110.3	115.8	113.2	106.5	106.3	109.6	109.3
1977	206.5	194.0	244.8	232.3	238.0	227.9	276.8	266.6
1978	177.9	181.1	208.3	211.5	233.7	138.9	268.0	272.7
1979	465.3	479.9	510.2	524.8	458.5	475.8	511.8	528.5
1980	280.3	295.1	344.1	358.7	395.3	415.4	475.6	494.8
1981	315.4	333.8	347.3	365.5	444.7	510.5	543.1	568.4
1982	368.2	378.5	409.2	419.3	545.5	610.8	664.3	684.4
1983	393.7	403.0	423.5	432.6	629.4	699.9	748.4	769.4
1984	576.5	506.0	618.8	628.1	870.8	948.0	1,013.3	1,036.4
1985	743.5	764.5	788.6	809.4	1,149.9	1,247.6	1,311.7	1,349.1
1986	932.5	947.5	1,001.6	1,016.4	1,457.3	1,559.1	1,659.9	1,695.0
1987	1,358.0	1,362.8	1,428.0	1,432.6	1,976.6	2,075.6	2,196.8	2,225.0
1988	1,150.1	1,170.1	1,237.9	1,257.7	1,987.8	2,113.9	2,249.6	2,295.8
1989	1,153.2	1,173.2	1,266.1	1,285.9	2,250.3	2,392.9	2,571.3	2,623.5
1990	1,265.9	1,282.2	1,415.6	1,431.7	2,679.8	2,838.8	3,082.9	3,138.7
1991	1,227.1	1,226.4	1,412.4	1,411.5	2,957.4	3,116.8	3,440.3	3,485.2
1992	1,239.6	1,218.1	1,401.7	1,380.0	3,225.8	3,378.0	3,727.9	3,756.1
1993	797.8	761.0	930.6	893.6	3,001.4	3,146.3	3,500.5	3,514.9
1994	1,020.8	. . .	1,121.5	. . .	3,455.9	. . .	3,973.3	. . .

Source: Author's calculations.

the adjusted stock of the normal capital flow basis will be overestimated, and vice versa. The same is also the case for the estimates based on Pastor's (1990) stock adjustment method.

The capital flight series derived through both the normal external claim and the Pastor (1990) basis are reported in Table 2. These series are derived as the difference in the adjusted stock of external claims over the period. Thus, the series in Table 2 are the annual changes in the corresponding entries of Table 5.

These estimates are only as good as the data on which they are based. First, the use of a proxy interest rate in the stock adjustment process introduces a downward bias in the estimates of capital flight for those years when the proxy rate is lower than the actual rate of return, and an upward bias when it is higher.

However, all the estimates of capital flight reported in Table 2 suffer from a number of fundamental problems common to all data series on

African economies. The reliability of trade data is quite low. Four data sources—the Bank of Uganda, the Ugandan Revenue Authority, the Ugandan Ministry of Finance and Planning, and the IMF's *Direction of Trade Statistics Yearbook*—report conflicting series on trade transactions for the country. Data on foreign direct investment and on interest income inflow are not regularly reported by the national or international organizations that normally publish such data. The same problem bedevils external debt series. Here the problem of availability and reliability is more serious for short-term external debt series.

The poor quality of the data compounds the basic problems encountered in any attempt to measure capital flight. The nature of capital flight compels one to resort to indirect methods of estimation that are inherently inaccurate. When such methods have to rely on data of poor quality, the problem of estimation becomes magnified. This is particularly true of this study. The quality of balance of payments statistics in Uganda has deteriorated since the 1970s as a result of economic mismanagement and the breakup of the East African Community. Although an effort is under way to improve the quality of the database, the exercise has just begun. As a result, the data on which this chapter is based still suffer from all the problems highlighted above. For example, no data are reported for foreign direct investment and interest income inflows for many of the years covered in this study. An attempt was made to check the validity of the reported net foreign investment inflow in the balance of payments using data from IMF (1994) and the definition of the overall balance in the introduction to that publication. Although nearly all the entries were confirmed, large discrepancies were observed for 1973 and 1980 (Appendix Table A1). In view of these problems, the estimates of capital flight reported in Table 2 have to be interpreted with caution.

There is also the problem of trade misinvoicing. An attempt to check the trade flow data for misinvoicing produced no evidence of systematic misinvoicing of the type that would suggest its use as a channel for capital flight. Chang and Cumby (1991) reached the same conclusion for Uganda, among other African countries, for the period 1972–87. For this chapter the reported values of imports by country of origin and by Uganda were compared for the period 1989–93. The same was done for reported export values by country of destination and by Uganda. All reported import and export value series were obtained from the *Direction of Trade Statistics Yearbook*. The trading partner countries covered accounted for a little over 90 percent of Uganda's imports and nearly 80 percent of its exports over 1980–93. The ratios of import values reported by Uganda to those reported by trading partners and of exports to the values reported by Uganda do not significantly differ from Uganda's c.i.f.-f.o.b. factor as reported in the *International Financial Statistics Yearbook*. Because of these findings, the estimates of capital flight are not adjusted for trade misinvoicing.

In general, the various capital flight estimates in Table 2 are not significantly dissimilar. In particular, all the estimates indicate wide variations in both the magnitude and the direction of capital flight over the 24 years covered by the study. The four variants of capital flight estimated on the normal external claims basis exhibit patterns of capital outflow that reflect the different definitions of the losses of foreign exchange on which their computations were based. Thus, variants I and III, and II and IV, respectively, exhibit positive capital outflows in 67 percent and 65 percent of the total number of years of observation. The same is true of the estimates based on the Pastor (1990) concept of capital flight as unrepatriated external claims of residents. Variants I and III of those estimates indicate positive capital outflows 79 percent of the time, whereas variants II and IV show positive capital outflows 83 percent of the time. The two versions of the hot money approach produced positive capital outflows over 64 percent of the period for which relevant data are available.

In terms of the magnitude of capital outflows, the hot money approach in general produced the lowest estimates, except for 1988. Estimates based on the Pastor concept of unrepatriated external claims are generally higher than those derived on the basis of the normal stock of external claims. These characteristics of the different estimates are not surprising.

By definition, the hot money measure is narrower than the other two. And the concept of capital flight as the change in the stock of unrepatriated external claims is broader than the definition based on normal capital flows. Hence, the results presented in Table 2 are consistent with the definitions underlying their estimation. The degree of capital flight has varied over the years in all the estimates presented. Capital inflows (that is, the negative outflows in Table 2) ranged from about 6 percent of imports in the late 1970s to about 70 percent in 1993. Capital outflows ranged from the equivalent of 7 percent of imports in 1974 to over 70 percent in 1979. Capital outflows during the periods 1976–79 and 1981–87 correspond to periods of political and economic instability. The period 1972–74 was characterized by persistent capital outflows, which, although small relative to the average outflows of the 1980s, represented an average of about 12 percent of imports or about 10 percent of exports of goods and services. This period corresponds to the expulsion of Ugandan Asians and the declaration of "economic war" by the Amin regime.

All the estimates indicate a significant tendency to reverse capital flight in the 1990s. The only exception to this trend was in 1994, when all the estimates reported show significant capital outflows. This is perhaps explained by developments in the world coffee market and the consequent mild coffee export boom experienced by Uganda at a time when coffee export marketing had been liberalized.

The results for 1980 deserve some comment. All the estimates, except the two hot money variants, indicate reverse capital flight for that year. Yet the available evidence suggests significant capital repatriation from Uganda during that year. The author's estimate of this repatriation is on the order of $167 million. The negative entry for that year may be due to the fact that one "source" of foreign exchange, as defined by the sources-and-uses approach, turned into a "user" of foreign exchange of such magnitude that it exceeded both the flow of external loans and the use of foreign exchange reserves.

In general, however, the estimates of capital flight seem to be strongly influenced by the availability of external loans and the performance of the current account. The estimates of the adjusted stock of external claims (Table 5) based on the normal capital flow concept are all similar to that reported in Chang and Cumby (1991) for Uganda. For the period up to 1987, the estimates of the four variants of normal capital flow range from $1.36 billion for variant I to $1.43 billion for variant IV. Chang and Cumby (1991) report an estimate of $1.4 billion for Uganda in their study of capital flight for a group of African countries.

Table 4 clearly indicates a strong tendency for Ugandan residents to accumulate assets abroad, especially after 1976. If one accepts the hypothesis that the social rate of return on capital at home is higher than the returns from investment abroad, this tendency would have implications for the development of the economy. One may argue that the hypothesis might not have been true during most of the years covered in this study because of the then-prevailing political and economic instability, but the same cannot be said for the 1990s. Under the current regime of political stability and economic reform, there is a strong case to be made for the repatriation of these assets. The other dimension of the problem is the likelihood that the earnings on these assets are not fully reported. Preliminary investigation suggests that this is a very strong possibility. Balance of payments data from both the World Bank (1993) and the IMF (1994) indicate that, between 1982 and 1990, a net investment income inflow was reported only once, in 1990. Yet the estimates of the stock of foreign assets held by Ugandan residents during this time span ranged between $368.2 million and $1.3 billion. The implication is that the government was denied the tax revenue that would have accrued from this foreign investment income had such earnings been repatriated through the official channel.

Finally, it must be noted that the adjusted stock of external claims in Table 5 represents a significant proportion of the country's stock of external debt for most of the years covered in this study. As a proportion of long-term external debt, variant I of the estimates on a normal capital flow basis ranges from the equivalent of only 5 percent of external debt in 1971 to as much as 86 percent in 1979. Although residents' external claims declined as a proportion of the foreign debt in the 1980–83 period, possibly because of the IMF-supported stabilization program then in place, they increased during the second half of the 1980s, accounting for as much as 72 percent of the external debt in 1987. The period 1984–87 was marked by civil war and abandonment of the IMF-supported program. The ratio of external claims to long-term foreign debt declined consistently from 1988 to 1993, when it was down to 30 percent or less than half its 1987 level. The trend of private external debt provides further evidence to support the hypothesis that capital flight is influenced by both political stability and macroeconomic performance. The downward trend in the ratio of external claims to long-term foreign debt during 1988–93 reflects an improvement of the economy, which in turn permitted the conscientious implementation of a program of economic reform and recovery.

Causes of Capital Flight

One of the objectives of this chapter is to attempt an explanation of the phenomenon of capital flight from Uganda. The discussion of the determinants of capital flight suggests a model that tries to explain the trends of capital flight by the performance of the macroeconomy. Also, the analysis of the trends in the ratio of the stock of external claims to the stock of long-term foreign debt indicates that capital flight appears to have responded to macroeconomic developments in Uganda. To quantify these observations, an attempt was made to estimate a simple econometric model of capital flight from Uganda. The basic model used in this exercise is of the following general form:

$$CF = f(P^*, g, e^*), \tag{8}$$

where CF is some measure of capital flight, P^* is the domestic rate of inflation, g is the growth rate of domestic GDP, and e^* is the parallel exchange rate premium as a proxy for currency overvaluation. The basic model was estimated for the flows of capital flight reported in Table 2. The estimates were based on variant I of the estimates based on the normal stock of external claims in that table. Various attempts to estimate Equation (8) for this series failed to produce any good econometric results. The explanatory variables were not significant in the various combinations in which they were tried. The explanatory power of the regressions was also very low and not significant. When used as the only explanatory variable, only the domestic rate of inflation turns out to be a significant determinant of capital outflow. The regression result for this bivariate model is:

$$CF = -0.549 + 0.176 \ln P^{*}$$
$$(1.7) \qquad (2.03)$$

$R^2 = 0.16$; $F(1, 22) = 4.1$ (0.06); SEE = 0.55
D-W = 2.32.

The capital flow series were deflated with data on exports of goods and services. Although inflation thus explains only 16 percent of the variation in capital outflows, the statistical properties of this equation are acceptable. The same outcome was obtained when the ratio of the adjusted stock of external claims to the stock of external debt was used as an indicator of capital flight. The regression of this index of capital flight on domestic inflation produced the following results:

$$\ln (ASEC/LTEXD) = 2.91 + 0.237 \ln P^{*}$$
$$(9.2) \qquad (2.7)$$

$R^2 = 0.26$; $F(1, 22) = 7.53$ (0.011); SEE = 0.55
D-W = 2.1

where *ASEC* is the adjusted stock of external claims and *LTEXD* is the stock of long-term foreign debt. The two equations reported above indicate that the rate of domestic inflation has a positive effect on capital flight. The inflation elasticity of the ratio of the stock of external claims to long-term foreign debt is on the order of 0.2; although this may not be very high, it is a clear indication of the macroeconomic instability of the motivation of capital flight.

Summary of Findings and Policy Implications

The interpretation of the results of this study as well as any policy implications that may be drawn from them must always be offered with a caveat. The most important reason for caution is the poor quality of the data on which the analyses are based. Having said that, the results of the analyses indicate that the Ugandan economy experienced capital flight of such magnitude relative to the size of its economy during the 1970s and 1980s that it should be a major focus of policy. The evidence on the stock of external claims by Ugandan residents clearly indicates that the potential exists for solving the country's growth-cum-debt problem. Some indication of the role of the macroeconomic environment in providing incentives for the outflow of capital is also provided by the modest econometric exercise reported here. This is supported by the attempt to interpret the trend of capital outflows in light of the country's economic and political experience.

The obvious policy implication of these results is that a precondition for the success of any effort by macroeconomic managers to attract and keep investment capital, both domestic and foreign, is a stable economic environment. Only then will investors develop confidence in the economy to the extent that they will risk keeping their assets within the country.

Appendix. Trends in Uganda's External Debt and Capital Flight

Table A1. Database for Capital Flight Estimates, 1970–94

(In millions of U.S. dollars)

	Long-Term External Debt	Short-Term and External Debt	Net Foreign Direct Investment	Current Account Balance	Change in Reserves	Banks' Net Foreign Assets	Foreign Income Inflows	Net Private Short-Term Capital	Net Errors and Omissions	Cross-Border Deposits
1970	138.0	0.0	4.2	20.3	–1.6	7.7	2.9	–15.2	–26.1	. . .
1971	172.4	0.0	–1.2	–85.8	34.4	3.1	3.1	0.6	6.9	. . .
1972	177.5	0.2	–11.9	16.4	4.4	0.6	2.4	–2.3	–40.0	. . .
1973	176.7	0.2	–1.4	43.0	–8.6	2.2	4.1	–11.4	–41.1	. . .
1974	202.5	0.5	1.7	–24.1	–12.2	2.8	4.3	1.2	–22.5	. . .
1975	208.1	1.5	2.1	–56.1	11.5	9.5	4.0	–6.1	29.5	. . .
1976	241.5	2.9	1.2	43.2	12.4	10.3	2.8	–11.9	–21.8	. . .
1977	299.9	38.8	0.8	68.1	0.5	20.2	3.4	–7.5	–21.9	. . .
1978	421.6	30.4	1.1	–137.4	2.1	25.9	5.9	–44.0	75.8	. . .
1979	540.5	44.9	1.6	39.5	–36.5	14.5	2.0	26.4	–171	. . .
1980	632.7	63.8	–166.4	–83.2	–26.1	14.3	1.4	0.0	64.6	. . .
1981	697.8	31.9	0.0	7.7	34.6	10.7	0.8	–18.0	–38.2	. . .
1982	852.0	41.0	0.0	69.9	31.5	18.8	0.0	0.0	–24.7	80
1983	984.4	29.8	0.0	–72.2	28.6	19.8	0.0	0.0	–36.6	100
1984	1,037.2	42.3	0.0	103.5	–26.5	19.6	0.0	3.3	21.6	100
1985	1,195.3	45.1	0.0	4.6	–17.3	8.1	1.5	72.5	–52.2	120
1986	1,353.9	69.1	0.0	–3.8	–36.2	14.1	2.9	117.6	–40.1	140
1987	1,868.7	70.0	0.0	112.0	20.3	24.3	0.0	–86.4	26.4	170
1988	1,881.6	87.8	0.0	195.2	2.4	9.1	0.0	–29.9	154.9	170
1989	2,142.4	112.9	0.0	–259.5	–1.8	9.1	0.0	–41.4	–38.0	160
1990	2,513.2	149.6	0.1	–263.3	–5.2	12.8	0.0	–19.5	9.5	180
1991	2,682.4	184.2	1.0	–169.8	12.7	29.8	2.8	–21.4	0.6	190
1992	2,840.0	158.0	3.0	–99.6	50.6	50.6	4.1	–9.5	9.0	160
1993	2,643.0	128.7	3.37	–135.7	–57.4	. . .	6.4	–41.3	5.14	160
1994	2,999.3	96.6	4.49	–27.7	–167.7	. . .	14.0	–102.02	–33.56	. . .

Sources: World Bank (1993, 1994); International Monetary Fund (1994); and Research Department, Bank of Uganda.

Note: Based on information in the introduction to *International Financial Statistics Yearbook* (*IFS*; IMF, 1994, pp. xvii–xviii), net foreign direct investment was estimated using the balance of payments table in the same publication. The formula used is given as net foreign direct investment = overall balance (*IFS*, line 78..d) less current account balance (*IFS*, line 77a.d) less other capital (n.i.e.) (*IFS*, line 77g.d) less errors and omissions (*IFS*, line 77e.d). This formula should give an estimate of net direct investment plus portfolio investment. Since for Uganda the balance of payments data indicate no portfolio investment, the formula provides an estimate of net foreign direct investment. The estimates were compared with reported net foreign direct investment (*IFS*, line 77 bad). The only observed discrepancies between the reported values and the author's estimates are for 1973 and 1980. *IFS* reports a net inflow of $5.2 million and nothing for 1973 or 1980. The data reported for these two years are based on the author's estimates.

Table A2. Alternative Estimates of Uganda's Unadjusted Stock of External Claims, 1970–94

	Reported Foreign Income Basis	Gross Private Capital Outflows (GPCX Residual Method)				Hot Money Approach	
		GPCX I	GPCX II	GPCX III	GPCX IV	I	II
1970	41.3	41.3	41.3	41.3	41.3	41.3	4.3
1971	55.6	23.1	27.7	23.1	27.7	38.4	33.8
1972	43.5	28.3	35.4	28.5	35.6	83.2	76.1
1973	43.9	77.7	83.2	77.9	83.4	134.1	128.6
1974	37.8	93.3	98.2	93.8	98.7	154.8	149.9
1975	39.3	33.4	31.6	34.9	33.1	124.7	126.5
1976	25.2	98.8	96.2	101.7	99.1	157.6	160.2
1977	44.3	225.6	213.1	263.9	251.4	177.1	189.6
1978	75.3	208.9	212.1	239.3	242.5	129.6	157.8
1979	15.4	405.4	420.0	450.3	464.9	338.9	355.7
1980	9.2	274.1	288.9	337.9	352.5	403.7	420.3
1981	6.1	312.3	330.7	344.2	362.4	463.5	476.5
1982	0.0	362.1	372.4	403.1	413.2	480.1	501.2
1983	0.0	393.7	403.0	423.5	432.6	515.7	537.8
1984	0.0	576.5	586.0	618.8	628.1	491.0	512.9
1985	13.0	756.5	777.5	801.6	822.4	482.2	492.6
1986	28.0	947.5	962.5	1,016.6	1,031.4	388.7	405.1
1987	0.0	1,330.0	1,334.8	1,400.0	1,404.6	438.5	465.1
1988	0.0	1,150.1	1,170.1	1,237.9	1,257.7	328.5	340.1
1989	0.0	1,153.2	1,173.2	1,266.1	1,285.9	407.9	419.5
1990	0.0	1,265.9	1,282.2	1,415.6	1,431.7	414.2	429.5
1991	25.5	1,252.6	1,251.9	1,437.9	1,437.0	418.0	450.3
1992	45.9	1,260.0	1,238.5	1,422.1	1,400.4	398.0	450.8
1993	121.4	873.3	836.5	1,006.1	969.1	...	...
1994	139.3	1,038.7	...	1,139.4	...	...	...

Source: Author's calculations.

Note: The first data column is the implied external claims based on the level of interest income reported in the balance of payments accounts. It is equal to the inflow of interest income from abroad deflated by the U.K. treasury bill rate. The estimates correspond to the concept of normal capital flows in the literature (Khan and Ul Haque, 1987, p. 3). The other columns are cumulated private capital flows based, respectively, on the estimates reported in Table 3 in the text. These are initialized with the 1970 estimate of the implied stock of external claims in the first column, based on the value of interest income.

References

Ajayi, S. Ibi, 1990, "Capital Flight and External Debt in Nigeria," paper presented at an African Economic Research Consortium Workshop, Abidjan, December.

Chang, K.P.H. Kevin, and Robert E. Cumby, 1991, "Capital Flight in Sub-Saharan African Countries," in *African External Finance in the 1990s*, ed. by Ishrat Husain and John Underwood (Washington: World Bank).

Cuddington, John T., 1986, "Capital Flight: Estimates, Issues, and Explanations," Princeton Studies in International Finance, No. 58 (Princeton, New Jersey: Princeton University Press).

———, 1987, "Macroeconomic Determinants of Capital Flight: An Empirical Investigation," in *Capital Flight and Third World Debt*, ed. by Donald R. Lessard and John Williamson (Washington: Institute for International Economics).

Cumby, Robert E., and Richard M. Levich, 1987, "On the Definition and Magnitude of Recent Capital Flight," in *Capital Flight and Third World Debt*, ed. by Donald R. Lessard and John Williamson (Washington: Institute for International Economics).

Dooley, Michael P., 1986, "Country-Specific Risk Premiums, Capital Flight, and Net Investment Income Payments in Selected Developing Countries" (unpublished; Washington: International Monetary Fund).

———, William Helkie, Ralph Tryon, and John Underwood, 1986, "An Analysis of the External Debt Positions of Eight Developing Countries Through 1990," *Journal of Development Economics*, Vol. 21, No. 2.

Erbe, Suzanne, 1985, "The Flight of Capital from Developing Countries," *Intereconomics: International Review of Trade and Development*, Vol. 20 (November/December).

International Monetary Fund, 1994, *International Financial Statistics Yearbook* (Washington).

Khan, Mohsin, and Nadeem Ul Haque, 1985, "Foreign Borrowing and Capital Flight: A Formal Analysis," *Staff Papers*, International Monetary Fund, Vol. 32, No. 4.

———, 1987, "Capital Flight from Developing Countries," *Finance & Development*, Vol. 24 (March).

Lessard, Donald R., and John Williamson, 1987, "The Problem and Policy Responses," in *Capital Flight and Third World Debt*, ed. by Donald R. Lessard and John Williamson (Washington: Institute for International Economics).

Mbire, Barbara, and M. Atingi, 1994, "Growth and Foreign Debt in Uganda," paper presented at an African Economic Research Consortium Workshop, Nairobi, May.

Morgan Guaranty Trust Company, 1986, "LDC Capital Flight," *World Financial Markets* (March).

Ng'eno, N.K., 1992, "Capital Flight in Kenya," research proposal presented at an African Economic Research Consortium Workshop, Nairobi, December.

Pastor, Manuel, Jr., 1990, "Capital Flight from Latin America," *World Development*, Vol. 18, No. 1.

Vos, R., 1990, *On the Measurement of Private Accumulation of Foreign Assets: The Case of the Philippines* (The Hague: Institute of Social Studies).

World Bank, 1985, *World Development Report* (New York: Oxford University Press).

———, 1993, *World Tables* (Washington).

———, 1994, *World Tables* (Washington).

———, and United Nations Development Program, 1990, *Uganda: An Agenda for Trade Liberalization*, UNDP-World Bank Trade Expansion Program, Country Report No. 6 (Washington).

Capital Flight from Tanzania 9

Timothy S. Nyoni

This chapter focuses on the measurement and determination of capital flight from Tanzania. Capital flight has been regarded as a major reason for the mounting foreign debt problems and inhibition of development efforts in developing countries (see, for example, Cuddington, 1986). In real terms, external debt in Tanzania increased from $677.4 million in 1971 to $3,863.6 million in 1993, growing at an average annual rate of 8.2 percent (Table 1).

Despite positive real net private transfers and short-term capital inflows during most of the years between 1971 and 1993, Tanzania's per capita GDP from the late 1970s to the early 1990s fluctuated at levels lower than those registered during the first half of the 1970s; the current account deficit worsened as well (Table 1). The current account was in persistent deficit throughout 1971–93. As a percentage of GDP, the current account deficit increased from an average of 6.7 percent during 1971–77 to 16 percent during 1987–93 (Table 1). These observations suggest that much of the capital inflow to Tanzania was probably not used for domestic investment or for reducing the current account deficit and external debt problems. If so, there is reason to suspect capital flight.

Conceptual differences in defining capital flight have led to concerns about the need for policy intervention to stem it and about the interaction between economic policies in the developing countries and those of industrial countries. Capital flight also raises questions about the role of international financial institutions, which lend to developing countries and act as depositories for capital exports from these countries.

There are conflicting views about the concept of capital flight. Some observers regard it as a symptom of a sick society characterized by the breakdown of social cohesion, reduction in growth potential, erosion of the tax base, failure to recover from the debt problem, and a redistribution of wealth from poorer to richer social groups (Lessard and Williamson, 1987). Others consider the use of the term "capital flight" unnecessarily pejorative. Why, for example, label capital movements from developing countries "flight," while those from the United Kingdom and other industrial countries are termed "foreign investments" (Pastor, 1990; Lessard and Williamson, 1987)? Part of the explanation

Table 1. Tanzania: Selected Indicators of Financial Flows and Economic Performance, 1971–93

	Total External Debt (In millions of 1997 U.S. dollars)	Per Capita GDP at 1977 Prices (1977=100)[1]	Current Account Deficit (In percent of GDP)	Net Private Transfers (In millions of 1997 U.S. dollars)[2]	Short-Term Capital Inflows (In millions of 1997 U.S. dollars)[1]
1971	677.4	97.5	8.1	. . .	266.8
1972	978.8	101.0	4.7	–51.7	265.7
1973	1,092.8	101.1	6.6	–33.4	284.7
1974	891.4	99.6	14.5	–16.7	135.3
1975	1,048.6	101.0	10.0	18.2	228.5
1976	1,330.5	102.1	1.1	14.3	67.5
1977	1,449.5	100.0	2.1	19.4	111.0
1978	1,589.2	98.7	11.6	24.8	188.3
1979	1,581.4	98.9	8.8	27.1	113.0
1980	1,582.6	98.6	11.4	19.5	139.8
1981	1,615.1	95.5	7.3	23.0	149.4
1982	1,917.9	93.4	8.7	26.5	127.2
1983	2,132.3	88.8	5.5	19.6	189.4
1984	2,343.7	89.2	7.4	63.6	7.8
1985	2,630.1	90.8	6.6	256.5	–50.7
1986	2,980.1	90.0	8.1	235.3	6.6
1987	3,333.0	91.9	16.1	319.6	39.1
1988	3,333.8	92.3	11.6	230.1	20.9
1989	3,190.5	93.4	10.3	186.4	13.0
1990	3,313.8	94.8	12.5	178.0	68.5
1991	3,623.7	97.5	11.8	461.7	60.7
1992	3,687.4	98.2	12.2	554.6	48.8
1993	3,863.6	99.4	12.9	562.6	41.2

Sources: Tanzania, Bureau of Statistics, *National Accounts of Tanzania,* various years; International Monetary Fund (1996); and World Bank (1987, 1994).

[1]Deflated by the import price index.

[2]Nominal transfers deflated by the export price index.

for the use of the term "capital flight" is the notion that capital should be flowing from capital-abundant (industrial) countries to capital-scarce (developing) countries. In economic theory, so-called capital flight from developing countries results from the natural and economically rational behavior of wealthy residents of these debtor countries to diversify their portfolios to protect themselves against the riskiness of any particular investment.

Any study on capital flight must first sort out what capital flight really is. Is capital flight something bad that requires policy intervention to stop or reverse it? Is it not true that capital flight would deter policymakers from making "wrong" political and economic decisions? Such arguments make it difficult to define the concept of capital flight. This is especially true because capital flight has had damaging consequences for the economies concerned despite any reflows that some countries have experienced. On the one hand, the damaging effects of capital flight may make rational foreign lenders hesitant to increase credits to the debtor countries. On the other hand, the behavior of individual agents to diversify their portfolios by keeping some of their wealth in foreign assets is postulated as rational by economic theory and accepted as normal in industrial and some developing countries.

The main objective of this chapter is to measure the magnitude and determine the causes of capital flight from Tanzania. After empirically determining the causes of capital flight, we shall discuss the policy implications of containing or reversing capital flight.

This introductory section is followed by a statement of the hypothesis, along with a discussion of the definition and measurement of capital flight. Next, political and macroeconomic developments in Tanzania are discussed, and an empirical analysis of capital flight is provided. The chapter concludes with a summary of the findings and implications for policy.

Capital Flight: Definition, Measurement, and Consequences

The main hypothesis of this chapter is that capital flight is a positive function of the growth differential between the GDPs of the United Kingdom and Tanzania, the parallel market premium, domestic inflation, the financial incentive for capital flight, capital availability, political and external shocks, and lagged capital flight. This hypothesis will be tested using the capital flight model specified below.

Definition

The term "capital flight" connotes illegal movement of capital from one country to another. This connotation implies that there may be "normal" or "legal" and "abnormal" or "illegal" flows (see, for example, Lessard and Williamson, 1987). Normal capital flows are those that are sanctioned by the government. Abnormal capital flows are illegal capital movements that take place without the government's approval. The question of the legality of capital flows, however, implies that the country concerned imposes exchange or capital controls. This then complicates the matter, since so-called capital flight is known to have taken place even in developing countries, such as Argentina,

Mexico, and Venezuela, that had no capital controls (Lessard and Williamson, 1987). Thus, it is difficult to come out with an operational definition and measurement of normal and abnormal capital flows.

The concept of capital flight refers to "capital that runs away" or "flees" abnormal risks at home regardless of whether or not the flight is legal (Lessard and Williamson, 1987, p. 2). Measuring capital flight thus defined requires an attempt to measure normal capital outflows and deduct these from total outflows. Dooley (1986) attempted this. Although Dooley's concept of abnormal outflows as those propelled by the desire to escape the control of the domestic authorities corresponds to the concept of capital fleeing abnormal risks at home, his method of measuring normal capital flows is controversial and unacceptable (Lessard and Williamson, 1987).

The emphasis in this chapter is on all resident capital outflows rather than "normal" outflows. This is primarily because there is no sensible way of separating normal from abnormal flows. Furthermore, the consequences of capital outflows to the national economy are the same whether the outflows represent normal portfolio diversification or abnormal flight. If normal capital outflows are small, the resulting economic cost from the resident capital outflows will be modest. However, the cost will escalate when normal capital outflows are reinforced by money running away from abnormal risks at home.

The justification for using the emotive term "capital flight" is in the extent of the damage that resident capital outflows inflict on the home economy. If the damage is small, one may be content with using the term "resident capital outflows"; otherwise, "capital flight" is the preferred alternative.

Measurement

It is difficult to measure capital flight for two main reasons. One is that the concept itself is ambiguous, which makes it obvious that different definitions of capital flight may yield different estimates of the problem. The other reason is that even if there may be a consensus that capital flight means "money that runs away," such capital is in most cases not reported to the domestic authorities or compilers of balance of payments statistics. This makes it difficult (if not impossible) to deduct capital that flees abnormal risks at home from total capital outflows. For these reasons, therefore, we shall not attempt to distinguish normal from abnormal capital outflows. We shall instead concentrate on measuring all resident capital outflows.

Table 2 presents the various items of the balance of payments and external debt for estimating capital flight. There are three main ap-

Table 2. External Debt and Balance of Payments Items for Measuring Components of Capital Flight

A	=	Changes in external debt
B	=	Current account balance
C	=	Net foreign direct investment
D	=	Net private short-term capital flows
E	=	Portfolio investment
F	=	Change in foreign assets of the banking system
G	=	Net errors and omissions
H	=	Changes in reserves

Sources: Ajayi (1995) and Olopoenia (1995).

proaches to the measurement of capital flight: the balance of payments accounts approach, the residual approach, and the bank deposits approach. We discuss each of them in turn.

The Balance of Payments Accounts Approach

In the pioneering studies of capital flight, the phenomenon was measured using the balance of payments accounts (see, for example, Cuddington, 1986). The objective in this approach is "to isolate short-term capital movements that might reasonably be considered capital flight" (Cuddington, 1986, p. 3). In this approach, changes in short-term foreign assets, often called "hot money," are considered speculative and an indication of recorded capital flows (Cuddington, 1986). The net errors and omissions item of the balance of payments is considered equivalent to unrecorded capital flows. According to Cuddington (1986), private short-term capital movements are either imprecisely reported or not reported at all, especially in countries that impose capital controls. The failure to precisely record short-term private capital flows shows up in the net errors and omissions entry of the balance of payments.

In the balance of payments approach, capital flight is measured as the negative of the sum of recorded short-term capital flows and unrecorded net flows or net errors and omissions.

That is,

$$KFB = -(D + G), \tag{1}$$

where *KFB* is capital flight measured by the balance of payments approach, *D* is net private short-term capital flows, and *G* is net errors and omissions (Table 2). Positive values of this capital flight (*KFB*) measure represent capital outflows, whereas negative values are capital reflows or reverse capital flight.

The balance of payments approach has several problems. In this approach, the short-term capital flows capture recorded capital flows, and the errors and omissions are supposed to capture unrecorded capital flows. However, not everything in the net errors and omissions entry is capital flows. Errors and omissions include not only unreported or smuggled exports and imports (which may be related to capital flight) but also items that are not related to capital flight, such as true measurement and recording errors and errors because of lagged registration. Hence, the balance of payments approach fails to adequately capture unrecorded capital flows.

Another problem with this approach is that the measure ignores capital that flees to finance long-term investments such as equity and real estate abroad. The approach also fails to distinguish clearly between short-term and long-term investments, especially when the two are close substitutes. Long-term bonds, for example, can be substituted easily for short-term investments without significant loss of liquidity (Eggerstedt and others, 1995).

The Residual Approach

The residual approach was developed by the World Bank (1985) and Erbe (1985) and was modified further by Morgan Guaranty Trust Company (1986). This approach arose out of the belief that the balance of payments accounts approach was not sufficient to estimate resident capital outflows.

In the World Bank (1985) and Erbe (1985) versions of the residual approach, capital flight is calculated as the difference between sources and uses of capital inflows. The sources of capital inflows are increases in external debt and foreign direct investment. These capital inflows are used to finance either current account deficits or increases in official reserves. Inflows that finance neither current account deficits nor increases in reserves constitute capital flight.

Capital flight in the World Bank (1985) and Erbe (1985) versions of the residual approach (KFW) is measured as

$$KFW = A + C + B + H, \tag{2}$$

where A is changes in external debt, C is net foreign direct investment, B is the current account balance, and H is changes in reserves (Table 2). Positive values for KFW represent capital flight, whereas negative values are capital reflows.

Morgan Guaranty (1986) adjusted the World Bank (1985) and Erbe (1985) measure for changes in foreign assets held by domestic agents other than the banking system. According to Morgan Guaranty (1986), capital flight is measured as

$$KFM = A + C + B + H + F, \tag{3}$$

where *KFM* is the measure of capital flight, *F* is changes in foreign assets of the domestic banking system, and *A*, *B*, *C*, and *H* are as defined above. As with the other residual measure of capital flight, positive values of *KFM* are capital flight, whereas negative ones are reverse capital flight.

The residual approach to the measurement of resident capital outflow faces the problem of inadequacies in the debt statistics. The statistics may not always be correctly recorded, especially if the private sector also borrows from foreign creditors. When some debts are denominated in currencies other than the U.S. dollar, changes in exchange rates may increase (or decrease) the debts even if no new borrowing has taken place (Zedillo, 1987). The changes in debts denominated in currencies other than the U.S. dollar should thus be adjusted for exchange rate variations.[1]

The Bank Deposits Approach

A third approach to the measurement of resident capital outflows involves measuring the increase in recorded foreign bank deposits of a country's residents. This is controversial because, even if there are statistical sources that distinguish between private and official holdings, it cannot be argued convincingly that all private funds held abroad are recorded by the relevant authorities. The difficulty in compiling bank deposits data is reinforced by the fact that some of the funds are deposited in banks that do not report to the IMF or other relevant authorities, whereas others may be held in nonbank foreign assets. Another difficulty arises from the desire of the depositors to hide their nationality in order to minimize any potential risk they may perceive. Therefore, foreign bank deposits owned by a country's residents are likely to underestimate resident capital outflow.

The Magnitude of Capital Flight from Tanzania: Unadjusted Measures

The magnitude of capital flight from Tanzania unadjusted for trade misinvoicing in 1977 is shown in Table 3. The corresponding measures

[1]I would like to thank Professor S. Ibi Ajayi for pointing out the need to adjust the change in external debt for exchange rate variations. However, since the sources used for the external debt statistics report the data in U.S. dollars, there is less need to adjust the external debt for exchange rate variations.

Table 3. Tanzania: Real Measures of Capital Flight Unadjusted for Trade Misinvoicing, 1971–93
(In millions of 1977 U.S. dollars)

	Balance of Payments Approach	World Bank Residual Approach	Morgan Guaranty Residual Approach[1]	Bank Deposits Approach[2]
1971	–233.18	–113.95	–72.17	. . .
1972	–305.30	174.70	154.97	. . .
1973	–241.68	113.54	88.76	. . .
1974	–166.63	–172.08	–157.98	. . .
1975	–198.11	–6.29	–37.61	. . .
1976	–60.85	227.25	221.61	. . .
1977	–180.10	356.20	375.70	. . .
1978	–197.77	–274.0	–330.14	. . .
1979	–131.13	–60.71	53.32	. . .
1980	–110.18	–130.73	–130.73	. . .
1981	–209.74	–176.57	–176.57	. . .
1982	–169.55	–164.90	–164.90	. . .
1983	–152.39	–49.27	–49.27	21.09
1984	–98.31	–72.91	–72.91	0
1985	80.47	–15.17	–15.17	21.57
1986	21.77	190.71	190.71	21.34
1987	–100.89	242.52	242.52	52.24
1988	5.08	–38.39	–38.39	12.55
1989	–24.50	–272.31	–272.31	24.14
1990	–191.17	267.21	267.21	66.80
1991	–50.27	–58.04	–58.04	5.71
1992	–74.96	–31.27	–31.27	–33.69
1993	–31.67	–173.33	–173.33	22.46
Totals				
1972–73	–546.98	288.24	243.73	. . .
1976–77	–240.95	583.45	597.31	. . .
1983–91	–585.17	163.07	163.07	191.76
1986–87	–79.12	433.23	433.23	53.58
1971–93	–2,821.04	–237.87	–186.00	214.25

Sources: Author's calculations based on data from World Bank, *World Tables*, various issues, and International Monetary Fund, *International Financial Statistics*, various issues.

[1]The two residual approaches coincide after 1979 because the banking system's foreign assets are zero.

[2]Data for calculating the bank deposits approach during 1971–82 were not available.

in current prices are shown in Table 4. Using estimates from the balance of payments approach, it can be seen that there were only two episodes of capital flight in 1971–93: during 1985–86, when capital flight totaled $102.24 million in 1977 prices, and during 1988, when it totaled $5.08 million in constant prices.

Table 4. Tanzania: Nominal Measures of Capital Flight Unadjusted for Trade Misinvoicing, 1971–93
(In millions of current U.S. dollars)

	Balance of Payments Approach	World Bank Residual Approach	Morgan Guaranty Residual Approach[1]	Bank Deposits Approach[2]
1971	–88.2	–43.1	–27.3	. . .
1972	–125.3	71.7	63.6	. . .
1973	–147.3	69.2	54.1	. . .
1974	–140.6	–145.2	–133.3	. . .
1975	–179.6	–5.7	–34.1	. . .
1976	–56.1	209.5	204.3	. . .
1977	–180.1	356.2	375.7	. . .
1978	–222.6	–308.5	–371.6	. . .
1979	–174.1	–80.6	70.8	. . .
1980	–172.1	–204.2	–204.2	. . .
1981	–321.2	–270.4	–270.4	. . .
1982	–251.6	–244.7	–244.7	..
1983	–216.8	–70.1	–70.1	30
1984	–138.2	–102.5	–102.5	0
1985	111.9	–21.1	–21.1	30
1986	30.6	268.1	268.1	30
1987	–154.5	371.4	371.4	80
1988	8.1	–61.2	–61.2	20
1989	–40.6	–451.2	–451.2	40
1990	–343.4	480.0	480.0	120
1991	–88.0	–101.6	–101.6	10
1992	–133.5	–55.7	–55.7	–60
1993	–56.4	–308.7	–308.7	40

Sources: Author's calculations based on data from International Monetary Fund (1996) and World Bank, *World Tables*, various issues.

[1]The two residual measures coincide after 1979 because banking system foreign assets are zero.

[2]Data for calculating capital flight by the bank deposits approach during 1971–82 were not available.

In 1971–93, in general, Tanzania experienced reverse capital flight totaling $2.82 billion in real terms (Table 3). The balance of payments measure—which is narrow by definition— understates the magnitude of capital flight and yields lower estimates than the broader residual approach.

The residual approach indicates higher values and more episodes of capital flight than the balance of payments measure (Table 3). The World Bank (1985) and Morgan Guaranty (1986) residual measures yield more or less the same magnitudes and episodes of capital flight. According to the residual measures, capital flight during 1972–73 ranged between $243 million and $288 million in constant prices. Another episode of capital flight occurred in 1976–77, when between $583 million and $597 million fled the country. During 1986–87 capital flight totaled $433 million, and in 1990 it totaled $267 million. During 1971–93 Tanzania experienced capital reflows of between $186 million and $238 million in real terms according to the Morgan Guaranty (1986) and World Bank (1985) residual approaches, respectively.

The bank deposits approach indicates that during 1983–91 a total of $192 million (in 1977 prices) fled the country. This approach, as discussed above, gives a lower estimate of capital flight relative to the residual approach. Hence, the residual approach gives higher estimates than either the balance of payments approach or the bank deposits approach.

The Morgan Guaranty (1986) residual approach captures more episodes of capital flight than does the other broad residual approach. As will be explained below, the capital flight episodes indicated by the residual approach reflect the major political and external shocks the country experienced. The balance of payments and bank deposits approaches are too narrow to be credible and are conceptually inferior to the residual approaches. We thus prefer the Morgan Guaranty measure of capital flight to the other approaches discussed in this chapter.

Trade Misinvoicing and Capital Flight

The three approaches to measuring capital flight have been criticized on several grounds, and none can be considered satisfactory. One weakness is that they ignore trade misinvoicing. In countries where currencies are overvalued and foreign exchange and trade controls are prevalent, invoices for imports or exports are often faked and the registration of imports is avoided. In such cases, balance of payments data are recorded imprecisely and do not fully reflect actual trade and capital flows. If smuggling and underinvoicing of imports conceal a larger current account deficit, capital flight (measured by the residual approach) will be overstated unless it is adjusted for trade misinvoicing.

Capital flight can be effected by overinvoicing imports and underinvoicing exports (Eggerstedt and others, 1995; Ajayi, 1992). By underinvoicing exports, exporters surrender only a part of their export receipts to the domestic authorities and may use the remaining receipts to build up their foreign exchange holdings, some of which may be shifted to foreign countries. When importers overinvoice imports, they obtain foreign exchange in excess of their import costs. The importers can then use this excess foreign exchange to add to their foreign assets in the domestic economy and abroad. Since such operations are not recorded in the balance of payments statistics, omissions of trade misinvoicing will yield an inaccurate measure of capital flows in the residual and balance of payments approaches. Some of the trade misinvoicing, however, may be detectable in foreign bank deposits if those involved in trade faking and smuggling deposit the money in (reporting) foreign banks.

Depending on the nature of trade policies in the domestic economy, trade misinvoicing may occur for motives other than financing capital flight. Thus, rather than imports being overinvoiced to transfer funds abroad, imports may be underinvoiced to lower the cost of customs duties and value-based quantitative restrictions (Eggerstedt and others, 1995). If there are export incentives, it will be more rational for exporters to overinvoice their exports to take advantage of the export subsidies and preferred access to subsidized credits. The net effect of underinvoicing imports and overinvoicing exports will be reverse capital flight.

Data on smuggling and unreported trade flows are hard to come by, especially because such activities are not reported to the domestic authorities. To track down trade misinvoicing and smuggling, one has to compare trade statistics of the trading partners. Since the imports of any one country are the exports of another country, the ratio of the free-on-board values of the imports and exports—called the valuation ratio—should be unity (Ajayi, 1996). If the valuation ratio is not unity, it is an indication of trade misinvoicing. However, there are other reasons—apart from capital flight motives—for the recorded values of the exports and imports not to match. These reasons include differences in the recording systems, improper identification of the origin and destination of goods, differences in valuation methods, and differences in time spans covered (Eggerstedt and others, 1995; Ajayi, 1996).

Trade misinvoicing is calculated as

$$X_{MIS} = XD - MW/k_W \tag{4}$$

and

$$M_{MIS} = MD/k_T - XW, \tag{5}$$

where X_{MIS} and M_{MIS} are, respectively, export and import misinvoicing; k_T and k_W are, respectively, the c.i.f./f.o.b. correction factor for Tanzania and its world trading partners; XD is Tanzania's exports to world trading partners as reported by Tanzania; MW is imports from Tanzania as reported by Tanzania's world trading partners; MD is imports from world trading partners as reported by Tanzania; and XW is exports to Tanzania as reported by the country's world trading partners.

When export misinvoicing (X_{MIS}) is negative, it reflects export underinvoicing and thus capital is flowing out of the country. Conversely, a positive X_{MIS} denotes export overinvoicing, which implies reverse

Table 5. Tanzania: Trade Misinvoicing in Real Terms, 1971–93
(In millions of 1977 U.S. dollars)

	Export Misinvoicing[1]	Import Misinvoicing[2]	Misinvoicing Adjustment[3]
1971	114.93	–14.42	–129.35
1972	197.38	–153.94	–351.33
1973	–18.22	–172.04	–153.81
1974	–44.85	–136.40	–91.55
1975	–28.33	39.57	67.89
1976	–45.16	–115.54	–70.38
1977	–33.37	–106.53	–73.16
1978	–96.09	–68.77	27.32
1979	–117.34	–105.32	12.02
1980	–95.34	–154.85	–59.51
1981	5.15	–82.22	–87.37
1982	–2.24	–10.29	–8.05
1983	–47.88	–39.12	8.75
1984	–51.20	–72.65	–21.45
1985	–97.69	–47.60	50.09
1986	–64.87	–97.97	–33.10
1987	–97.71	–141.49	–43.78
1988	–120.95	–118.85	2.10
1989	–193.57	–131.95	61.62
1990	–20.00	–58.21	–38.21
1991	–15.45	–65.62	–50.16
1992	–26.75	–76.91	–50.16
1993	–17.71	–70.81	–53.09
1971–93	–917.26	–2,001.92	–1,084.67

Sources: Ajayi (1996) for the misinvoicing concept and formula; and International Monetary Fund, *Direction of Trade Statistics Yearbook*, various issues, for trade flows.

[1]Export misinvoicing (X_{MIS}) was calculated as $X_{MIS} = XD - MW/k_W$, where *XD* is exports to world trading partners as recorded by Tanzania, *MW* is imports from Tanzania as recorded by world trading partners, and k_W is the world c.i.f./f.o.b. correction factor. The world export price index for Tanzania was used as the deflator.

[2]Import misinvoicing (M_{MIS}) was calculated as $M_{MIS} = MD/k_T - XW$ where *MD* is imports from world trading partners as reported by Tanzania, *XW* is exports to Tanzania as reported by world trading partners, and k_T is Tanzania's c.i.f./f.o.b. correction factor. The world import price index for Tanzania was used as the deflator.

capital flight. When import misinvoicing (M_{MIS}) is positive, it reflects import overinvoicing. A negative M_{MIS} represents import underinvoicing. Import overinvoicing connotes capital outflows, whereas underinvoicing of imports implies capital inflows. To adjust our measures of capital flight, we take the sum of import overinvoicing and the negative of export underinvoicing, since capital flight appears with positive values in our measures.

Trade misinvoicings in constant and current prices are presented in Tables 5 and 6, respectively. The general case during 1971–93 appears

Table 6. Tanzania: Trade Misinvoicing in Nominal Terms, 1971–93[1]
(In millions of current U.S. dollars, unless otherwise noted)

	Export Misinvoicing	Import Misinvoicing	Misinvoicing Adjustment[2]	Export Misinvoicing as Percentage of Trading Partners' Imports to Tanzania	Import Misinvoicing as Percentage of Trading Partners' Exports to Tanzania
1971	26.41	–5.45	–31.86	10.38	–2.09
1972	47.35	–63.18	–110.53	17.65	–18.36
1973	–8.90	–104.85	–95.96	–2.48	–23.92
1974	–36.13	–115.09	–78.96	–7.73	–15.55
1975	–20.05	35.87	55.92	–4.80	6.01
1976	–34.71	–106.51	–71.81	–6.53	–17.43
1977	–33.37	–106.53	–73.16	–5.67	–14.80
1978	–90.26	–77.40	12.86	–14.84	–7.23
1979	–118.83	–139.83	–21.01	–17.44	–13.63
1980	–116.28	–241.88	–125.60	–18.20	–19.34
1981	5.59	–125.91	–131.50	0.96	–12.52
1982	–2.32	–15.27	–12.95	–0.50	–1.66
1983	–47.88	–55.66	–7.78	–11.09	–7.78
1984	–51.85	–102.14	–50.29	–11.57	–12.71
1985	–94.15	–66.18	27.97	–23.93	–7.20
1986	–70.44	–137.73	–67.29	–15.93	–17.21
1987	–82.25	–216.67	–134.42	–20.96	–23.86
1988	–113.62	–189.47	–75.85	–27.62	–21.26
1989	–181.84	–218.63	–36.80	–38.96	–24.65
1990	–18.30	–104.56	–86.26	–4.11	–9.64
1991	–13.95	–114.86	–100.91	–3.42	–10.47
1992	–22.20	–136.97	–114.77	–4.83	–10.17
1993	–14.70	–126.11	–111.41	–2.97	–10.26
Average 1971–93				–9.33	–12.86

Sources: Ajayi (1996) for the misinvoicing concept and formula; and International Monetary Fund, *Direction of Trade Statistics Yearbook*, various issues, for trade flows.

[1]Export and import misinvoicing are defined in Table 5.

[2]Misinvoicing adjustment is the sum of import misinvoicing and the negative of export misinvoicing. When this sum is positive (negative), it reflects capital flight (reflows).

to be that of export and import underinvoicing as reflected by negative values in either case. Export misinvoicing as a percentage of imports from Tanzania as reported by the country's trading partners averaged –9.33 percent during 1971–93. (See International Monetary Fund, *Direction of Trade Statistics Yearbook*, for information on Tanzania's trading partners.)

Import misinvoicing as a percentage of exports to Tanzania as reported by the country's trading partners averaged –12.86 percent during 1971–93 (Table 6). Expressed in 1977 prices, export underinvoicing during 1971–93 totaled $917 million; import underinvoicing in the same period amounted to $2 billion (Table 5). During 1971–93, therefore, there was net reverse capital flight of about $1.1 billion.

The fact that exports and imports in Tanzania are underinvoiced suggests that export misinvoicing in the country is done mainly for capital flight motives, whereas import misinvoicing is done for reasons other than financing capital flight. Using an econometric analysis, Mpango (1996) found that in Tanzania imports are underinvoiced mainly to evade import duty.

Since there is evidence of trade faking in Tanzania, it is appropriate to adjust the capital flight measures for trade misinvoicing. The adjusted capital flight measures in constant and current prices are shown in Tables 7 and 8, respectively.

Capital Flight Measures Adjusted for Trade Misinvoicing

After adjusting for trade misinvoicing, the capital flight measures are significantly changed, and in some cases (especially in the bank deposits approach) capital flows in the reverse direction relative to the unadjusted measures (Tables 3 and 7).

According to the balance of payments approach, capital flight occurred only in 1985 and during 1988–89, when $174.87 million in real terms fled the country (Table 7). The general case for the rest of the years was one of capital reflows. During 1971–93, reflows totaled $3.9 billion. According to the bank deposits approach, there were several episodes of capital flight, and net capital flight during 1971–93 totaled $46.84 million. However, as discussed above, the balance of payments and bank deposits approaches are narrow measures and show only the minimum levels of capital flight.

The adjusted residual approaches indicate higher levels of capital flight than under the balance of payments and bank deposits approaches. Three episodes of capital flight are jointly reported by the two residual approaches, in 1975–77, 1985–87, and 1990. According to the residual approach, between $484.05 million and $501.52 million in real terms fled Tanzania during 1975–77, $391.28 million during 1985–87, and $229.0 million in 1990 (Table 7). The Morgan Guaranty (1996) approach reports an additional episode, that of 1979, when $65.35 million fled the country.

One can contemplate many other modifications to the measures of capital flows than trade misinvoicing and others discussed above.

Table 7. Tanzania: Capital Flight Measures in Real Terms Adjusted for Trade Misinvoicing, 1971–93
(In millions of 1977 U.S. dollars)

	Balance of Payments Approach	World Bank Residual Approach	Morgan Guaranty Residual Approach[1]	Bank Deposits Approach[2]
1971	–362.53	–243.29	–201.52	. . .
1972	–656.63	–176.63	–196.36	. . .
1973	–395.49	–40.28	–65.05	. . .
1974	–258.18	–263.63	–249.52	. . .
1975	–130.21	61.60	30.28	. . .
1976	–131.23	156.87	151.23	. . .
1977	–253.26	283.04	302.54	. . .
1978	–170.45	–246.76	–302.82	. . .
1979	–119.10	–48.68	65.35	. . .
1980	–169.69	–190.24	–190.24	. . .
1981	–297.11	–263.94	–263.94	. . .
1982	–177.60	–172.95	–172.95	. . .
1983	–143.64	–40.52	–40.52	29.84
1984	–119.76	–94.36	–94.36	–21.45
1985	130.57	34.92	34.92	71.67
1986	–11.33	157.61	157.61	–11.76
1987	–144.66	198.75	198.75	8.46
1988	7.18	–36.29	–36.29	14.65
1989	37.12	–210.69	–210.69	85.76
1990	–229.38	229.00	229.00	28.59
1991	–100.44	–108.21	–108.21	–44.45
1992	–125.12	–81.43	–81.43	–83.85
1993	–84.76	–226.42	–226.42	–30.63
Totals				
1975–77	–514.70	501.52	484.05	
1985–87	–25.43	391.28	391.28	68.37
1971–93	–3,905.69	–1,322.52	–1,270.65	46.84

Source: Author's calculations.
[1]The two residual approach measures coincide after 1979 because the banking system's foreign assets are zero.
[2]Data for calculating capital flight by the bank deposits approach during 1971–82 were not available.

Such modifications would include adding interest income earned on bank deposits held abroad and income from tourism. All these aspects are taken into consideration when capital flight is defined as resident capital outflow (Lessard and Williamson, 1987).

A better picture of the magnitude of capital flight may be seen from some capital flight ratios. In analyzing capital flight ratios in Tanzania, we use our preferred Morgan Guaranty residual measure and express

Table 8. Tanzania: Capital Flight Measures in Nominal Terms Adjusted for Trade Misinvoicing, 1971–93
(In millions of current U.S. dollars)

	Balance of Payments Approach	World Bank Residual Approach	Morgan Guaranty Residual Approach	Bank Deposits Approach
1971	–120.06	–74.96	–59.16	–31.86
1972	–235.83	–38.83	–46.93	–110.53
1973	–243.26	–26.76	–41.86	–95.96
1974	–219.56	–224.16	–212.26	–78.97
1975	–123.68	50.22	21.82	55.92
1976	–127.91	137.69	132.49	–71.81
1977	–253.26	283.04	302.54	–73.16
1978	–209.74	–295.64	–358.74	12.86
1979	–195.11	–101.61	49.79	–21.00
1980	–297.70	–329.80	–329.80	–125.60
1981	–452.70	–401.90	–401.90	–131.50
1982	–264.55	–257.65	–257.65	–12.95
1983	–224.58	–77.88	–77.88	22.22
1984	–188.49	–152.79	–152.79	–50.29
1985	139.87	6.87	6.87	57.97
1986	–36.69	200.81	200.81	–37.29
1987	–288.92	236.98	236.98	–54.42
1988	–67.75	–137.05	–137.05	–55.85
1989	–77.40	–488.00	–488.00	3.20
1990	–429.66	393.74	393.74	33.74
1991	–188.91	–202.51	–202.51	–90.91
1992	–248.27	–170.47	–170.47	–174.77
1993	–167.81	–420.11	–420.11	–71.41

Sources: Author's calculations.

it as a percentage of total external debt, GDP, and merchandise exports and imports. These ratios are presented in Table 9.

Capital flight as a percentage of total external debt was most severe during 1975–77, when it averaged 11.39 percent. In 1979 it was less than 3 percent, and in 1985–87 the average was 3.16 percent. The ratio was 6.44 percent in 1990. As a percentage of merchandise exports, capital flight averaged between 29.69 percent and 48.06 percent during 1975–77 and 1985–87, respectively. In 1990, capital flight reached the remarkable level of 96.55 percent of the country's merchandise exports. For imports, capital flight averaged 24.63 percent during 1975–77 and 15.49 percent during 1985–87; in 1990, capital flight was equal to 33.19 percent of the country's imports (Table 9). Capital flight

Table 9. Tanzania: Capital Flight Ratios, 1971–93[1]

	Capital Flight as a Percentage of			
	Total external debt	Merchandise exports	Merchandise imports	GDP
1971	–18.11	–22.58	–17.13	–4.30
1972	–11.59	–14.84	–13.04	–3.00
1973	–7.52	–11.51	–9.56	–2.24
1974	–26.83	–53.17	–32.14	–9.46
1975	2.18	5.85	3.26	0.85
1976	11.13	27.02	23.84	4.55
1977	20.87	56.18	46.78	8.69
1978	–19.85	–75.37	–36.15	–8.60
1979	2.37	9.12	5.18	1.13
1980	–13.32	–56.60	–30.28	–6.42
1981	–15.33	–65.56	–37.87	–6.78
1982	–8.84	–62.40	–27.06	–3.86
1983	–2.48	–20.32	–10.99	–1.27
1984	–4.51	–38.34	–20.10	–2.74
1985	0.18	2.09	0.79	0.11
1986	4.68	59.78	21.99	4.43
1987	4.61	82.31	23.69	7.45
1988	–2.53	–35.46	–13.27	–3.71
1989	–9.12	–117.56	–45.60	–11.97
1990	6.44	96.55	33.19	10.13
1991	–3.14	–55.91	–15.76	–4.75
1992	–2.54	–42.54	–12.98	–4.49
1993	–6.13	–90.93	–32.32	–12.12
Averages				
1975–77	11.39	29.69	24.63	4.69
1985–87	3.16	48.06	15.49	4.00
1971–93	–4.32	–18.44	–8.50	–2.10

Sources: Author's calculations.

[1]Capital flight refers to the Morgan Guaranty (1986) measure adjusted for trade misinvoicing. The ratios were of nominal variables in U.S. dollars.

as a percentage of GDP ranged from 0.11 percent in 1985 to 10.13 percent in 1990. These figures indicate that, despite the reflows that occur, when capital flees the country it may reach critical levels and may have undesirable consequences for the domestic economy.

Consequences of Capital Flight

Whether or not a country imposes capital controls, the immediate consequence of capital flight is to reduce foreign exchange reserves, which may, in turn, require increased external borrowing to finance development expenditures. When both foreign exchange reserves and external borrowing capacity have been exhausted, the country will be forced to initiate balance of payments adjustment through either devaluation or equivalent expenditure switching policy, or by expenditure reduction. Devaluation will result in the reduction of domestic saving required for financing domestic investment and hence reduce future growth potential. The reduction in expenditure or demand also reduces output in the current and in future periods.

In countries that impose capital controls, capital flight is associated with a rising parallel market premium as the demand for foreign exchange increases owing to the need to finance capital flight. The premium will also result in the drain of some foreign resources from official reserves into the parallel market. In the extreme case, the diversion of reserves into the parallel market may exhaust the country's foreign exchange reserves, forcing both the government and the private sector to increase their foreign borrowing.

Capital flight also has some consequences for income distribution, especially if the country follows the "origin" principle of taxation, since there may be little foreign investment that can be taxed. Even if Tanzania followed the "residence" principle of taxation, it would be difficult to tax flight capital since such capital is normally not reported to the tax authorities.

It is not easy to reach any strong conclusions on the consequences of capital flight without an empirical analysis, which, however, is beyond the scope of this chapter.

Political and Macroeconomic Developments in Tanzania During 1967–93

Episodes of capital flight from Tanzania reflect political and external shocks, which in turn have an impact on the performance of the macroeconomy. The shocks referred to here include the 1967 Arusha Declaration on African socialism and the consequent nationalization of private banks, manufacturing, estate farms, and wholesale and retail trade. Another political shock was the 1971 Buildings Acquisition Act, which nationalized private buildings and real estate. Other shocks included the 1973 oil price hike, the breakup of the East African Community in 1977, the 1978 Kagera War, the second oil price shock in 1979, the crackdown on "economic saboteurs" in 1983, the presidential elections of 1985 and 1990, and the implementation of economic recovery programs in 1986 and 1989.

Table 10. Tanzania: Per Capita GDP, International Reserves, Inflation, and Parallel Market Premiums, 1967–93

	Per Capita GDP (In 1997 Tanzania shillings)	International Reserves[1] (In millions of 1997 U.S. dollars)	Inflation[2] (In percent)	Parallel Market Premium[3] (In percent)
1967	1,235	257.19	13.04	21.85
1968	1,266	341.00	15.38	19.05
1969	1,261	338.29	16.67	21.85
1970	1,277	260.00	2.86	41.46
1971	1,287	262.40	5.56	62.46
1972	1,333	498.54	7.89	112.89
1973	1,334	296.18	9.76	106.55
1974	1,315	62.32	20.00	89.34
1975	1,333	92.38	25.93	179.51
1976	1,348	146.13	6.62	161.34
1977	1,320	281.80	11.72	159.35
1978	1,303	106.35	11.73	69.91
1979	1,306	68.04	13.81	45.99
1980	1,302	16.64	30.20	156.10
1981	1,260	17.31	25.37	233.33
1982	1,233	4.63	29.27	251.29
1983	1,172	19.40	26.96	255.48
1984	1,178	26.56	36.12	273.45
1985	1,199	16.60	33.33	280.65
1986	1,188	56.27	32.40	392.35
1987	1,213	37.78	29.98	172.33
1988	1,219	82.71	31.20	112.51
1989	1,233	57.70	25.82	83.78
1990	1,252	210.71	19.71	49.90
1991	1,287	225.96	22.29	59.02
1992	1,296	394.35	22.07	36.34
1993	1,312	244.95	25.32	11.04

Sources: Computed using data from World Bank (1995); Tanzania, Bureau of Statistics; Bank of Tanzania; International Montary Fund (1996); and Kaufmann and O'Connell (1992).

[1]World price of Tanzanian exports was used as the deflator.

[2]Changes in the average domestic consumer price index.

[3]Parallel market premium (*PREM*) defined as 100*(*EU* – *EO*)/*EO*, where *EU* and *EO* are, respectively, the unofficial and the official nominal exchange rates between the Tanzania shilling and the U. S. dollar.

Tanzania's economic performance was better during the late 1960s to the mid-1970s than in the late 1970s and early 1980s. During 1967–75, for example, per capita GDP in real terms grew at an average annual rate of 1.0 percent; during 1976–85 it declined at an average annual rate of 1.3 percent (Table 10).[2]

[2]The averages and growth rates referred to in this section were computed from Table 10.

International reserves in constant prices declined at a relatively low annual rate of 12.0 percent during 1967–76, compared with the drastic annual decline of 21.5 percent during 1976–85 (Table 10).

During 1986–93 growth was restored and the balance of payments crisis was ameliorated. Real per capita GDP during 1986–93 grew at an average annual rate of 1.4 percent, while international reserves in constant prices increased at the impressive rate of 23.4 percent a year.

Domestic inflation seems to have been fairly constant throughout 1967–93, when it averaged 20.4 percent. During our capital flight sample period of 1971–93, inflation averaged 21.9 percent (Table 10).

The performance of the economy has implications for capital flight. Poor economic growth is an indication of low profitability of domestic investment; capital will thus tend to flee the country. A balance of payments crisis is a symptom of possible devaluation as one of the measures to correct the balance of payments deficit. Since a devaluation reduces the value of domestic financial assets, private agents will protect the real value of their assets by acquiring foreign assets, some of which will find their way out of the devaluing country.

The performance of the Tanzanian economy and the political aspirations of the country decided the nature and level of government intervention in the economy. Government intervention, in turn, had varying impacts on resident capital flows.

Before the 1967 Arusha Declaration on African socialism and self-reliance, Tanzania had a minimum level of government intervention in economic affairs. This noninterventionist policy was supported by conservative fiscal and monetary policies (Kaufmann and O'Connell, 1997). During this time, there was less incentive for capital flight, especially during the operation of the East African Currency Board, when there were no capital controls within the sterling area. The desire for capital flight from Tanzania was intensified following the dismantling of the East African Currency Board in 1965 and the promulgation of the Arusha Declaration of 1967 (O'Connell, 1990). The dismantling of the currency board was followed by the prohibition against moving capital out of East Africa (that is, outside Kenya, Tanzania, and Uganda).

Following the Arusha Declaration, the government of Tanzania nationalized all the "commanding heights of the economy." The major private import-export firms were nationalized and replaced by the State Trading Corporation. The banking sector was also nationalized, and the National Bank of Commerce took over the activities of trade finance. In line with the Arusha Declaration, the Building and Acquisition Act was passed in 1971, under which most buildings and real estate belonging to the private sector were expropriated. The act increased expropriation risks and the incentive for capital flight.

Government control of the economy—especially capital and foreign exchange controls—was evident in the parallel market premium. The controls drove a wedge between the parallel and official market exchange rates, giving rise to a premium, the behavior of which reflected the changing nature of the controls (Ndulu and others, 1995). The trade and foreign exchange controls remained relatively low during 1967–71, as reflected in low parallel market premiums, which averaged 33.33 percent in that period. With the heightening of the nationalization policies after 1971, coupled with balance of payments crises, trade and foreign exchange controls were intensified; this gave rise to a booming parallel market in foreign exchange in which the premium increased from 62.46 percent in 1971 to a peak of 392.35 percent in 1986, growing at an average annual rate of 13.03 percent. With the more liberal policies beginning in 1986, the controls were eased and the parallel market premium declined to 11.04 percent in 1993, falling at an average annual rate of 60.04 percent between 1986 and 1993.

In response to the mini–balance of payments crisis in 1974, the government instituted and then intensified capital and foreign exchange controls (Kaufmann and O'Connell, 1992 and 1997). Despite the strict and severe trade and exchange controls instituted in the early 1970s, the balance of payments showed no significant improvement and the economic decline continued. The country was then forced to implement some structural adjustments. Beginning in mid-1984, the government instituted the own-fund import license scheme, under which individuals with access to their own (unofficial) foreign exchange sources were allowed to obtain import licenses without being asked about the source of their funds. Licenses issued under the own-funds scheme accounted for about 40 percent of total import licenses issued in 1988. The share of own-funded imports in total imports is estimated to be larger than that of the licenses, probably exceeding 50 percent of total imports (Kaufmann and O'Connell, 1992).

The capital flight that occurred during 1985–87 could be partly explained by the need to finance own-funded imports. The value of such imports is therefore the reverse of capital flight. The sources of funds for own-funded imports are the decumulation of foreign exchange and illegal trade. Individuals with their own foreign exchange (abroad) may sell it in the parallel foreign exchange market or use it directly to purchase own-funded imports. Those who do not hold foreign exchange may receive grants or borrow from relatives and associates abroad. Illegal trade includes, among other things, smuggling of minerals, elephant tusks, rhinoceros horns, and export crops (mainly coffee), as shown in Table 11. However, not all foreign exchange generated through illegal trade is used to finance own-funded imports.

Table 11. Tanzania: Some Reported Cases of Corruption, 1987–94

	Amount Involved		
	In millions of U.S. dollars	In percent of exports	Description
1987	0.18	0.06	Smuggled elephant tusks ($0.07 million), smuggled coffee ($0.11 million)
1988	0.31	0.08	Reported traveler's checks stolen from the National Bank of Commerce
1989	8.86	2.13	Smuggled elephant tusks
1990	1.45	0.36	Money lost primarily through fake contracts at the Tanzania Breweries Limited ($0.61 million) and smuggled garments ($0.67 million)
1991	0.16	0.04	Gold and gemstones seized at the Dar es Salaam International Airport
1992	59.22	14.78	Money lent to government institutions that has not been accounted for
1993	43.50	26.85	Payments for services not rendered at the Ministry of Home Affairs
1994	3.20	0.63	Open general license and debt conversion program funds illegally paid to a private businessman ($3.19 million) and illegal drugs ($0.01 million)

Source: Msambichaka and others (1994).

Some of it may be used to increase private foreign assets abroad and thus constitutes capital flight.

Economic reforms were further enhanced with the introduction and implementation of economic recovery programs in 1986 and 1989. The main item of the reforms included devaluation of the local currency. The recovery programs were supported by massive inflows of foreign aid that increased the availability of capital (Nyoni, 1995). These capital inflows and the devaluations of 1986–87 provided a great incentive for capital flight during these two years and in 1990.

Another important political development was the crackdown on "economic saboteurs" in 1983. Under this policy, many private entrepreneurs were jailed or were forced to go into hiding with their capital (Bagachwa and Maliyamkono, 1990). The "lucky" ones managed to acquire foreign assets and shift them to foreign countries.

The combination of uncertainties following the breakup of the East African Community in 1977, together with increased capital availability and looser exchange controls following the 1976 coffee boom, led to a massive exodus of capital during 1975–77, totaling $484.05 million in real terms using the adjusted Morgan Guaranty approach (Table 7). The risks associated with the 1978–79 Kagera war and the 1979 oil price hike seem to explain the capital flight of $65.35 million that occurred during 1979.

The uncertainties associated with the 1985 and 1990 presidential elections and the increased availability of capital following the implementation of the 1986 and 1989 economic recovery programs seem to explain the capital flight that occurred during 1985–87 and in 1990, when flight capital in 1977 prices totaled $391.28 million and $229.00 million, respectively.

Another plausible explanation for the capital flight that occurred in the last half of the 1980s and early 1990s in Tanzania is corruption. Corruption in the country is well documented in Msambichaka and others (1994), Chachage (1994), and Mbatia (1994). The reported amounts of money involved are sometimes quite substantial, reaching up to 27 percent of the country's exports (Table 11). Money obtained through corruption is most likely be deposited in foreign banks to avoid detection and prosecution at home.

From the discussion of the measurement of capital flight and trade misinvoicing, one may say that the conduits of capital flight in Tanzania include foreign exchange bureaus, illegal trade, corruption, and trade misinvoicing. Foreign exchange can also be carried physically across the borders through legal or illegal means. Money obtained through illegal trade or corruption can only safely flee the country through illegal means. Funds purchased through foreign exchange bureaus or other official sources are allowed by law to be taken out of the country for financing current account transactions. Capital can then flee the country through overinvoiced imports that are financed by foreign exchange purchased in either the official or the parallel market. Capital can also flee the country through underinvoiced exports. The foreign exchange obtained from trade misinvoicing may be used by those involved to increase foreign asset holdings by domestic residents.

Empirical Analysis of Capital Flight in Tanzania

Causes of Resident Capital Outflow

The discussion in this chapter of the causes of capital flight is based mainly on Lessard and Williamson (1987) and Pastor (1990). Other contributors to the subject include Cuddington (1986), Dornbusch

(1985), and Khan and Ul Haque (1985). In discussing the causes of resident capital outflows one must also look at the circumstances in both source and haven countries and identify factors that would distinguish "normal" from "abnormal" flows.

In general, "resident capital outflow results from a difference in perceived, risk-adjusted returns in source and haven countries" (Lessard and Williamson, 1987, p. 215). The risk (and the returns) may be economic or financial. Economic or social returns are the total returns to a given society derived from a particular investment and adjusted for price distortions and externalities. Financial or private returns are the total returns that accrue to private investors and are calculated at market prices, net of both explicit and implicit taxes.

Capital flight occurs when the overall investment climate is negative for domestic investors. "Overall investment climate" refers to factors that influence the financial attractiveness of source country assets relative to the world standard. These factors include domestic inflation, fiscal deficits, the real interest rate differential between the domestic economy and other economies, expected devaluation, and the differential in expected rates of profitability between the domestic economy and other economies.

Increasing domestic inflation reduces the real value of the domestic currency. To protect the real value of their domestic currency holdings, private agents may substitute foreign assets for these holdings. Some of these foreign assets may be siphoned out of the country, thus constituting capital flight. Increasing fiscal deficits create inflationary expectations and increased tax liabilities to the private sector, since the deficits will have to be financed by either printing money or selling government bonds (Ajayi, 1995). To avoid increased tax liabilities and protect the real value of their assets, domestic investors will reduce their domestic assets and increase foreign assets, some of which will be shipped abroad.

When there is financial repression or there are ceilings on interest rates, real interest rates will be negative, and this will fuel capital flight. Capital flight will also occur if real interest rates on savings in the domestic economy are lower than those obtainable in foreign countries.

Other factors explaining capital flight include devaluation and the relative profitability of the economy. Depreciation of the local currency will reduce the value of domestic assets. When the currency is considered overvalued, a devaluation is expected. The expectation of devaluation will, in turn, propel the exodus of capital from the domestic economy. Capital flight is also caused by low anticipated profitability in the domestic economy relative to that in other countries. Thus, if growth in the real sector in Tanzania is lower than real growth in, say, the United Kingdom, it is a signal that profitability in Tanzania is low; capital will flee to the United Kingdom, where the expected profitability is higher.

Another explanation for capital flight is political instability and the potential for confiscation (Khan and Ul Haque, 1985; Lessard and Williamson, 1987). With high expropriation risks, capital flight will occur even if the relative profitability of capital is higher in the domestic economy than abroad.

Capital availability is a potential cause of capital flight (see, for example, Pastor, 1990; Cuddington, 1986). Increased capital availability may be due to increased foreign aid inflows, a boom in export earnings, or disbursement of public and publicly guaranteed loans. In countries where both the private and the public sector can borrow abroad and private investors may purchase government debts, private investors can shift their own capital abroad and acquire publicly guaranteed external loans at home. When domestic investment is no longer profitable, so that the loans become unserviceable, the private sector may avoid payments on the debt obligations by either "declaring bankruptcy or pressuring the local government to bail out private borrowers through the assumption of their liabilities" (Pastor, 1990, p. 8). When this happens, there will be increased external debt simultaneous with increased capital flight as capital becomes more available. The government thus ends up with the debts, and the elites with the dollars (Duwendag, 1989).

As Lessard and Williamson (1987) point out, it may not always be possible to take into account all the factors that explain international capital flows. Some economists have decided to take only a subset of the factors by focusing on the overall investment climate (see, for example, Cuddington, 1986; Conesa, 1987; Dornbusch, 1985). The emphasis in this doctrine is on overvaluation in terms of the real exchange rate, on fiscal deficits, and on inflation. Others emphasize discriminatory tax treatment of residents versus nonresidents, financial repression, capital denominated in different currencies, and asymmetric investment guarantees (Dooley, 1986; Khan and Ul Haque, 1985; Eaton, 1987; Ize and Ortiz, 1987).

Earlier Studies

Most studies on capital flight have been done for Latin America. Cuddington (1986) and Conesa (1987), for example, emphasized the overall investment climate, while Dooley (1986) focused on the discriminatory treatment of resident versus nonresident capital. Studies on capital flight from Africa include those by Ajayi (1995) for Nigeria,

Awung (1996) for Cameroon, Baruani (1995) for Tanzania, Ng'eno (1994) for Kenya, and Olopoenia (1995) for Uganda.

Cuddington (1986) estimated the economic determinants of resident capital outflow for four major flight countries: Argentina, Mexico, Uruguay, and Venezuela. In his portfolio-adjustment model, the factors that explained resident capital outflow were the expected inflation rate, the foreign interest rate, the domestic interest rate, and disbursement of public and publicly guaranteed loans. Depending on the perceived risks and returns, domestic investors will allocate their wealth among domestic financial assets, domestic inflation hedges such as land, and foreign financial assets. An increase in the foreign financial assets owned by domestic residents constitutes resident capital outflow.

The empirical findings by Cuddington (1986) differed from country to country. For Mexico, the author found that capital flight was highly correlated with currency overvaluation, disbursements of public debt, and lagged capital flight. In Argentina and Uruguay, only the lagged real effective exchange rate and the lagged error of the model were correlated with capital flight. In Venezuela, the only statistically significant determinants were overvaluation and foreign interest rates.

The model results of Conesa (1987) are similar to those of Cuddington (1986), except that Conesa had 16 annual observations whereas Cuddington had only 9, and Conesa had (lack of) growth as an additional explanatory factor. The other difference between the two studies is that, unlike Cuddington (1986), Conesa (1987) did not attempt to estimate overvaluation in terms of the real effective exchange rate, but used the level of government external borrowing and reserves as proxies for overvaluation. Like Cuddington (1986), Conesa's (1987) results also differed from country to country.

In a study of seven developing countries—Argentina, Brazil, Chile, Mexico, Peru, the Philippines, and Venezuela—Dooley (1988) found that capital flight was significantly determined by domestic inflation, financial repression, and a measure of the country risk premium.

The study by Ajayi (1995) provided a link between capital flight and external debt in Nigeria. He concluded that most capital flight from Nigeria was recorded in the balance of payments and external debt statistics and that capital flow is explained not only by economic factors but also by political instability.

Baruani (1995) did an economic analysis of capital flight from Tanzania. The author measured capital flight using both Cuddington's (1986) balance of payments approach and the World Bank (1985) residual approach. This chapter complements the Baruani (1995) study with adjustments for trade misinvoicing and the Morgan Guaranty (1986) residual approach and the bank deposits approach.

Econometric studies on Africa seem to suggest that capital flight results mainly from macroeconomic mismanagement, especially domestic inflation. Olopoenia (1995), for example, found that inflation was the only significant variable (with a positive coefficient of 0.176) propelling capital flight from Uganda. The Ng'eno (1994) study for Kenya found that the coefficient for inflation was positive 0.9, whereas that for lagged capital flight was positive 0.7.

The R^2 in Ng'eno's study was 0.98, which contrasts sharply with a similar study by Olopoenia (1995) for Uganda in which the R^2 was less than 0.30. In an earlier study on economic analysis of capital flight, Ajayi (1992) found that capital flight from Nigeria was triggered by the real interest rate differential, growth of the domestic economy, changes in the nominal exchange rate, the fiscal deficit, and the foreign interest rate adjusted for changes in the nominal exchange rate. The models in Ajayi (1992) had low adjusted R^2 ranging from 0.32 to 0.49. The low explanatory power in Ajayi (1992) and Olopoenia (1995) raises concern about the difficulty of estimating capital flight in African countries, which arises mainly from short sample periods, low data frequency, and poor quality of the data.

The Data

In carrying out econometric analysis of capital flight, we used annual data for 1971–93. However, after transforming the data into first differences, the estimation sample was reduced to 20 years, covering only 1973–92. The brevity of the sample period was dictated by the availability of data, most of which are compiled on an annual basis.

The main data sources for the empirical analysis were the IMF's *International Financial Statistics* and *Direction of Trade Statistics*, the World Bank's *World Tables* and *African Economic Indicators*, and Kaufmann and O'Connell (1992). The data on political and external shocks were obtained from the author's own observations and from Bagachwa and Maliyamkono (1990). Data on domestic interest rates, inflation, and GDP were obtained from the Tanzanian Bureau of Statistics (1995a, 1995b) and various issues of the Bank of Tanzania's *Economic and Operations Report*.

The Model and Model Results

Following Cuddington (1986), Lessard and Williamson (1987), and Pastor (1990), we specify an implicit capital flight model as follows:

$$KF_t = KF(KF_{t-1}, GUTD_t, PREM_t, DINF_t, FINC_t, KAV_t, POS_t, EXS_t), \quad (6)$$

Table 12. Definitions of Variables in the Regression Model

Expected sign	Variable	Definition
	KF_t	Capital flight in 1977 prices measured using the Morgan Guaranty approach (deflated by import price).
+	KF_{t-1}	Lagged capital flight.
+	$FINC_t$	Financial incentive for capital flight. It is measured as $FINC = (i^{UK} - (i^{TZ} - \Delta e))$ where i^{UK} is the U.K. deposit interest rate; i^{TZ} is the Tanzanian deposit interest rate; and Δe is devaluation or the change in the Tanzania shilling–pound sterling nominal exchange rate.
+	EXS_t	Dummy variable for external shock. $EXS = 1$ for year with shock, 0 if otherwise.
+	POS_t	Dummy variable for political shock. $POS = 1$ for year with shock, 0 if otherwise.
+	$PREM_t$	Premium on the U.S. dollar in the parallel market. Measured as $100*(EU - EO)/EO$, where EU and EO are the unofficial or parallel market and the official Tanzania shilling–U.S. dollar nominal exchange rates, respectively.
+	$DINF_t$	Domestic inflation in Tanzania. Measured as the change in the average consumer price index.
+	KAV_t	Availability of capital. Measured as net long-term capital flows deflated by the world price of imports.
+	$GUTD_t$	Growth differential. Measured as $GUTD = g^{UK} - g^{TZ}$ where g^{UK} and g^{TZ} are, respectively, growth rates of U.K. and Tanzanian real GDP.

where t is a time subscript, KF is capital flight in 1977 prices (measured by the Morgan Guaranty approach adjusted for trade misinvoicing), KF_{t-1} is lagged capital flight, $GUTD$ is the difference between the U.K. and Tanzanian real GDP growth rates (serving as a proxy for the relative profitability of investment in the domestic real sector), $PREM$ is the parallel market premium (as a proxy for foreign exchange controls and the degree of real exchange rate overvaluation), $DINF$ is domestic inflation, $FINC$ is the financial incentive for capital flight as defined in Table 12, KAV is a measure of capital availability proxied by net long-term capital flows expressed in 1977 prices, and POS and EXS are, respectively, dummy variables for political and external shocks. Capital flight is an increasing function of all the explanatory variables specified above. The regression variables are further explained in Table 12 and data for these variables are given in Table 13.

Table 13. Data for Selected Variables Used in the Regressions[1]

	GUTD	*PREM*	*EXS*	*POS*	*FINC*	*DINF*	*KAV*
1971	–2.19	62.46	0	1	3.69	5.56	364.04
1972	–3.22	112.89	0	0	2.44	7.91	264.12
1973	4.30	106.55	1	0	–3.65	9.76	228.88
1974	–4.20	89.08	0	0	2.10	20.00	147.78
1975	–6.41	179.89	0	0	2.83	25.92	227.67
1976	–3.83	161.34	0	0	–5.08	6.62	111.08
1977	1.96	159.35	1	0	0.03	11.72	96.60
1978	1.33	83.99	1	0	2.51	11.73	120.83
1979	0.38	45.99	1	0	19.49	13.81	169.76
1980	–5.15	156.10	0	0	15.53	30.10	185.08
1981	–0.79	233.33	0	0	–4.75	25.38	192.83
1982	1.13	251.29	0	0	–4.34	29.16	232.56
1983	6.05	255.48	0	1	21.55	26.96	167.50
1984	–1.06	273.45	0	0	20.38	36.12	–32.93
1985	1.13	280.65	0	1	8.89	33.33	14.81
1986	1.02	392.35	1	1	223.75	32.40	857.01
1987	–0.27	172.33	0	0	93.10	29.99	144.44
1988	0.77	112.51	0	0	32.48	31.20	163.72
1989	–54.32	83.78	1	1	19.50	25.82	172.97
1990	4.07	49.90	0	1	7 90	19.71	215.89
1991	–7.66	59.02	0	0	1.35	22.29	130.37
1992	–4.06	36.34	0	0	3.04	22.07	91.07
1993	–1.91	11.04	0	0	20.01	23.46	180.74

Sources: International Monetary Fund (1996); World Bank (1995) and *World Tables*, various issues; Kaufmann and O'Connell (1992); Bagachwa and Maliyamkono (1990).

[1]The variables are as defined in Table 12.

The variables were first tested (results not shown) for stationarity using the augmented Dickey-Fuller test (Hendry, 1989). The only variables found to be stationary were the contemporaneous and lagged capital flight, the U.K.-Tanzania real growth differential, and the two dummy variables for external and political shocks.

The regression analysis was carried out using PC-GIVE version 8 software developed by Hendry (1989). Attempts to run a cointegration model yielded very poor results (not reported here) with no explanatory variable significant at the conventional significance levels. The main problem could be that of the short sample period and low-frequency annual data. To avoid spurious regression, we ran the capital flight model by using the variables in first differences.

The empirical model is explicitly specified as

$$\Delta KFt = \alpha_0 + \alpha_1 \Delta KF_{t-1} + \alpha_2 \Delta GUTD_t + \alpha_3 \Delta PREM_t + \alpha_4 \Delta DINF_t + \alpha_5 \Delta FINC_t + \alpha 6 \Delta KAV_t + \alpha 7 \Delta EXS_t + \alpha_8 \Delta POS_t + \mu_t, \quad (7)$$

Table 14. Tanzania: Determinants of Capital Flight

Variable	Coefficient	Standard Error	*t*-Value
Constant	–43.263	72.892	–0.594
ΔKF_{t-1}	–0.555	0.202	–2.744
$\Delta GUTD_t$	7.056	2.884	2.446
$\Delta PREM_t$	1.306	1.157	1.129
$\Delta DINF_t$	–3.982	7.348	–0.542
$\Delta FINC_t$	2.531	1.962	1.290
ΔKAV_t	–0.883	0.503	–1.755
POS_t	144.280	127.330	1.133
EXS_t	51.109	139.700	0.366

R^2 = 0.63; $F(8,11)$ = 2.31; RSS = 445636.77; Adjusted R^2 = 0.36; period = 1973–92

Source: Author's calculations using ordinary least-squares estimation.

where α_i ($i = 1, \ldots, 8$) are coefficients; KF_t, KF_{t-1}, $GUTD_t$, $PREM_t$, $DINF_t$, $FINC_t$, KAV_t, EXS_t, and POS_t are as defined above; μ_t is the error term; and Δ is the difference operator for the indicated variables.

The regression results are presented in Table 14. The model has a goodness of fit of 0.63. We also attempted to run the model without capital availability or lagged capital flight. Omitting either of the two variables reduced the R^2 by more than 50 percent. This strengthens the *F*-test for the R^2 that the explanatory variables are jointly significant and explains 63 percent of the variations in capital flight.

At the level of individual variables, the only statistically significant variables in explaining capital flight from Tanzania are the U.K.-Tanzania real GDP growth differential. The growth differential variable bears the expected positive sign. Lagged capital flight, however, bears an inverse sign, suggesting that lagged capital flight in Tanzania is associated with reverse capital flight.

As mentioned above, since the model passes the *F*-test for goodness of fit, all the variables in the model are jointly significant. Capital flight is then jointly determined by the U.K.-Tanzania real GDP growth differential, domestic inflation, political and external shocks, lagged capital flight, the parallel market premium, financial incentives for capital flight, and capital availability. Looking at the coefficients of the variables, it can be seen that political and external shocks in Tanzania have the overriding impact of propelling capital flight from the country.

Conclusion

Summary of the Findings

This chapter has analyzed the magnitude and determinants of capital flight from Tanzania. Capital flight was measured by the balance of payments approach, the World Bank (1985) and Morgan Guaranty (1986) versions of the residual approach, and the bank deposits approach. We argued that the measures should be adjusted for trade misinvoicing to get more accurate estimates of capital flight. We found that the Morgan Guaranty measure was more robust than the other two measures. The adjusted Morgan Guaranty measure indicates that capital flight episodes in Tanzania occurred during 1975–77, 1979, 1985–87, and 1990. The total amount of capital that fled the country during those years was $1.2 billion in 1977 prices.

The analysis of the causes of capital flight was carried out using both historical and empirical approaches. From the historical analysis, we found that trade misinvoicing and smuggling were important mechanisms of effecting capital flight. For this reason, the capital flight measures were adjusted for trade misinvoicing.

Corruption was also found to be an important vehicle for effecting capital flight from Tanzania. Cases of corruption were identified to include stealing of foreign exchange from the state-owned National Bank of Commerce, foreign exchange lost through fake contracts in public enterprises and government departments, and siphoning out of aid monies.

Political instability increased fears of expropriation risks and damage to private property. Such risks, in turn, increased the desire for capital flight. Instances of political instability were cited to include the nationalization policy following the 1967 Arusha Declaration on African socialism, the 1971 Buildings Acquisition Act, the Kagera war of 1978–79, the crackdown on "economic saboteurs" in 1983, and the presidential elections of 1985 and 1990.

From the empirical analysis, we observed that the only statistically significant factor explaining capital flight from Tanzania was the U.K.-Tanzania real GDP growth differential. Lagged capital flight was also statistically significant but was associated with reverse capital flight. It was also observed that capital flight was jointly determined by the U.K.-Tanzania real growth differential, lagged capital flight, external and political shocks, the parallel market premium, domestic inflation, capital availability, and financial incentives for capital flight.

Policy Implications

We can draw several policy implications from the historical and empirical analyses. To control capital flight, it is important to restore public confidence in the government and the sustainability of macroeconomic policy. This, in turn, requires a realistic exchange rate, positive but moderate real interest rates, robust economic growth, and an honest government.

The econometric analysis of capital flight showed that the exodus of capital from Tanzania was strongly determined by the U.K.-Tanzania real growth differential. This underscores the importance of a pro-growth bias of official policy in the country. It is important to avoid excessive austerity in monetary and fiscal policies so as not to choke off production. Pro-growth policies include market liberalization and export promotion measures.

To control capital flight and recapture flight capital requires getting the macroeconomic fundamentals right; that is, policymakers should avoid the habit of allowing the local currency to be overvalued and thus minimize the necessity of devaluation. This may be achieved by allowing the currency to float or by setting it at an appropriate level and making sure that inflation is controlled so that the currency is not overvalued in real terms. This also warns against expansionary fiscal and monetary policies, as these generate expectations of inflation and the desire for capital flight. For this policy to be effective, it is important to maintain public confidence that the policy will not be reversed under any circumstances.

Restoration of public confidence in the sustainability of macroeconomic policy also requires setting domestic interest rates above international rates. However, care must be taken not to set the rates too high, since too-high interest rates will discourage domestic productive investment and trigger capital flight.

Even if the macroeconomic fundamentals are set right, a country may continue to experience repeated bouts of capital flight if corruption is rampant. Some of the income illicitly gained from bribes on public sector contracts or from import licenses is likely to be shifted abroad to avoid detection and prosecution in the home country. Policy change is thus necessary to reduce such illicit incomes as well as incentives for corruption and capital flight. The establishment of a uniform tariff rate structure, lower tax rates, and an end to the rationing of underpriced foreign exchange and credits will greatly reduce incentives not only for corruption but also for trade misinvoicing and capital flight.

From both the historical and the econometric analyses, we found that political shocks are important in propelling capital flight. Hence, policymakers should strive to maintain peace and calm in the country and avoid policies that are hostile to the private sector and property. Such hostile policies include the crackdown on "economic saboteurs" and the expropriation of private property.

References

Ajayi, S.I., 1992, "An Economic Analysis of Capital Flight from Nigeria," World Bank Policy Research Working Paper No. 993 (Washington: World Bank).

———, 1995, "Capital Flight and External Debt in Nigeria," Research Paper No. 35 (Nairobi: African Economic Research Consortium).

———, 1996, "An Analysis of Capital Flight and External Debt in Severely Indebted Sub-Saharan African Countries," paper presented at the IMF Conference on Financing Low-Income Countries, Washington, December 10–11.

Awung, W.J., 1996, "An Economic Analysis of Capital Flight in Cameroon," final research report presented at a research workshop organized by the African Economic Research Consortium, Nairobi, May.

Bagachwa, M.S.D., and T.L. Maliyamkono, 1990, *The Second Economy in Tanzania* (London: James Currey).

Bank of Tanzania, *Economic and Operations Report* (Dar es Salaam), various issues.

Baruani, M.S., 1995, "An Economic Analysis of the Determinants of Capital Flight in Tanzania, 1967–1990" (unpublished, University of Dar es Salaam).

Bureau of Statistics, 1995a, *National Accounts of Tanzania, 1976–1993* (Dar es Salaam).

———, 1995b, *Selected Statistical Series, 1951–1991* (Dar es Salaam).

Chachage, S., 1994, "Corruption in Tanzania: Some Issues for Consideration," paper presented at the workshop on Corruption and Drug Trafficking in Tanzania, Dar es Salaam, October 12.

Conesa, E.R., 1987, *The Causes of Capital Flight from Latin America* (Washington: Inter-American Development Bank).

Cuddington, J.T., 1986, *Capital Flight Estimates, Issues, and Explanations*, Princeton Studies in International Finance No. 58 (Princeton, New Jersey: Princeton University Press).

Dooley, M.P., 1986, "Country-Specific Risk Premiums, Capital Flight, and Net Investment Income Payments in Selected Developing Countries" (unpublished; Washington: International Monetary Fund).

———, 1988, "Capital Flight: A Response to Differences in Financial Risks," *Staff Papers*, International Monetary Fund, Vol. 35 (September).

Dornbusch, R., 1985, "External Debt, Budget Deficits and Disequilibrium Exchange Rates," in *International Debt and the Developing Countries*, ed. by G.W. Smith and J.T. Cuddington (Washington: World Bank).

Duwendag, D., 1989, "Capital Flight from Developing Countries," *Development and Cooperation*, No. 3.

Eaton, J., 1987, "Public Debt Guarantees and Private Capital Flight," *World Bank Economic Review*, Vol. 1 (May).

Eggerstedt, H.R., B. Hall, and S. van Wijnbergen, 1995, "Measuring Capital Flight: A Case Study of Mexico," *World Development*, Vol. 23, No. 2.

Erbe, Susanne, 1985, "The Flight of Capital from Developing Countries," *Intereconomics: Review of International Trade and Development*, Vol. 20 (November/December).

Hendry, D.F., 1989, *PC-GIVE: An Interactive Econometric Modelling System* (Oxford: Institute of Economics and Statistics).

International Monetary Fund, 1996, *International Financial Statistics Yearbook 1995* (Washington).

———, *Direction of Trade Statistics Yearbook* (Washington), various issues.

Ize, A., and G. Ortiz, 1987, "Fiscal Rigidities, Public Debt, and Capital Flight," *Staff Papers*, International Monetary Fund, Vol. 34 (June).

Kaufmann, D., and S.A. O'Connell, 1992, "The Macroeconomics of the Unofficial Foreign Exchange Market in Tanzania," in *Economic Reforms in Sub-Saharan Africa*, ed. by A. Chhibber and S. Fischer (Washington: World Bank).

———, 1997, "Exchange Controls and the Parallel Premium in Tanzania, 1967–1990," in *Parallel Exchange Rates in Developing Countries*, ed. by M. Kiguel, J.S. Lizondo, and S.A. O'Connell (New York: St. Martin's Press).

Khan, M., and N. Ul Haque, 1985, "Foreign Borrowing and Capital Flight: A Formal Analysis," *Staff Papers*, International Monetary Fund, Vol. 32 (December).

Lessard, D.R., and J. Williamson, 1987, "Capital Flight: The Problem and Policy Responses," in *Capital Flight and Third World Debt*, ed. by D.R. Lessard and J. Williamson (Washington: Institute for International Economics).

Mbatia, J.K., 1994, "Drug Trafficking in Tanzania," paper presented at the Workshop on Corruption and Drug Trafficking in Tanzania, Dar es Salaam, October 12.

Morgan Guaranty Trust Company, 1986, "LDC Capital Flight," *World Financial Markets* (March).

Mpango, P.I.N., 1996, "Evasion of Import Duties: An Economic Analysis of the Case of Tanzania" (unpublished, University of Dar es Salaam).

Msambichaka, L.A., G.D. Mjema, and M.O.A. Ndanshau, 1994, "Corruption and Drug Trafficking in Tanzania: The Practice and Hazards," paper presented at the Workshop on Corruption and Drug Trafficking in Dar es Salaam, Tanzania, October 12.

Ndulu, B.J., J. Semboja, and A.V.Y. Mbelle, 1995, "Trade Liberalization in Tanzania: Episodes and Impacts," a research report for the Collaborative Research Project in Trade Liberalization and Regional Integration in Africa, coordinated by the African Economic Research Consortium, Nairobi.

Ng'eno, N.K., 1994, "Capital Flight in Kenya," paper presented at the African Economic Research Consortium Workshop, Nairobi, May 28–June 3.

Nyoni, T.S., 1995, "Foreign Aid and Economic Performance in Tanzania," final research report submitted to the African Economic Research Consortium, Nairobi, September.

O'Connell, S.A., 1990, "The Parallel Foreign Exchange Market in Tanzania," paper submitted to the Bank of Tanzania, Dar es Salaam.

Olopoenia, R.A., 1995, "Capital Flight from Uganda, 1971–1994: Estimates, Causes and Consequences," paper presented at the African Economic Research Consortium Economic Research Workshop, Nairobi, May 27–June 2.

Pastor, M., Jr., 1990, "Capital Flight from Latin America," *World Development*, Vol. 18, No. 1.

World Bank, 1985, *World Development Report 1985* (New York: Oxford University Press).

———, 1987, *World Tables 1987* (Washington).

———, 1994, *World Tables 1994* (Washington).

———, 1995, *African Development Indicators 1994–95* (Washington).

Zedillo, E., 1987, "Mexico," in *Capital Flight and Third World Debt*, ed. by Donald R. Lessard and John Williamson (Washington: Institute for International Economics).

Capital Flight in Kenya 10

N.K. Ng'eno

The withholding of quick-disbursing aid by donors in November 1991 contributed to one of the worst episodes of balance of payments crisis in Kenya's history. The crisis brought to the fore the debate on capital flight, as it became evident that capital flight continued even as the foreign exchange crisis deepened. At the time capital flight was viewed as the major cause of slow economic growth, declining investments, and mounting external debt. The growth of GDP declined from 4.5 percent in 1990 to 2.1 percent in 1991, and declined further to 0.5 percent and 0.2 percent in 1992 and 1993, respectively. Long-term outstanding debt rose by 10 percent between 1990 and 1991, and the balance of payments deficit was 12 percent of GDP in 1990 (Ng'eno, 1997). Foreign direct investment declined from $19 million in 1991 to $6 million and $2 million in 1992 and 1993, respectively (World Bank, 1994).

The data relied on nonbank cross-border deposits, reported in the IMF's *International Financial Statistics,* as a measure of capital flight. Total capital flight from this source was $2.53 billion at the end of 1992, equivalent to 37 percent of the country's total external debt.

While accepting that capital flight was a problem, the government disputed its magnitude, but began nonetheless to take some steps to deal with it. The government on many occasions reminded Kenyans of the illegality of operating foreign accounts, and in 1991 it gave a one-month amnesty to holders of foreign assets. The most significant step, however, was to relax foreign exchange controls beginning in the early part of 1993, which led to the convertibility of the shilling in June 1994. Ng'eno (1997) provides a detailed narrative on economic reforms in Kenya since the 1970s.

The reforms were intended to restore confidence in the economy and thereby stem capital flight and promote foreign investment and increased exports, and, ultimately, a higher rate of economic growth. The reforms were so successful in attracting foreign exchange inflows that by September 1994 holders of foreign currency accounts were being encouraged by the central bank to retain their funds abroad to stabilize the exchange rate.

The capital flight debate in Kenya mirrors the common problem surrounding the issue in the literature. Studies on capital flight have not established a consensus on the right definition, method of measurement, or causes and effects of the problem. There is indeed no consensus as to whether capital flight is a problem or not. These issues need to be addressed, at least to some acceptable degree, if capital flight estimates are to be useful for policy purposes.

The extent of capital flight in Kenya, like that of many other sub-Saharan African countries, has not been given much attention in the literature. The available estimates of capital flight in Kenya (for example, Chang and Cumby, 1991) are sketchy and inconclusive. Ajayi (1996) provides estimates of Kenya's capital flight in 1980–91.

This chapter aims to analyze the extent of the problem of capital flight in Kenya using different methods of estimation and to determine empirically the causes of capital flight, with emphasis on the role of macroeconomic variables. The chapter first addresses the conceptual and practical problems related to the definition of capital flight and discusses the causes and effects of capital flight. It then reviews the different methodologies used for estimating capital flight and provides empirical results obtained by estimating a simple capital flight function. These results are used to discuss the policy implications of capital flight in Kenya.

Capital Flight: Definition, Causes, and Effects

Capital flight is simply the movement of capital from one country to another, motivated by differentials in returns to capital across countries. The movement of capital from developing to developed countries has generated much controversy, however.

The use of the word "flight" to describe the movement of capital from developing to developed countries connotes illegal or unsanctioned movement, but this cannot be true of all capital flows. This has led to attempts to distinguish normal or legal capital flows from "abnormal" or "illegal" flows. Assuming the existence of controls on the capital account, normal capital outflows would be those that occur with government approval, and capital flight would be movement of capital not sanctioned by the authorities. In practice, it is difficult to distinguish between normal and abnormal capital flows. Because of this problem, Kindleberger (1987) and Walter (1987) suggested that capital flight should simply be defined as all capital that "flees," irrespective of the motive. Such a measure, while neutral, would be too general to be of use in assessing the problem of capital flight. An alternative definition used by the World Bank (1985), Erbe (1985), Morgan Guaranty Trust (1986), and Chang and Cumby (1991) is "the change in the private sector's net foreign assets." This definition is still too broad but is the most commonly used measure.

The other issue that arises in the analysis of capital flight is the existence of "cross-transfer" of capital between developed and developing countries. Theory predicts that capital-scarce developing countries would have higher returns to capital than capital-abundant developed countries. This should lead to net capital inflows to developing countries. However, simultaneous foreign borrowing and lending (private capital outflows) by developing country residents is common. Increased external indebtedness of developing countries has indeed been accompanied by high capital flight.

Several explanations have been given for this phenomenon. One is the existence of abnormal risks, or what Khan and Ul Haque (1987) call "expropriation risks." The underlying assumption behind this explanation is that developing country residents invest in developed countries as a means of diversifying their portfolios. Investing in the domestic economy is perceived to be risky because of poor economic performance, inefficient capital markets, and/or fragile political systems. Moreover, the risks of expropriation of assets are higher in developing countries than in developed countries. This argument does not explain why foreign residents would want to invest in developing countries, but this problem of cross-transfer of capital could be explained by the existence of asymmetric risks between residents and nonresidents (Dooley, 1986, 1988). The asymmetric risks may arise from different tax treatment and credit guarantees offered to domestic and foreign residents. A tax system that discriminates in favor of foreign investment may induce increased foreign capital inflow and an outflow of domestic capital trying to avoid taxes and other risks. This is quite common in developing countries, where governments try to attract foreign capital inflows and promote exports by offering substantial tax incentives to foreign investors. Government guarantee of foreign debt can also induce capital inflows, and when domestic investments do not enjoy similar guarantees, capital is more likely to flee to safer havens. At the extreme, public and publicly guaranteed external debt could be contracted by local investors who at the same time acquire foreign assets. This is the most likely scenario in many developing countries facing high capital flight. These explanations led Khan and Ul Haque (1987) and Dooley (1986, 1988) to define capital flight as the unreported stock of foreign claims that generate income that is not recorded in the balance of payments.

The choice of a measure of capital flight depends on the issues of importance to the country under consideration. Chang and Cumby (1991) argue that if capital flight reduces domestic investment, then the outflow of capital, whether reported or not, should be considered a measure of capital flight. However, if the issue of interest is the effect of capital flight on the domestic tax base, then the unreported capital outflow is the appropriate definition. The two problems coexist in Kenya. This chapter will therefore not limit itself to particular measures.

Capital flight results from macroeconomic and political instability. A poor investment climate, characterized by high poverty, low savings and investment rates, a narrow technological base, and poor performance of the economy, also contributes to capital flight. The macroeconomic variables that play a major role in capital flight are inflation, domestic and foreign interest rates, and exchange rates. Inflation causes capital flight by reducing the value of domestic assets such as money and savings. Similarly, an overvalued currency implies a high probability of devaluation, which would reduce the value of domestic assets. Low or negative interest rates are common in the financially repressed economies of developing countries. The large difference between domestic and foreign interest rates makes it attractive to acquire foreign assets. However, it is possible that even if domestic interest rates were higher than foreign interest rates, political instability, which leads to high expropriation risks, would make it profitable to invest ("save") abroad.[1] Thus, in the face of expropriation risks, higher foreign interest rates may not necessarily explain capital flight. The performance of the economy can also serve as an indicator of the profitability of investments. Poor economic growth can encourage capital flight in search of better returns.

Capital flight has several negative effects on the economy. First, it reduces domestic investment and therefore depresses economic growth. Second, it reduces the domestic tax base, which may force the government to resort to distortionary taxes that introduce inefficiencies in the market, thus reducing economic growth. Third, by increasing foreign exchange, which could be siphoned out, capital inflows can contribute to capital flight. This is especially true where corruption results in the flight of public and publicly guaranteed debt. Last, capital flight creates a need for higher foreign borrowing and therefore leads to higher indebtedness, and also slows the solution of the debt problem. Creditors would be unwilling to supply new money on favorable terms when most of it is likely to be repatriated to developed countries.

Measurement of Capital Flight

The following methods have been most commonly used to estimate capital flight: the residual method, the Dooley method, the "hot money" method, the nonbank cross-border deposits method, and the trade misinvoicing method.

[1]The first case in Kenya of capital flight induced by political events was at independence in 1964, when white settlers transferred their capital abroad (Ng'eno, 1991).

Residual Method

This method estimates capital flight as a residual based on the balance of payments identity. The residual is measured as the difference between capital inflows and official allocation of funds as recorded in the balance of payments statistics. This method was developed by Dooley and others (1983) and has been applied by the World Bank (1985), Erbe (1985), Morgan Guaranty Trust (1986), and Cumby and Levich (1987). The variants of this model are discussed by Chang and Cumby (1991) and Gajdeczka (1990).

The most basic form of this method can be specified as follows:

$$CF = dD + NFI - CAD - dR, \quad (1)$$

where

CF = capital flight

dD = change in external debt

NFI = net foreign direct investment flow

CAD = current account deficit

dR = change in official reserves.

This method was used by the World Bank (1985) and Erbe (1985). It assumes that the residual represents the net foreign claims by the private sector, so that if $CF > 0$, then capital flight exists, and $CF < 0$ represents capital inflows.

Morgan Guaranty (1986) modified the World Bank and Erbe method by excluding from the estimation of capital flight the acquisition of short-term foreign assets by the banking sector. However, foreign claims by other private sector agents are considered capital flight. This method can be specified as follows:

$$CF = NFI + dD - CAD - dR - dFCB, \quad (2)$$

where $dFCB$ is the increase in net foreign claims by commercial banks.

Cline's method (Claessens and Naude, 1993, and Cumby and Levich, 1987) in turn modified the Morgan Guaranty method by excluding the following items from the current account: travel (credit), reinvested foreign investment income (abroad and domestically), and other investment income (credit).

Cline's rationale for the exclusion of these items in method is that they are beyond the control of the foreign exchange authorities and therefore should not be treated as capital flight. The problem in Kenya's case is that earnings from tourism form a large part of the current account. The exclusion of these earnings would overestimate the extent of capital flight. Cumby and Levich (1987) suggest that low estimates from Cline's method would indicate that controls on the capital account have been successful in reducing capital flight.

Dooley Method

Dooley (1986) defines capital flight as a stock of privately held foreign assets that earn income but is not reported to domestic authorities and is therefore not recorded in the balance of payments accounts. The stock of private sector external claims is derived from adjusted capital flows in the balance of payments accounts and the stock of external debt as reported by the World Bank.

The Dooley estimate, however, can be obtained more easily by subtracting the imputed stocks of reported assets from the World Bank residual measure (Claessens and Naude, 1993). The problem with this is that the imputed stock of reported assets is made up of new capital flows and interest earned abroad but not repatriated, which is a stock. The imputed stock of reported assets would not be a pure measure of flows and therefore distorts the Dooley measure of capital flight.

"Hot Money" Method

The "hot money" method, associated with Cuddington (1986), is the simplest measure of capital flight, comprising short-term capital plus errors and omissions. Errors and omissions are used as proxies for unreported short-term capital outflows. This measure reflects speculative private capital movements that can easily move in and out of the country depending on economic conditions; hence the term "hot money."

This measure is too restrictive because it excludes long-term assets. Cumby and Levich (1987) and Eggerstedt and others (1993) argue that unreported short-term capital is not the only item in the errors and omissions account of the balance of payments. The other items in the account would include measurement errors, unrecorded imports, and lagged registration. Eggerstedt and others argue further that long-term capital cannot be easily distinguished from short-term capital. Moreover, there is no particular reason why agents cannot acquire long-term foreign assets in highly developed foreign capital markets as a hedge against unfavorable economic conditions in their countries.

Despite these shortcomings, estimates obtained from this method are useful and may be treated as lower-bound estimates of capital flight. The estimates can be used as benchmarks for evaluating estimates from other methods.

Nonbank Cross-Border Deposits Method

This method measures capital flight as the change in deposits held by a country's residents in foreign banks. It is based on the assumption that foreign assets held by residents abroad are mainly in the form of bank deposits. Khan and Ul Haque (1987) argue that this measure is more reliable because capital flight is directly recorded, not estimated as in the other methods. Vos (1990), however, notes that nonbank private deposits held abroad may not be accurately recorded, because some of the funds are held outside reporting institutions and the nationalities of depositors are not always known or easy to establish. Foreign assets are also not always held in the form of bank deposits but may be stocks, bonds, treasury bills, or real estate.

Similar to estimates obtained from the hot money method, nonbank cross-border bank deposits may be taken as lower-bound estimates of assets that can be repatriated easily. The estimates can also be used as easy measures of the extent of capital flight.

Trade Misinvoicing

Trade misinvoicing is one way of effecting capital flight. Bhagwati (1964), Bhagwati and others (1974), Gulati (1987), and Vos (1990) have shown that overinvoicing of imports and underinvoicing of exports are important means of capital flight in developing countries. Misinvoicing occurs as a result of high trade taxes, quantitative restrictions, and exchange controls, all of which are common regimes in developing countries.

This chapter analyzes the role of trade misinvoicing in capital flight using the Bhagwati (1964) methodology. The methodology uses partner country trade statistics to determine the level of misinvoicing and hence capital flight. The analysis starts with the assumption that for purposes of repatriating capital, exporters will underinvoice exports while importers will overinvoice imports.

It is worthwhile to note that the imports and exports used in determining overinvoicing are valued c.i.f. and f.o.b., respectively. This makes it difficult for the data to be compared on a consistent basis. This problem is corrected in this chapter by adjusting Kenya's imports from the partner countries and imports of the partner countries from Kenya (Kenya's exports) by an f.o.b.-c.i.f. ratio obtained from the IMF's *International Financial Statistics* (1996). Trade data are obtained from the IMF's *Direction of Trade Statistics*.

Trade misinvoicing can therefore be expressed as

$$IM = (M_k / CIF - FOB \text{ factor}) - M_p \qquad (3)$$

$$EM = (X_p/CIF - FOB \text{ factor}) - X_k, \tag{4}$$

where

IM = import misinvoicing

EX = export misinvoicing

M_k = imports by Kenya from partner country as reported by Kenya

M_P = exports to Kenya as reported by partner country p

X_p = imports from Kenya as reported by partner p country

X_k = exports to partner country as reported by Kenya.

Positive signs for Equations (3) and (4) indicate misinvoicing, that is, overinvoicing of imports and underinvoicing of exports, implying capital flight. Negative signs indicate reverse capital flight or underinvoicing of imports and overinvoicing of exports. The net effect of misinvoicing on capital flight can be obtained by adding import misinvoicing (IM) and export misinvoicing (EM).

Data from Kenya's major trading partners—the United Kingdom, Germany, France, Italy, the United States, the Netherlands, Japan, India, the United Arab Emirates, Tanzania, and Uganda—are used to estimate the extent of trade misinvoicing. These countries account for 60 percent of Kenya's imports and exports. The regional diversity of the countries will allow us to determine whether the source or the destination of trade affects the level of misinvoicing. Yeats (1991) suggests that it does.

Estimates of Capital Flight

Estimates of capital flight in sub-Saharan Africa are scanty. Empirical studies on capital flight are predominantly confined to the Latin American countries. Chang and Cumby (1991) estimate capital flight for 36 sub-Saharan African countries, including Kenya. Ajayi (1996) estimates capital flight for 25 severely indebted countries of sub-Saharan Africa, also including Kenya. Ajayi (1991) provides capital flight estimates for Nigeria using a variety of methods, and Olopoenia (1995) provides estimates for Uganda. Using the residual method and the cross-border bank deposits method, Chang and Cumby (1991) estimate Kenya's stock of capital flight between 1967 and 1987 to have been \$0.6 billion and \$1.2 billion, respectively. The study also found that there was misinvoicing of both imports and exports. Yeats (1991) found that Kenya's exports to sub-Saharan Africa were underinvoiced by 12.3 percent in 1982/83 and that exports of manufactured goods were underinvoiced by 32.8 percent. The same study found that

Table 1. Components of Capital Flight

A.	Current account balance (August 27, 1998) A1: Travel: Credit A2: Reinvested earnings on direct investment abroad A3: Reinvested earnings on direct investment domestically A4: Other investment income: credit
B.	Net direct foreign investment
C.	Other short-term capital of other sectors: net C1: Other assets
D.	Portfolio investment, other bonds
E.	Change in deposit money bank's foreign assets
F.	Change in reserves
H.	Change in external debt
G.	Net errors and omissions

World Bank method:	(H + B + A + F)
Morgan Guaranty method:	(H + B + A + E + F)
Cline method:	$(H + B) + (A - (A_1 + A_2 + A_3 + A_4) + E + F$
Cuddington method I:	–(G + C)
Cuddington method II:	–(G + C1)

Sources: Data for A, B, C, D, F, and G, International Monetary Fund, *Balance of Payments Yearbook;* data for E and cross-border bank deposits, International Monetary Fund, *International Financial Statistics;* and data for H, *World Bank World Debt Tables.*

Kenya's exports to the European Community, the United States, and member countries of the European Free Trade Association were underinvoiced by 24.3 percent, 27.1 percent, and 68.2 percent, respectively. Ajayi (1996) established that there were instances of overinvoicing of exports and underinvoicing of imports in Kenya. While indicating the possible causes of capital flight, these results also highlight the inconsistent outcomes from the use of different methodologies and even data types to estimate capital flight.

Estimates of Kenya's capital flight are derived using the World Bank, Morgan Guaranty Trust, Cline, and Cuddington methods for the period 1971–95. Data on cross-border bank deposits could only be obtained from 1981 onward. The notations used by Cumby and Levich (1987) and Claessens and Naude (1993) are shown in Table 1.

The estimates of capital flight using cross-border bank deposits are presented in Table 2. The stock of capital flight peaked at $2.6 billion in 1990 and remained above $2 billion in 1989. The stock of capital flight is substantial, accounting for an average of over 30 percent of external debt

Table 2. Kenya: Cross-Border Deposits of Nonbanks by Residence of Depositor, 1981–95

	Total Deposits (In millions of U.S. dollars)	Change in Deposits (In percent)	Ratio of Total Deposits to External Debt (In percent)	Ratio of Total Deposits to GNP (In percent)
1981	20		6.2	0.3
1982	1,120	110	33.5	18.1
1983	1,070	–60	29.4	19.3
1984	990	–80	28.1	16.6
1985	1,360	370	32.4	23.0
1986	1,500	140	31.8	21.5
1987	1,840	340	32.0	24.0
1988	1,810	–30	31.3	22.2
1989	2,101	200	35.8	26.3
1990	2,640	630	37.4	32.6
1991	2,530	–110	33.9	33.4
1992	2,220	–310	32.1	29.4
1993	2,080	–140	29.2	40.8
1994	2,130	50	29.7	32.1
1995	2,230	100	30.1	25.8

Source: International Monetary Fund, *International Financial Statistics,* various issues.

since 1982 and over 20 percent of GDP since 1985. The estimates decline, however, when measured as the year-to-year change in deposits. The measure indicates that there was reverse capital flight between 1991 and 1993 and that subsequently capital flight was low. It would seem puzzling that there were substantial returns of capital during 1991–93, given that this was also a period of serious political turmoil and economic decline. It is possible, however, that the capital was repatriated to finance the elections of 1992 and as a clearly positive response to foreign exchange and exchange control liberalization at the time.

The residual and Cuddington estimates are shown in Table 3; it is evident from these measures that capital flight peaked in 1979, 1987, and 1990. With the exception of 1987 these were also years of balance of payments crisis. This implies that the flight of capital was used to hedge against the poor economic conditions. Capital flight in 1987 must have resulted from the availability of large foreign exchange reserves owing to the mini-boom in tea in 1986. The periods in which capital flight bottomed out (1984, 1992, and 1994) were also marked by poor economic performance, which reduced the availability of savings to be expatriated. Decline in capital inflows, especially after 1990, also contributed to lower capital flight.

Table 3. Kenya: Estimates of Capital Flight, 1971–95
(In millions of U.S. dollars)

	World Bank	Morgan	Cline	Cuddington I	Cuddington II
1971	91.9	95.1	295.7	10.3	10.3
1972	245.1	250.7	263.7	8.8	1.7
1973	387.9	372.2	486.2	8.6	–8.2
1974	506.1	495.6	730.0	13.1	–25.9
1975	427.3	429.2	507.1	13.2	–13.1
1976	501.2	493.6	449.1	12.5	0.2
1977	357.4	363.7	276.1	2.2	1.8
1978	751.6	743.2	1,403.8	–0.9	–52.6
1979	1,510.6	1,492.2	1,277.3	11.9	–216.5
1980	1,237.3	1,235.7	1,821.9	–9.6	–151.2
1981	590.0	592.9	787.9	45.0	–80.8
1982	858.5	876.7	920.5	–98.3	–110.8
1983	666.2	671.3	623.6	12.7	–25.9
1984	29.6	33.7	280.7	–2.1	–68.5
1985	755.4	756.2	1,103.4	30.1	–78.5
1986	666.4	659.8	916.7	19.5	–71.5
1987	1,409.9	1,416.0	1,937.2	–142.4	–206.6
1988	671.4	665.1	888.2	–31.5	–91.5
1989	794.3	775.6	1,140.2	–37.6	–120.3
1990	1,626.5	1,622.6	2,203.2	–0.4	–214.9
1991	653.0	651.3	1,052.4	–41.6	–52.4
1992	–297.1	–259.3	81.1	–110.3	–110.3
1993	591.3	350.6	564.6	–257.5	–257.5
1994	–434.2	–510.7	466.3	–5.8	–5.8
1995	315.1	300.9	1,092.2	–11.4	–11.4

Sources: Author's calculations.

The results also indicate that estimates from the residual method have similar trends. These trends are similar to those obtained by Cumby and Levich (1987) and Vos (1990). There is little difference between the estimates obtained from the World Bank and Morgan Guaranty methods. This is not surprising since the only difference between the two is the addition of net foreign claims by commercial banks to the Morgan Guaranty method. The estimates obtained using Cline's method are higher than those of the World Bank and Morgan Guaranty methods. This is also to be expected because Cline's method excludes, among other items, tourism earnings, a major element of Kenya's current account.

Cuddington's method generates the lowest estimates of capital flight. The peaks of the Cuddington estimates follow a pattern similar to those obtained with the residual method.

Table 4 presents misinvoicing of exports by country. Misinvoicing of exports is high for exports to the United Kingdom, the United States, and Germany, and to a lesser extent for exports to Italy and France. The incidence of misinvoicing is low for exports to India, the United Arab Emirates, Tanzania, and Uganda. This indicates that exports to industrial countries have been used as conduits for capital flight. It could also suggest, as argued by Gulati (1987), that data from these countries are more accurately recorded, thus showing up as high capital flight.

It is also evident from Table 4 that misinvoicing has mainly been in the form of underinvoicing of exports and that this has been a major problem for exports to the United Kingdom, Germany, France, Italy, the United States, and Japan. The problem has been consistent for exports to the United Kingdom throughout 1974–95 but rose in Germany, Italy, and the United States after 1985. This result confirms the finding that exports to industrial countries have been used for capital flight. Exports to Tanzania, Uganda, and the Netherlands are overinvoiced, implying that they are used to repatriate capital. Exports to the Netherlands, however, began to be underinvoiced after 1991. The direction of misinvoicing for exports to India and the United Arab Emirates is not clear.

The extent of misinvoicing of imports is shown in Table 5. Imports from all the countries for almost all the years were underinvoiced, implying that imports were used to bring capital back through unofficial channels. This situation was caused by the restrictive trade regime, especially the high import taxes and quantitative restrictions that were prevalent in Kenya before 1993. The underinvoicing of imports would also have been used to obtain foreign exchange outside the foreign exchange control system under the import licensing regime.

Generally, the highest underinvoiced imports are those originating in the United Kingdom, Germany, France, Italy, the United States, the Netherlands, and Japan. These are followed by imports from India and the United Arab Emirates, but those from Tanzania and Uganda are the least underinvoiced. This confirms again that trade with industrial countries is the major source of misinvoicing.

The net effect of total misinvoicing, that is, the sum of export and import misinvoicing results, indicates that underinvoicing of imports outweighs the underinvoicing of exports (Table 6).

This suggests that trade policy plays a major role in the misinvoicing of trade. This is confirmed by the dramatic decline in misinvoicing from 1992, following the dismantling of the import licensing and exchange control regimes in 1993.

It is evident from the overall results that the level of capital flight is sensitive to the method of estimation. It is also true that the cross-

Table 4. Kenya: Export Misinvoicing, 1974–95

(In millions of U.S. dollars)

	United Kingdom	Germany	France	Italy	United. States	Netherlands	Japan	India	United Arab Emirates	Tanzania	Uganda
1974	43.7	11.2	5.4	3.0	18.0	–8.5	8.8	8.6	. . .	–7.1	–7.6
1975	20.2	10.4	7.4	2.5	14.5	–3.9	11.0	2.7	. . .	–9.2	–13.6
1976	16.8	–0.5	5.3	–3.1	18.1	–7.8	6.4	0.1	. . .	–10.4	–7.8
1977	99.6	8.9	11.8	–2.2	25.5	–46.3	3.3	2.2	. . .	–4.7	0.1
1978	57.5	39.6	15.8	–6.0	5.0	–22.3	5.3	0.5	. . .	–4.4	0.0
1979	72.7	1.6	16.8	7.7	8.0	–16.7	7.7	0.2	–0.5	–1.4	–0.2
1980	66.4	33.5	16.8	5.0	38.9	–13.9	5.6	–1.2	–0.5	–5.5	–1.7
1981	49.6	–1.2	16.7	4.2	11.4	–13.0	4.0	–1.2	0.6	–3.8	–1.0
1982	5.5	7.4	1.0	0.6	–53.7	1.7	0.3	–1.0	–0.5	–0.8	–1.4
1983	6.7	8.2	0.8	0.8	2.9	1.8	0.4	–1.2	0.8	–0.3	–0.6
1984	64.2	14.5	17.5	–3.8	11.9	–21.0	6.8	–0.4	0.6	–6.3	–0.3
1985	62.3	33.7	17.8	9.5	47.5	–16.7	2.2	3.2	0.6	5.0	–0.1
1986	8.8	45.7	19.8	8.2	82.4	10.9	1.9	2.2	3.3	–0.5	26.6
1987	28.6	30.2	23.8	16.1	33.3	–8.2	6.6	3.2	0.6	2.5	–1.1
1988	54.2	–120.1	27.6	20.6	12.2	–31.3	7.5	4.1	–0.3	–0.2	–0.2
1989	50.8	33.9	25.4	18.4	23.1	–4.5	5.3	1.2	1.6	–2.0	–0.3
1990	108.4	6.6	28.1	26.3	32.3	–2.9	8.3	9.7	1.5	–6.7	–1.7
1991	45.2	64.0	27.7	18.7	30.1	13.7	4.5	1.1	2.4	–1.7	–0.1
1992	38.4	75.2	39.2	20.8	35.0	17.6	7.1	2.8	–0.5	–2.3	–0.8
1993	50.2	24.7	24.8	12.5	50.2	19.1	6.3	–0.2	3.1	–5.4	–0.6
1994	20.5	9.8	5.2	1.9	5.8	3.8	–0.1	–0.4	–0.1	–7.3	–1.0
1995	16.8	12.6	5.6	1.0	6.1	4.2	0.4	–0.5	–0.3	–9.4	–1.4

Source: Author's calculations.

Table 5. Kenya: Import Misinvoicing, 1974–95

(In millions of U.S. dollars)

	United Kingdom	Germany	France	Italy	United. States	Netherlands	Japan	India	United Arab Emirates	Tanzania	Uganda
1974	–28.3	–1.2	1.3	–2.6	1.4	4.8	–5.7	–2.3	. . .	–3.5	–1.4
1975	–25.2	3.5	2.7	3.6	10.3	0.6	–1.4	–3.1	. . .	–0.3	1.1
1976	–12.3	8.4	–4.2	–1.9	6.0	5.1	–6.4	–1.4	. . .	–3.7	–0.2
1977	–6.0	0.8	–20.3	–12.9	–9.1	–3.4	–5.6	–8.6	. . .	0.5	–4.1
1978	–47.4	–9.3	0.6	–5.4	–47.1	9.4	–0.1	–1.8	. . .	0.7	–4.1
1979	–38.4	16.5	–21.8	–15.2	18.6	–3.5	–12.3	–21.9	–35.3	–0.2	–0.3
1980	–220.8	6.9	–5.4	–9.2	1.7	5.0	17.1	–9.5	–54.7	0.5	–0.4
1981	–57.5	–9.3	–4.5	–1.7	–28.8	0.4	–3.7	–10.1	–20.3	–0.5	–0.3
1982	–13.9	–5.9	–3.6	–2.2	–4.8	–1.6	–5.0	–8.7	–8.4	0.2	–0.3
1983	–9.1	–6.4	–0.2	–1.9	–3.7	–2.5	–6.7	–10.1	–7.3	–3.3	–0.3
1984	–51.8	2.1	0.7	–3.2	–15.0	–6.4	–15.5	–5.2	30.4	–0.5	–0.1
1985	–34.3	–2.2	12.6	–7.3	–41.1	–0.5	–14.7	–12.2	23.0	2.4	–0.1
1986	–53.8	–39.5	–135.6	–23.1	–7.2	–15.2	–28.4	–11.5	25.1	2.3	–0.1
1987	–114.6	–17.3	–55.8	–17.7	–27.1	–14.7	–54.4	–8.7	–10.3	3.3	0.7
1988	–119.1	–8.1	–53.3	0.3	–15.5	–47.4	–53.6	–12.1	–10.9	3.2	–0.3
1989	8.1	–4.3	–81.5	–51.9	–41.0	29.3	14.0	–14.9	–12.3	2.0	0.7
1990	–130.2	–51.3	–23.4	–14.5	32.8	–18.8	11.9	–9.6	–6.7	–3.4	0.0
1991	–163.4	–36.9	–33.3	–33.1	–24.1	–23.9	–10.0	–11.0	–13.4	–0.1	–0.1
1992	–65.4	–18.4	–19.5	–17.7	5.8	–14.6	–26.2	–6.4	–14.9	–0.3	0.3
1993	–49.2	1.5	–20.2	–1.1	–30.2	–10.9	–35.5	–19.6	–12.7	–1.1	0.2
1994	–16.4	–8.1	–7.2	–5.3	–10.1	–3.0	–10.0	–5.4	–13.1	–0.4	0.0
1995	–20.7	–10.7	–5.8	–9.1	–6.5	–4.6	–14.6	–12.0	–14.7	–0.7	–0.1

Source: Author's calculations.

Table 6. Kenya: Total Misinvoicing, 1974–95

(In millions of U.S. dollars)

	United Kingdom	Germany	France	Italy	United. States	Netherlands	Japan	India	United Arab Emirates	Tanzania	Uganda
1974	15.4	10.0	6.7	0.4	19.4	–3.7	3.0	6.3	. . .	–10.6	–9.1
1975	–5.1	14.0	10.1	6.2	24.8	–3.4	9.6	–0.3	. . .	–9.5	–12.5
1976	4.6	7.9	1.1	–5.0	24.1	–2.7	0.0	–1.3	. . .	–14.1	–8.1
1977	93.6	9.7	–8.5	–15.0	16.4	–49.6	–2.3	–6.4	. . .	–4.2	–4.0
1978	10.1	30.3	16.4	–11.4	–42.1	–12.9	5.3	–1.4	. . .	–3.7	–4.1
1979	34.3	18.1	–4.9	–7.5	26.6	–20.2	–4.6	–21.6	–35.8	–1.7	–0.5
1980	–154.4	40.4	10.4	–4.2	40.7	–9.0	22.8	–10.7	–55.1	–5.0	–2.1
1981	–7.8	–10.5	12.2	2.5	–17.3	–12.6	0.3	–11.2	–19.7	–4.3	–1.3
1982	–8.4	1.5	–2.6	–1.5	–58.5	0.1	–4.7	–9.8	–8.8	–0.6	–1.7
1983	–2.4	1.9	0.7	–1.1	–0.8	–0.7	–6.4	–11.3	–6.5	–3.7	–0.9
1984	12.3	16.5	18.2	–7.0	–3.1	–27.4	–8.7	–5.7	31.0	–6.9	–0.4
1985	28.0	31.4	30.4	2.2	6.4	–17.2	–12.6	–9.1	23.7	7.4	–0.3
1986	–45.0	6.2	–115.8	–14.9	75.2	–4.3	–26.5	–9.4	28.4	1.8	26.5
1987	–86.0	12.9	–32.0	–1.6	6.3	–22.9	–47.7	–5.5	–9.7	5.8	–0.4
1988	–64.9	–128.2	–25.7	20.9	–3.3	–78.8	–46.1	–8.0	–11.2	2.9	–0.5
1989	58.9	29.6	–56.1	–33.5	–17.9	24.7	19.3	–13.7	–10.7	0.0	0.4
1990	–21.8	–44.7	4.7	11.8	65.1	–21.7	20.2	0.1	–5.2	–10.1	–1.7
1991	–118.1	27.1	–5.6	–14.4	6.0	–10.2	–5.4	–10.0	–11.0	–1.8	–0.2
1992	–27.0	56.8	19.7	3.1	40.8	3.0	–19.1	–3.6	–15.4	–2.6	–0.5
1993	1.0	26.2	4.6	11.5	20.1	8.2	–29.2	–19.7	–9.6	–6.5	–0.4
1994	4.1	1.7	–1.9	–3.4	–4.3	0.9	–10.1	–5.8	–13.2	–7.7	–0.9
1995	–3.9	1.9	–1.1	–8.1	–0.4	–0.5	–14.3	–12.5	–15.0	–10.1	–1.6

Source: Author's calculations.

border bank deposit and Cuddington estimates are too narrow and therefore form lower-bound estimates of capital flight, while the World Bank and Morgan Guaranty estimates are the upper bound. The trade misinvoicing estimates indicate how policy distortions can lead to undesirable effects with wide-ranging macroeconomic consequences.

A comparison of the estimates of the residual method and trade misinvoicing clearly shows that the residual method generates the best estimates of capital flight. The estimates of this method are more reliable because they are based on coherent and well-tested data. Estimates from Cline's method are problematic, because they overestimate capital flight. The World Bank and Morgan Guaranty methods therefore provide the best estimates of capital flight for Kenya.

Empirical Analysis of Capital Flight

Empirical studies on capital flight have been limited by data availability. Pastor (1990) reviews the available empirical literature, which mainly covers studies of Latin American countries. The study also specifies a model that estimates capital flight as a function of changes in inflation, interest rates, degree of currency overvaluation, net long-term capital flows as a percentage of GDP, difference between domestic and U.S. growth rates, tax revenue as a percentage of GDP, and value of labor share in income. The study used pooled data (eight countries over 14 years) to estimate the model. All the coefficients were found to have the right sign (positive, except the difference between the domestic and U.S. growth rates) and were significant, except tax revenue as percentage of GDP.

Cuddington (1986, 1987) uses individual country data to estimate the determinants of capital flight. The 1986 study modeled capital flight as a function of domestic and foreign interest rates, inflation, and the depreciation of currency. The model was estimated for Argentina, Brazil, Chile, Korea, Mexico, Peru, Uruguay, and Venezuela. The study estimated capital flight as a function of domestic and foreign interest rates, inflation, real effective exchange rates, and foreign aid disbursements using data from Argentina, Mexico, and Venezuela. The variables were found to have the correct signs (positive) and were significant in all the countries. The Cuddington studies are limited by the fact that they are restricted to fewer than 12 observations.

Following Cuddington (1986, 1987), we specify an asset portfolio adjustment model that assumes that domestic agents diversify their portfolio by holding domestic and foreign assets. The study uses quarterly data from 1981:Q4 to 1995:Q1. This gives a reasonable number of observations, which allows for dynamic specification of the model. The

Table 7. Unit Root Tests

Test	Variable			
	CF	*RD*	*RER*	*RY*
Weighted-symmetric	–1.088 (0.966)	–2.718 (0.177)	–1.934 (0.692)	–0.672 (0.990)
Dickey-Fuller	–1.075 (0.933)	–2.298 (0.435)	–1.210 (0.908)	–2.708 (0.233)
Phillips-Perron	–5.757 (0.765)	–30.428 (0.008)	–3.662 (0.905)	–6.030 (0.743)

Note: *CF*, capital flight; *RD*, difference between foreign and domestic interest rates; *RER*, real effective exchange rate; *Y*, real income. Figures in parentheses are the probability values for the null.

data are obtained from the IMF's *International Financial Statistics*, but GDP data were obtained by interpolation. In this study nonbank cross-border deposits are used as the dependent variable and assumed to be a function of GDP, the real effective exchange rate, and relative returns, measured as the difference between the real foreign interest rate and the domestic interest rate.

The general functional form of the model is as follows:

$$CF = f(RD, Y, RER) \tag{5}$$

where

R = domestic interest rate

RW = foreign interest rate

RD = relative returns $(RW - R)$

RER = real effective exchange rate

Y = real GDP.

It is postulated that *RER* is positively correlated and *Y* negatively correlated with capital flight. The coefficient of *RD* cannot be determined a priori but is expected to be positively correlated to *CF* if $RW>R$ and negatively correlated otherwise.

The model was tested for the order of integration of the variables, and it was found that the variables were integrated of order one, implying stationarity (Table 7). Cointegration was tested using the Engle and Granger (1987) two-stage procedure. Since cointegration was established, the variables were entered into the equation in first differences. The model was reduced starting with six lags for each variable.

The estimates for Equation (5) are shown in Table 8. The coefficients of all the variables are significant, but that of *Y* has an unexpected sign.

Table 8. Solved Static Long-Run Equation for Capital Flight

Variable	Coefficient	Standard Error
Constant	–0.133	0.027
Y	5.097	0.802
RER	1.046	0.125
RD	–0.196	0.043
ECM	–0.047	0.050
*D*93(3)	0.150	0.036
Sessional	–0.042	0.026
Step dummy (91)	0.991	0.229

Note: The null hypothesis that coefficients are zero is rejected. Wald test $chi^2(7) = 86.63$ [0.0000]**.

The positive effect of currency appreciation on capital flight is confirmed. Real income was used as a proxy for the investment climate; that is, higher income is expected to raise the credibility of policy reforms and therefore reduce capital flight. But the results indicate the opposite effect. It is plausible, however, that where policies are not credible, an increase in income provides an opportunity for increased outflow of capital. The positive coefficient of *Y* can therefore be rationalized in the face of noncredible economic reform. The negative coefficient of relative interest rates indicates that the positive effects of foreign interest rates on capital flight have been outweighed by the negative effects of domestic interest rates. In other words, real domestic interest rates are higher than foreign interest rates. This phenomenon has been common in the 1990s with interest rate liberalization and relaxation of exchange controls.

The coefficient for *ECM* is low and insignificant. It is also evident that there were seasonal effects. Two dummies, *D*91 and *D*93(3), introduced to account for interest rate liberalization and capital flight in 1991 and the third quarter of 1993, respectively, were found to be significant.

The model confirms that real exchange rate appreciation encourages capital flight. It also suggests that if reforms are not credible, economic growth would lead to increased capital flight. The increases in incomes then simply provide the means for greater accumulation of foreign assets.

Conclusion

This chapter has derived estimates of capital flight using the residual method, the cross-border bank deposits methods, and the trade misinvoicing method. The determinants of capital flight were also estimated.

The chapter establishes that estimates of capital flight depend on the method used, but estimates derived from the residual method have similar trends. Estimates from cross-border deposits and the Cuddington method should be treated as a lower bound, while the World Bank, Morgan Guaranty, and Cline estimates are the upper bound. There is no objective rule for determining the best estimates for Kenya, but the World Bank and Morgan Guaranty estimates are more reliable since they are derived from consistent and well-tested data.

Results from trade misinvoicing indicate that underinvoicing has been a major problem and that it has been prevalent with exports to developed countries. Exports to Tanzania and Uganda have been overinvoiced. These results suggest that exports to industrial countries have been used for capital flight, while those to developing countries have been used to repatriate capital. Imports from all countries were underinvoiced throughout the period, suggesting the use of imports to transfer capital held abroad into the country without going through official channels. The net effect of total misinvoicing also indicates underinvoicing of imports, suggesting that trade policy plays a major role in trade misinvoicing. This conclusion is supported by the decline in trade misinvoicing from 1992, a period in which trade and exchange control regimes were relaxed.

The estimated model of capital flight indicates that real exchange rate appreciation encourages capital flight. The model also suggests that economic growth in the face of reforms that are not credible would result in increased capital flight.

In general, the chapter establishes that sound macroeconomic policies are the right way to deal with the problem of capital flight. It is evident that Kenya's move in this direction has contributed to the marked reduction in capital flight. This is shown by the low trade misinvoicing in 1994 and 1995 and the net inflows of capital as shown by the Cuddington and cross-border deposits methods. Indeed, the positive change in cross-border deposits in 1994 and 1995 reflects the legitimization of ownership of foreign assets through the total removal of exchange controls. The trends of capital flight derived from the other residual methods also point to the reduction of the problem since serious economic reforms began.

References

Ajayi, S.I., 1991, "Capital Flight and External Debt in Nigeria," paper presented at the African Economic Research Consortium Workshop, Nairobi, May 26–30.

———, 1996, "An Analysis of External Debt and Capital Flight in the Severely Indebted Low-Income Countries in Sub-Saharan Africa," paper presented at the IMF–World Bank Conference on External Financing for Low Income Countries, Washington, December 9–12.

Bhagwati, J.N., 1964, "On the Underinvoicing of Imports," *Bulletin of Oxford University Institute of Economics and Statistics*, Vol. 26.

———, A. Craggier, and C. Webulswasdi, 1974, "Capital Flight in LDCs: A Statistical Analysis," in *Illegal Transactions in International Trade*, ed. by J.N. Bhagwati (Amsterdam: North-Holland).

Chang, K.P.H., and R.E. Cumby, 1991, "Capital Flight in Sub-Saharan African Countries," in *African External Finance in the 1990s*, ed. by I. Husain and J. Underwood (Washington: World Bank).

Claessens, S., and D. Naude, 1993, *Recent Estimates of Capital Flight*, Policy Research Papers (Washington: World Bank).

Cuddington, J.T., 1986, "Capital Flight: Estimates, Issues and Explanations," Princeton Studies in International Finance No. 58 (Princeton, New Jersey: Princeton University Press).

———, 1987, "Macroeconomic Determinants of Capital Flight: An Econometric Investigation," in *Capital Flight and Third World Debt*, ed. by D.R. Lessard and J. Williamson (Washington: Institute for International Economics).

Cumby, R.E., and R.M. Levich, 1987, "On the Definition and Magnitude of Recent Capital Flight," in *Capital Flight and Third World Debt*, ed. by D.R. Lessard and J. Williamson (Washington: Institute for International Economics).

Dooley, M.P., 1986, "Country-Specific Risk Premiums, Capital Flight and Net Investment Income Payments in Selected Developing Countries" (unpublished; Washington: International Monetary Fund).

———, 1987, "Comment," in *Capital Flight and Third World Debt*, ed. by D.R. Lessard and J. Williamson (Washington: Institute for International Economics).

———, 1988, "Capital Flight: A Response to Differences in Financial Risks," *Staff Papers*, International Monetary Fund, Vol. 35 (September).

———, W. Helkie, R. Tryon, and J. Underwood, 1983, "An Analysis of External Debt Positions in Eight Developing Countries Through 1990," *Journal of Development Economics*, Vol. 21, No. 2.

Eggerstedt, H., R.B. Hall, and S. van Wijnbergen, 1993, "Measuring Capital Flight: A Case Study of Mexico," Working Paper No. 859 (Washington: World Bank).

Engle, R.F., and C.W.J. Granger, 1987, "Co-integration and Error Correction: Representation, Estimation and Testing," *Econometrica*, Vol. 55, No. 2.

Erbe, S., 1985, "The Flight of Capital from Developing Countries," *Intereconomics*, November/December.

Gajdeczka, P., 1990, "The Measurement of Capital Flight and Developing Country Foreign Assets," paper presented at the Kiel Institute Workshop.

Gulati, S.N., 1987, "A Note on Trade Misinvoicing," in *Capital Flight and Third World Debt*, ed. by D.R. Lessard and J. Williamson (Washington: Institute for International Economics).

International Monetary Fund, *International Financial Statistics*, various issues (Washington).

Khan, M.S., and N. Ul Haque, 1987, "Capital Flight from Developing Countries," *Finance & Development*, March.

Kindleberger, C.P., 1987, "A Historical Perspective," in *Capital Flight and Third World Debt*, ed. by D.R. Lessard and J. Williamson (Washington: Institute for International Economics).

Morgan Guaranty Trust Company, 1986, "LDC Capital Flight," *World Financial Markets*, March.

Ng'eno, N.K., 1991, "Kenya's Export Performance," in *Trade and Development in Sub-Saharan Africa*, ed. by J. H. Frimpong-Ansah, S. M. Ravi Kanbur, and P. Svedberg (Manchester: Manchester University Press).

———, 1997, "The External Debt Problem of Kenya," a revised version of the final report presented at the African Economic Research Consortium Workshop, Nairobi, May 24–28, 1992.

Olopoenia, R.A., 1995, "Capital Flight from Uganda," draft final report presented at the African Economic Research Consortium Workshop, Nairobi.

Pastor, M., Jr., 1990, "Capital Flight from Latin America," *World Development*, Vol. 18, No. 1.

Vos, R., 1990, *On the Measurement of Private Accumulation of Foreign Assets: The Case of the Philippines* (The Hague: Institute of Social Studies).

Walter, I., 1987, "The Mechanism of Capital Flight," in *Capital Flight and Third World Debt*, ed. by D.R. Lessard and J. Williamson (Washington: Institute for International Economics).

World Bank, 1985, *World Development Report 1985* (New York: Oxford University Press).

———, 1994, *World Debt Tables*, Vol. 2 (Washington: World Bank).

Yeats, A., 1991, "On the Accuracy of Economic Observations: Do Sub-Saharan Africa Trade Statistics Mean Anything?" *World Bank Economic Review*, Vol. 4, No. 2.

Contributors

Ajayi, S. Ibi, Department of Economics, University of Ibadan, Ibadan, Nigeria

Atingi, Michael, Research Department, Bank of Uganda, Kampala, Uganda

Iyoha, Milton A., Department of Economics and Management, University of Benin, Benin City, Nigeria

Khan, Mohsin S., International Monetary Fund, Washington, D.C., United States

Mbire, Barbara Barungi, Witwatersrand University, Johannesburg, South Africa

Ng'eno, N.K., Cabinet Office of the President, Nairobi, Kenya

Nyoni, Timothy S., Economic Research Bureau, University of Dar es Salaam, Tanzania

Olopoenia, Razaq A., Department of Economics, University of Ibadan, Ibadan, Nigeria

Osei, Barfour, Department of Economics, University of Ghana, Legon, Ghana